UNIVERSITY OF NOTRE DAME

Liturgical Studies

VOLUME IV

Liturgical Studies

LITURGICAL COMMITTEE OF THE UNIVERSITY OF NOTRE DAME

Liturgical Piety
REV. LOUIS BOUYER (OF THE ORATORY)

Church Buildings and Furnishing
REV. J. B. O'CONNELL

The Bible and the Liturgy
REV. JEAN DANIELOU, S.J.

Worship: The Life of The Missions
REV. JOHANNES HOFINGER, S.J.

The Meaning of Sacred Scripture
REV. LOUIS BOUYER (OF THE ORATORY)

•

IN PREPARATION

The Primitive Liturgy
REV. JOSEF A. JUNGMANN, S.J.

The Psalter as a Christian Prayer Book
REV. BALTHASAR FISCHER

The Prayer Life of the Church
REV. BONIFAAS LUYKX, O.PRAEM.

The Sacred Scripture and the Spiritual Life
VERY REV. MSGR. FRANCIS H. DAVIS

Church Architecture for Our Time
HERMANN BAUR

Liturgical Studies

WORSHIP: THE LIFE

OF THE MISSIONS

BY

JOHANNES HOFINGER, S.J.

JOSEF KELLNER, S.J.

PAUL BRUNNER, S.J.

JOHANNES SEFFER, S.J.

OF THE INSTITUTE OF MISSION APOLOGETICS
MANILA, P. I.

Translated by Mary Perkins Ryan

UNIVERSITY OF NOTRE DAME PRESS

1958

IMPRIMI POTEST: Hsinchu (Formosa), die 17 Junii, 1956.
P. Josephus Onate, s.j., Visitator.

IMPRIMI POTEST: Theodore J. Mehling, c.s.c., Provincial

NIHIL OBSTAT: Eugene P. Burke, c.s.c., Censor Deputatus

IMPRIMATUR: ✠ Leo A. Pursley, D.D., Bishop of Fort Wayne

June 15, 1958

Preface

This fascinating book presents to us the missionary impact of the current liturgical renewal. "The apostles were sent out into the world to preach," Father Hofinger reminds us, "to announce the Good News to all peoples. But their missionary mandate was in no way exhausted by this. All real Catholic missionary activity begins with the preaching of the faith; but its final aim is the establishment, the development, the bringing to perfection of a new family of God on earth, thanks above all to the life given in the sacraments." Worship of God by His creatures is the end-product sought by each missionary band that takes up its task among each new tribe or people over the earth. Father Hofinger's thesis is that properly conducted worship not only honors God but in missionary fashion draws more of God's children into the fold to honor Him in worship.

The primary task of liturgy is worship. "In the missions as everywhere else," Father Hofinger explains, "the primary task of the liturgy is to worship the Father 'in spirit and in truth,' and to this end everything else must be subordinated with generous missionary zeal, as being indeed the crown and the completion of our missionary activity."

But the liturgy renders additional services beyond its principal goal of worship. There is great catechetical value in properly conceived liturgy. "The superiority of teaching by means of worship over any other form of Christian preaching consists in the fact that *the liturgy gives what it teaches*," asserts Father Hofinger. "Christian worship is thus a treasure-house of catechetical wealth. The more fully we appreciate our apostolate, the more we missionaries appreciate its value. . . . Like Christ, are we not called to dispense, not only knowledge about the divine life, but also this life itself, as abundantly as possible: *Ut vitam habeant et abundantius habeant*" (John 10:10)?

Christian worship, then, forms apostles. Properly conducted worship, with properly conceived liturgy, should prompt Catholics both old and new in the faith to go to their neighbors outside the fold and say, "Come and worship with us."

Involved in the current liturgical renewal is the vast problem of the reappraisal of Christian liturgy in the light of the past and of the rapidly evolving present. Father Hofinger is among those who make a strong plea for more active participation of the Christian millions in the life of worship in the Church. "This active participation of the people," he explains, "was expressed in the very way in which the (early) Christians spoke about the Mass. The current term for the action of the laity was *celebrare missam*, to celebrate the Mass. In addition, during the first eight centuries, the participation of the laity in the Eucharistic Sacrifice was expressed by various verbs with the word 'Mass' as their direct object: to carry out, concelebrate, make, offer, say, hold. . . . When we compare these expressions, in which the active part of the laity shines out so clearly, with the expressions in use today—'to hear Mass,' 'to go to Mass,' 'to assist at Mass'—can we deny that a change in attitude has come about, a different way of thinking about the Holy Sacrifice?"

Father Hofinger bewails the defects which crept into the liturgy in Antioch and other places in the East from the fourth century on through a great falling-off in the active participation of the people in the essential parts of the Mass. This was further accentuated after the eighth century when the apostolate, which had passed into the German and Slavic peoples of Northern Europe, called for adaptations in the liturgy which, to thinkers of Father Hofinger's school, were not always successfully rendered. The present day effort is prompted in part through a desire to correct the harm done to Christian liturgy in these centuries.

The pages of this book devoted to the past are wonderfully enlightening, but those that dwell on constructive phases of the vital present are of still greater appeal. For the practical missioner, one of the most important subjects treated is communal worship in the absence of a priest.

Of the fifty million Cahtolics in the new Churches of Asia and Africa, it is estimated that more than half are geographically so situated that they are unable to attend Mass on Sunday. For them, Sunday services without the presence of a priest is recommended. "Such services," says Father Hofinger, "cannot, of course, actually replace the incomparable homage that we render to the heavenly Father with Christ in the Mass. Nevertheless even in such a celebration the Christian community can render to God a most fitting homage, one that is also presented to the Father by Christ."

Incidentally, Father Hofinger's detailed study of this question will prove immensely interesting to many missionaries who are strongly impressed by the inadequate liturgical values in the various services currently available for the worship of God in the thousands of priestless communities over the earth.

THE MOST REV. RAYMOND A. LANE, M.M., D.D.
Titular Bishop of Hypaepa

Maryknoll Fathers,
Maryknoll, N. Y.

Feast of Sts. Peter and Paul, 1958.

Contents

PART ONE

ESTIMATE OF THE SITUATION

CHAPTER ONE

Our Concern for the Liturgy in the Light of Missionary History

JOHANNES HOFINGER, S.J.

Many people still remember the astonishment caused by the bold reforms of Pius X, above all by his decrees on Holy Communion. A large number of the clergy shared these feelings, very loyal and conscientious priests along with the rest. They simply could not understand such a radical about-face. What an unheard-of innovation — to set aside a tradition sanctioned for some fifteen hundred years, not in this or that part of the Church, but almost everywhere! There must have been "good grounds" for this tradition; indeed, was it not to be thought of as the work of the Holy Spirit? But this radical Pope did not seem to be very concerned about the powers of the Holy Spirit in this regard. Here precisely, was the really distressing aspect of the matter.

During the Middle Ages, certainly a thoroughly Catholic period, even great saints, if they were not priests, did not approach the Lord's table more than a few times a year. True, after the Reformation, it was understandable that particularly fervent Christians should be urged to communicate more frequently and even be allowed to receive as often as once a week, provided, of course, that they went to confession beforehand. But now, all of a sudden, any ordinary Christian who took his religion seriously had to be admitted to the Communion rail every day if he wished, without going to Confession each time, and only because he wanted to "share" more perfectly in Holy Mass. But was not this very idea of "sharing," this desire of the laity to take an active part in the Mass, a very dangerous thing, against which, as a prudent man, the Pope should have been on guard? How could the Holy Father have failed to consider such an obvious danger? Perhaps the only charitable answer was that, after all, he was getting old. . . .

But, in actual fact, the Holy Father not only tolerated this desire of the faithful, to take their active part in the Holy Mysteries; he made it a principal — perhaps *the* principal — point in his wonderful program: *instaurare omnia in Christo:* to renew all things in Christ. Such a renewal in Christ presupposes a new mentality, a return to the mind and spirit of Christ. Even in the earliest documents in which he initiated his work of reform, the Holy Father tells us, in phrases of classic precision, where the source of this renewal in Christ is to be found: "The primary and indispensable source of this spirit is the active participation of the faithful in the sacred mysteries and in the public and solemn prayer of the Church." (Motu proprio, *Tra le sollecitudini,* Nov. 22, 1903). St. Pius X is thus the real founder and the great promoter of the pastoral-liturgical movement of recent years. This movement is the full implementation of his program: the awakening and the renewal of Christian life through as active a participation as possible in divine worship.

Anyone who is at all familiar with the reforming work of the Pope of the Eucharist, knows that it was the care of souls and not historical reasons that motivated his acts. He worked for the restoration of frequent Communion and for the active participation of the faithful in the liturgy generally; but not because historians could easily prove that these were common practices in the earliest ages of the Church. As a pastor of souls, he saw clearly that the ancient practice was infinitely more in accord with the very nature of Christian worship, that it possessed a unique power to renew Christian life, a power that we could not do without in the dreadful religious impoverishment of our times. This was reason enough for him to return to the practice of fifteen hundred years ago, not, of course, in the sense of returning to a state of things that had disappeared once for all, but with the idea of making a wise use of the past for the benefit of the present.

The historical study that we are about to present is, we hope, inspired by the same pastoral spirit. The question is, what does the history of the first Christian centuries and of the Middle Ages teach us about the value of Christian worship in our missionary work and about the way in which this worship should be carried out in the missions?[1] We shall begin, then, with a description of worship in the early Church and its effects on missionary work, and then indicate the great changes that took place in the Middle Ages and how these changes affected the missions.

1. Modern missionary science, which generally prefers historical topics, has unfortunately done little work up to the present time on the history of Christian worship in the missions. Profound studies in this field would certainly render valuable service to the work of evangelization, especially if they were always carried on with an awareness of present-day missionary problems.

Divine Worship in the Missionary Church of the First Centuries

Throughout the centuries which we consider as being Christian antiquity, the Church everywhere was primarily a missionary Church. Only at the end of this period was the enormous missionary territory of the old Roman empire transformed into a Christian region. Even during the fifth century, there were many pagans in the empire still to be converted; divine worship, then, had a typically missionary character. It had, of course, already undergone many great changes: the extreme simplicity of the first few centuries had rapidly given way to the many elaborations characteristic of the great basilicas of the fourth and fifth centuries. From the fourth century on, marked differences developed between various rites: different forms of celebration were perfected around the great Patriarchal Churches. The rite of the Roman Church showed more and more clearly its own special characteristics, as also did the rites of the Churches of Antioch, Jerusalem and Alexandria. But the missionary quality of Christian worship remained untouched. Until the end of the Patristic period, and even into the sixth century, divine worship was carried out in a way which, from a missionary point of view, must be described as highly valuable.

What especially strikes those of us who here and now are messengers of the Gospel — what, indeed, arouses a holy envy — is the *wonderful adaptability* of the worship of those first centuries. For the primitive Church, overflowing with youthful vitality and spontaneity, such adaptability involved no complicated problems; it was taken for granted. Worship was not thought of in any other way. Any attempts to bring about rigid uniformity, any renunciation of the principle of adaptation, would certainly have met with general and resolute opposition. This adaptability was considered to be a precious heritage from Apostolic times, and, whenever any limitations eventually came to be considered, there was immediate and voluble appeal to the sacred traditions of the Apostles. We might do well, then, to consider briefly the character and the chief reasons for the existence of this adaptability.

The *language of divine worship* was at that time everywhere the language of the country: in the Western empire, therefore, it was Latin. We should notice the significant fact that the Latin actually used in worship comes somewhere between the classical Latin of a Cicero and the common speech of daily life. Ambrose, Augustine, Gregory, the guiding lights of the ancient Church, had themselves been formed by classical culture, and they expressly rejected the idea of using classical Latin. But they would equally have opposed the idea of introducing into the liturgy the "slangy" vocabulary of ordinary uncultured people. In the eastern part of the empire, alongside the liturgy in Greek, liturgies in other languages developed: Syrian, Armenian, Coptic. And this fact is also significant, for in the Eastern empire, Greek was recognized and used as the universal language of the educated. But Christian worship was the business of the whole Christian community, and therefore of all the people and not only the educated classes.

But the possibility of liturgical adaptation was not limited to language. The various liturgies that grew up in the different parts of the ancient Church, while maintaining their unity on essential points, developed various ways in which particular rites were carried out and the liturgical texts elaborated: both their ceremonies and their texts show the influence of the *special temperament of the people concerned*. For example, compare the objective quality, the austere simplicity, the clearly defined outlines of the Roman liturgy, with the external richness, the affectivity and the dramatic appeal of the Byzantine rite. Even the dogmatic battles of the time, which so profoundly stirred the Christian soul, are registered in the various liturgies: for example, the violent discussion on Christology in the East, and, in the Gallican liturgy of the West, the debates on the necessity and nature of grace.

Furthermore, the liturgy of the Church borrowed without hesitation a great deal from the art of the times and from ancient culture generally, with its wide variety of forms of expression. It borrowed also from the rites of pagan worship, but this was probably done unconsciously. The effort to develop Christian worship was naturally affected by the associations and experiences of the contemporary pagan world. Without deliberate design, a young and spontaneous Christianity took advantage of the means of expression derived from pagan worship and adapted them to the expression of Christian thought and feeling.

But in spite of this adaptability, the Church retained the unity and the unique Christian character of her sublime worship. In studying the development of the liturgy at this time, we hardly know whether to admire most the boldness and the spontaneity of the various adaptations, the many ways in which Christian religious feeling was left free to express itself, or the perfect unity retained in essentials — a unity the more striking since it can in no way be accounted for by any strict uniformity imposed by Rome.[2] Its basis was simply the living unity of the faith and of Christian thought, reverence for the traditions of the Church even in matters of discipline, and a profound sense of the true nature of Christian worship. And, furthermore, the intense realization of common

---

2. Rome was concerned very early with liturgical questions that concerned the universal Church, as is shown, for example, by the position it took in the dispute over the date of Easter. This controversy also shows clearly the kind of difficulties encountered by Rome in imposing her solution of such questions.

unity, underlying all particular Churches, bringing all the faithful together in the one Catholic Church, created a mentality which, amid all adaptations and differences, was vitally concerned with this unity, inducing Christians of one place to be willing to learn from those of another.

But while we admire the wonderful liturgical adaptability, so full of boldness and spontaneity, in these first Christian centuries, we should beware of seeing in it a direct model for the missionary Church of today — even supposing that Rome were to give the necessary authorization. In our age of religious subjectivism and divisive nationalism, the Church has special need of a closer unity than was required in the Roman empire whose own structure, taken as a whole, was comparatively unified. And besides, the generally vital sense of the rightful value of Christian worship and the respect of all particular Churches for liturgical tradition made it less necessary to have a uniform legislation imposed by the Pope. Today, if there were no strict guidance from Rome, we should soon fall into liturgical chaos. And perhaps, greater liturgical uniformity might have been attempted in early Christianity if the divisions and schisms of later times could have been foreseen. The Church of today enjoys the fruits of many centuries of experience, and the central power of the Roman primacy has gained in force and extension. Thanks to this, we have an assurance of unity that the ancient Church did not explicitly possess in the same way. The question, then, is whether today, in the spirit of the primitive Church, liturgical adaptations can be made to correspond to the needs of our people, especially in the missions where this question takes on a special urgency.

But what, after all, was the main reason for this adaptability in the early Church? The need to make our missionary work more effective urges us today to ask insistently for some adaptations of the liturgy in general, to state that such adaptations are necessary for the spread of the Catholic religion and for its taking root among the peoples in missionary lands. But this apostolic point of view, though it is motivated by the best intentions, still does not go to the heart of the matter.

For we should be on the wrong track entirely if we were to think that the adaptability of the liturgy of the early Church had only a missionary purpose. The Church of that time certainly was fully conscious of being the Church of the pagans. She felt herself responsible for "those outside," and wished that they should find in her an understanding and welcoming mother, a second homeland. But, in establishing the forms of her worship, she thought little of those outside her fold, who in any case were not allowed to assist at her worship and so could not feel its attraction. Her liturgical adaptability seems to us much more to be the obvious and self-explanatory result of her attitude toward Christian worship itself. In the eyes of the ancient Church, the Christian community, gathered together to celebrate the worship of God, was the active agent in carrying out the liturgy, always, of course, in dependence on the hierarchy. She did not think of it primarily as the liturgical action of the hierarchy cut off from that of the Christian community, nor as the worship of the universal Church in which each Christian could take part as he pleased. She considered it to be the action of the concrete Christian community celebrating "its" worship and by so doing uniting itself in the wonderful work of the whole Church, acting in its spirit and under its direction. This fundamental attitude explains the great adaptability of the liturgy at that time, and also the *intensive active participation of the people in divine worship* — a participation which is so evident in the liturgy itself and which was so powerful a missionary force.

This active participation of the people was expressed in the very way in which *Christians spoke about the Mass.* The current term for the action of the laity was *celebrare missam,* to celebrate the Mass. In addition, during the first eight centuries, the participation of the laity in the Eucharistic Sacrifice was expressed by various verbs with the word "Mass" as their direct object: carry out, concelebrate, make, offer, say, hold, etc.[3] Particularly frequent was the expression "to sing" the Mass; it was so deeply rooted that it was still employed even after Low Mass had come into use. We even find such expression *cantare missam sine cantu* or *sine nota* (to sing a Low Mass). When we compare these expressions, in which the active part of the laity shines out so clearly, with the expressions in use today: "to hear Mass," "to go to Mass," "to assist at Mass," can we deny that a change in attitude has come about, a different way of thinking about the Holy Sacrifice? Obviously, the peoples in missionary countries have also been influenced by this change. For the Western expression "to hear Mass," for instance, there is the corresponding Chinese phrase: *wang missa,* "to look from afar at the sacrifice of the Mass" which the priest is offering at the altar — as if any pagan could not see and hear "from afar" what is going on at the altar!

The early Christians on the other hand had a most vivid sense of the fact that their part in the Mass was not only to hear and to look but *to do something,* to carry out a holy action that presupposed the consecration and special powers received at Baptism. The real Christian

3. *Agere, concelebrare, conficere, consecrare, dare, dicere, explere, facere, offerre, peragere, tenere, tractare.* See G. Ellard, S.J., *The Mass of the Future,* Bruce, Milwaukee, 1948, p. 68 ff.

faith and the good will of a catechumen was not enough to enable him truly to take part in the Mass, and therefore the catechumens were dismissed after the "liturgy of the Word." In the sacrificial action itself they could have done nothing more than "be spectators," "assist devoutly." But the missionary Church of those ages did not want any spectators at the Sacrifice, however well-disposed and devout; she wanted only those present who were able to take active part in the Sacrifice.

This was clearly the opinion of those who made the regulations governing worship. But what did the simple faithful themselves think of their own part in the Mass? On this point we have the magnificent testimony of the martyrs of Abilene, near Carthage. In the persecution of Diocletian, fifty Christians were arrested at the end of the Eucharistic celebration. The record of their trial before the proconsul of Carthage, Annulius, has come down to us. The decisive question for all those arrested was the same: had they actually taken part in the service that preceded their arrest, and if so, why? The authorities would have been satisfied if they had denied that they had taken part, or if they had given some excuse for it on grounds of violence or undue influence. The prisoners were even tortured to "make it easier" for them to give such excuses. But under torture, the lector Emeritus explained his participation in this way: "We cannot live without the Mass." Felix publicly confessed himself to be a Christian; then the proconsul said: "I asked if you took part in the gathering. Answer this question." And Felix answered: "As if a Christian could live without the Mass or the Mass be celebrated without Christians! Do you not know, Satan, that it is the Christians who make the Mass and the Mass that makes the Christians, in such a way that one cannot exist without the other?" And the other Christians answered, in the same way, that they had acted as Christians and celebrated the Mass.[4]

The form of the liturgy corresponded to this attitude. In every part, it gives evidence of the active participation of the community, from the response of the congregation to the priest's first greeting to the liturgical dismissal of the people, a dismissal which itself presupposes active participants, for passive spectators have no need to be sent away. In the circus or the theatre of that time, there was no official dismissal, everyone came and went as he pleased; but there was such a dismissal at the end of popular gatherings and assemblies in which each person was "active" as being a member in good standing of the community, taking part in the discussion about accepting orders from above or ratifying a governmental decision.

4. Migne, *PL* 8, 705-715.

The active part of the faithful in the Mass was shown most particularly in the chants sung together; the prayers said in dialogue with the priest (or the deacon); the *"oratio fidelium"*; the action of standing facing the East while the priest was praying; the general participation in the offertory and in Communion; the giving to one another of the kiss of peace; the praying with hands raised; the giving of the responses, which were understood as answers to the priest's invitation to take part in the action, addressed precisely to the congregation, and as the expression of that participation; and, finally, the Amen by which the congregation solemnly acknowledged the prayer of the priest as their own prayer. It is a significant that in the first, very sketchy, description we possess of the primitive celebration of the Eucharist, the Amen by which the people responded to the eucharistic prayer of the bishop is mentioned twice, so important did Justin, apologist and martyr of the second century, consider this Amen to be.

Obviously, these expressions of active participation customary in the first Christian communities do not call for any slavish imitation on our part; no such imitation would solve our problem — even if the liturgical legislation of the Church were to authorize it. It would, in fact, place a further obstacle in the way of the real adaptation which is needed today. Should we not rather take our inspiration from the spirit behind these particular manifestations and so work out a form of worship in missionary countries which will assure to Christians today an equally intense active part in the worship of the Church?

We can also admire the active part taken by the people in early Christian times in the administration of the sacraments. The assembly of the faithful had a most important role in the progressive initiation of catechumens into the sacrament of Baptism, in the choice and the examination as to the fitness of candidates for the priesthood, even in the sacrament of Penance which we today consider to be the most personal and "private" of all. The community was liturgically associated with the rite excluding sinners, with their return along the painful road of penitence, and finally with their reconciliation. No missionary today would dream of wishing to return, for example, to the ancient discipline of penance; but can we not learn many lessons from the spirit that inspired the ancient Church in order to work out forms of the liturgy of the sacraments that are better adapted to the needs of our people? Should not our Christians become more aware of the fact that the divine gifts we receive in the sacraments are given to us as being members of the one and indivisible Mystical Body of Christ? Should not the whole Christian community be more profoundly concerned with the blessings given to one of its members in the sacraments, blessings which finally profit the whole community? What fruitful effects for missionary work would flow, for example, from a closer cooperation of the whole community in the progressive initiation of catechumens, both in the liturgy itself and outside it?

But in order to understand the influence of worship in the religious formation of Christians in the early Church, we need to consider not only its adaptability and the active participation of the faithful in it, but also its other outstanding characteristics: richness of doctrinal content, intelligibility and affective power.

Our present liturgy is certainly very rich in *doctrinal content*. The Roman liturgy, in particular, has, perhaps, kept intact more faithfully and fully than any other, the heritage of the first Christian centuries, its fullness, its dignity and its marvellous focussing on the mystery of our redemption by Christ. But even from this aspect, we must remember that the primitive liturgy had an obvious advantage over ours. Aside from the difficulties raised by the Latin language, the liturgy as it is arranged today is catechetically less rich than was the early liturgy with all its instructive lessons from Holy Scripture. We shall return to this point when we speak of the use of the Bible in our missionary worship.

In our present situation, it is the *intelligibility* of ancient Christian worship that appears particularly enviable. Even if permission were given to celebrate the liturgy in the language of each country, Christian worship as it is today would still remain difficult to understand, especially in the missions. The liturgical texts are — at least for many missionary peoples — too concise, too difficult for the people to pray as their own prayers. In the ancient Christian liturgy, the liturgical prayers were much more simple and popular in style; born of Christian prayer and the cultural environment of the time, they were more comprehensible and therefore appealing to the Christians of those days, who, on their part, were familiar with Holy Scripture, with its ideas and images and modes of expression, and so were much better prepared than the majority of Christians today to understand the liturgy itself.

In this regard, the *clearly defined structure of early Christian worship* played an important part. For a liturgical ceremony to be easily comprehensible, it does not suffice to have each separate prayer easy to understand. The ceremony as a whole should reveal its meaning by its structure and pattern. The principal parts of the Mass, for instance, should appear clearly as such, and should be self-explanatory by their readings, songs, gestures. In the Mass celebrations of the sixth and seventh centuries, we can easily recognize the entrance-rite, then so beautiful; the reading service, so clearly distinct from the sacrifice (what a profound impression must have been given by the "liturgy of the Word" thought of as the solemn hearing of the word of God); the sense of sacrifice clearly expressed in the offertory procession; the great eucharistic prayer constituting the climax of Christian worship, followed by the participation of all in the divine banquet, the counterpart to the offertory procession in which everyone also took part.

The early and simpler form of worship was also more *truly moving* than our present form. Later developments brought a greater degree of solemnity, but worship became less interior, less direct. Our *Kyrie,* more ordered than were the supplications of the primitive Christian congregation, has become a beautiful melody when sung at a high Mass. We can see that this is fitting; but we can see also, from the missionary point of view, the value of the ancient, more moving form. In the same way, has not the disappearance of the ancient *oratio fidelium* at the end of the Fore-Mass lessened the affective power of worship; and the fact that we do not carry out the responses of the Mass as did the first Christians has had the same effect. The progressive extension of rubrical regulations to the least details of worship has had its good effects but has also reduced the spontaneity and the appeal of our ceremonies. Is it too much to ask that worship in the missions should have more appeal and more spontaneity, above all in the not at all infrequent case of those people who do not find in the severe restraint of the ancient Romans the authentic expression of their religious life? This difficulty did not exist in the ancient liturgy. The Roman style suited the needs of the Christians belonging to the western part of the empire. The ardent Africans knew how to manage, and the Easterners were never forbidden to give to their worship forms better adapted to their temperament.

What, then, was *the missionary effectiveness of this primitive Christian worship* whose characteristics we have tried to describe? By "missionary" value or effectiveness, we do not mean primarily any direct influence on those outside the Church, any missionary propaganda. Today we are, perhaps, too preoccupied and anxious to discover the most effective way of reaching those outside. The Christians of the first centuries showed little of this concern. Their worship, in any case, consciously and clearly renounced this kind of missionary action: pagans were allowed, at most, to take part in the reading service, which was by its nature directed essentially to the baptized faithful and to catechumens. And yet the worship of these centuries was a missionary force of the first order; regular participation in that worship made of the faithful fully-formed Christians and "missionaries."

In the first place, it gave them, from the catechumenate on, the *necessary religious instruction.* We can state without exaggeration that the Christians of that time — and particularly the many who did not know how to read — owed their knowledge of the faith almost entirely to their participation in Christian worship. In its richness of doctrinal content, its organic ordering of all its teaching around the chief doctrines of Christianity, and its adaptation to the psychology of the faithful, divine worship carried out in a most wonderful way its missionary role of giving religious instruction. Anyone who assisted regularly at it acquired the necessary Christian knowledge. In hearing, in praying, and in acting, he grew up in the Christian religion. The missionary Church of the first centuries has irrefutably proved that it is possible to give basic religious instruction by means of divine worship alone. Should we not, in view of the missionary situation today all over the world, draw some valuable lessons from this historic fact? Moreover, worship teaches in function of life and action; Christians learn by bringing to worship from the beginning their personal religious activity; thus knowledge and life form one whole.

Another great merit of primitive worship was that it was a *perfect school of Christian prayer*. The characteristics of classic Christian prayer that we admire today in the Roman liturgy were clearly marked in the primitive liturgy: the theocentric and Christocentric orientation through Christ to the Father; the primacy of the prayer of praise and thanksgiving, related to the prayer of petition in function of the life and the spirit of the whole community; the climax in the Sacrifice and Communion. Christians not only understood the liturgical prayers, but considered them as "their" prayers, even though they were recited by the priest or bishop. So the great eucharistic prayer, the core of all Christian prayer, enlisted the active participation of the faithful by the introductory dialogue, by their enthusiastic joining in the Sanctus of the celebrant and of the hosts of heaven, by the final Amen to the Canon recited *aloud* by the priest. Thus public Christian prayer was wholly liturgical, yet it did not set up any needless obstacles to private prayer. In those days no form of public "popular" prayer, composed for another purpose, went on concurrently with the Mass. The liturgy itself was an effective initiation into the spirit of Christian prayer, and so rendered a service to missionary work of the highest order, a service that has never been equalled in any subsequent period. As catechumens learned the faith by hearing God's message and responding to it in the reading service, so neophytes were transformed into the spirit of Christ by taking part in the Sacrifice.

The martyrs of Abilene show us how the Mass bound a *Christian community together* in time of persecution. Their bishop had gone away before the persecution began: the priest Saturninus was their leader in continuing Christian worship. They knew the danger of holding a liturgical service during the "indescribable torments" of the Diocletian persecution. But "they could not live without the Mass." In those days, excommunication, involving exclusion from common worship, was the greatest and most dreaded penalty for sin. In thus creating and developing the spirit of Christian fellowship, the liturgy carried out a great missionary work: it provided an oasis in the midst of persecution and unceasing oppression, a protection against the harmful influences of the pagan world, a unifying and dynamic force for missionary propaganda, an object of admiration to the pagans and a reason for conversion.

Christian worship thus *formed apostles.* There was no direct orientation toward the missionary apostolate, although there were public prayers for catechumens and for pagans. But in taking part in the solemn thanksgiving of the liturgy, Christians became aware of the riches of their redemption in Christ, and so, urged by motives of gratitude, they became active heralds of Christ. Have we no need of such heralds today?

Now that we have examined some of the qualities of the liturgy in the early Church, let us compare it with the liturgy as celebrated in later periods, in order to arrive at a just estimate of its value.

The Worship of the Missionary Church in the Middle Ages

At the end of the fifth century, the Christianization of the Roman empire was completed so far as the long-established peoples were concerned. But the Church then faced a new missionary task, of world-wide historical importance, the conversion of the "barbarians" of the North, of the German and Slavic peoples. Did means that had already proved their worth continue to be used? Or, if new tactics were adopted, what were the reasons for so doing, and what were the results in missionary work? Let us first consider the historical facts.

Long before the Church began to devote herself to any large scale effort to convert the Germanic and Slavic peoples, we have evidence that from the fourth century on, in the East — at Antioch to begin with — there was a great falling-off in *the active participation of the people in the essential parts of the Mass.* This began with a neglect of Communion, and soon led to a failure to take part in the offertory and in the Sacrifice itself. For, at the time, the faithful considered the Sacrifice and the sacrificial banquet as so closely related that the man who refused to receive Communion thereby showed his lack of interest in the Sacrifice. Why should he bring up to the altar any bread and wine at the time of the offertory procession? Thus numerous texts of the fourth century show that many Christians gave up, not only going to Communion, but also taking part in the Sacrifice; they left after the Readings.[5]

By insisting on the obligation of assisting at the Sacrifice, the Church finally succeeded in having the faithful remain until the Canon was finished, and in this way the continuation of the offertory procession was assured for a while. But its real significance had vanished; no longer was it intimately related to taking part in the sacrificial banquet. Little by little, from the ninth century on, *instead of the bread and wine originally offered, other things and, soon, money were offered.* The clergy, perhaps had little objection to this change: the donations were used for their maintenance. But from the point of view of participation in the Eucharistic Sacrifice, the old custom was infinitely more expressive. From the very fact that the faithful presented the material for the Sacrifice, it appeared clearly as *their* Sacrifice; their gifts represented themselves; they themselves became symbolically the material of the Eucharistic Sacrifice; the Lord took them up into His Sacrifice.

As this process continued, the abandonment of active participation extended to the other parts of the Mass. *The people more and more yielded their "speaking part"* to a choir of clerics, and to the assistants. Even the choir soon became superfluous, for the priest carried out its functions also by reciting the texts to be sung. This development and its results is shown in concrete form in the "Missale plenum," the Mass-book complete in one volume, which, in the thirteenth century, began to take the place of the sacramentary, lectionary and antiphonary. If the priest was to carry out all these functions, obviously he needed to have all the texts in one book. The choir and clerical assistants became a kind of "decoration" for the feast days. Only the server was left to show that the priest, in the private Mass that became more and more customary, celebrated Mass *for* the people, though he had no need *of* them. In the eighth and ninth centuries, Mass was celebrated without even a server, but this abuse did not take permanent hold.

With this falling off in the active participation of the people, there came about a corresponding separation of the priest from the congregation, a separation most evident in the *silent recitation of the prayers of the Sacrifice itself, especially of the Canon.* This was now considered to be the affair of the priest, not of the people; it obviously seemed better that he should recite these prayers in a low voice.

During all the epoch that now concerns us, that is, from the beginning

5. Especially significant texts are: Chrysostom, *In Eph. hom.* 3 (*PG* 62, 29); Synod of Antioch 341, can. 2 (*PL* 67, 60); Canons of the Apostles about 400, can. 10 (*PL* 67, 142); Cesarius of Arles, *Serm.* 73, 2 (*PL* 39, 2276 f.).

of the Middle Ages until their height, *the ceremonies of public worship continued to develop*. Rites and prayers multiplied to form a rich and complex whole, but one which continually became more complicated and difficult to grasp. And the newly-admitted prayers and rites, in spite of their beauty and their profound significance, did not always conform to the primitive form of the Mass (we find, for instance, prayers in the singular, prayers addressed to Christ and to the Holy Trinity, sequences), and obscured in a certain way the clear lines of the original structure (as do the prayers of the offertory, for instance, and those after the final dismissal). All this enrichment was, as history bears witness, the work of a deep piety, of a zeal anxious to celebrate the central mystery of our religion in a magnificent way. Thus this process brought about, *in place of the direct contact with the people, a great increase of pomp and ceremony*, and even, in the great cathedrals, the development of an elaborate ritual inspired by the ceremonies used in royal courts, and equally remote from the people.

This worship of the Middle Ages was no longer the worship of a missionary Church. The Church carried it out even in the regions of her missionary activity, but it no longer had, as did the worship of the primitive Church, a truly missionary character. It became more and more the cult of an established Church, of a Church that was, one might say, triumphant, who now appeared more as a resplendent queen before her subjects than as a mother teaching her children and praying with them.

This same period was one of great activity. The Church found herself confronted with a new state of affairs. For the first time she had to deal with people who needed *not only to be Christianized, but also to be civilized*. This new situation had a special influence on the choice of a liturgical language.

How did it happen that Latin became *the language of the liturgy* even in the German missions? At the time when the Church undertook the work of a systematic and intensive evangelization of these regions, that is, in the seventh and eighth centuries, the liturgical language differed quite perceptibly from the popular language. Even in Roman lands, the language of the people had grown away from the Latin of the Church, so that, from this time on, we observe sadly how the people become less and less able to follow the wonderful texts of the liturgy. But nobody, at the beginning of the Middle Ages, even in once Roman regions, would have dreamed of using in worship the decadent Latin of daily speech. Everyone, even simple people, would have thought this a profanation, for the Romance languages had not yet become sufficiently developed for liturgical use.

Even before undertaking the large-scale evangelization of Germany,

Latin had in some sense been adopted as the liturgical language for peoples of Germanic origin. The evangelization of Germany itself took place after that of the Germanic tribes which migrated into Latin-speaking regions. Those who settled in these countries formed a minority of the whole population, and there seemed to be no call to formulate a special liturgical language for their benefit. These newly-arrived conquerors were uncivilized at first, but they were pupils eager to acquire the old Roman culture, and they became Romanized in a comparatively short time.

Later on during the evangelization of Germany, Latin continued to be used as the language of worship. In the face of the wonder felt by these Nordics at the superior culture of the Latin, and in the face of the very aristocratic character of the classic German mission, there seems to have been no serious opposition on the part of these new converts. As they admired the culture of the south, so they admired its solemn and mysterious liturgy. And can we say that there were no political considerations involved? It would be putting it too strongly to say the use of Latin in the liturgy was politically premeditated. But the sense of the need for political unity, inherited from the Romans and living on in the Roman Church, certainly led naturally to a solution of the language question which would assure more stability and unity in the world situation of those times. Bitter experiences with the Eastern Churches who were then hastening toward separation from Rome, made it seem desirable to bind the flourishing missionary Church of Germany as closely as possible to Rome. The Latin language, the common language of the Church, fostered and strengthened this union far more effectively than it does today. For at that time the language of Rome was not only the language of worship which had to be understood by the clergy; it was the only cultured language of Western Christendom, which had to be learned by anyone who wished to attain a high degree of culture or to carry on any literary or scientific work. The clergy of Germany had a great appreciation of Latin formation. They would have thought it beneath the dignity of Christian worship and the holy mysteries to celebrate them in a "lingua barbarica." This was the reason behind their irritation with and their violent attacks against Sts. Cyril and Methodius, the great apostles of the Slavs. For these actually tried, with the express permission of Rome, to establish the ancient Slavic language as the language of the Church in Slavic countries. It was not in Rome that understanding of this important question was lacking. But in any case, the inability of the ordinary people to understand the language of the liturgy militated in every way against their active participation in Christian worship.

Another force working along the same lines was the *new mode of theological thinking*. In former times, Christian worship was considered to be the thanksgiving of the Christian community, which, gathered around Christ, its risen Head, and presented by Him to the Father, was enabled to offer to the Father fitting worship. But the new Christian mentality turned its regard primarily on the *mysterium tremendum*, to which we should respond with feelings of fear, of sinfulness and unworthiness. The fact that religious fear became more and more prevalent in these times is admitted by all historians, and we do not need to go into its causes in any detail. But let us notice the part played in this development by the emphasis placed on the divinity of Christ in preference to His function as Mediator, the effect of the controversy with the Arians; and also the part played by the growing worldliness of the times which increased the individual's awareness of his own unworthiness. The results of this new attitude were manifested particularly in the infrequency of Communion. Saints such as Caesarius of Arles and Gregory the Great laid down such severe conditions for the worthy reception of Communion that ordinary Christians could receive it only very rarely. And, obviously, this diminution in the number of Communions was due also to the growing loss of fervor among Christians and to the people's ignorance of the close relationship between the sacrifice of the Mass and Communion.

During this period, the Christian congregation, gathered together in the presence of God and hierarchically organized, was less and less considered to be the subject of Christian worship. The liturgy was seen as being above all the *worship of the whole Church* carried out by the celebrant in its name. The simple faithful took on more the role of spectators admitted to the heavenly drama and favored with the Lord's gifts. And so the perfect execution of the ceremonies carried out by the priest in the name of the Church was increasingly emphasized. "Juridical" representation by the priest took the place of the worship offered by Christians themselves as living members of Christ. The priest offered the sacrifice in their name. He was even thought to communicate in their name, according to some opinions of the time.[6]

And in consequence also of this predominance of the *mysterium tremendum*, the Mass came to be thought of less as our "Eucharist" to the Father, and more as the coming down of God to us at the consecration, requiring as our first duty to adore the Host and Chalice at the Consecration and elevation. So the central act of the Mass was

6. Josef Jungmann, S.J., *The Mass of the Roman Rite*, Vol. II, p. 364.

no longer found in our self-donation to the heavenly Father in union with Christ, but rather in the adoration we pay to Christ.

The effects of these changes *on missionary work* are what interest us here above all. The historical facts hardly allow us to avoid making the judgment that because of the profound changes which began with the dawn of the Middle Ages, Christian worship in great part lost its missionary power.

We see first of all an unfortunate lessening of its *catechetical value.* A language unintelligible to the Christian community and increasingly complicated ceremonies prevented the liturgy from accomplishing its missionary work of instruction. The people of the Middle Ages did, it is true, understand and love religious symbols. And they loved the liturgical ceremonies, though they did not understand them. But liturgical actions and symbols, apart from the language with which they form a whole, have very limited teaching value. In former times, the liturgy, both in the texts designed as instruction and in its prayers, gave the Christian people an inexhaustible wealth of catechetical teaching, actually fulfilling the task of catechetics properly so called. What more was needed was taken care of by the oral teaching inserted in the liturgy itself. But today, on the contrary, formal catechesis has to bear the whole burden of instruction, and this overburdening is particularly felt in the missions where the priest cannot find the time to give all the necessary teaching.

During the Middle Ages, the general level of religious knowledge was very low. It was considered quite sufficient for ordinary Christians to know the Our Father, the Apostles' Creed, the Commandments of God, and, later on, the seven Sacraments. The decadence of preaching and of catechesis during the first half of the Middle Ages made the situation worse. The whole catechetical development of the following centuries, the growth of popular medieval piety, the formation of the great popular devotions, the growth of a religious literature in the language of the people, the establishment of many schools in the cities, were all needed in order slowly to raise the level of religious knowledge. And in spite of all this, the general knowledge of fundamentals remained distinctly inferior to that of the Christians of the first centuries, a historical fact that is explained by the small extent to which the most abundant source of religious teaching was opened up to the faithful. If this lack did not produce, in the Middle Ages, the harmful effects that it does today both in the missions and in once Christian countries, this is due on the one hand to the modest cultural level of the people at that time and, on the other, to the profoundly Christian atmosphere of medieval life.

To the same degree, during these ages, the liturgy *ceased to be the classic school of Christian prayer.* This was another great loss from the missionary point of view: is not the Christian formed, above all, by prayer? The great popular devotions, so fruitful for the Christian people and for the Church in general, can never fully replace the liturgy as a school of prayer.

And, finally, Christian worship lost to a great degree its power of *forming the community.* Another value lost, with incalculable consequences in missionary work! The progressive loss of active participation and its replacement by an attitude of passivity weakened the sense of a living community and of personal cooperation in communal Christian life. The motives for taking part in worship became chiefly the hope of gaining spiritual benefits — certainly a sound enough hope — and the need to satisfy a grave obligation. Since everyone was content with merely passive participation, and since catechumens and pagans were admitted to the sacrifice and there was no external difference between their kind of "participation" and that of the baptized, the Christian no longer had the sense of the special Christian dignity of taking part in the Mass, but saw rather, in distinction to catechumens and pagans, the obligatory character of his attendance at Mass on Sundays.

We shall finish our sketch here without going into modern missionary history, since there is no need to do so in order to achieve the purpose of this chapter. There is no question, obviously, of bringing accusations against this period of missionary history. Complaints do nothing to solve present problems, and the changes that took place from the beginning of the Middle Ages could hardly have been prevented; experience and awareness were both lacking. But can we not, and should we not today draw from the study of this historical development many valuable lessons for our apostolate?

CHAPTER TWO

Basic Missionary Values of the Liturgy

JOHANNES HOFINGER, S.J.

Our historical study has shown us how effective Christian worship can be as a missionary force, and how effective it actually was during the early ages of the Church. But our study has also shown us that not all forms of worship have the same missionary value: every solemn rite may be, from this aspect, less valuable than a simple one that is intelligible and truly popular. The elaborate liturgy that flourished in the cathedrals and abbeys of the Middle Ages, for example, must certainly be considered inferior in apostolic effectiveness to the unostentatious cult of primitive Christian communities. Our brief historical sketch has already indicated wherein the apostolic values of the liturgy are to be found, but now we need to study these values systematically in order to determine what are their essential and permanent elements.

Public worship in the missions has a threefold task to fulfill: catechetical, pastoral, and cultual — the last of these being, of course, the most fundamental.

The Catechetical Value of the Liturgy

The missionary knows that he has been sent, first of all, to proclaim the Good News to those who lack the faith; to establish the kingdom of God by teaching Christian doctrine to the baptized and the unbaptized; to strengthen the beginnings of Christianity in his territory. He can accomplish each of these tasks much more effectively with the aid of services in which the catechetical values of Christian worship are effectively brought out.

Experts in catechetics today unanimously recognize the catechetical value of properly conducted worship. Since the beginnings of the modern catechetical movement, we have been forced, in the countries where it has made progress, to bring out these values more and more and to place them at the service of religious education. As the catechetical renewal in its first period interested itself primarily in questions of *method,* it was from this point of view that Christian worship was first studied and appreciated.

The worship of the Church actually constitutes an "intuitive" form of instruction of the first order, and this is especially valuable in the missions. Does not our scholarly teaching of religion run the risk of being too abstract for peoples who think in concrete and imaginative concepts? Do not our mission schools in general lack the material means needed for giving a more intuitive form of elementary catechetical instruction? Our catechumens need to be initiated into Christian truths by way of their senses, and the liturgy wonderfully satisfies this need, offering not merely an image but an actualization of religious reality. A real chalice that the catechumen can look at closely and perhaps kiss respectfully impresses and teaches him much more effectively than does a picture of a chalice. A priest actually coming to the altar in the presence of the catechumens and beginning to celebrate the Mass holds their devout attention much more closely than any description or reproduction of these same liturgical actions. We Catholic missionaries are often too little aware of our wealth in this regard. In our churches with their decorations, in the objects and actions used in the liturgy, Christian truths find an expression that is strikingly concrete and even dramatic. And the liturgy is far more than an abundantly illustrated catechetical manual that brings the mysteries of our faith within reach of catechumens and Christians, children and adults alike, and recalls them unceasingly to their memory. To proclaim in common prayer our faith in these great mysteries obliges us to make a personal commitment, allows us to make them our own by practice. If the principle of "learning by doing," so inculcated by modern teaching methods, can ever be fully applied, it is here. And we can add to this the rich variety of feasts, the religious atmosphere of the ceremonies, the living experiences of the various rites.

But while we should willingly recognize and make full use of these methodological resources, we should realize clearly that in themselves they do not constitute the decisive catechetical value of the liturgy. This consists primarily in the fact that here *the very substance of Christian faith and Christian life is taught* in the most direct and effective way. The catechetical requirement of concentration on the core of the Christian religion is here realized in an exemplary way; it is always the basic mysteries of our religion which our Mother Church has us ceaselessly pray and sing. Consequently there resounds through the whole liturgy, as a kind of thorough-bass, the mystery of mysteries: that is, our redemption by Christ, our return to the Father by Christ, our divine Brother and Savior. Without any question, this is the central theme of the whole liturgy, and it shines out with special clarity in the two great liturgical realities which have special catechetical importance even in the initiation of children and catechumens: the celebration of the Mass and the liturgical year.

This "mystery of Christ," as St. Paul so strikingly calls it (Col. 4, 3), is unquestionably the proper theme of the Church year, whose two basic cycles, centered in Christmas and Easter, celebrate the mystery of our salvation from different but complementary points of view. The mystery of Christ and our participation in it also form the basic matter of the celebration of the Holy Sacrifice. This central mystery of our belief is here seen also in its relationship with the other basic doctrines of Christianity. As in the teaching of St. Paul (see especially Eph. 1, 3-14; Col. 1, 27-2, 3; 4, 3; Rom. 16, 25 ff), so in the Eucharistic Sacrifice, it appears as "the" mystery, purely and simply, *mysterium fidei,* which synthesizes all the other doctrines of the Christian faith in a sublime unity.

How clearly also in the celebration of the Holy Sacrifice does the theological and Christological character of our religion shine out: Christ, the great gift of the Father, Christ, our way to the Father.[1] Anyone who takes part wholeheartedly in the Mass and the liturgical year cannot continue to lack a fundamental knowledge of Christian truth or the truly religious attitudes which are more important than any detailed knowledge.

But the final and decisive reason for the superiority of teaching by means of worship over any other form of Christian preaching consists in the fact that *the liturgy gives what it teaches.* It makes us directly participate in the mystery of Christ as it presents this mystery to us. If there is in Christianity a time and place in which we participate in the mystery of Christ, in the true sense of the term, it is certainly when we take active part in the worship of the Church. Holy Scripture teaches us that this is true of the sacraments.[2] For even greater reason, it is true of the Eucharistic Sacrifice, in which the Lord associates in His sacrifice the Church, His Bride, the members of His Mystical Body, in which He offers with them and they with Him. Theologians differ as to the way in which the saving work of Christ is actualized and carried

---

1. See Chapter 7 on teaching the Mass.
2. For Baptism: Rom. 6, 3-14; Col. 2, 12; Gal. 3, 28; I Cor. 12, 13. For the Eucharist, especially John 6, 53-58; for Marriage, Eph. 5, 32.

out in Christian worship. But they have always unanimously agreed that the worship of the Church truly involves a mysterious participation in the redeeming work of Christ, in such a way that in the liturgy we not only partake of the fruits of the redemption but also take part actively in Christ's mystery and in His worship. This is true above all of the Eucharistic Sacrifice, of the sacraments also, and, to an essentially lesser degree, of the other ceremonies of the liturgy. It follows, then, on the one hand, that the active agent in each liturgical ceremony is the mystical Christ, the Head with His members, and, on the other, that the action of the mystical Christ is intrinsically and inseparably related to the saving work of Christ.

Christian worship is thus a true treasure-house of catechetical wealth. The more fully we appreciate our apostolate, the more we missionaries appreciate its value. Are we not carrying on the work of Christ among our pagans? Like Him, are we not called to dispense, not only knowledge about the divine life, but also this life itself, as abundantly as possible: *Ut vitam habeant et abundantius habeant* (John 10, 10)? And Christian worship properly carried out has the incomparable advantage of imparting a truly religious knowledge of this heavenly life, of making it appreciated, of communicating it in abundance. In this respect, it excells every other form of catechetical instruction, and nothing else can take its place.

This would be true even if we could establish in the missions, along with our worship, a school system that would give flawless instruction in religion. In those countries which have an excellent Catholic school system — such as Holland, Germany, the United States — the necessity is seen more and more clearly of complementing the best religious instruction in school with the teaching given in Christian worship. *And what of us in the missions?* In spite of all our efforts to raise the level of our Catholic schools and to use them as fully as possible in the service of our apostolate, we recognize grave lacks, we see the necessity of a renewal of our catechetical teaching. And even if our religious teaching in the schools were of the highest quality, how many Christians are reached by it only to a small degree, or not at all? And what of the neophytes, to whom we owe special care; before Baptism we take great pains to give them the necessary instruction, but after Baptism they need fuller instruction and much encouragement. The school does not reach them at all, and our own words only occasionally. What a great role, therefore, belongs to the liturgy!

The question then arises: how can our Christian worship be carried out so as fully to realize its catechetical potentialities? In our fourth chapter, we shall describe the qualities that a celebration must have in order to do so, and in subsequent chapters we shall study the chief forms of the liturgy in this light and give concrete examples. Here let us mention only three of the indispensable qualities of a catechetically valuable celebration: rich doctrinal content, the clear and eloquent expression of it, the cultivation of a personal and active attitude toward it in the prayers and liturgical activities.

The Pastoral Value of the Liturgy

Obviously no real separation can be made between catechetical instruction and pastoral care: they intermingle continually. But by the pastoral value of the liturgy in the missions we mean especially its contribution to the establishment and development of a true Christian life in a Christian community. The question is not only one of the Christian life of individuals, but also of cultivating and developing a true Christian community.

Let us ask, first of all, what do we missionaries, as shepherds of souls, expect of our Christians and our Christian communities, not dreaming of impossibilities, but conceiving an ideal that can be approximated in reality. In the missions as everywhere else, the Church gathers in the weak and sinful, those whom the Lord came to seek in the highways and the byways. We have to take account of this fact; but we need also to have clearly in view an ideal which it is possible to realize. To have meaning and to make progress, then, our missionary work should, it would seem, be directed primarily toward the following pastoral goals:

a) *To inspire joy and gratitude for the riches of the Christian religion.* This is a fundamental attitude, implied by adherence to the Christian message. Authentic Christianity is found where religious values are not merely known intellectually but are also lived and generously professed. Such Christianity requires a "eucharistic" attitude in prayer, and therefore it gives the primacy to thanksgiving. In mission countries, this feeling of gratitude, this assurance of possessing a great treasure, protects our Christians against the dangers of their pagan environment and makes them the heralds of the values and the truth of Christianity.

b) *To cause Christians to give a good example.* According to the will and the command of the divine Master, Christians ought to be "the city set on a mountain." Their very existence ought to attract the attention of pagans. For those outside the fold, the "visibility" of the Church is above all the example of the Christian community, not that of the isolated Christian alone. They are won by the example of true charity and true humility. Without this humility, the sense of possessing such great riches would degenerate into the pride of belonging to a special caste, often met with in those who have been Christian for a long time. And every missionary knows by experience how sterile is such an attitude.

c) *To utilize to the greatest extent possible the chief sources of Christian life:* the sacraments, the word of God, prayer. In view of the fact that Christians in missionary countries cannot receive the sacraments frequently, cannot assist often at holy Mass, it is necessary to make sure that they receive the sacraments as fruitfully as possible when they do receive them, that they take part in a celebration of the Mass which is as perfect as possible. The missionary can preach but seldom in isolated communities; the word of God as given in the liturgical readings must supply this need. And, so far as prayer is concerned, not every cherished form of prayer nourishes and forms Christian life to the same degree. The highest formative power belongs to liturgical prayer when it is thoroughly understood and consciously carried out.

d) *To foster the internal union* of the Christian community, the profound sense of belonging to the universal Church and of being under her protection. The isolated Christian who lacks this sense of communal strength easily gives in to the influence of his un-Christian environment and, at the least, loses his missionary dynamism; he becomes a crypto-Christian.

e) *To create an apostolic mentality.* Those who have to spread Christianity are not only the missionaries and official catechists, but also and especially the ordinary Christians. They must, therefore, live their religion as a free gift from heaven which obliges them to communicate it to others. Here we touch on an important aspect of evangelization; and, reflecting for a moment on the history of the missions, we cannot avoid this question: how did the primitive missionary Church, with so few means at her disposal, obtain such great missionary results, while our missionary work today, with more means than ever at its disposal, has such a comparatively modest success? No single cause alone explains this fact; but, when we consider the matter closely, we cannot avoid the conclusion that in early times the laity played a much more active part than they do today in the missionary apostolate of the Church. What we need above all is not a more perfect organization of the lay apostolate, but more lay people aware of the greatness and the splendor of their vocation and consistently striving to conform their whole existence to its requirements.

Every missionary will recognize his own desires in these pastoral aims. The question then arises: *How can the fostering of Christian worship in the missions help us to attain these goals?*

The pastoral aspect of the liturgy must not, of course, be thought of as separate from other missionary activity; the liturgical renewal is not a kind of universal panacea rendering everything else unnecessary. It must be accompanied by an intensive proclamation of the word of God: by preaching and by catechesis. Nevertheless, the celebration of Christian worship, carried out with great care and adapted to the pastoral circumstances of each place, constitutes an indispensable means of attaining the pastoral goals described above.

a) *The liturgy creates a "eucharistic" attitude.* At the very heart of the efforts toward a liturgical renewal is the fostering of the most perfect and intense celebration of the Eucharist. Our Christians should be ever more fully inspired by this solemn Act of Thanksgiving; it should be the chief formative influence in their lives, their lives of grateful love. And this presupposes that in our preaching and our catechesis, we make Christianity known as a whole world of incomparable riches.

b) *The liturgy rightly understood is an initiation into Christian living.* The liturgy is far more than a ceremony working from without. And so we should strive primarily not for greater splendor in our ceremonies, but for a better understanding of the mystery, for greater personal participation. The divine life, here drawn from its sacred source, itself obliges us to a new way of life, as was stated clearly by the great missionary of the primitive Church: "Let us walk in newness of life" (Rom. 6, 4). It is easy to show — and we should insist upon this with our Christians — how Christian charity and humility must accompany an attitude that it is truly eucharistic and sacramental. Rich in heavenly gifts, we should, after the example of our heavenly Father, practice openhearted charity; since we have received everything as a free gift, we should be the more humble. What light the holy mysteries cast upon our Christian vocation! And, when we compare our weakness with the grandeur of this vocation, what lessons in humility! What have we to glory in as compared with our pagan neighbors? We can only glory in the inexhaustible riches of Christ given to us for no merit of our own, and in our own weakness which corresponds so poorly to these riches and which too often hides or misrepresents them in the eyes of the pagans.

c) *Christian worship opens up the sources of Christian life:* the sacraments, the word of God, prayer. The liturgical renewal desires, above all, forms of worship which will foster interior participation in the sacrifice and the fruitful reception of the sacraments. It does not aim — except secondarily — to increase the external beauty of worship, but to cause the people to participate in it, body and soul. It desires to put the word of God contained in Holy Scripture once more at the service of souls, not only by the reading of it in private, but also by the public liturgical reading which is an essential element in Christian worship. And it is concerned, finally, with a profound renewal of the prayer of our Christian communities and of all those who are one with the praying Church.

d) *Christian worship creates and develops the sense of community which is so greatly needed in the missions.* The more active the participation of the people, the more effective is worship in building up the sense of Christian community. The spectators at a play do not think of themselves as in any way forming a community, but the actors are living and drawing closer the bonds that bind them together as a troupe each time the play is presented. In truly popular worship, the Christian congregation acts, prays, listens, sings, sorrows and rejoices. Nowhere so strongly as in worship can the Christian realize his membership in a glorious, world-wide community, including earth and heaven. Here "the Church" should appear to him as the community of the redeemed, in ordered hierarchical action, celebrating, praying, acting with its Leader and its Head.

e) *Christian worship forms apostles,* "missionaries from among the people," not *ex opere operato,* but by active participation in which Christians discover their wealth and their happiness. Worship should incite our people to take part in the apostolate, not so much by direct invitation — the Roman liturgy is very reserved on this point — as by awakening them to the realization of their heavenly wealth and of the love of God freely given, which in gratitude they should strive to proclaim and to communicate.

The Value of the Liturgy as Worship

The catechetical and pastoral values of the liturgical revival which we have been considering up to now are obviously oriented toward greater missionary effectiveness. But it should be clear that a well-developed form of Christian worship is not primarily concerned even with these important missionary values. The basic value of the liturgy is not to be sought in its catechetical and pastoral power. In the missions, as everywhere else, the primary task of the liturgy is to worship the Father "in spirit and in truth," and to this task everything else must be subordinated with generous missionary zeal, as being, indeed, the crown and the completion of our missionary activity.

In the missions, as throughout the whole Church, we celebrate Christian worship above all to offer to our heavenly Father our homage of grateful love and profound adoration. To care for the carrying out of this worship is one of the essential tasks of the missionary. But how can this duty of worship find due place among all our other activities? Have we no need of the active collaboration of our Christians in order to fulfill it rightly? Perhaps we are here posing a question that has been considered too little up to the present time.

The "divine Missionary" Himself clearly defined our mission once and for all when He said: "Go, make disciples of all nations, baptizing them . . . teaching them to observe all the commandments that I have given you" (Matt. 28, 19). The apostles were sent out into the world to preach, to announce the Good News of Christ to all peoples. But their missionary mandate was in no way exhausted by this. All real Catholic missionary activity begins with the preaching of the Faith; but its final aim is the establishment, the development, the bringing to perfection of a new family of God on earth, thanks above all to the life given in the sacraments.

To the "go and teach" of the missionary mandate of Christ is added the "baptize," and to this in turn the crowning "teach them to observe all things . . . ". Hereby is added the obligation of watching over the new Christians with ceaseless pastoral care after their incorporation into the community of God's children, so as to lead them to perfection, to their new divine life. To be sure, this pastoral work presupposes an indefatigable work of teaching and instruction. But our obligation as missionaries is not fully carried out by a merely intellectual introduction to a virtuous life, but in the ideal living of the sacramental life of the new family of God, above all, in carrying out the command given by our Savior on the eve of His Passion: "Do this in memory of Me" (1 Cor. 11, 24).

The life of the new people of God reaches its climax here on earth in the celebration of the Holy Sacrifice; and, in contrast to the missionary activity of Protestants which contents itself with the "service of the Word," true Catholic missionary work is, essentially, ordered to the fostering, step by step, of full participation in the holy mysteries — and this participation itself presupposes truly Christian life and activity, as well as careful preparation for the work of worship itself.

Here we touch upon a most important point in the missionary apostolate. Every missionary strives to save as many souls as possible in his given territory. The "give me souls" of St. Francis Xavier has been the light, both before and after his time, leading thousands of missionaries to heroism in the apostolate. This desire, as the missionary knows well, is that of his divine Master Who came on earth as a "missionary" in the fullest sense of the word, "to seek and save that which was lost" (Luke 19, 10). But was the winning of souls the final aim of Christ in His work of evangelization? Obviously not. Even above the salvation of men, the glory of His heavenly Father was His guide. If He was concerned with the salvation of souls, it was, finally for love of the Father. For His sake these "children of wrath" (Eph. 2, 3) were to be taken up and refashioned into loving and obedient children. Considered in this light, was not the missionary work of Christ a work of worship, carried out above all in His sacrifice on the cross? And does not its completion demand that He include those whom He has redeemed in this total giving, and cause them to participate actively in it? And when does this take place, if not above all, in the Eucharistic Sacrifice that He left to us?

Like Christ Himself, the Christian missionary strives to gather together the new people of God, to bring them up, to establish the kingdom of God, to raise up children to the heavenly Father by the sacrament of Baptism, and to form by the celebration of the liturgy those who will "adore Him in spirit and in truth," as the Father desires (John 4, 23 ff). But the homage paid to God's sovereignty, the total gift of self to the heavenly Father, the ideal adoration of the children of God, attain their culminating point on earth in Christian worship, precisely when the Christian community with Christ and by Christ offers itself to the Father in heaven. Christian worship is, therefore, in itself — without taking into consideration its catechetical and pastoral values — the end of all missionary activity, rightly understood.

It is clear, therefore, that the fostering of worship is the very center of missionary work, but it is clear also that the impeccable observance of the rubrics alone will not solve the problem. It is a question of leading the members of the Mystical Body of Christ to take a personal and active part in the sacrifice of their Head by means of the intense and active participation of the congregation. The celebrating priest cannot fulfill the part of the people by juridically representing them, any more than in the human body the heart can breathe for the lungs. The children of God themselves must be led "to adore in spirit and in truth" in our worship. And how can this be achieved unless the forms of worship are adapted to the special genius of each people? Thus we come back to our point of departure: the necessity to promote a more active participation by the people in liturgical worship and a greater degree of adaptation of liturgical forms so as to foster this participation.

In this chapter, we have also seen that in our efforts to promote the liturgy we should have before our eyes above all its function as worship. Far from being lessened by this, the effectiveness of our apostolate will be fully assured by it. Here also the word of the Lord is applicable: "Seek first the kingdom of God . . . and all these things will be added to you besides" (Matt. 6, 33).

CHAPTER THREE

The Urgent Need for Liturgical Renewal

JOHANNES HOFINGER, S.J.

The fact that the liturgy possesses such great missionary values might lead us to believe that the present liturgical movement must have received a warm welcome in the missions and have fructified the missionary apostolate. In general, however, this has not been the case, owing, as we shall see, to a number of special circumstances. For the most part, indeed, the liturgical renewal has still to be carried out in the missions, and it is most urgent that we set about this work as soon as possible, both because of the liturgical situation in the missions, and because of the pressing needs of the present time.

The State of the Liturgical Renewal in the Missions

Since any detailed description would go beyond the scope of this book, we shall content ourselves with giving an estimate of the whole situation, seeking not so much to support it with proofs, as to illustrate it, especially by examples drawn from the Chinese missions. Any such estimate cannot, of course, be just and accurate in all respects, for it cannot take into account the infinite variety of real life. In the mission countries, there are, from the liturgical point of view, real oases, here and there a desert, many steppes; even in the same region, striking differences are to be found. But in any case, neither our own experience nor the reports received from a variety of places reveal any profound penetration into, or realization of, the new effort toward "pastoral liturgy" in any important missionary area as a whole. During recent years, the Steyl Fathers in some Indonesian missions have made great use of liturgical worship for missionary purposes, the most prominent promoter and representative of these efforts being His Excellency, Bishop

31

William van Bekkum, Apostolic Vicar of Ruteng in Indonesia. In times past, the Benedictines of St. Odile were outstanding in their liturgical apostolate in Korea; but unfortunately the war has done away with all that. In spite of these attempts, and a certain amount of success, we are forced to admit that in missionary countries progress has been slow in the fostering of the liturgy. We missionaries are still, on the whole, among the "sluggish" whom the Holy Father sought to arouse from their apathy by his Encyclical *Mediator Dei*. The consoling thought that in the missions we have avoided the exaggerations to be found in some other places does not in any way authorize us to sleep the sleep of the just.

The condition of Catholic worship in China may be taken as fairly typical here. Missiologists do not consider China to be a backward missionary country. Indeed, one of the most eminent scholars, Johannes Beckmann, who is able to judge the actual situation from first hand observations, has stated, both in speech and writing, that before the advent of Communism, the missions in China were well in advance of many others.

First of all, certain things have been achieved there which might well lead to sound developments in the future. For centuries, community prayer has been the rule in the missionary Church of China. Such prayer is zealously carried out. The Chinese Christian has at his disposal many prayer-formulas, of high literary merit, taught both at home and in school. In their content, they are superior to the rather mediocre formulas of many Western prayer books of the last century. Moreover, the Christian in China realizes the fact that the Christian community should pray together during liturgical services, above all during the Holy Sacrifice. Even if there are very few present, the faithful assist at a low Mass by chanting together on the traditional tone the Mass prayer customary in their region. This promotes the active, regular and evident participation of the assembled community in worship.

Yet the actual form of this participation is far from being satisfactory. The prayers recited by the people are not, either in form or in content, near enough to the liturgical texts; the literary idiom of these prayers is too little understood by the less cultured people. But other grave deficiencies exist as well. The people pray, but they do not exercise to a sufficient extent their other chief function: to hear and to welcome the word of God in the spirit of faith. There is no colloquy between God and His people, a colloquy in which God should be allowed to take the initiative. The faithful are continually speaking to God, or, rather, making vigorous "acclamations," and, "having presented their compliments," so to speak, they go away without having given their Father in heaven any opportunity to speak to them. It is true that on Sundays and feast days, the prayer of the people is interrupted, after the Gospel, by the reading of the Gospel in Chinese; but the "Good News" is not an organic part of the celebration, nor is it understood to be an indispensable part. It is sad to see how the priest and the people go their separate ways: the priest recites the liturgical texts to himself in a low voice; the Christian people sing to themselves. At the climactic point of the Mass, the people, if they have finished their singing ahead of time, watch the priest attentively, in order to be able to take up their devout "cursus" immediately after the Consecration. Moreover, the people themselves and, it seems, many priests, are quite unaware of the deficiency of such a form of celebration. As we said in an earlier chapter, the absence of personal participation is taken for granted in the Chinese word for the laity's action at Mass: *wang missa,* to watch from afar what is being done at the altar.

We might inquire whether there do not exist in China, or in other missions, any forms of community Mass better adapted to their purpose. Such forms certainly do exist. Technically speaking, it is quite possible, in China for instance, to arrange a high Mass in which the people sing the Ordinary of the Mass in Latin in a very creditable way, and certainly with enthusiasm and remarkable unanimity. But are the people capable of expressing in these incomprehensible Latin texts either their Christian joy or, most particularly, the true significance of their participation in the Mass? In order to do so, they need to use simpler forms which would inculcate, as a living reality, the true meaning of the celebration of the Holy Sacrifice.

To arrive at a reasonable estimate of the liturgical situation in the missions, we need to take into account, of course, the *special difficulties* that face any liturgical renewal under mission circumstances. The zealous missionary always has the painful feeling that he has preached far too little. More than one apostle, interpreting mistakenly the word of St. Paul, says that he has been sent to preach the doctrine of Christ and not to administer the sacraments with great liturgical solemnity nor to busy himself with liturgical details which may be justified in Christian countries saturated with religion, but are inconceivable under missionary conditions. Yet with what great zeal would these same missionaries not devote themselves to the liturgical apostolate if they became aware of the kerygmatic power at work in the liturgy, if they realized that it possesses effectiveness that catchesis and preaching can never equal!

It might also be noted that the continual moving about of the missionary scarcely favors any taste he might have for beautiful ceremonies, and neither does the rarity of liturgical services in isolated parishes. Many small communities are visited only three or four times a year. Then, too, the faithful are not very numerous in these isolated communities: a hundred Christians are considered a large congregation. Moreover no trained personnel exists in such communities, and, as far as the missionary is concerned, time is lacking in which to educate the Christians who could be trained. Again, the extreme simplicity and poverty of many communities, the very modest standards of their schools, certainly handicap the progress of liturgical worship. And, finally, both the difficulties and the problems multiply greatly when one makes any serious attempt to adapt the form of participation in public worship to the native temperament.

All these obstacles could be overcome if in the formation of young missionaries, foreign as well as native, pastoral liturgy were given its due place, a place that has up to the present time too often been denied it. There are many reasons for this regrettable oversight. For a long time, although the situation has improved somewhat in the last decades, the preparation of professors in missionary seminaries was not equal to the importance of their task. The best men were entrusted with the major courses in theology and philosophy, and the teaching of the secondary branches was confided to men less well-trained. We may also note, in this connection, the paralyzing effects of the failure of many missionary seminaries to keep in touch with the currents of spiritual progress at work in Christian countries, the result, partly, of the unavailability of good libraries.

A recognition of all these difficulties is necessary for any sound judgment of the liturgical situation in the missions, and also for any successful promotion of the liturgical renewal. Missionaries themselves, like their superiors, are for the most part realistic men of action who do not wish to waste their time or to commit themselves to dangerous experiments. They can only be won over by becoming convinced of the extraordinary importance for the missions of a true liturgical renewal, one that will actually work in the given concrete situation.

Our times demand a worship that has its full missionary effectiveness. Once again, we might expressly emphasize that we in no way view the liturgical renewal as a universal remedy for the needs of our times. Our thesis is not that the missions today need nothing but a liturgical renewal. Our thesis is simply this: in order to carry out our missionary task today, we need above all a worship that is fully developed from a missionary point of view.

This need arises most obviously from *the catechetical situation in the missions today.*

In spite of great differences in many respects, all missions today have a *special concern for their schools*. The task of evangelization has become in great part a kind of school work; even the instruction of catechumens is carried out by methods similar to those used in the schools. This is not the place to discuss how this condition has come about, still less to depreciate the mission schools and their methods of teaching religion, or to cast doubt upon their great usefulness. The missions have made enormous sacrifices to establish their schools, and in the future they will watch zealously over their maintenance and development. They are certainly justified in so doing.

But what will happen if, one of these days, the schools are rendered powerless by force? We shall find ourselves in a very difficult situation, for our whole program of evangelization depends very much upon them. The situation would be aggravated still more if, along with the religious instruction, the preaching of the missionary and of his catechists were interfered with. Yet *the experience of recent years* proves without any doubt that when atheistic Communism comes into power, it brings with it the destruction of mission schools. And this threat comes not only from Communism; it exists in the countries where any totalitarian system takes possession of the schools, as has happened recently in South Africa. When colonies become independent, they tend, even without any Communistic interference, to reduce, if not to stop entirely, the work of mission schools. If this tendency does not yet show itself openly in certain countries, it is because they still feel the need of "provisional" help from these schools.

But community worship and preaching during sacred services are in much better case. Even atheistic Communism tries to disguise its hostility against religion and to preserve the appearances of a certain freedom of religion. It is easy, of course, for authorities to paralyze worship celebrated by a priest by driving out foreign priests under some political pretext or by refusing to let them into the country, while at the same time making it difficult for native priests to get the necessary authorizations to visit parishes deprived of their priests. But community worship held without a priest is much more difficult to attack.

Here Communism has taken us by surprise. We were in no way prepared for this kind of persecution, and this fact excuses us somewhat. In China, we were the first to be swept away. We lacked experience. After the blow has fallen, it is easy to talk about it without reproaching anyone. But what would we have done or tried to do if we had known in advance about this persecution and its particular characteristics?

If we had known that our schools were going to be destroyed, we would not, of course, have abandoned them; we would have used them up to the last moment, especially the secondary schools, to do everything possible to form lay apostles. Thanks be to God, we did succeed in forming a large number of young people and students who, in the present persecution, are a priceless aid to the Church and to her apostolate; the work both of evangelization and of religious preaching has fallen particularly on them. Wherever they are sufficiently numerous and have succeeded in keeping some contact with one another, the dangers resulting from the persecution have been at least partly neutralized.

But besides this formation of an élite, we would also have adapted our religious services to those new requirements. When the school has disappeared, the task of giving Christian teaching to the faithful, both children and adults, falls back almost entirely on public worship, on religious services, as it did in the first ages of Christianity and during persecutions. Certainly, Christian instruction would need also to be given by lay catechists; the word of God to be proclaimed with even more zeal than in times of peace; teaching and preaching need to be carried out on the occasion of every religious service. But this is not enough. Even if the missionary is allowed to remain in the country and to go about freely, he cannot preach and celebrate in all his stations at the same time, and, furthermore, the regular teaching of religion by catechists, outside the services, is easily interfered with. Thus the task of giving sufficient religious instruction must be assumed by the various forms of public worship: by those services conducted by a priest, but, even more, religious services that can be held by the Christian community in the absence of a priest. (We shall devote two chapters later on in this book to the question of such services.)

Priests sometimes say that Christians in missionary countries appreciate Holy Mass much more fully than do average Christians in our own lands. Why, then, is there so much need for a liturgical renewal in the missions? Thanks be to God, this objection has a great deal of truth in it. Christians in missionary countries, taken as a whole, do greatly appreciate Holy Mass and assist at it with fervor, even when the form of community participation leaves something to be desired in its adaptation to the needs of the people. A living faith can profit greatly from it. But should we not do everything in our power to make that profit even greater? And should we not also take into account a time when public worship, celebrated with or without a priest, may have to fulfill the catechetical task now carried out by the school?

In any case, Communism is not satisfied with what it has gained already; it is still at work, trying to bring other mission countries under its yoke. In them also it will proceed as it has done in China, in North Korea, and in North Vietnam. We should not be worried by vague conjectures or doubtful prophecies; but we must face the evident dangers of the present situation and take the necessary measures. A ten per cent probability of fire is enough to make a man take out insurance on his house. Is there not at least the same degree of likelihood that some mission areas now enjoying full liberty will suffer from a Communist invasion?

It is no less obvious that when Communism actually does reach out its iron hand over mission regions, it is too late to make preparations against it in the domain of the liturgy. *The necessary transformations must be made in a time of comparative peace,* and must be well established before missionaries begin to be driven out and otherwise restricted. What is the situation in China today? Could we possibly, after the persecution had broken out, have undertaken those modifications in the prayer-life of our Christian communities which would have assured to public worship its full religious and catechetical effectiveness?

But, someone might object, surely it would not be desirable to organize our whole apostolate in relation to Communism? Granted; obviously, nobody would think of calling in the firemen before there is any fire. But everyone wants the firemen and their equipment to be ready and thinks it desirable to take out fire insurance before the alarm actually sounds.

The essential point, however, is this: *even if the danger from Communism were to disappear,* as we all hope and pray it will, are there not many other compelling reasons for giving to Christian worship its proper effectiveness in the missions? Let us consider only one: in insisting so much on the teaching of religion in schools, our missionary work of evangelization has taken on, without our intending it, an undue character of rationality. Should it not be the task of worship, viewed under its catechetical aspect, to re-establish the equilibrium here, drawing its inspiration from modern catechetics?

However impressive the work carried out by the school and its religion courses during the last few centuries, and however great its services may be in the future, our apostolate does not have so many means at its disposal that it can afford to neglect the catechetical values of worship. And the same conclusion forces itself upon us if we consider *the age of transition in which we live.*

For such an age demands a greatly increased vitality. We all have the feeling that the missionary apostolate has entered a new stage with the overthrow of colonialism and the emancipation of the non-white peoples. What the future will be depends in great part on what happens in this period of transition. We must summon all our energy to make the voice of Christ heard among these peoples who are now awakening, to form them in the spirit of Christ. More than ever before, these peoples find themselves at the crossroads; which way will they choose? We all grieve to see our means and our opportunities of exercising a formative Christian influence among these peoples so cut down. We do not feel that we are in control of this critical condition. How then, under such conditions, can we allow an educational force of the first magnitude to be only half-utilized?

But, someone might object, Christian worship does not reach the masses in missionary countries, the masses whom we most especially wish to interest and to win for Christianity in this time of transition. And even if it somehow were to reach them, Christian worship is primarily for Christians. This is quite true, and therefore nobody dreams of relying only on a liturgical renewal. But, and let us clearly understand this fact, our missionary influence on those outside the Church depends in great part on the religious level attained by the Christians, on their own Christian vitality. Everything that can help us to foster this vitality must necessarily be profitable to our apostolate to the pagans. Observe what happens in connection with spiritual exercises. We do not preach retreats — with some few exceptions — to unbelievers, but to Christians. If we succeed, however, in awakening in our Christians, by means of retreats, a greater understanding of their Christian vocation and a greater religious zeal, our missionary work has obtained certain gains from it. Was there any limit to the missionary effectiveness of the Spiritual Exercises given by Ignatius Loyola to the professor, Francis Xavier?

What is actually our chief difficulty in our missionary apostolate at the present time: Is it primarily the small number of Christians? Or is it not rather that our Christians, taken as a whole, have too little vitality to exercise any profound influence on their unbelieving neighbors? Has not every powerful movement begun with a small number of men fully possessed by their ideal? If only we could fill our Christians with the spirit of Christ! How great is the need to do so at the present time! But what has the highest authority in the Church had to say in this very question? St. Pius X expressed himself in these words: "The primary and indispensable source of the true Christian spirit is the active participation of the faithful in the sacred mysteries and in the public and solemn prayer of the Church." And the liturgical reforms of the present Pope have no other meaning.

It is the task of the missions to act in accordance with these directives.

CHAPTER FOUR

Qualities That Should Characterize the Celebration of the Liturgy in the Missions

JOHANNES HOFINGER, S.J.

We have already pointed out the outstanding values of the liturgy in relation to our missionary work, and, in the following chapters of this book, we shall give practical suggestions as to how these values might be brought out in the celebration of the various rites. But first let us review briefly the principal qualities which must characterize public worship in the missions if the essential values of the liturgy are to be made fully available to our people.

The official Roman liturgy is a model for *richness in doctrinal content*. It is here that we should seek inspiration when we undertake the task of composing suitable texts for forms of community worship to be used in the absence of a priest. This richness of doctrinal content guarantees not only the catechetical function of public worship, but also its specific function as worship. The liturgy is essentially the worship of the new people of God, a cult of adoration and thanksgiving offered to God Who reveals and gives Himself to us in His works of creation and redemption. Our services, then, should continually recall to our minds these "marvellous works of God." And this is obvious, above all, when Christian worship is seen to be a real sharing in the mystery of Christ.

The *intelligibility* of Christian worship is, therefore, a most important cultual necessity. God expects from His new people that "adoration in spirit and truth" (John 4, 24) which Christ spoke of as being the distinctive characteristic of worship in the messianic age. Should not this quality be particularly evident in missionary countries where we are laying the foundations for the establishment and growth of the kingdom of God among a new people? Obviously, this adoration in spirit and in truth does not mean that the people need to understand every

39

word of the ceremonies. But is it possible to deny the fact that an accumulation of unintelligible prayers and ceremonies makes this adoration in spirit and in truth far more difficult for the people to render? And, under missionary conditions, a basic understanding of the rites cannot be assured by explanations given outside the services themselves, since the time needed to do so is lacking, nor by the use of translations.

It is sometimes taken for granted that the rites of the Church have already been made intelligible to the people in the majority of missions by means of the prayers and hymns given them to say and sing during the Mass and other liturgical ceremonies. But these prayers and hymns often render only imperfectly the rich doctrinal content of the liturgy. And, since they are carried on as a kind of accompaniment to the action of the priest rather than being a means of active participation in the liturgical ceremonies, they do not help to form a worshipping community. Priest and people should be united together: the Christian community carries out its worship under the leadership of the hierarchy, and this truth should clearly appear in the external form of the people's participation. And so we arrive at another necessary quality of Christian worship in the missions — and, obviously, not here only: it should be carried out *communally*.

Christian worship is a great deal more than a gathering of many Christians in one place in order to pray each man for himself. Christian worship requires that the community be praying. Our living union with Christ, our invisible Head, and with His visible representative, the celebrant, should be clearly and beautifully evident. There must be united action by the priest and the people; this, by the very nature of the liturgy, which calls for the carrying out together of various roles. It should be quite evident, from the way in which the ceremonies are carried out, that the celebrant is the leader, but also that he forms a liturgical whole with the congregation, that he draws the people into his prayer and his action. This has always been a basic concept of Catholic liturgy.

The liturgical texts themselves, from the most ancient times, leave us in no doubt on this subject. Is not this the meaning of the plural form that predominates in the most primitive texts? Is not this the formative concept behind their composition? And is not this the significance of the many phrases in which the celebrant addresses himself expressly to the people before beginning the main actions and prayers: that he wants to draw them into his action and his prayer?

In missionary countries, this visible community action is of the *utmost importance.* It is absolutely vital for our Christians in pagan lands, our neophytes and catechumens, to discover and deeply experience the mystery of the Church, at least during the time of worship. The more apparent is their active participation in the prayer and the action of the priest, the more they come to understand that their participation in worship signifies also their active collaboration in the apostolate of the hierarchy. Any "catholic action" that is rightly conceived and carried out is not limited to a program of external activities; it is born at the very heart of our religion, and it is here that it must first express itself.

To make real this communion between the priest and the people, we must above all restore the practice of having the people *give the responses,* by means of which the congregation feels that it is being really addressed by the priest and so responds to him wholeheartedly. But can these achieve their purpose if the people are addressed and must respond in Latin? Certainly, some short Latin phrases can be learned by heart by almost anyone; but can the liturgical purpose of these responses be achieved by phrases mechanically memorized?

This "community of worship," primordial in the liturgy of Christian sacrifice and prayer, should be evident also in the liturgy of the sacraments, as is indicated in the texts themselves. Here also, the people are not to remain mere spectators.

The active participation of the congregation must, obviously, be not any kind of "activity," but the *activity of prayer, activity vivified by the Spirit.* There are two reasons for insistence on this point. First, the majority of the peoples in missionary countries take a natural pleasure in liturgical ceremonies, being gifted for liturgical participation. It is up to us to cultivate these inclinations as fully as possible. But the same peoples often are found to have a tendency to remain satisfied with the external beauty of Christian ceremonies, as they were with the external show of their pagan rites before they were baptized. This tendency to be satisfied with ritual for its own sake does not disappear with Baptism. The missionary, therefore, needs to make available to his people the religious realities made manifest and given in visible forms in the sacramental actions of the Church; and he needs also continually to inculcate the *meaning* of the ceremonies. It is, of course, much easier to lay down this requirement than to carry it out. For carrying it out means engaging in a long and difficult struggle that is unremitting in its demands.

And if Christian worship in the missions is to enlist the intense but truly spiritual active participation of the congregation, it must also be characterized by simplicity and closeness to the people.

The ceremonies need to be *simple,* that is, easy to understand and to execute, for Christian worship has to take account of the needs of small and poor communities with few, if any, fully trained personnel, whose priests can visit them only rarely. Would that we might be dispensed from the rubrical requirements which may be fully justified in a religious community or in a large and well-administered parish in a Christian country, but which cannot help seeming utopian in a missionary situation and arouse the determined opposition of realistic missionaries!

In asking for ceremonies that are easy to understand, we are thinking particularly of the part of the people. We desire to assure the intense active participation of the whole congregation by means of forms of expression that are authentic and beautiful, but also natural and easily learned. This is a problem the solution of which will cause many a headache, and need much careful experimentation. But two things must always be taken into account. First, the fact that common actions are much easier for the people to learn than words; we need, therefore, to give them liturgical actions and gestures to carry out which will clearly express their active participation. This, in any case, is in harmony with the native temperament of most peoples in missionary countries, for to a far greater degree than most western peoples, they feel the need to express religious experiences in bodily movements.

And the second thing to be kept in mind is that the Church has always made it very easy for the simple faithful to take their active part in her worship by giving them as their "role," not long texts, but responses or acclamations that are easy to sing or say. The people themselves love such a form of participation which is at once simple and expressive, a fact which is proved by their preference for litanies.

When we missionaries visit even our smallest and most inaccessible communities, we always take our *catechist* with us, and therefore we have at our disposal at least a potential liturgically formed assistant. It is up to us, therefore, to train these catechists; and it may well be that it is on taking advantage of their potentialities that we can build our whole program. Our catechists can perform very valuable services as prayer-leaders, so that the people will have only the simple responses and singing to carry out. Catechists can also help in the work of training the people to take their active part in worship when the missionary himself is unable to find the time to do so.

Communal worship must also be *close to the people,* answering the needs of the Christian, appealing to his heart and will. The more the services are truly popular in the best meaning of the word, the more they are "of the people," the better will they fulfill their functions of worship, of catechesis, of building up the community. Such worship comes from the heart and reaches the heart; it can really be lived by the Christian community as its own worship, expressing its particular spirit and special qualities. And is this not what the Father in heaven desires when His well-beloved children come to honor Him in the simplicity of their hearts? The catechetical value of the liturgy also increases the more "popular" it becomes, for everything that is proclaimed gains in effectiveness the more deeply it resounds in the minds and hearts of the people. And during a ceremony that is truly popular, the Christian feels himself at home, the Christian community is drawn together more closely and awakens to its own special quality of life, its own special value.

It is here that adaptation of liturgical forms to the needs of people should play its part. And this should present no canonical difficulties, for if we apply the principle, *sacramenta propter homines*, to the very sacramental elements instituted by Christ Himself, should we not also apply it, and even more fully, to the additional forms and ceremonies with which, out of regard for our needs, our Mother the Church administers the sacraments?

In fostering this quality of nearness to the people, a most important role must be given to sacred music. To this vital question, we shall devote three chapters later on in this book.

And, finally, liturgical worship in missionary countries should borrow from the arts connected with the theatre a certain *dramatic quality:* first of all in the texts for the people's use, in which an oriental vividness might sometimes be preferable to Roman reserve and sobriety; and then in the gestures by which the people manifest their active participation reverently and devoutly. The great delight which the peoples of most mission countries take in the dramatic arts and their need to manifest the inner sentiments of their souls by appropriate bodily gestures are precisely the factors which offer such excellent opportunities for the cultivation of the dramatic aspect of worship, opportunities which we of the West might well envy.

In this connection, certain people both in missionary and Christian countries sometimes ask themselves whether it might not be preferable in some missionary territories to use one of the Oriental rites, as being temperamentally nearer akin to these peoples than the Roman rite. This suggestion, which certainly has some merit, nevertheless does not seem at all acceptable in this form; and this, for two reasons. Even though the Roman rite is characterized by a certain reserve and sobriety which is not so desirable in relation to the temperament of many mission peoples, nevertheless it is also characterized by one particular missionary value not found to the same degree in other rites. Its simplicity, its essential intelligibility, its peculiarly rich doctrinal content centered on the mystery of Christ, its insistence on the mediation of Christ, all recommend it most especially for use in the missions. Its lack of external dramatic action may be made up for by a better understanding of its inner structure on the part of the people, and also by some relaxation of the rubrics. (We shall return to this point in the final chapter of this book). Because of its essential simplicity, above all, the Roman rite seems to us to be the most adaptable to the needs of the missions. Other rites may have certain elements which recommend them, but in view of all the factors involved in this question, these other rites would be less suited to missionary use than the Roman.

And the second reason is not less important: a suggestion of this kind is completely impractical because generally unacceptable. In the present situation, the vast majority of missionaries would be opposed to such a liturgical revolution. Again, Rome would be much more apt to grant the authorizations required for needed or highly desirable adaptations of the Roman rite than it would be to grant permission for the use of an Oriental rite. And, in fact, such use would not be desirable from the viewpoint of the unity of the Church. Nonetheless, even though the introduction of a new rite into mission countries need not be considered even as a remote possibility, it is true that the study of the Oriental rites can offer many valuable suggestions about the forms, especially of the people's participation, to be used in missionary countries.

And we should keep in mind above all that the renewal of the liturgy is not primarily a matter of the renewing of liturgical prescriptions, but rather a renewal of our appreciation of the liturgy itself and a renewal of the way in which we celebrate the actual liturgy of the Church today.

PART TWO

THE WORSHIP OF THE NEW COVENANT

CHAPTER FIVE

The Celebration of Mass

Josef Kellner, s.j.

One particular characteristic of the Catholic Church is that she requires her faithful to take part in Sunday Mass as their chief religious obligation. She does not require of all some set form of daily prayer, as is the case in Islamism, for example, which is what might be expected from the command of the Lord: "that we ought always to pray." The Church sees the Eucharistic Sacrifice as being precisely "the culmination and center, as it were, of the Christian religion."[1] In this community of prayer and sacrifice, the faithful find "the principal source of the true Christian spirit"[2] and "the source of all holiness."[3]

Taking this truth as its starting point, the liturgical renewal, both in Christian and missionary countries, has tended, since the very beginning, towards a more profound understanding of Holy Mass and a closer participation of the faithful in the Holy Sacrifice. Once this important end has been attained, at least to a certain degree, it is not difficult to awaken a greater understanding of the other aspects of worship, such as the Sacraments, the sacramentals, etc. For they are all related in one way or another to the Eucharistic celebration as to their center.

What matters above all in Christian worship is interior participation. "The more the faithful take part in this sublime sacrifice, the more do

---

1. *Mediator Dei, Acta Ap. S.*, 39 (1947), p. 547. Cf. A. Bugnini, C.M., *Documenta Pontificia ad Instaurationem Liturgicam Spectantia*, Romae, 1953, p. 120, and *The Sacred Liturgy*, Vatican Library Translation, n. 66, p. 27, pub. by the National Catholic Welfare Conference, Washington, D. C.
2. See *Divini cultus sanctitatem, Acta Ap. S.* (1929) 35; Bugnini, 61 (trans. White List of the Society of St. Gregory in America, N. Y., 1954).
3. *Roman Missal*, Feast of St. Ignatius of Loyola, Secret. July 31st.

they profit from the blessings of eternal salvation."[4] Pius XII says still more explicitly: "The chief element of divine worship must be interior, for we must always live in Christ and give ourselves to Him completely, so that in Him, with Him and through Him, the heavenly Father may be duly glorified."[5] The divine Bridegroom wills to assure to His bride, *here and now,* participation in His prayer and His offering to the Father.

This interior participation is essentially a matter of the Christian heart at prayer. The hierarchical Church can by no means substitute itself for us, as individuals or as a community gathered together for worship; neither can the hierarchical Church directly give this participation to those who pray, nor impose it upon them. Its part is to make the way smooth, to remove obstacles, to awaken understanding by means of religious instruction and by the form of the Mass celebration itself. Later chapters will deal with other particular aspects of this manifold task; here we shall begin with the vital question of the form of the Mass celebration.

In the missions, even more than in Christian countries, the celebration of the Mass should make it clear that *the Holy Sacrifice is the heart and the climax of Christian worship.* Our catechetical instruction should, of course, never grow weary of stating that the Mass *is* Christian worship; but this theory should be confirmed and not contradicted by the way in which the services are conducted. It is contradicted, for example, if Benediction of the Blessed Sacrament, processions, and so on are celebrated more imposingly than the Mass, with more candles, more decorations, a greater number of assistants, more music, and the like. Orientals especially judge from what they see, not from what they are taught theoretically. They assess the value and importance of a ceremony primarily on the basis of its magnificence. In the Oriental missions, should we not, therefore, adapt ourselves to the native temperament, even if the rubrics call for twelve candles for Benediction with the ostensorium and do not prescribe or permit for the Holy Sacrifice more than two, four, or six, as the case may be?

If, now and then, the afternoon or the evening seem more favorable for carrying out a solemn celebration, we have today, thank God, the possibility of an evening Mass, a possibility that we should not neglect. In the missions, Christians do not hesitate to travel a long way in order to come to the church on great feast days. Not a few of them who would be prevented from coming at other times of day could assist at an afternoon Mass. But whenever a morning celebration satisfies the needs of the faithful and gives the day its festal quality, let us beware of

4. Bugnini, p. 54.
5. *Mediator Dei,* N.C.W.C. Trans. n. 24.

introducing — for reasons of personal piety, for example — Mass in the afternoon or evening.

In the missions, as everywhere else, there are *various forms of Mass celebration:* low Mass with or without prayers and singing, dialogue Mass, high Mass (*missa cantata*), solemn high Mass, pontifical Mass. The high Mass (*missa cantata*) is the ideal to be sought in the missions, and a great feast of the Church cannot be thought of without it. We need to work towards it as towards a superior kind of celebration. But is a *missa cantata* the form of Mass celebration most fitted to give our Christians a deepened understanding of the Eucharistic Sacrifice? Let us state it simply: the *missa cantata* is by no means an ideal form from the *pastoral point of view,* for it neither is, nor is it capable of being, a way of achieving real understanding of the Mass even if we make use of all the concessions granted to the missions by Pius XII in his encyclical *Musicae Sacrae Disciplina.* For, as things are at present, we cannot make free use of the language of the country, as is done, for instance, in the German high Mass with the people singing in German. The wider use of this form of celebration would, according to the encyclical, necessitate an express authorization by the Holy See; we must, therefore, keep to the language of the Church in the singing, the readings and the responses. But even for those Christians who are capable of learning the Latin chants, this foreign language always remains a more or less incomprehensible tongue; it never allows them to gain a deepened understanding of the sacred ceremonies. The liturgically ideal form of Mass celebration and the pastorally most effective are two different things, at least in mission countries.

The form generally called the "community Mass," that is, a Mass with prayers and hymns, answers more fully, though not ideally, to the pastoral requirements of worship in the missions; such a form of celebration is particularly suited for use on ordinary Sundays and in small communities. In such a celebration, there can be more or less singing, according to circumstances. To avoid disorders, certain principles laid down in the first centuries of the Church,[6] should always be followed.

1. The celebration should be permeated with the spirit of the liturgy: it should always have its congregational character, its looking to the glorified Savior, its attitude of reverence and thanksgiving, its sense of recollection, sincerity and "interiority," of hierarchical ordering. This spirit of the liturgy is indispensable. There is no need, however, to be tied down to any particular texts, for instance, in the sung parts. Here we should take account of concrete circumstances and of the spiritual

6. See J. A. Jungmann, S.J., *The Mass of the Roman Rite,* Vol. I., Benziger Bros., N. Y., 1950, p. 32.

needs which are to be satisfied by the teaching given in the readings. When, for instance, the homily is customarily connected with the Gospel, the reader might, in accordance with the priest's directives, substitute for the Epistle of the day, which may deal with an entirely different theme, a more appropriate passage from Scripture.

2. The principal parts of the Mass must be clearly marked and differentiated: the entrance, the readings, the preparation of the offerings, the action of the sacrifice, the communion, the conclusion of the Mass. Thus, for example, the readings should never be supplanted by singing; the part of the people during the Offertory, formerly expressed by the Offertory procession, should not completely disappear; the hymns, if there are any, sung during the central part of the Mass, that is to say between the Offertory and Communion, should be clearly related to what is being done at the altar.[7] But the entrance hymn, the hymns sung between the readings, and the closing hymn should all be inspired simply by the spirit of the day.

3. It seems most important to us that the close union between the priest and the congregation should be indicated externally, wherever this can be done. The vital contact between the nave and the altar, provided by the responses, for example, cannot be replaced by any reading of the same thing in a book, even in the missal. For the same reason, it is desirable that the celebrant himself should give the readings to the people, at least the Gospel.

4. However simple the ceremonies need to be, we must not neglect the element of variety. Eastern peoples especially appreciate ceremonies that have a certain dramatic quality: a procession, an expressive gesture, a symbolic action.

5. As far as possible, every community Mass ought to include some hymns. Singing gives to the Holy Sacrifice a festal quality: is not song the appropriate language of the soul and of the Christian community assembled for a solemn celebration? "A congregation that is devoutly present at the sacrifice," says the Encyclical Mediator Dei, "in which our Savior together with His children redeemed with His sacred blood sings the nuptial hymn of His love, cannot keep silent, for 'song befits the lover' and, as the ancient saying has it, 'he who sings well prays twice.' "[8] Singing, Hacker says, "belongs to the very essence of Christian worship,"[9] above all to Eucharistic worship. Its fundamental tone is the

7. See the excellent study of this question in: Dr. Josef Hacker, *Die Messe in den deutschen Diözesen-Gesang-und-Gebetbüchern*, Munich, 1950, pp. 52-76 and 129 ff.
8. *Mediator Dei*, N.C.W.C. Trans. n. 192.
9. Hacker, p. 75.

grateful joy of the redeemed children of God, which moves them to sing "Alleluia." A community which, gathered together with its priest to celebrate the Eucharistic Sacrifice, is not allowed to sing, is condemned to something unnatural. "A people that does not sing is a dying people; a religion that does not sing will die."[10]

6. In the missions, we should avoid any celebration of the Mass in which the participation of the congregation is reduced to rising and to making the sign of the Cross at the Gospel. Such celebrations too easily produce — especially in tropical climates — a state of spiritual torpor, from which it is impossible to rouse the people unless we give them more activity. Participation should include, so far as the missions are concerned: the responses (other than the prayers at the foot of the altar and the *Suscipiat*); the Amen expressing the people's affirmation after the prayer of the priest and at the end of the Canon; the hearing of the liturgical readings; one or more hymns; participation in the Offertory, in the great Eucharistic Prayer, and in Communion, expressed in one way or another by appropriate prayers, gestures, etc.

7. Devotional prayers said during the Mass should be carefully screened, and, so far as is found necessary, progressively transformed into forms that are richer and more vital.

8. We must allow some room for silence, but these pauses should not be unduly prolonged. Here again the liturgy itself is our model: it indicates that we should pray in silence *"per aliquod temporis spatium"* — for a short time.[11] If the pause is prolonged, the people will not know what to do, and here again we must take into account the restless temperament of those who live in tropical climates.

Concerning *the different parts of the Mass*, we should like to make the following remarks:

The entrance rite is very rich and complex in the present Roman Mass: the prayers at the foot of the altar, the Introit, the Kyrie, the Gloria, the Collect. If we base the community Mass on the regulations for high Mass, the prayers at the foot of the altar are not part of the role of the congregation.[12] The Introit, designed to give the fundamental tone and thought of the day, can be replaced by a hymn that resembles the Introit as closely as possible: let us call this briefly the "hymn of the day."[13] The Kyrie and the Gloria should remind us of our essential

10. *Diözesangesangbuch für die Bistümer Gurk*, Linz, St. Pölten, 1939, preface.
11. *Ordo Hebdomadae Sanctae Instauratus*, Feria IV, De Missa.
12. See Josef Gulden, "Grundsätze und Grundformen der Gemeinschaftsmesse in der Pfarrgemeinde," in *Volksliturgie und Seelsorge*, by Karl Borgmann, Colmar, O. J., 1942, pp. 101-104.
13. For further details on this topic, see the next chapter.

attitudes toward God: our dependence upon and need of His help as creatures and imperfect human beings (the Kyrie): our joy and thanksgiving as the redeemed children of God (the Gloria). Both the Kyrie and the Gloria can be recited or sung. This song of praise, the Gloria, should be among the prayers known by heart, among which there usually are only two prayers of praise: the Gloria Patri and the Apostles' Creed. The Collect concludes this part of the Mass.

The Reading Service. The world of Holy Scripture is the world of the Orient: it is often found to be more akin to Orientals than to Westerners. In any case, how can we deprive our Christians of the revealed word of God? We must "proclaim" the divine message, not simply "give a reading" of it.[14] And we are hurrying things unduly if we do not give the necessary time and attention to the transitional singing after the Epistle. A Psalm sung in responsorial form, connected with the preceding reading, will not fail to awaken a living echo in the hearts of the faithful. Or along the same lines, more general aspirations such as: "He who is of God hears the words of God" (John 8, 47), or "Blessed are those who hear the word of God and keep it" (Luke 11, 28), alternating with some verses of Psalm 18 or 118, can answer the purpose of the transitional chants. Or again, the repetition of "Alleluia" or of "His mercy is everlasting"[15] would be suitable.

The Gospel is the climax of the Reading Service. And then the Creed offers an over-all view of and a general conclusion to, the Good News that has been announced. At the same time it makes us ready for the "Eucharist" of the Holy Sacrifice, insofar as it reminds us why we are to give thanks to the Father. In the missions, where Christians can assist at Mass only rarely, and where, in consequence, every Mass ought to take on a certain festive character, we are inclined to encourage those who promote the use of the Credo, at least in the short and familiar form of the Apostles' Creed.[16] And in order clearly to distinguish the fore-Mass from the Mass of the faithful, we would make our own the desire of the International Liturgical Meeting held at Maria-Laach (July 12-15, 1951): "The fore-Mass ought to take place not at the altar itself, but in the choir (*in choro*) as is done at a Pontifical Mass and at Vespers."[17] Even in a humble mission chapel, we could arrange a chair on the Epistle side where the priest could celebrate the fore-Mass "ad sedes."

14. We shall discuss the question of the readings in Chapter 8.
15. For the time after Septuagesima, see Psalm 135.
16. J. Hofinger, S.J., "The Apostles' Creed is a Real Prayer" in *Lumen Vitae,* X (1954), pp. 193-208.
17. *Die Liturgiereform,* taken in part from Herder-Korrespondenz, Fribourg, 4 (1952), p. 21.

Some liturgists have voiced the hope that the Mass of the Faithful should be preceded by a preparatory act of contrition, a general confession which would come after the Credo.[18] This wise suggestion has always been observed in the missions. Thus according to the usage existing in our Chinese mission, on his arrival, usually in the morning just before Mass, the missionary is conducted by the Christians to the church, where he blesses them with holy water after the recitation of the Confiteor in Chinese, and gives them his blessing. Often almost all the Christians go to Confession, especially in small communities seldom visited by a priest. Is not confession the principal act of purification and penitence? The morning prayers, which are usually recited together before Mass, also contain an act of contrition and the Confiteor.

The Preparation of the Offerings. "At every community Mass, the altar should not be arranged before Mass; the sacred vessels and, above all, the elements of the sacrifice should not be placed upon it until immediately before the offertory, as is done in a solemn high Mass.[19] The idea that the sacrifice of Christ becomes in the Mass our personal sacrifice was clearly expressed in the offertory procession of ancient times, in which the Christians brought up to the altar the materials for the sacrifice. The Oriental, so receptive to ceremonial-dramatic representations, understands this idea much more easily and willingly by means of a corresponding action, especially by an offertory procession, a custom which survives here and there or is being brought back into use. Gerald Ellard, S.J., rightly recommends for large congregations an offertory procession carried out by some "selected representative offerers."[20] Offertory hymns expressing the above ideas should accompany this procession and also some appropriate gesture, made by the whole congregation, could manifest the desire to offer (along the lines of the gesture made by the priest in offering the bread: his forearms extended horizontally, palms upward). The preparation of the offerings by the priest is the time during which we should revive another element of primitive liturgy: "the general prayer of petition" or "the prayer of the faithful" or "the universal prayer." This "General Prayer" after the Readings and the Oremus of the offertory, can and should be re-established for the sake of the faithful attending low Mass. The form of a litany, with the announcement of the intentions of the faithful and a fixed response to be given by the people, would seem preferable to the form of the "solemn

18. J. A. Jungmann, S.J., "Der vorbereitende Bussakt und die stillen Gebete bei der Feier der heiligen Messe," in *Liturgisches Jahrbuch,* 3 (1953) pp. 297-300.
19. *Die Liturgiereform,* pp. 21 ff.
20. G. Ellard, S.J., *The Mass of the Future,* Bruce, Milwaukee, 1948, p. 285.

prayers."[21]   We certainly need, at some point during the Mass, a place in which Christians can present to God their great and small petitions. This place cannot be the Prayer or Collect which has another function and does not take long enough, nor can it be the Eucharistic Prayer, for this would be to supplant more essential elements, nor the *Pater* which fulfills the function of a "blessing" before the Eucharistic banquet. But after the *Oremus* and the presentation of the offerings, our own prayers find their true place: here we offer to God *"preces et hostias";* here is a space of time long enough to initiate our neophytes in a practical way into the spirit of Christian prayer; and here, finally, as happened originally, the "Secret" of the priest comes in as a wholly natural conclusion.[22]

The Eucharistic Action. In addition to the dialogue between priest and people introductory to the Preface, and the *Amen* to the final doxology of the Canon,[23] there are various ways of having the congregation take their liturgical part in the sacred Action. The congregation can listen, standing and in silence, to the Preface recited aloud by the priest in Latin, and continue it in their own language, bringing together the ideas of thanksgiving and of sacrificing, as these are found in the most ancient parts of the Canon, in the singing of the Sanctus. The texts suggested for a community Mass (see Chapter 7) incline to this solution. Or instead, during the Preface of the priest, the leader might translate the Latin text, followed by the Sanctus of the congregation. The time up until the "per Ipsum" is devoted to silent prayer, the attention of the congregation, from time to time, being drawn to the main ideas of the Canon by short phrases: the first part of the *Te igitur; Qui pridie; Unde et memores; Supra quae; Supplices; Per Ipsum.* This method is suitable for more exacting savants. In the chapter following, we are giving only suggestions for a project along these lines, for the profundity of thought in the Preface, the Sanctus and the prayers of the Canon is not easy to grasp in its entirety, because of the conciseness of the text. In any case, some provision must be made for the singing of the Sanctus, since this is the oldest chant in the Mass. And should we not lay stress upon the great Eucharistic Prayer between the Consecration and the

---

21. *Die Liturgiereform,* pp. 21 ff.
22. If the Secret should once more be sung or said aloud by the celebrant, as was requested at Maria-Laach, we should like to suggest that it be called the *Postoblatio* just as we speak of the *Postcommunio.*
23. This *Amen* would regain its resonance and its proper setting if the suggestion made at Maria-Laach were put into practice of making the *Per Ipsum* once again audible to the congregation. *Liturgiereform,* p. 23.

Pater by some special gesture of prayer and adoration?[24]   One thing is certain: on this point it would be difficult to go beyond the desires of Oriental peoples.

The Eucharistic Banquet. The *Our Father* recited standing, slowly and respectfully, constitutes a preparation for Communion, as is proved afresh by the Communion rite for Good Friday. Here also we learn that if the chant accompanying the breaking of the sacred host is not superfluous, still it is not so important, since the breaking itself takes a very short time. All the same, the breaking and the commingling require a word of explanation. In the texts suggested for a community Mass, we have tried to bring together these various elements in three prayers. We would wish also, as did the Congress at Maria-Laach, that here some ceremony of "reconciliation" might be introduced for the faithful.[25] The distribution of Holy Communion should be accompanied by a hymn, which, preferably, along the lines of many diocesan hymn books in Germany, would develop the thought of the sacred banquet as did the primitive Church,[26] rather than being more or less a "hymn of the day" as is the Communion verse in our present missal.[27] The personal colloquy with the Lord, who has become our Eucharist, now has its place in the interior prayer of each communicant after the reception of the sacred food. The Communion hymn should be inspired by the theme of the community of all the members of the Mystical Body, a community which has been realized in Communion, or by the fact that the Eucharistic bread is the fruit of the sacrifice, the food that strengthens us for the struggle of life.[28]

Conclusion of the Mass. When the congregation has answered *Amen* to the priest's blessing, the celebration concludes with a hymn in which all join. On the feast days, the thought of the day might be expressed; otherwise a general hymn of praise should close the ceremony.

We shall indicate in the following chapter how a community Mass in the missions might be presented.

---

24.   Perhaps by extending the arms, as the celebrant does in the Dominican rite, or by a profound bow, as is indicated at the altar in the Roman Ordines (see Jungmann, *The Mass of the Roman Rite,* Vol. II, pp. 172 ff.) and as the Indian painter, Angelo da Fonseca, shows us in a manner most expressive and typically Oriental in his picture, *Prayer.* See Sepp Schüller, *Christliche Kunst aus fernen Ländern,* Düsseldorf, 1939, p. 52.
25.   *Die Liturgiereform,* p. 23.
26.   Jungmann, *The Mass of the Roman Rite,* Vol. II, p. 392.
27.   Hacker, p. 66.
28.   Hacker, p. 68.

CHAPTER SIX

Text for a "Community Mass"[1]

Josef Kellner, s.j.

The following text has been designed especially for use in the missions where the celebration of "community Masses" has not been uniformly regulated. Its special quality flows from the basic pastoral idea to be inferred from the liturgical reform of recent years: the liturgy and the congregation are once more to be brought closer together so as to become properly related to one another. We have, therefore, intentionally neglected matters of secondary importance; we have brought out as clearly as possible the fundamental ideas and leading thoughts of the liturgy (especially during the Canon); we have restored the contracted intercessory prayer of the offertory (*Oremus*) to its full form (General Prayer). Finally, we have assigned to each individual and group of participants their proper "role," while at the same time the existing rubrics are scrupulously observed. The simplification to the great lines of the structure of the Mass should reduce the need for explanatory remarks to a minimum, while clarifying both the understanding and the conduct of the Mass celebration. To be sure, even here preparation and practice are both needed if due perfection of execution is to be attained. This is particularly true of the chants to be sung by the congregation, among which the favorite songs of the Church, the Psalms, should not be lacking.

1. The complete text, with musical notation for singing, variations for the liturgical feasts and seasons, etc., is published in pamphlet form by the Institute of Mission Apologetics, Box 1815, Manila, P. I., and may be obtained from the Institute or The Liturgy Program, Notre Dame University, Notre Dame, Ind. (15c a copy). The Psalm texts used are taken from the Fides translation (Fides Publishers Assn., Chicago).

Preparatory Prayers (to be said while the priest is vesting)

Leader—Lord God, heavenly Father, by Thee and for Thee all things were made. Look kindly upon us, the work of Thy hands, and grant that we may adore Thee in spirit and in truth and make adequate reparation for our sins. Through Christ our Lord.

All—Amen.

L—Lord God, heavenly Father, Thou hast loved us above every other creature. Through water and the Holy Spirit, Thou hast given us a new life in Baptism, freeing us from the powers of darkness and bringing us into the kingdom of Thy beloved Son. Grant that we may joyfully offer Thee a sacrifice of thanksgiving. Through the same Christ our Lord.

A—Amen.

L—Lord God, heavenly Father, Thou hast redeemed us and sanctified us through Thy Son, and made of us a chosen people, a kingly priesthood, a holy nation: grant that through this sacrifice we may love Thee and our brothers more truly. Through the same Christ our Lord.

A—Amen.

THE OPENING

We pass through the gateway from this world to God
(from the beginning of Mass to the Collect, incl.)

Entrance Hymn

L—We stand up.

L—Come, let us worship the Lord: we are His people and the sheep of His pasture.

A—Come, let us . . .

L—Sing with joy to the Lord, all you lands: serve the Lord with gladness, come into His presence rejoicing.

A—Come, let us . . .

L—Know that the Lord He is God, He made us and we are His: we are His people and the sheep of His pasture.

A—Come, let us . . .

L—Come into His gates with thanksgiving, into His courts with praise: give thanks to Him and bless His name.

A—Come, let us . . .

L—For the Lord is good, His mercy is everlasting, His faithfulness endures from generation to generation.

A—Come, let us . . .

The Kyrie

Priest—Kyrie eleison   A—Kyrie eleison
P—Kyrie eleison   A—Christe eleison
P—Christe eleison   A—Christe eleison
P—Kyrie eleison   A—Kyrie eleison
P—Kyrie eleison

The Gloria

P—Gloria in excelsis Deo
L—Glory to God in the highest
A—And on earth peace to men of good will. . . .

The Collect

P—Dominus vobiscum.
A—Et cum spiritu tuo.
P—Oremus
L—(reads the text from the Missal, concluding with the appeal to "our
Advocate with the Father":) We ask this of Thee, Father, through
our Lord Jesus Christ, Thy Son, who is God, living and reigning
with Thee in the unity of the Holy Spirit for ever and ever.
A—Amen.

THE READINGS
We listen to God's Good News
(up to and including the Gospel or the Creed)

L—We sit to listen to God's Word.

The Epistle or Lesson

L—(faces the community and reads the Epistle from the Missal while
the priest is reading it in Latin.)

The Intermediate Psalm (Gradual, Alleluia or Tract, Sequence).

L—Alleluia, alleluia, alleluia.
A—Alleluia . . .
L—Praise the Lord, all you nations, give Him glory, all you peoples.
A—Alleluia . . .
L—All powerful His mercy towards us, the Lord is true to His promise
forever.
A—Alleluia . . .
L—Glory be to the Father and to the Son and to the Holy Spirit,
A—Alleluia . . .
L—As it was in the beginning, is now and ever shall be forever and ever,
Amen.
A—Alleluia . . .

L—All stand to honor the Gospel.

The Gospel

P—Dominus vobiscum.
A—Et cum spiritu tuo.
P—Sequentia sancti evangelii secundum . . .
A—Gloria tibi, Domine.
L—(faces the community and reads the holy text from the Missal while the priest is reading it in Latin.

The Sermon (if there is to be one)

The Creed

P—Credo in unum Deum
L—Let us profess the Apostles' Creed.
A—I believe in God, the Father almighty. . . .

THE OFFERTORY
We respond to God's Good News by gifts and prayers
(up to and including the Secret)

P—Dominus vobiscum.
A—Et cum spiritu tuo.
P—Oremus.

The Offertory Psalm (for feast days or when there is an offertory procession).

L—Lord, in honor of Thy name, we offer gifts and prayers.
A—Lord, in honor . . .
L—Lord, I am Thy servant, the son of Thy handmaid, Thou hast loosed my bonds.
A—Lord, in honor . . .
L—I will offer the sacrifice of praise, and call on the name of the Lord.
A—Lord, in honor . . .
L—I will fulfill my vows to the Lord in the presence of all His people.
A—Lord, in honor . . .

The Offertory Prayer (for other days).

L—We offer Thee, most gracious Lord, our gifts for consecration, bread and wine as symbols of ourselves. By these gifts we offer to Thee our persons and all our works, our joys and our pains, our successes and our failures, our life and our death. We humbly pray that just as this drop of wine mingles with the wine in this chalice, so may we become sharers of the very sacrifice, which our

High Priest, Jesus Christ, continuously offers in His Church and here today renews in our midst.

The General Prayer

L—We all kneel to implore God's mercy.

Let us pray fervently that the almighty God, the Father of mercy, through our Mediator Jesus Christ, may listen favorably to our prayers.

A—Have mercy, O Lord, have mercy.

1. For the Holy Church

L—Let us pray for the Holy Church: may God our Lord preserve and protect her. May He sanctify and spread His kingdom throughout the world.

A—Have mercy . . .

2. For the Pope

L—Let us pray for our Holy Father, Pope N.N. May God our Lord inspire in him knowledge of what is good for the Church, and strength to accomplish it.

A—Have mercy . . .

3. For Civil Authorities

L—Let us pray for the rulers of our country and those of all nations. May God our Lord direct their thoughts and their actions toward justice and peace and true prosperity.

A—Have mercy . . .

4. For Clergy and Religious

L—Let us pray for all bishops, priests, religious, seminarians and lay helpers. May God our Lord strengthen them in their holy vocation.

A—Have mercy . . .

5. For the afflicted

L—Let us pray for all those who are afflicted by illness, hardship or temptation: May God our Lord allow them to experience the strengthening power of the Cross of Christ.

A—Have mercy . . .

6. For relatives, benefactors and friends

L—Let us pray for our relatives, benefactors and friends. May God our Lord grant them health and all blessings, both of body and soul.

A—Have mercy . . .

7. For the dead

L—Let us pray for our beloved dead. May God our Lord admit them into His most blessed Presence in the eternal glory of paradise.

A—Have mercy . . .

8. *For enemies and sinners*

L—Let us pray for our enemies, for all evildoers and sinners. May God our Lord bring them back to the right path, and to our merciful Father in heaven.

A—Have mercy . . .

9. *For separated Christians*

L—Let us pray for our separated brethren. May God our Lord bring them once again into union with us in the true Church of our Lord Jesus Christ.

A—Have mercy . . .

10. *For pagans and unbelievers*

L—Let us pray for those in the darkness of paganism or unbelief. May God our Lord enlighten them with the light of His truth.

A—Have mercy . . .

11. *For our own intentions*

L—Let us pray for ourselves. May God our Lord strengthen us in His love and His grace, and graciously hear our humble petitions.

A—Have mercy . . .

(If the above is concluded before the priest has finished the washing of the hands, there is a silent pause. When he has turned to the servers and said *Orate, fratres,* the Leader says in conclusion:)

L—Accept, O holy Father, through the intercession of the blessed Virgin Mary and all the Saints, the prayers and offerings of Thy faithful. May our offering, through the grace of the Holy Spirit, become the sacrifice of our High Priest, Jesus Christ, to the glory of Thy name and the well-being of all Thy holy Church.

The Secret

L—(reads the text from the missal with the usual conclusion:) We ask this of Thee, Father, through our Lord Jesus Christ Thy Son . . .

P—Per omnia saecula saeculorum.

A—Amen.

L—We stand for the great Thanksgiving.

THE SACRIFICE

We give thanks while our offerings become Christ's
(up to the Lord's Prayer exclusive)

The Great Eucharistic Prayer, Part One

P—Dominus vobiscum.

A—Et cum spiritu tuo.

P—Sursum corda.

A—Habemus ad Dominum.

P—Gratias agamus Domino Deo nostro.

A—Dignum et justum est.

P—Vere dignum et justum est . . . nos Tibi . . . gratias agere . . . per Christum Dominum nostrum . . . dicentes:

The Great Eucharistic Prayer, Part Two

L—Holy,

A—Holy, holy, Lord God of hosts. Heaven and earth are full of Thy glory. Hosanna in the highest.

The Great Eucharistic Prayer, Part Three

L—Thanks be to Thee, O Father, and praise through Jesus Christ: He is the Head of the Church, His Mystical Body.

A—Heaven and earth are filled with Thy glory.

L—Thanks be to Thee, O Father, and praise through Jesus Christ: He is our advocate with Thee and our mediator.

A—Heaven and earth . . .

L—Thanks be to Thee, O Father, and praise through Jesus Christ: He is our High Priest for all eternity.

A—Heaven and earth . . .

L—Thanks be to Thee, O Father, and praise through Jesus Christ: He is our Host sublime.

A—Heaven and earth . . .

The Consecration and Elevation

(When the priest raises the consecrated Host, all pray silently:) Accept, O heavenly Father, the Body of our Lord Jesus Christ, which was sacrificed on the Cross for our salvation.

(When the priest raises the chalice with the Precious Blood, all pray silently:) Accept, O heavenly Father, the Blood of our Lord Jesus Christ, which was shed on the Cross for our salvation.

The Great Eucharistic Prayer, Part Four

L—Receive, most holy Father, our gift, the Lamb of God: in memory of the wonderful incarnation of Christ, our blessed Lord.

A—Hail to Thee in the highest.

L—Receive . . . : in memory of the redeeming death of Christ our Savior.

A—Hail to Thee in the highest.

L—Receive . . . : in memory of the glorious resurrection of Christ our great King.

A—Hail to Thee in the highest.

L—Receive . . . : in memory of the eternal Glory of Christ our Brother.
A—Hail to Thee in the highest.
L—Receive . . . : in memory of the second coming of Christ our just Judge.
A—Hail to Thee in the highest.
(After the priest has struck his breast, saying *Nobis quoque peccatoribus.*)
L—O triune God, through our Lord Jesus Christ, in these divine Mysteries celebrated by our holy community, be all honor and glory to Thee for ever and ever.
P—Per omnia saecula saeculorum.
A—AMEN.
L—All stand for the Our Father.

The Banquet

We regain our consecrated offering, Christ, as our food
(up to and including the Postcommunion)

The Lord's Prayer
P—Oremus.
L—Urged by our Savior's bidding and guided by divine teaching, we make bold to say:
A—Our Father, who art in heaven . . .

The Breaking of the Sacred Host
P—Per omnia saecula saeculorum.
A—Amen.
P—Pax Domini sit semper vobiscum.
A—Et cum spiritu tuo.

Prayers before Communion
L—O Lord Jesus Christ, Thou didst say to Thy apostles: "Peace I leave you, my peace I give you": we pray Thee to give Thy people this peace now and forever. Lamb of God, Who takest away the sins of the world,
A—Have mercy on us and grant that we may be one.
L—O Lord Jesus Christ, Thou didst say to Thy followers: "I am the Vine, you are the branches": we pray Thee, break unto us this Bread of life, that we may be in Thee, and Thou in us. Lamb of God, Who takest away the sins of the world,
A—Have mercy on us and grant that we may be one.
L—O Lord Jesus Christ, Thou didst pray to Thy Father: "That they may be one as Thou, Father, in me and I in Thee, that they also may be one in us": we pray Thee, make all those who partake of

this Bread, to become one in Thy love. Lamb of God, Who takest away the sins of the world,

A—Have mercy on us and grant that we may be one.

L—All kneel.

The Sacred Banquet

P—Ecce Agnus Dei . . .

L—Behold the Lamb of God, behold Him who takes away the sins of the world.

A—Lord, I am not worthy that Thou shouldst enter under my roof, say but the word and my soul shall be healed. (Three times).

L—All stand.

The Communion Psalm

L—Taste and see how good is the Lord to His faithful.

A—Taste and see . . .

L—At all times will I bless the Lord
His praise is ever in my mouth.

A—Taste and see . . .

L—O glorify the Lord with me,
together let us praise His name.

A—Taste and see . . .

L—I sought the Lord and He heard me;
He rescued me from all my fears.

A—Taste and see . . .

L—Gaze at Him and be bright with joy,
no shame darkening your faces.

A—Taste and see . . .

L—Turn from evil, do good:
seek after peace and pursue it.

A—Taste and see . . .

L—The eyes of the Lord are on the good,
His ears attentive to their cries.

A—Taste and see . . .

L—The Lord is near to the broken-hearted,
He will save the bruised in spirit.

A—Taste and see . . .

The Postcommunion

P—Dominus vobiscum.

A—Et cum spiritu tuo.

P—Oremus.

L—(reads the Postcommunion from the missal, ending like the Collect:)
We ask this of Thee, Father, through our Lord Jesus Christ, Thy
Son, who is God, living and reigning with Thee in the unity of
the Holy Spirit, for ever and ever.
A—Amen.

THE CONCLUSION

We pass through the gateway from God to the world—with Christ
(the Mass is brought to an end by the official dismissal and by
the blessing of the priest)

The Dismissal

P—Dominus vobiscum.
A—Et cum spiritu tuo.
P—Ite, missa est (*or* Benedicamus Domino)
A—Deo gratias.

Last Blessing

L—Bless us, Father,
A—That we may fulfill in our lives the task we have begun in our
Sacrifice.
L—We kneel for the Blessing.
P—Benedicat vos . . .
A—Amen.
L—All stand.

The Final Hymn

L—Praise the Lord, for He is good,
A—Everlasting His love.
L—Praise Him, the God of gods,
A—Everlasting . . .
L—Who alone does great wonders,
A—Everlasting . . .
L—Who made the heavens in wisdom,
A—Everlasting . . .
L—Who spread the earth above the waters,
A—Everlasting . . .
L—Who made the great lights,
A—Everlasting . . .
L—With a strong hand and arm outstretched,
A—Everlasting . . .
L—He cleft the Red Sea asunder,

A—Everlasting . . .
L—And led out Israel through its midst,
A—Everlasting . . .
L—He overwhelmed Pharaoh and his army in the Sea,
A—Everlasting . . .
L—He gives food to all living things,
A—Everlasting . . .
L—Praise the God of heaven . . .
A—Everlasting His love . . .

CHAPTER SEVEN

Teaching the Mass

JOHANNES HOFINGER, S.J.

As we have seen, a well-thought-out form of participation in the Mass will make it much easier for the Christian people to understand the holy mysteries and to take part in the ceremonies. But even the most perfect form of celebration can never render instruction on the Mass superfluous; some solid catechetical teaching will always be necessary. Nevertheless we should make one important distinction. So long as the ceremonies are not self-explanatory, our teaching will need to spend considerable time on the structure of the Mass in order to give our people a truly religious understanding of it. But when the celebration itself makes the essential structure clear, then this aspect of the instruction can be brief, and the main part of the available time be devoted to a clear and concrete explanation of the dogma of the Holy Sacrifice.[1]

The essential task of Mass instruction is that by means of frequent exhortations, given with great conviction, the missionary should arouse in catechumens and Christians alike, from the very beginning, an appreciation of the Mass as one of the keystones both of Christian doctrine and Christian life.

The essential task of Mass instruction in the missions is not a detailed explanation of the ceremonies, however useful this might be. The faithful need above all to *understand the Mass itself,* its meaning, its central position in our religion, its intimate relationship with all the other truths of Christianity. This does not, of course, mean that we should give our

---

1. The missionary can profit greatly from the catechetical studies made in Christian countries, though obviously he needs to keep in mind the special circumstances of missionary teaching. Concerning instruction in the Mass, we should especially recommend: *La Maison-Dieu,* N. 42, 1955; *Lumen Vitae,* X, 1955, N. 2-3.

hearers theological speculations or scholarly theses, but a Christian synthesis that is simple, clear, vital and centered in the mystery of the Mass, that *compendium vitae and doctrinae christianae*. For this should be the essence of our teaching: to make our faithful understand, appreciate and live, according to the spirit of Christ and the Church, not this or that ceremony of the Mass, but the Mass itself in its most comprehensive and profound meaning.

The way in which we view our whole faith has a great influence on our understanding of the Holy Sacrifice. For instance, if our faith is presented as a summary of obligations on the observance of which our salvation depends, then it is difficult to bring out the grandeurs, the joys, the riches of our religion. The mind which is preoccupied with the "burden of the faith" does not open up to welcome the Gospel, does not feel towards God any great gratitude. But when the faith is presented in a doctrinal synthesis which renders faithfully the Gospel of our Lord Jesus Christ, that is to say, the Good News of our sanctification in Christ, then every generous listener will feel profound gratitude to God and will see in the Eucharistic Sacrifice the great means which God Himself has given us of showing our gratitude in a fitting way.

The Mass is essentially *the sacrifice of thanksgiving* of the redeemed children of God; and therefore all Christian training in gratitude should converge on our teaching on the Mass. Only Christians who are filled with gratitude are ready to take their full part in the Holy Sacrifice. True gratitude, which is not content to respond to a great gift by some polite formula but inspires us with affectionate devotion toward our benefactor, is an emotion normal to our very nature, and to awaken it in our people is worth all our efforts. *Gratia supponit naturam.* We cannot reasonably expect that those who are unused to feeling and expressing gratitude will react intensely and in a practical way to the benefits given them by God. In the missions, have we perhaps not somewhat neglected this *training in true gratitude?* We have taught our Christians to receive, but have we taught them to give thanks as they should?

The effectiveness of our instruction on the Mass also depends greatly on our *exposition of the fundamental Christian truths.* The following are some instances that are particularly relevant to mission countries.

Always and everywhere — and above all in Christianity, by reason of the sublimity of its sacrifice — any religious sacrifice presupposes a *great idea of God,* the interior and spontaneous recognition of His infinite grandeur and of our complete dependence. Every means which the catechist can use to inspire in his catechumens this respect and submission to God prepares them for a fruitful participation in the Mass.

God, infinitely powerful and infinitely great, manifests Himself first of all in *creation*. Paganism has obscured and falsified the idea of the divinity. The catechist, therefore, first of all by the Christian teaching on creation and then by that on the infinite goodness of God, must give the catechumen that noble idea of God from which alone can spring "adoration in spirit and in truth."

Even more than the doctrine on creation, the doctrine of our *redemption* reveals the infinite generosity of the divine love toward us, the innumerable benefits for which we give thanks in the Eucharistic Sacrifice. Noah, saved from the Flood with his whole household, offered to God a sacrifice of thanksgiving; and so we offer with Christ, the new Noah, the sacrifice of the New Covenant to thank God for our deliverance, for our redemption. The positive aspect of the redemption — the participation in the divine life which comes to us in Christ — is often too little brought out in missionary preaching. And this is most unfortunate, since this lack is felt in the celebration of the holy mysteries. *Si scires donum Dei* (John 4, 10) : if you understood and truly appreciated the incomparable divine gift of baptismal grace, you would show your gratitude at Holy Mass. In the missions above all, we need to associate Baptism closely with the Holy Eucharist, the thanksgiving and sacrificial banquet of the baptized.

The instruction on *the Church* should speak *ex professo* of the community of the faithful gathered together for Eucharistic worship. The more our Christians see the Church as the community of the redeemed children of God, the realization on earth of the Kingdom of God, rich in all the blessings of the messianic age, the more will they love, during the Mass, to affirm their unity with one another and to celebrate worthily with their brothers and, above all, with Christ, the sacrifice of thanksgiving.

Our teaching on *prayer* should lay the basic foundations of education in the Eucharist, and be accompanied by a practical initiation into Christian prayer, an initiation which is careful to vitalize all the various phases of religious formation. Nobody can truly appreciate the Mass or feel its greatness in the depths of his being, unless he first realizes the nature of Christian prayer, unless his whole prayer life is in harmony with the Holy Sacrifice. Thus Christian prayer addresses above all the heavenly Father through Christ our Lord; it recognizes the primacy of praise and thanksgiving above petition; it manifests a keen awareness of the communal character of our prayer in which the "I," aware of its weakness, lets itself be carried to God in the current of the praying community. This does not mean, of course, that every prayer public or private should follow liturgical forms. We should never fall into that kind of suspicious puritanism which is unsympathetic to the more simple and popular forms of piety and feels that great devotions such as the cult of the Sacred Heart, of the blessed Virgin, or the Way of the Cross are, as it were, obstacles to true devotion which need to be prudently but firmly set aside. Nevertheless, our Christian training of our catechumens should, more than ever, insist on the true meaning of prayer: an elevation of the soul which, upheld by the realization of our divine adoption, mounts spontaneously up to the heavenly Father, to rest on His heart.

In mission countries, above all, it is fatal to allow in our Christians' prayer life, two completely different currents which, far from complementing, succeed only in neutralizing one another. The faithful will remain ignorant of the most perfect forms of prayer contained in the community celebration of the Mass if they are not first made familiar with the interior rhythm of fundamentally Christian prayer. Here, we believe, is one of the most urgent tasks of Christian preaching, relative both to Eucharistic worship itself and to the whole development of a vigorous Christianity.

Our lessons in *Christian living* — Christian morals — can best present Christian conduct as one of the blessings and effects of the Eucharistic Sacrifice, by which we give ourselves wholly to God with Christ. The offering of oneself at Mass calls for the same offering carried out in action; liturgical worship, far from being a mere outward ceremony, demands the worship of one's whole life. In order to show concretely and practically what is the quality of life answering to the sublime greatness of the Eucharistic Sacrifice, our teaching should develop the positive aspects of morality.

Thus true teaching on the Mass and the whole teaching of the faith should continually interpenetrate. Even without expressly mentioning our sacrifice, every exposition of any Christian truth should make it easier to understand. And further, every apostle who is convinced of the primordial rôle of the Eucharistic Sacrifice in our religion and who finds in it the inspiration of his priestly life, will have no difficulty in drawing the attention of his flock to the close connection existing between the articles of our belief and the Mass, and so make it better known and loved.

Mass Instruction in the Limited Sense

Such teaching on the Mass in relation to the whole of Christian doctrine is only the first stage; the doctrine of the Holy Sacrifice must be treated *ex professo* at the most opportune moment.

In the *religious instruction of beginners* (children and those who are beginning their instruction for Baptism), the unfolding of the history of salvation brings us to the teaching on the Mass after the account of the Last Supper. For the more advanced catechumens, we might do well to give first the history of the Last Supper, of the Passion, of the redeeming and victorious death of Christ. When we have spoken of the Resurrection, we could go to the Mass, which would then appear as the continuation of the sacrifice of Christ and its completion in the sacrifice of the Church.

Later *systematic religious instruction* has two places for direct teaching on the Mass. First, in the exposition of the sacraments: the sacrament of the altar is not only "a visit of Jesus to our souls to help us to be good," but the sacrificial banquet of the baptized, the incomparable "return-gift" of the heavenly Father for the priceless offering we have made to Him at Mass, the heavenly bread, the mysterious food and strength of God's children. Here we must make our hearers understand not only the difference but also the close relationship between the sacrifice and the sacrament, the sacrament as the fruit of the sacrifice. As we see it, the essential teaching on the sacrifice of the Mass should be given here: a fundamental article of Christian doctrine should not be divided up.

Later on, in dealing with prayer, the treatment of the Holy Sacrifice should be taken up again; the Mass is the prayer *par excellence* of the Christian community, the ideal lesson and practice in Christian prayer. So far as time allows, we can here go into the details of the ceremonies — without ever losing sight of the whole — but the first instructions should necessarily be devoted to the chief parts of the Mass and their function.

Theologically speaking, the fundamental treatise on prayer is the traditional place in which to give instruction on the Mass. But pedagogical effectiveness, so important in missionary method, makes it preferable to give it in the course of treating the sacraments, giving additional explanations in the teaching on prayer.

It is of the utmost importance to present the sacrifice of the New Law under the proper aspect. Experts on catechetics in Christian countries are in accord on this point; and the directives given by many bishops are authoritative. It is surely desirable that our missionary work also should profit from such experience.

The liturgy itself teaches us to see the Mass as, above all, the "Eucharist," that is *the solemn thanksgiving of the redeemed children of God,* who, all united with their Head, with Christ, offer themselves to the heavenly Father. In the minds of the faithful, the sacrifice of the Church, in and with Christ, should appear above all as being a sacrifice of thanksgiving. This point of view does not in any way neglect the essential relationship of the Mass to the sacrifice of the Cross; on the contrary, it gives a better understanding of it. Far from being a mere "double" of the sacrifice of the Cross, the Eucharistic Sacrifice is its continuation and completion in the mystical Christ. The sacrifice of the Cross, which delivered us from sin and from death, expresses chiefly the expiatory homage of the Son of God, who represented his fallen brothers in the sight of the heavenly Father Whom we had offended. But in the Mass, the victorious Savior presents Himself to the Father with the fruits of His victory, that is with His redeemed brethren, and gives thanks for their deliverance which has already been accomplished. On Calvary, we were completely passive; in the Mass, we have become active. We are, as it were, carried away by the joyful realization of our redemption and of our incorporation into the divine life in Christ, by the happiness of knowing that we are even enabled fittingly to express our thanks. Yet we never should lose sight of the fact that the value and the acceptability of our offering in the Father's sight comes not from us, but from Christ our Head, who renews His sacrifice in our midst and associates us in it.

To present the Mass as above all a sacrifice of thanksgiving is desirable also from the point of view of efficient teaching. The effectiveness of our instruction on the Mass depends on *the harmony that we establish between our catechesis and the actual celebration of the holy mysteries:* from this fact flows the necessity of insisting on the liturgical structure of the Mass. But there can be no doubt that in this liturgical structure, the sacrifice of the Church, especially considered as a sacrifice of thanksgiving, stands out everywhere.[2] And certainly in our missionary preaching, with the limited time at our disposal, we cannot allow too great a separation between the liturgy of the Mass and our teaching on it. Our great concern must be to draw from the liturgical action itself the inspiration which will give our Christians an understanding of the Mass.

In this connection, we might ask to what extent the sacrificial customs of the pagans can help us in the explanation of the Eucharistic sacrifice. Here we certainly need a great deal of tact. Whether we can make

2. "That the Mass is also the sacrifice of Christ is taken for granted in the Roman Mass Ordo, but is not actually expressed directly." So Jungmann in *The Mass of the Roman Rite*, Vol. I, p. 180, Benziger, N. Y., 1955. For the proper significance of the Mass, see the same work, p. 175-195. One could wish that this important question might be treated in as exhaustive, profound and basic a way by dogmatic theologians as well.

use of such customs or not depends on whether there exists, among the people concerned, sacrificial actions that are religiously elevated and a religious symbolism that is generally understood. Furthermore, any comparison that we make with our sacrifice should be one that comes naturally in the course of our explanation and gives us the opportunity to bring out the meaning and the transcendence of the Mass. We should beware of wasting precious time on a laborious explanation of pagan customs. In the Chinese missions in former times, for example, we could most fruitfully remind our hearers of the solemn sacrifice which the emperor as the "Son of Heaven" offered each year on the Altar of Heaven. In any case, such comparisons are little by little losing their value, for the present generation is losing any knowledge of such rites.

But we can bring home to our people the wonderful meaning of the ceremonies of the Mass if we use explanations that are simple and *well illustrated.* In China, for instance, a comparison with the customary New Year festivities is very suggestive. Each New Year, Chinese children, led by their oldest brother, give their parents the homage of their gratitude by carrying out the traditional "prostration," and they are invited then by the parents to take part in a family meal. And so, in the same way, at Mass we are led by our oldest Brother, our Head, to pay homage to the Father in heaven, and in return for this homage, we are invited to the heavenly banquet. Such a consideration of the sacrifice helps our Chinese Christians to understand the main lines of the Mass; it allows them to grasp, before they are given any detailed explanation of the ceremonies, the meaning of, and the relationship between, its main parts: the readings, the offertory, the sacrifice, the sacrificial banquet.

The readings are more important than they are shown to be in most of our catechisms. For the lessons, the Gospel and the sermon are not designed simply as moral instruction to prepare us for the sacrifice; they are to remind us of the blessings given us by God. Before the Paschal meal, the Jews recounted the wonderful deeds of God in their behalf at the time of their deliverance from Egypt; so we recall the incomparable "great deed" of our redemption before celebrating the thanksgiving of the New Law. This is the best preparation of the heart. If only preachers would understand in this sense the task of giving a sermon at Mass; to proclaim the *magnalia Dei,* to make the people aware both of the riches that God gives us and of their duty to respond with gratitude!

Then the Creed, concluding the first part of the divine service, would regain its true significance: our profession of faith in the blessings given us by the eternal love of the Father . . . the only response possible to the announcement of the Good News, which is essentially the news of the eternal love of God for us.

Inspired with these ideas, we go on to the sacrifice itself. The offertory makes us aware of our powerlessness to respond adequately to God's love. But, in the hands of our Brother and High Priest, this humble offering of bread and wine is changed by the *consecration* into the Body and Blood of the eternal Son of God. By Him, with Him, and in Him, we offer God a worthy holocaust, we take part in our Savior's offering of Himself and of us. And, at *Communion,* we in turn receive from the Father, in the form of food, the gift that we have offered to Him.

Once this main line of the Mass is understood and assimilated, the principal end of our teaching has been attained. If there is no time for more, the rest must be made clear in and by the actual celebration of the Mass. And since, unfortunately, sufficient time is almost always lacking in the missions, we need to search more zealously than ever for a form of Mass celebration by which the Christian mysteries will explain themselves and reach our peoples' hearts.

CHAPTER EIGHT

Scripture Readings in Christian Worship

JOHANNES HOFINGER, S.J.

The catechetical value of Christian worship depends in great part — though of course not exclusively — on the liturgical readings: what is chosen and how it is arranged; the adaptation of these readings to the different phases of the ceremonies; the manner of presentation; how their themes are brought out by the homily during the Mass, and by the preaching and teaching outside the Mass on themes in one way or another connected with the readings. We shall, therefore, consider first the questions involved in the choice of scriptural pericopes to be used in reading during the celebration of divine worship, with a priest or without one, in the missions. And to give these questions their due importance, we need to enlarge the scope of the discussion to include the general importance of Holy Scripture and the use to be made of it in our whole work of evangelization.

The Importance of Holy Scripture in the Work of Evangelization

This importance is shown, first of all, in a historical reality in the life of the primitive Church. In the golden age of the early missionary Church, the instruction of Christians themselves and of aspirants to Baptism was carried out almost entirely in divine worship itself by the reading of long extracts from Scripture, and by the homily directly related to the celebration and to the scriptural reading. During this period, there was no catechesis in our present use of the word; and as far as me know there was not even any ecclesiastical catechesis given to those who had been baptized as children.[1] Catechetical instruction was given only, outside of the services themselves, to candi-

1. J. A. Jungmann, S.J., *Catechetics*, Brussels, ed. *Lumen Vitae*, 1956, p. 11.

dates for Baptism. At the beginnings of the catechumenate, that is, before the time of Constantine, the catechumens were first carefully instructed for some three years in the new moral standards that they would have to live by. This teaching was inspired in great part by the "teaching" books of the Old Testament — Origen mentions especially Esther, Judith, Tobias, and the Wisdom books — and consisted of a reading accompanied by commentaries and practical applications. This first initiation into Christianity included prayer and the laying-on of hands; thus it also had the character of worship. In the later form of the catechumenate, during the fourth and fifth centuries, a period which showed a notable diminution as to missionary catechesis, this program disappeared entirely.

The candidates for Baptism were next given, for several weeks preceding their reception of the sacrament, a special course of instruction in Christian truth, an intensive teaching that gave, in a fairly systematic way connected with the Apostles' Creed, a general idea of fundamental Christian doctrine. This was associated with exorcisms and the imposition of hands, and so was essentially oriented to the approaching celebration of the baptismal mystery and included in the sacred realm of liturgical action. The Catecheses of St. Cyril of Jerusalem are models of this kind of instruction; we possess nineteen of his pre-baptismal Catecheses and five of his "mystagogic," given after Baptism.

Thus the missionary Church in its golden age made use only of catechetical teaching which formed part of the whole structure of her worship or at least was closely connected with the liturgy. The reading of Scripture during the services predominated. The catechetical effects were, in general, surprising: the Christians of that time bore witness to an impressive store of religious knowledge, one that in any case was life-giving; from their community celebration of Christian worship, they drew the elements of a Christianity that was intelligently and intensely lived. In calling this period the "golden age" of missionary activity, we do not mean so much the number of conversions as the quality of the preparation given for Baptism. Never during the ages that have followed, has the Church succeeded so well in transforming catechumens into real Christians during the period of preparation for Baptism. By this work, so superior in its quality, the missionary Church of that time laid a solid foundation, on which the centuries to come might have built with confidence.

Today, on the other hand, Holy Scripture frequently plays a minimal role in the instruction of catechumens and the newly baptized, and even in the instruction of Christian youth in mission lands. Of course, there must certainly be some happy exceptions, the existence of which we have no intention of denying. But generally, we should say, present-day religious instruction in the missions is chiefly given by means of what is called "systematic" teaching that follows the plan of the catechism, or by means of preaching on theses that draw their teaching value from Scripture and Tradition, but do not bring out the value of the sacred text itself.[2]

Among the *reasons for this change* was the fact that the liturgical language, Latin, was no longer understood by the people. As the various Romance languages developed, the people in Latin countries gradually became incapable of following the liturgical readings well enough to understand them, and this was even more the case in the countries comprising the German mission. Christian worship thus lost a great part of its former catechetical value, and it was only by very slow degrees that "systematic" religious instruction began to make up in part for this unfortunate loss.[3]

The increasingly complex exposition of Christian doctrine was another factor. Such an evolution was, of course, natural and good, since the Bride of Christ must continually study more profoundly the saving truth entrusted to her by her divine Bridegroom, truth which is not only a treasure to be guarded, but a seed capable of developing by its own intrinsic nature. But this doctrinal development made the old simple and concrete terminology seem inadequate. Under the influence of Scholastic Theology, the proper relationship of which to catechetical instruction was not always very clearly thought out, the people were considered to need a presentation of the truths of salvation given in formulas or in the "system" of the schools, whose distinctions, definitions and subdivisions were, for the most part, taken over as essential elements of catechetical teaching. And so this systematic kind of teaching of religion was emphasized instead of the biblical-liturgical teaching of the early Church.

Since the sixteenth century, moreover, the *defensive attitude* adopted against heretics who held that the Bible was the only source of faith, reduced still further the part of Scripture in religious instruction, and, at the same time, gave recognition to systematic instruction — often mistakenly put on the same footing as "Tradition" — as having the predominant role.

2. In any case, this was the result of the enquiries made by Johannes Thauren, S.V.D., published twenty years ago under the title, *Die religiöse Unterverweisung in den Heidenländern*, Vienna, 1935. The great progress made since must be taken into account, but if the general situation is considered as a whole, there has been no radical change since that time.
3. J. Hofinger, S.J., "The Catechism Yesterday and Today," *Lumen Vitae*, 1956, 479-486.

We might wonder why the so timidly Scriptural catechesis of the Middle Ages and especially of the period after the Council of Trent should have had any influence on the instruction given in the missions, when during these centuries no serious struggles with Protestantism took place in missionary countries. The answer is clear. Just as preaching generally was too little aware of its own laws as distinguishing it from scholastic theology, so the special qualities of missionary preaching were not thought out in distinction to the instruction then given in Christian countries under the influence of a defensive attitude against Protestantism. This lack of thought cannot be blamed on the valiant missionaries of the time. We should rather ask why, on the part of theology, the nature and special qualities of the preaching of Christian truth were not more clearly recognized and safeguarded.

We might also inquire whether the less frequent use made of Scripture in the missionary preaching and teaching of the last few centuries bears any relation to the secondary role given to Holy Scripture in the ascetic and theological formation of future missionaries. The fact is undeniable; and we need, therefore, to discover the causes that little by little have deprived Holy Scripture of the fundamental role that belonged to it in the priestly formation of the early Church, while, during the same period, the dogma of the inspiration of Scripture had been more and more clearly resolved. Is the explanation entirely satisfactory that this change came about chiefly because of the abundance of other ascetical literature produced since the early ages of the Church, or because of the defensive attitude adopted against Protestantism?

But whatever may be the reasons which, in the course of centuries, have caused us to some extent to lose sight of the importance of Holy Scripture in missionary teaching, we should recognize the fact that even today missionary work does not take sufficient account of this importance. There are few indeed who would think of beginning their work of evangelization with the Bible. The proof is to be found in the fact that the best manuals devote only a few short paragraphs to the subject of the missionary use of the Bible, if they do not pass it over in silence.[4] In all the abundant missionary literature with which we are flooded, even an occasional substantial article on this subject is hardly to be found. During the last hundred years — and we can say this with no risk of exaggeration — there have been written incomparably more

4. See Jos. Schmidlin, *Katholische Missionslehre,* 2d. ed., Münster, 1923, p. 409 ff. in which it is almost entirely a question of translation of the Bible. The best manuals of recent years leave out this chapter entirely, for example, Pio de Mondreganes, O.F.M., Cap., *Manual de Missiologia,* 2nd ed., Madrid, 1947; Saverino Paventi, *La Chiesa missionaria,* 2 vols., Rome 1949/50; André Seumois, O.M.I., *Introduction à la Missiologie,* Schöneck-Beckenried, 1952.

articles on the missionary value of the arts, of modern technical devices, and probably even of agriculture, than on the missionary value of the Bible; and certainly more than on anything connected with the use of the Biblical readings during the celebration of Christian worship in the missions.[5]

In such a situation, we need to study carefully *the intrinsic reasons for the incomparable missionary value of the Bible.* Among these, some of the greatest are:

1. The word of God, in the formal sense of the term, is to be found only in Holy Scripture. It is true that the treasure of the tradition of the Church, in particular the decisions of the *magisterium* transmit divine revelation to us, pure and unmixed with error. But if we take really seriously the Catholic dogmas on revelation and inspiration, it cannot be a matter of indifference to us to know just "how" God has spoken to us. And this above all in the missions, where the apostle must to the greatest possible extent present himself as the faithful messenger sent by God, and teach as such; and, both in the content and in the form of his preaching, must strive to resemble, not in any servile way but disinterestedly and faithfully, Him who sent him. And it should further be understood that the people to whom God speaks with such respect — children of God at least in their calling — have a sacred right, among all the catechetical and pastoral possibilities that exist, to learn not only *what* the heavenly Father has said to them, but also *how,* in concrete fact, He did speak.

2. Moreover, the whole New Testament is the immediate fruit of the missionary situation of the primitive Church whose first task and first care was the missionary preaching of the Good News. The writings of the New Testament reveal to us today how God called, formed and spoke to the first Christians. This is true of the Acts of the Apostles and of the Epistles, but in a certain sense it is true above all of the Gospels, which are to be considered as the inspired condensation of the primitive missionary catechesis.

3. It is most important in missionary preaching that the catechumen

5. We know only of the following articles, of which none treats directly the question of liturgical Scripture readings: Max Meinertz, "Die Heilige Schrift und die Mission," in *Missionswissenschaftlicher Kursus in Köln* (196), pub. by J. Schmidlin, Münster, 1916, pp. 64-66; Sigismond, O.C., "Le Culte du livre sacré," in *L'âme des peuples à évangeliser,* Louvain, 1928, p. 130 ff. Thomas Ohm, O.S.B., "Die Heilige Schrift als Missionsmittel," in *Zeitschrift für Missionswissenschaft,* 1937, p. 85-89 (this is the most noteworthy of the articles listed here); "Le rôle de la Bible en mission," in *Bulletin des Missions,* 1937, p. 114-122 (this is a good though somewhat free summary of the preceding article); J. Ross, S.J., "Die Bibel dem Volke, auch in der Mission," in *Actio Missionaria,* Tokyo, 1938.

or the newly baptized realize, as fully as possible, that God is speaking directly to him, and that he live in the light of this realization. Experience shows that this idea is received much more easily from the liturgical reading of Scripture than from systematic catechesis, above all in the missions where the teaching of the catechism is so often given by a lay catechist, not perfectly trained, rather than by the missionary priest. To say this does not deny the catechetical values of a solid teaching of the catechism — values which the liturgical reading of Scripture cannot give to the same degree.[6] We do not mean to substitute Scripture reading for the teaching of the catechism. The question is, rather, how the teaching of the catechism might be improved by the use of Holy Scripture, and how the too exclusively "systematic" teaching of religion might be strengthened, completed, and even in difficult times replaced by religious services with Scripture readings.

4. The great missionary value of Holy Scripture arises also from the fact that its modes of thought and expression are closer to the mentality of the peoples to be converted than is the language of our catechisms and systematic teaching, which is too dependent on the abstract concepts of scholasticism. But the ideal solution is not to be found in simply using this abstract catechesis and Biblical readings side by side, but in bringing systematic catechetical teaching slowly closer to the simple and concrete ways of expression used in Holy Scripture.

5. A more extensive use of Holy Scripture, above all of the New Testament, would help to bring about that simplification and concentration of our missionary teaching which we need so greatly today; our attention, which tends to wander off into peripheral zones of devotionalism would be brought back to the essential and central elements of our message. This undeniable weakness of our missionary teaching cannot be directly attacked; to do so would expose us to most unfortunate misunderstandings. But if Holy Scripture regained its due place in our missionary work, then the essential and central truths of the faith would quite naturally become the subject of our thoughts.

The Use of Holy Scripture in Missionary Work

The two ways in which our work of evangelization can make use of Holy Scripture are: by readings[7] with or without commentaries, and by the close connecting of both preaching and catechesis with the text, the content and the modes of expression of Holy Scripture. Here we

6. J. Hofinger, S.J. "The Catechism Yesterday and Today," *Lumen Vitae,* 1956, 479-486.

7. See the profound article of H. Schürmann, "Eine dreijährige Perikopenordnung für Sonn-und-Feiertage," in *Liturgisches Jahrbuch,* 2, 1952, pp. 58-72.

can take up only the first question: that of *readings,* in relation to the present world-wide need in the missions for an intensive use of Scripture in public worship. For if the faithful in the missions are to become familiar with the text of Holy Scripture, they will do so primarily by means of extensive and carefully ordered readings given during the services themselves. This is why we are asking for *more Scripture reading during the services in missionary countries.*

The reasons for such a request are obvious.

1. Only by this means can Holy Scripture with its incomparable religious values once more become the common heritage of the Christian people, that is to say, of the whole Christian community. Anyone who has any knowledge of the social and cultural conditions in most missionary countries, knows that it would be extremely difficult to bring about any intensive and persevering private reading of the Bible, and in some places it would be entirely out of the question. If circumstances allow it, we should of course, cultivate private reading, but we must realize that in this way, Holy Scripture will never reach the whole community of Christians of good will. For practical reasons, then, we recommend liturgical reading of Holy Scripture rather than private, basing our conviction on the following fundamental ideas.

2. Holy Scripture is addressed above all, and by its very nature, to the "community"; from its beginnings, it was designed for use in common worship. This is true first of all of the immediate purpose that ruled over the composition of each of its books and played an essential part in the development of the text, to the extent at least that both the Old and the New Testaments, except for some short passages, were addressed essentially to the community. This fact is clear from the theology of Holy Scripture. Apart from the personal intention of each of the sacred writers, Holy Scripture is the source of Revelation inasmuch as it gives us, not edifying private revelations, but the divine message addressed to the whole people of God in the Old and New Testaments: it contains essentially what God wishes to say to His chosen people, and, through His Church, to all mankind called to salvation. And it contains this *in the way in which* He wishes to speak to the Church. The liturgical reading of Scripture clearly brings out this theological fact, all the more when the community "gathered together in the presence of God and realizing this presence," hears the word of God. It is hardly necessary to add that, especially in the missions, the assembled community ought to feel itself a people called by God from among the mass of its pagan neighbors, a people to whom God wishes to speak *personally.*

3. Again, the missionary can only rarely celebrate Holy Mass and distribute Holy Communion in small and remote stations. We should,

therefore, take care to provide the starving Christian community with the bread of the word of God all the more abundantly and carefully.[8]

4. Moreover an intensive reading-service of the word of God will greatly enhance these unavoidably infrequent Masses. The more the Christian community realizes through the reading service the wonderful blessing of God's call and invitation to a personal relationship with Himself, the more it will love and understand the celebration of the Christian sacrifice. Is not the Mass above all an act of thanksgiving for our call and for our redemption? And should not the community celebrate and live the Mass with this intention?

5. The situation in the missions today suggests three other reasons which we have already discussed and need only mention here. In the course of centuries, our teaching of religion has become too *exclusively academic*, and this fact imposes on Christian worship a most important supplementary role, a role which it cannot carry out unless the Scripture readings are carefully selected and arranged.

6. Catechetical instruction given in an academic way may reach the aspirants to Baptism and the Christian young people who are of school age, but by its nature it *is not adequate to continue the formation of adults* who have been recently baptized.

7. In the face of the present communist danger, it would be absolutely *inadequate and unjustifiable to cultivate only the academic teaching of religion.*

Arrangements of Liturgical Scripture Readings

Since conditions vary so widely in mission countries, only general suggestions can be made. One fundamental rule, however, should always be followed: *the readings should be chosen and arranged in such a way that by regularly attending divine worship an aspirant to Baptism could receive a fairly adequate instruction in Christian doctrine in the course of one year.*

This rule is fully justified even in normal times: during his cate-chumenate, the aspirant to Baptism needs to be initiated to a sufficient extent into Christian truth, not only by a systematic course of instruction in preparation for Baptism, but by the practice of his religion, beginning with that of Christian worship. But now we must also take account of the possibility of an overthrow of normal conditions. The time may come when extensive instruction for Baptism, given by a priest or a

8. L. H. Kahlefeld, "Ordo Lectionum," in *Lit. Jahrbuch*, 3, 1953, p. 59. The author brings up the special importance of readings from the Old Testament. So that the community may hear the most important parts of the New Testament during the Sunday service, he recommends a four-year cycle, rather than the three-year one proposed by Schürmann.

trained catechist, may become impossible except during divine worship, a time in which instruction for Baptism will have to be limited to a simple summary and repetition of the knowledge gained during the celebration of Christian worship. In such times of trouble, for which we ought to be prepared, the rule given above would apply in all strictness.

In going into more detail on this question, we need to distinguish between the Scripture readings of the Mass, and readings during services to be held in the absence of a priest.

The readings now given in the Roman Missal answer only imperfectly to the needs of the missions for Scripture readings in the Mass. We do not need to mention the obvious difficulties that have been pointed out by liturgists and pastors alike,[9] but we might mention two more. Missionaries often say, quite rightly, that many of the Epistles are too difficult, for example Gal. 4, 22-31 (Laetare Sunday), I Cor. 3, 4-9 (12th Sunday after Pentecost), Gal. 3, 16-22 (13th Sunday after Pentecost). And, also, they find the lack of unity between the Epistle and Gospel of the Sundays after Epiphany and the Sundays after Pentecost most unfortunate. They have to take into account the needs of simple people; furthermore, there is not time to give profound explanations. From this fact arises the very understandable desire for Sunday Masses in which the readings, chants and prayers have a unified theme which will be readily available to the people. By this, both the value of the prayers and the value of the readings and chants would be remarkably enhanced. Obviously, there is no question of imposing any rigid logical unity upon the Mass Propers, but rather of introducing a supple unity of theme expressed in a variety of ways suitable to a ceremony addressed to the whole people.

But these special mission problems do not, as we see it, make a special lectionary for the missions desirable. There are, in fact, many grave reasons against proposing any such solution: the constant transition of missionary territories to the status of "home-countries," so that it would be impossible to define, in order to determine who was to use such a special lectionary, what constitutes a "mission," if one took into account, as one would need to, not the juridical definition of a mission but the general pastoral situation. Again, the rigid conservatism of many missions would prevent them from becoming at all enthusiastic about a new lectionary which was not that of the universal Church, as would also the great desire felt in the missions to participate in the life of, and the various currents at work in, the whole church. It is most important that the Christians of small mission communities be able to carry out

9. On this subject, see also E. Stommel, "Messpericopen: Zur Frage ihrer Neuordnung," in *Trierer Theologische Zeitschrift*, 61, 1952, 205-213.

their worship, which often seems so impoverished, with the vivid realization of their intimate association in the glorious unity of the whole Church, knowing that their millions of brethren in Christ are celebrating the same worship with them, reciting the same prayers, hearing the same Good News. And we should also take note of the present untimeliness of any special requests. For each particular solution requires profound study of all the related problems, and needs precious time to be worked out. Considering the world-wide missionary situation today, there is no time to be lost.

The proposal already made to have a *four-year cycle of liturgical readings* introduced into the Roman rite would correspond to the needs of the missions. The reasons given for the general adoption of such a cycle hold good also in the mission field. In the missions, as well as elsewhere, a greater variety of readings would more easily attract the attention of the average Christian and would offer to the priest an abundant source of inspiration for his preaching. And in the missions, as well as at home, it is certainly desirable that Christians become familiar in some way with all the riches of Christian revelation, without losing the necessary concentration on essentials. In connection with this requirement, one important condition should be laid down: with such a four-year cycle of readings, it would not be possible to read all the principal texts of Scripture each year; yet in the course of each of the four years, all the main themes of Christian revelation should be not only brought out, but adequately developed.

Liturgists and pastors of souls have often proposed a more frequent use of the *Old Testament* in the form of a supplementary reading to be used at discretion. And here we should point out the great missionary value of readings from the Old Testament, the narratives and the Psalms being especially welcomed by our people. In missionary teaching, the great figures of the Old Testament should play an important part. But if they are to be introduced into religious instruction, some knowledge of them is necessary, otherwise they will become more of an obstacle than a help. And even aside from these figures, the Good News of the New Testament needs to be supported by the Old. The wonder of God's nearness, realized in Christ, only takes on its full significance against the background of the lofty idea of God revealed in the Old Testament.[10]

The actual way in which the most instructive readings from the Old Testament might be given to the people should be determined in relation to circumstances. In the missions, the celebration of the Mass is

10. It does not follow that we should explain the Old Testament in any detail in our elementary catechesis.

often preceded by a lengthy period of hearing Confessions; and again, since the visits of the missionary are so rare, he must preach at some length during Mass. A supplementary facultative reading from the Old Testament will bear no fruit unless the reform of the Mass readings, so desirable in other respects, does not unduly lengthen the ceremony taken as a whole.[11]

The missions are also greatly concerned in the eventual grant of a *reasonable amount of liberty* in the choice of liturgical readings. Without this liberty, a satisfactory solution of the problem is almost impossible. We do not need a special lectionary for the missions, but we do need the permission to set aside the common lectionary, according to circumstances, when missionary needs require or urge us to do so. For example, the missionary should be allowed to use the Masses for Easter and Christmas again and again during the seasons after these great feasts when he is hastening from one of his stations to another to bring them the Easter message or to announce the coming of the Savior.

And it would be equally desirable, above all in visiting his small stations, that the missionary be able to choose a reading suitable to the importance of these infrequent celebrations. During these rare visits, the missionary has to teach the central doctrines of faith and morals and, in spite of the little time at his disposal, explain, at least during the course of several years, all the chief truths of Christianity. But he cannot possibly do so if he has to give a homily on the Gospel of the day, which on weekdays is usually the feast of some minor saint. The pastoral character of these visits to small stations, therefore, makes it desirable not to take the subject of his preaching from the readings of the actual Proper of the day. But it would be far better if he could use readings in the Mass of such doctrinal-liturgical significance as to make it possible to take the theme of his reading from them, and so to base it entirely on the word of God. All such cases where it seems necessary to depart from the common lectionary could easily be regulated by some clear prescriptions of the ecclesiastical authorities, so that there would be no danger of liturgical arbitrariness. Then we would have a freedom that was both objectively established and properly regulated in its exercise.

11. In the Chinese missions, we found the custom was to have the people recite a long series of prayers, in addition to their regular morning prayers which were themselves lengthy, during the time that the missionary was hearing confessions. A study needs to be made of the possibility of introducing a reading from the Old Testament during this time. Above all, the morning prayer customary on Sunday in the missions needs the addition of a short reading that will give some motives for zeal during the remainder of the week. A lengthy recitation of prayers that is not varied from time to time by a reading or some moments of silent prayer, easily becomes routine and perfunctory.

This desire, based on the very nature of things, would give a certain flexibility to the present rigid uniformity, and so effect a real and comprehensive *conformity*. This principle, generally, is one on which the liturgical renewal depends both in the missions and in Christian countries.

The readings of Holy Scripture during services held in the absence of a priest is also a most important question, which we shall discuss in Chapter XI of this book.

CHAPTER NINE

The Psalms in the Missions

Paul Brunner, s.j.

St. John Chrysostom compares the Christians of his day to people who sit on a hidden treasure or carry purses that they cannot open, because they recited the psalms without understanding them (on Ps. 140, 55). To whom would he compare our Christians in the missions today? Not only do they not understand the psalms; but most of them do not even know that the psalms exist or that the Psalter was for centuries in fact, and still remains in theory the Church's official book of prayers, for the faithful as much as for the clergy. The missionary who ventures to recommend the use of the psalms causes no less surprise, not to say scandal, than would have a pastor of the time of St. John Chrysostom, St. Ambrose or St. Augustine who forbade his flock to recite them. At that period, everyone realized that the Psalter was written by the Holy Spirit Himself for the use of God's children under the New Covenant as well as the Old, that the whole book is prophetic, being fulfilled in Christ; each psalm in some way speaks *of* Christ, or *to* Christ, or else Christ speaks through it.[1] But in our own day, it seems that everyone who is aware of the existence of the psalms is convinced that they are Old Testament prayers *not* meant for Christians. Anyone who talks of giving them back to the faithful is considered a freak with a mania for the archaic.

And yet, if the prayers of our faithful are to possess the vigor, the riches, the "eucharistic" quality and the theocentricity of authentic Christian prayers, it is essential to give back to them the familiarity with

---

1. Cf. Balthasar Fischer, "Le Christ dans les Psaumes," *La Maison-Dieu*, no. 27. 1951, 3rd quarter, p. 92.

the psalms which has been lost in the course of the last centuries. Let us unearth this treasure, let us teach them that, in God's mind, the Psalter is not meant to be a book reserved for monks, priests and nuns; the Holy Spirit composed it to be the song book of the people of God journeying to the heavenly Jerusalem. Let us give back to the faithful the part they have lost in the chorus to the "praise of the glory of His grace," which should resound from His "chosen people" over the whole world. The small host which the baptized laity offer for sacrifice is not made of different bread from the priest's host; nor does God will that the matter of "the offering of our lips" (Ps. 118, 108) given Him by the laity should be other than that of the priest.

Let us state at once that we do not wish to take away from our Christians other forms of devotion with which centuries of faith have enriched popular piety. We do not mean to suggest that it is necessary to pray only with the inspired psalms if we are to pray as God wishes. No, what we want to do is to bring private piety back to the school of the official prayer of the Church, so that inspired prayer should play a larger part in private prayer. Is it normal that Christians should use all sorts of prayer formulae but not those which have been given us by God Himself? The object of the psalm revival has been stated with precision by Cardinal Schuster, and his words apply to the missions as well: "The private piety of present-day Catholics would gain much, if, letting themselves be influenced by our common Mother, the Church, who appoints for her ministers the weekly recital of the Psalter, they too would make more use of this prayer book which was inspired by the Holy Spirit and adopted for our example by our Saviour, Jesus Christ Himself."[2]

The Psalms as used in the Worship of the IVth and Vth Centuries

We have chosen the Church of this period for discussion because it is analogical in many ways to the Church in the missions today. After the era of the martyrs, the flood of conversions presented an urgent problem of how to assimilate and educate the ignorant masses. The Church then possessed no special teaching personnel, nor schools, nor books. The great problem of religious education was solved mainly by the liturgy, in which the psalms played an important part. They formed the accompaniment to the three processions of the ancient Mass: the Introit, sung while the celebrant and clergy went up to the altar; the Offertory, while the faithful presented their offerings; the Communion,

2.   Cardinal Schuster, *Sacramentary*, Vol. II, p. 156.

while they received back their gifts changed into the Body of Christ.[3] A psalm was inserted also between the lessons of the Mass of the Catechumens. God spoke to the people by the Scriptures and this word of God, which is both promise and invitation, awoke in their hearts a responsive echo of love, gratitude and trust. And this response to the word of God could not be better expressed than by the word of God itself; the inspired word of the psalms. The same Spirit who spoke by the voice of the lector answered by the voice of the people, a double movement, so to speak, of diastole and systole.

The congregation had no books for their part in the singing; the clergy had no time for choir practice: the Church, as a good pedagogue, adopted the responsorial form as she had learned it in the synagogue, to make her people sing. A cantor intoned the refrain, which the congregation repeated after him. Then he sang the verses of the psalm; the people supplied the refrain between each two verses or two strophes. The responsorial form has the advantage of ensuring both continuous participation by the community and a variety of formulae, without necessitating a choir nor musical training of the singers. Hence, it is particularly suitable for our missionary communities which lack choirs, organists and any facilities for the musical training of the faithful.

The celebrant, bishop or priest, chose the refrain to be repeated in chorus by the congregation. Sometimes this was the text of the psalm itself; we read that St. Athanasius, blockaded by the emperor's troops in the church of Theonas at Alexandria, ordered the deacon to intone Psalm 135 and caused the people to repeat the second half of each verse: *Quia in aeternum misericordia ejus*.[4] St. John Chrysostom made the congregation sing at Easter the refrain: *Quemadmodum desiderat cerva rivos aquarum. . . .*[5] The use of the Alleluia psalms was also inherited from the synagogue. When they prayed the Hallel, the Jews interposed an Alleluia in the middle of a verse, according to ancient sources, thirteen times altogether.[6] St. Hippolytus of Rome tells us that when the psalms were read at the beginning of the Agape, the faithful said Alleluia. We find this Alleluia today in one and another form in the liturgy of the Mass, both in the East and West.[7]

The singing of the psalms in the Mass of the catechumens attained

3. Cf. J. A. Jungmann, *The Mass of the Roman Rite*, Benzinger, I (1951), p. 320 et seq.
4. Cf. Athanasius, *De fuga*, c. 24, *PG*, 25, 676 A.
5. Cf. J. A. Jungmann, "The Pastoral Effect of the Liturgy" in *Orates Fratres*, vol. 23, Oct. 1949, p. 485.
6. Cf. J. A. Jungmann, *The Mass of the Roman Rite*, I, p. 422, note 6.
7. *Ibid.*, pp. 422-23.

its full development in the time of St. Augustine. In the *Enarrationes in Psalmos,* he speaks of the psalm "which we have heard sung and to which we have replied." How enthusiastically he alludes to this community singing: "We have sung the psalm. We encouraged each other; we cried with one voice, with one heart: *Venite exultemus.*"[8]

The frequent repetition of such psalm refrains engraved them in the memory as are the catechism formulae of our own childhood; they provided preachers with texts and key phrases for their catechesis. These verses also provided the faithful with a stock of ejaculatory prayers which have the enormous advantage — not possessed by our modern ones — of being inspired. Having been repeated so constantly throughout the services, these verses were imprinted in the subconscious and emerged as an accompaniment to the day's occupations. St. Jerome bears witness: "One continually hears the psalms in the fields and vineyards of Palestine. The plowman at his plough sings the Alleluia; the reaper, the vinedresser, the shepherd, sing something from the psalms of David."[9] St. Jerome would rejoice to hear what was recently told me by a traveller from Hong Kong to Manila: "The sailors scrubbed the decks while humming Père Gélineau's version of the psalms." The singing of the psalms thus continued in daily life the lessons learnt during the services and impregnated it with a holy atmosphere. The "rumination" of formulae, simple, but pregnant with profound sentiments of adoration, thanksgiving, repentance and trust, constitutes a remarkable catechetical method. Moreover, the bond was forged which linked together the official prayer of the Church and private devotion. There was no such division as exists today between the expressions of official worship, essentially theocentric, Christocentric and Biblical, and the expressions of popular devotion, concerned mainly with human needs and formulated without any reference to the sacred text. Private prayer was then the participation and continuation of official worship; it remained communal even when performed in private, as is today the private recitation of the breviary. This does not mean to say that popular devotions have not enriched Christian piety in the course of ages, but simply that the danger arises, when these are used exclusively, of creating such a barrier between the prayer of the Church and the prayer of her children that they no longer have any taste for, or comprehension of, her prayer, to the great detriment of authentic piety.

We must not, however, imagine that in the patristic period Christians had nothing but the psalms on their lips and knew their psalter by

8. Cf. J. A. Jungmann, "The Pastoral Effect . . . ," p. 485.
9. Quoted in Dom W. Walker, O.S.B., "The Psalms in Catholic Life," p. 120, in *The Proceedings of the National Liturgical Week,* 1944, Chicago, 1945.

heart. Father J. A. Jungmann quotes from a sermon by St. John Chrysostom: "Most of you know dirty songs by heart, but which of you is able to say even one psalm?" The following quotation, however, throws a more favorable light on the psalm equipment of his parishioners: "Yet, another time (St. John Chrysostom) supposes that all knew by heart at least the morning Psalm 62 ("O God, my God, to Thee do I watch at break of the day") and the evening Psalm 140 (". . . the lifting up of my hands as an evening sacrifice" . . .). At Naples, the candidates for Baptism had to learn, besides the short Psalm 116, also Psalm 22 (the Lord is my shepherd) and to recite them in thanksgiving for Baptism, Confirmation and the Eucharist."[10]

From the point of view of the liturgical revival in the missions, it is particularly interesting to note that the "psalm enthusiasm" of the fourth and fifth centuries was not the result of a rectilinear evolution from the psalmody of the temple and synagogue. We might, perhaps, be tempted to believe that the Church incorporated the Psalter in her liturgy in virtue of inherited Jewish tradition. Since the Savior did not leave to His Apostles any euchology of the New Covenant, the Church might be supposed to have adopted the Jewish custom, which had been consecrated by Christ, this use being maintained and developed even when the majority of converts had lost all links with Judaism. Actually the reality is different. At the beginning the role of the psalter in the worship of the Church was limited, it seems, to that of a *book of liturgical readings,* like the other books of the Bible. Of St. Paul's invitation: "Singing in your hearts to God by His grace . . . psalms, hymns and spiritual songs" (Col., 3, 16), the early Christians applied themselves chiefly to the last two. On the model of the inspired psalms, the young charismatic Church produced a harvest of hymns, called *psalmi idiotici,* that is to say, psalms produced by human agency in contrast to those of divine origin.[11] The Gloria of the Mass is an example of this hymnal literature which has mainly disappeared. The Psalter, as the *book of liturgical songs,* does not therefore derive in a direct line from Jewish tradition; it is the result of a "biblical revival" by which the Church dropped the *psalmi idiotici,* of which the Gnostics had made undesirable use, to turn consciously to a book more suited to the aspirations of the Christian soul.[12] It was not, therefore, respect for tradition, but pastoral reasons which introduced the Psalter as the hymn book of the liturgy; in the same way, it is not to recover a tradition, however respectable, that we are attempting to restore the Psalter to our people

10. Cf. J. A. Jungmann, "The Pastoral Effect . . . , " p. 485.
11. Cf. J. A. Jungmann, *The Mass of the Roman Rite,* I, p. 346.
12. Cf. B. Fischer, *Op. Cit.,* p. 91.

in the missions, but because it is the prayer book most suited to the needs of the Christian soul.

Pastoral Reasons for the Use of the Psalms in the Missions

Because God is its Author, the Psalter is a prayer book without an equal. In order that men should praise Him worthily, God has praised Himself.[13] Christ made use of it to express His filial homage, His trust, His anguish, to His Father.[14] The Church employs it in all times and places to acquit herself of her *opus divinum* and to sing her epithalamium to her heavenly Spouse. It is a prayer which purifies the soul and unites it to its Creator by the quasi-sacramental effect of the words of God in which it is expressed. A prayer which gives voice, in the praise of God, to the whole gamut of sentiments which He has placed in man's heart: joy and anguish, repentance and trust; a prayer which corresponds to all the situations of a human life. A theocentric prayer, preserving man from the perpetual temptation to identify prayer with request and to confine his prayer to his earthly interests. These reasons for using the psalms are as valid for Christian countries as for the missions. But their theocentric character is particularly important in countries where the work of evangelization is still in its infancy.

For in the missions, we have to do with recent converts. Their motives for conversion are not always purely disinterested, especially in the case of the mass conversion of a whole village or a tribe brought by its chief. Religion runs the risk of remaining for them a kind of contract, *do ut des,* and prayer the small change for conciliating the favors of the Almighty. We need, therefore, even more in the missions than elsewhere, prayer formulae which are strongly theocentric and which draw the soul out of the circle of self-interest and raise it to the prayer of praise and thanksgiving. Christians ought to be initiated on earth into what will be their eternal activity before the throne of the Lamb; thanksgiving to the Father Who has called them in Christ Jesus "from darkness to His wonderful light." Where shall we find formulae of praise more appropriate for centering the soul on God than in the Psalter, called in Hebrew *Sepher Tellihim,* "the book of Divine praise?" He who takes the psalms seriously abandons either himself or them.

Besides these qualities which recommend the Psalter to Christians of all times and places, it has several which make it particularly well suited to the mentality of the peoples in mission countries. Let us

13.   "Ut bene ad hominibus laudetur Deus, laudavit se ipse Deus" (S. Augustine, *Enarr.* in Ps., 144).
14.   Cf. Adalbert Hamman, "La prière de Jésus," in *Bible et vie chrétienne,* 10, May, 1955.

define what we mean by this mentality. What is there, in fact, in common between the manner of thought of the Chinese and of the Indian, who reached the summits of human civilization long before the European, and the mentality of certain peoples in Africa who have remained at the patriarchal stage? In contrast to the Graeco-Latin mentality we can characterize this mentality as, in general, synthetic, suggestive, associative, concrete and linked to nature. (For the sake of simplification, we shall call this the Oriental mentality, although we are also including the mental structures of the African and Australian peoples insofar as they are similar to those of the East.) The psalms possess these same qualities to a high degree.

Synthetic. The occidental mind has transposed its theological analysis into its prayer and has endowed its devotional books with formulae which are masterpieces of composition. Think of our "Acts" of the theological virtues: the Act of Faith, for example, is a marvellous summary of the theological treatise of faith; it reminds us that faith is the firm adhesion of the mind to the truths revealed by God and transmitted by the Church: the *objectum quod;* and this adhesion has as its formal motive the veracity of God: the *objectum quo.* We have these developed "Acts" for each element in our spiritual organism, Acts of Charity, of Hope, of Contrition, of Humility, of Trust. . . . We find the same spirit of analysis at work in the usual forms of morning and evening prayers, or in the request for a particular virtue. . . . The Oriental mind does not care for these dichotomies; it does not feel the need for identifying, labelling and expressing its inner sentiments with logical precision. It is more at ease in a prayer which places it before God in a simple *attitude,* which is the result of complex acts. It is less interested in the idea than in what we might call the radiation, the resonance of each idea in the whole person. This is exactly the type of prayer which the Psalter provides. Take for example the Good Shepherd psalm. Is it an Act of Faith, Hope, Love, Trust or Humility? It is all these acts in one. The whole spiritual organism sets in motion at the same time the various components of the attitude of the human being before his God, harmonics of a dominant note of trust. Without identifying them, the Christian praying this psalm covers the whole gamut of the theological virtues. He is not producing a formal Act of Faith, but is applying his virtue of faith to a concrete thing: the providence of the Good Shepherd who will not let him lack anything, who causes him to rest in the shade, defends him in danger, gives him food and lodging in His own dwelling. These manifestations of the goodness of God awaken hope as the pledges of His benevolence in the future; they provoke the love of gratitude. Would our faithful pray any the worse if they occasionally replaced the

"Acts" of the morning and evening prayers or their thanksgiving after Communion by psalm 22? Almost all the psalms reveal a similar complexity of the soul's uprisings blended in a simple attitude. This is what makes them at once so rich and so natural, because they are not products of the study or the prie-dieu, but spring from a concrete situation which has called forth the response of the psalmist's whole being.

Suggestive. Another feature which makes the psalms suitable to the oriental mind is their power of suggestion. Western thought tends to express itself in definite concepts which are mutually exclusive and proceed according to relationships of causality, consequence or opposition. In the East, the ideal of expression is one, not of definition, but of suggestion. The accomplished speaker does not set out a notion in black and white but envelops it in a certain misty halo which leaves his hearer the task of completing and interpreting it. The meaning is above and beyond the expression. China, in particular, is past master in this kind of divination of the thought of another. It is said that in the time of Confucius the ambassadors of various kingdoms transmitted their messages by means of musicians playing airs from the "Book of Odes," the official collection of poems. It was for the questioners to identify the text corresponding to the melody and to guess the allusion contained in the poem. This is typical of the oriental manner, which loves to express itself in hints and veiled allusions. The psalms are poetry, and oriental poetry, and as such they possess a suggestive value which attracts the oriental soul. But there is more than that. Since its "fulfillment" by Christ (cf. Luke 24, 44) and its adoption by the Church as the official euchology of the New Covenant, the whole Psalter has undergone a transposition which enriches its literal expression with a further prophetic and typological meaning. This does not only apply to those psalms which are explicitly recognized as messianic by Catholic exegesis; the primitive Church Christianized or "Christologized" the whole Psalter. "Where one hears a single voice, that of David, the king, a man, the innocent persecuted or the just man saved, the primitive Church loves to hear the voice of Christ: *"Filium ad Patrem, id est Christum verba ad Deum facientem,"* as Tertullian expressly says when speaking of the Psalter: the voice of the true David, of *the* King, *the* persecuted Innocent, *the* Just Man saved. Where once sounded the voice of the former people of the Covenant of the Old Testament, we hear the voice of the new and real Israel, the voice of the Church. The morning jubilation of David in Psalm 3: "I lie down and I sleep, now I wake again for the Lord upholds me" becomes for Justin, Irenaeus, Hippolytus and Cyprian the exultation of the Risen Christ, of Easter morning; the joy of the liberation of Israel in psalm 123: "The net has been broken and we are set free" becomes for Origen "the joy of the Church at her deliverance."[15] From the missionary point of view, then, the prayer of the psalms presents a mentality which loves to suggest its real thought behind the obvious significance, a whole world of meanings which leave for what one might call the fourth dimension of the mind ample matter on which to exercise itself.

Associative. The progress of the world of thought in the psalms is not rectilinear but concentric. In general, the psalm does not advance from one idea to another: by means of parallelism, it lingers over the contemplation of an idea, goes about considering it under different aspects. The passage to the following idea is achieved less by causality or consequence than by association of images, comparisons, analogy of situations and sentiments. This want of logic — according to our Graeco-Latin ideas — makes it sometimes hard for people used to discursive methods to employ the psalms in prayer and meditation. But *there* precisely lies their suitability to the Oriental, more intuitive than discursive in his habits of thought. To realize the truth of this, one has only to read some pages of the ancient and modern Chinese or Indian philosophers.

The majority of the Christians in mission countries, under their conditions of life, live according to the rhythm of nature. They rise and retire with the sun, they count the days according to the moon's phases and calculate the weather according to the state of the sky, they fear the storm which will destroy the harvests, long for water in time of drought and dread it during the rainy season. These natural elements which frame the daily life of our Christians do not as a rule figure in our classic prayer books. But, sun and moon, seasons and atmospheric phenomena, fauna and flora, are incorporated in the prayer of the psalmist, either as matter for praise, or comparison, or like a stealthy escape in the midst of more abstract psalms, resembling those miniature landscapes which one can divine through the window in the interiors of the Dutch masters.[16]

Concrete. Finally, the psalms offer us a type of concrete prayer. The prayers in our manuals generally oscillate between two poles: either they are so dogmatic that they are above the intellectual capacity of the average Christian and do not allow the heart to express itself, or else

15. Cf. Fischer, "Le Christ dans les Psaumes," in *La Maison-Dieu,* no. 27, 1951, p. 93. For the justification of the Christological interpretation, that of the primitive Church, cf. *ibid.,* p. 105 et seq.
16. Examples: Psalms 122, 1-6; 36, 20-35; 41, 8; 51, 10, etc.

they neglect any doctrinal content and drown in sentimentality. In the missions, it is all the more important to have formulae rich in doctrinal content because prayer is, with liturgical readings, almost the only means of practicing the religious knowledge which the faithful have learnt in the catechumenate. In fact, our country people have neither books nor magazines; they only rarely have the chance of hearing the missionary. In many places, it is true, in the course of the Sunday meetings presided over by a catechist, the community recites or rather chants in two choirs alternate parts of the catechism. But it must be admitted that this bookish knowledge of questions and answers is no direct nourishment of devotion. These abstract formulae do not go from the mind to the heart. Formulae are needed which turn these doctrinal pills into a substantial food for the heart's prayer. And this is exactly what the Lord has Himself taken care to give to His people in the Psalter. The Psalter is revelation in the form of prayer, prayer which is dogmatic without being abstract, from the heart without being sentimental. Of course, we do not find in it all the articles of the Creed; that is why, in the New Testament, we cannot be content to pray only the psalms. But most of the truths of Faith are contained in them if not literally, at least in type, in prophecy or in virtue of the plenary sense. The Trinity is not mentioned, but by the addition of the doxology, the Church has imprinted the Trinitarian stamp on the psalms. As for the One God, where is He revealed more than in the psalms as "Some One," as the living God Who acts, loves, punishes, saves, alone works wonders. No euchology in the world places us before Him in such authentic attitudes, as nothing before Him Who Is, redeemed before a God Who saves, sinners before a God Who forgives, children before a Father. It is so important for the neophytes coming from paganism to form a real conception of the living God, free from heathen representations. Their idea of God will be the cornerstone on which the entire edifice of their faith will rest. If this idea is false at the beginning, the whole presentation of the Christian Mystery will be false. In order to give them a true likeness of God, let us therefore put our neophytes and Christians in contact with the psalms in which He has Himself painted His own portrait.

Better than abstract arguments, quotations from the religious poetry of Oriental people show how the psalms are a form of prayer suited to them. How many themes similar to those of the Psalter can be met with, often expressed in analogous words. Here for instance are some Chinese specimens from the "Book of Odes"[17] of the time of Confucius. This is the portrait of the Heavenly King who governs with majesty:

17. Quotations from B. Karlgren, *The Book of Odes,* Stockholm, Museum of Far Eastern Antiquities, 1950.

Grand is God on High,
He is the ruler of the people below,
Terrible is God on High
His charge has many rules

(Karlgren, 255, 1)

This is not the God of Aristotle and the philosophers, who, having once given the initial push which set in motion the mechanism of the universe, retires into his Olympian solitude to leave the world to function by means of secondary causes. The God of the "Book of Odes" bends over the earth, He knows everything that happens, good as well as evil; He directs events. Nothing happens but by His will; no one resists His decrees.

Be reverent, be reverent,
Heaven (God) is splendid
(His) charge is not easy (to keep)
Do not say: "(He) is very high above;"
(He) ascends and descends in (his) workings
And daily inspects us who are here.

(K., 288, 1)

We also meet with the complaints of the just man who is oppressed similar to those which resound from one end to the other of the Psalter:

The arrogant men are pleased,
The toiling men are anxious;
Blue Heaven, blue Heaven,
Look at those arrogant men,
Pity these toiling men.

(K., 200, 5)

In the expression and use of images, we find an inspiration resembling that of the Psalmist. The regularity of the movement of the sun and moon, the solidity of the holy mountain and the luxurious vegetation of the great trees are symbols and proofs of the prosperity of the just and of heavenly blessings:

Like the moon's advancing to the full,
Like the rising of the sun,
Like the longevity of the southern mountains,
Which are never injured, never falling,
Like the luxuriance of the fir and the cypress . . .
(Heaven's protection is) everlasting for you.

(K., 166, 6)

Other themes link the "Book of Odes" to the Psalter: that of universal corruption, the happiness of brethren living together, the praise of the sacred mountain chosen by God, the praise of the Temple, the joy of perpetuating ancestral tradition, longevity the blessing of heaven, as is a numerous family, etc. These resemblances simply mean that the authors of the "Book of Odes," like the Psalmist, have touched the eternal chords which, in every age and every latitude, vibrate in the human soul.

Conditions for a Revival of the Psalter

If we want the Psalter to become once again what it used to be, Christian and popular prayer *par excellence*, it is indispensable to make a selection. To put the entire Psalter indiscriminately in the hands of all would be as harmful to our cause as would be the indiscriminate distribution of complete Bibles for a biblical movement in the missions. Our faithful, not ready for a direct contact with the Scriptures as a whole — and we have no means of preparing them for it — would soon reject the psalms as a form of prayer strange, difficult, even shocking in some places. This brings us to consider an objection which more than one reader has had in mind from the beginning of this article: the psalms are too difficult. Written in the setting of quite a different civilization, they presuppose, if they are to be understood, an equipment of geographical, historical, ethnological and Biblical knowledge which even priests do not always possess. How can we dream of expecting it from the faithful? If we sometimes hear missionaries, and these not the least zealous, express the wish that Rome would concede to the missions the general faculty of commuting the Breviary into a recitation of the rosary, is it reasonable to want to impose on the children a yoke which their fathers would not bear? As a matter of fact, the objection answers itself as soon as one formulates it with exactitude. "There are difficult passages in the Psalter." But the difficulty vanishes if we imitate the Spouse of Christ in the composition of her liturgical texts. She does not imagine that she is going contrary to the intention of her Spouse in choosing from the treasures of Scripture a relatively small amount of the text which is suited to the needs and capacities of all her children.

Principles of choice. As the official euchology of the Church, the Psalter ought to put on the lips of the faithful a prayer which both expresses and engenders the fundamental dispositions of the Christian soul. In the *Motu proprio, In cotidianis precibus,* which forms the preface to the new Latin translation promulgated in 1945, His Holiness Pius XII indicates three of the fundamental traits which the Holy Spirit engraves in the soul which recites the psalms devotionally: love, courage, compunction. This is an invitation to choose by preference those psalms which express and develop these three virtues.

The most perfect manifestation of love is the prayer of disinterested praise, or *eucharistic* prayer. It expresses our deepest reason for existence, the glory of God, and anticipates on earth the canticle which we shall sing eternally before the throne of the Lamb. The Lauds psalms provide ample matter for our choice here.

The Holy Father also wishes that the prayer of the psalms should develop the courage necessary for the soldier of God in this evil world. That is just what the psalms of combat provide. Many of them are born of a warring context. The universe of the Psalmist is peopled by enemies, snares, ambushes, the clash of arms, which sound strangely in our modern pacifist ears. However, it is not by chance that God chose a warrior as the principal bard of Israel. He wanted to intimate to us that the life of man upon earth is a military service. That is as true of the life of the religious in his cloister, of the mother of a family and of the peasant in his isolated farm as of the workman in the Babylon of the great cities. A state of watchfulness is the normal atmosphere of all Christian life, which is a military service. That is true of the life of the religious in his march in the desert towards the Promised Land. But it is even more true of our neophytes on the missions, for whom conversion often spells annoyances from their family, their tribe, underground or bloody persecution by the mighty of this world. What consolation for them to raise to heaven, with the persecuted Just Man, Christ Himself, the calls for help and the cries of trust which resound from one end of the Psalter to the other. As for the imprecations against one's enemies, we shall say later on what should be thought of them from the missionary point of view.

Finally, the psalms develop compunction, the source of the true spirit of penitence, the third dimension of the authentic Christian life. The psalms wage pitiless war on self-sufficiency and bring into bold relief the consciousness of human weakness. The Psalmist makes one think of a tightrope dancer always on the verge of losing his balance, but always just seizing hold of the bounty of the Most High. There is no other prayer which so fully develops the consciousness of our nothingness which the divine Mercy alone, by its ever-renewed forgiveness, maintains in existence. We shall therefore prefer to choose the psalms which engender love by unselfish praise, courage and compunction.

Christological Prayer. What has just been stated was true also for the praying people of the Old Testament. But we live in the New; Christ has already come. Our prayer should be Christological. First, in the sense that we like to echo the psalms which the Incarnate Word

Himself used during His mortal life, so that our prayer to God our Father may coincide with that of the First-Born. Cardinal Schuster wrote: "The Holy Gospels tell the life of Jesus in all its details and give His teaching, but the psalms of David show us His inner life, reveal to us His preferences, sentiments, battles, anguish; they teach us the accent of profound love with which He prayed to His heavenly Father. All His life, Jesus addressed Him in words of the Psalter, and on the Cross, during His last agony, Psalm 21 was on His lips. We might compare the Psalter to a book of sacerdotal prayers which the eternal Pontiff recited while He offered His Father the sacrifice of His own life."[18] We will therefore try to familiarize our Christians with the passages which we find in the New Testament on the lips of Jesus. His "morning prayer," Psalm 39, by which, the Epistle to the Hebrews tells us (10, 5-7), He formulated His first oblation to the Father when He came into the world: "Behold I come . . . To do your will, my God, is my delight." His "evening prayer," when, the "day's" work ended, He gave His soul into His Father's Hands: (Psalm 30, 6). Psalm 41, 6, 12 which comes into the prayer in Gethsemane: "Why are you sad, O my soul." Psalm 21 which Jesus recited on the cross (Matt. 27, 46; Mark 15, 34). With Psalm 68, we penetrate into the sanctuary of the heart of Jesus at the moment when, High Priest after the order of Melchisedech (Psalm 109, 4), He offered on the altar of the Cross the definitive sacrifice of the new and eternal Covenant. The great Hallel (Psalm 135) takes on a new distinction when we realize that Christ sang it with His apostles after the Last Supper.[19] In addition to the psalms whose prophetic or typological fulfillment by Christ is vouched for by an inspired text or the unanimous testimony of tradition, the primitive Church has left us a whole series of Christological or ecclesiastical interpretations,[20] most of which have been incorporated in the liturgy. These interpretations, the fruits of the Church's meditations on the Heart of her Spouse, cannot produce their letters-patent of nobility which would prove their origin in Christ. But were they not suggested by the Spirit of Jesus? In any case, Christianity has for centuries made them into jewels dear to all those who "feel with the Church." For this reason we also will give them a paramount place in the Psalter of the faithful.

Principles of elimination. Generally speaking, we should leave aside from the Psalter destined for the people of the missions those elements

---

18. Lib. Sacr., II, p. 156.
19. Cf. A. Hamann, "Le prière de Jésus," in *Bible et vie chrétienne*, 10, 1955, p. 8; see also J. A. Jungmann, *The Mass of the Roman Rite*, I, p. 9.
20. See other examples above, quoted by B. Fischer.

which are explicable only by historical, geographical or theological knowledge which it is impossible to impart even to select groups (Ex.: Psalms 87; 47; 106; 107, etc.).

There is such wealth in the Psalter that we need not regret these losses, among which we should include the comminatory psalms. Their imprecations are the product of a period before the "benevolence and humanity" of the Word Incarnate had shone forth. Explanations and distinctions make this rough material fashioned at the time of the Law of retaliation still usable today in the prayer of the New Covenant and justify their place in the Roman Breviary. The Biblical movement in European countries has perhaps endowed the faithful with enough historical sense to understand the exegesis of the comminatory psalms and mentally to substitute the sin for the sinner. In the missions we have not yet reached that point; even had we the time — which is not the case — to explain the curses of the psalmist, our flock would not understand. They would still be scandalized by the holy King taking pleasure in washing his feet in the blood of his enemies (Psalm 67, 24). (We are speaking of the psalms to be chanted by the congregation and do not deny that the entire Psalter could be put into the hands of the elite).

Some psalms are too long to be comfortably recited in public; in others we come across historical or geographical names which bewilder our people and create the impression that the psalms are foreign and exotic prayers (e.g. 135, 19-20). Or again a revengeful wish breaks the charm of an idyll (Psalm 136, 7-9: "Beatus qui apprehendet et allidet parvulos tuos ad petram"). We cannot suggest these as prayers to our young Christian communities. Must they then be deprived of the jewels of the Psalter because of one or two difficult verses? Would it not be more in conformity with the intentions and customs of the Church to cut out, with all the respect due to the Word hidden beneath the human words, that which is an obstacle to simple souls? The same principle which justifies the use of extracts from the Bible justifies a choice among the psalms. No doubt the unity of the sacred poem is destroyed thereby, but in the mission, for the love of souls, the aesthete has often to yield to the pastor.

When to Sing the Psalms?

First of all, the psalms have a definite place in the central act of the liturgy: the sacrifice of thanksgiving of the redeemed people of God. In the Introit, the Gradual and Communion, as given in our present Roman missal, the psalms are usually used, but reduced to one or two verses. (We do not include the psalms *Judica me* and *Lavabo,* since these are personal to the priest). Let us, then, give back to these songs of the Mass their original function and length.

As the entrance hymn, the invitation of the Breviary, Psalm 94, is indicated. It is the invitation to God's people to enter into the sanctuary to offer the sacrifice of praise and thanksgiving. The congregation joins in the chant by repeating each verse after the choir or soloist: "Come, let us adore the Lord." Or Psalm 99, in which the congregation sings the refrain: "Come, praise the Lord, we are the people of His pasture." Or Psalm 42: with the refrain: "I will go up to the altar of God, the God of my joy."

For practical reasons, the gradual psalm should be relatively short. The text in the missal can be sung by a soloist, and the Alleluia by the congregation. If it is feared, as is often the case with us, that the texts of the missal may be above the comprehension of the faithful, the soloist sings the *"Laudate Dominum"* (Psalm 116) with the following refrain by the congregation: "Praise the Lord, all people, sing Alleluia forever."

As the procession with the offerings has disappeared from our liturgy, the psalm which used to accompany it no longer has any purpose. We would prefer to substitute the "General prayer."[21] Where it is customary for members of the congregation to bring the offerings to the altar, the soloist could sing a psalm in harmony with the feast of the day, with this traditional refrain: "O Lord God, in the simplicity of my heart, joyfully have I offered all things." (1 Par., 29, 17).[22]

The traditional chants for the Communion are Psalm 144 with the refrain: "On you rest the eyes of all creatures, You give them their food in due season"; Psalm 33 with the refrain: "O taste and see that the Lord is good";[23] Psalm 114 with the refrain: "How make return . . ."; Psalm 41 with the refrain: "As the deer longs for the running waters . . ."; Psalm 22 with the refrain: "The Lord is my shepherd . . ."

The missal provides us with concluding hymns: Psalm 50 and the canticle of Daniel (3, 57-88). The great Hallel (Psalm 135) with the refrain: "For His love is eternal" will be especially dear to us, for it was sung by Our Lord Himself at the end of the first Mass in the Cenacle.

It is equally desirable to give the psalms a place in the morning and evening prayers. A good formula is that which provides both a fixed and a variable part. This has been in use for a long time in the euchology of the Mission of Hsien Hsien (China); variable readings and prayers

---

21. See Chapter V, p. 53.
22. Cf. Jungmann, *The Mass of the Roman Rite,* II (1955), p. 30.
23. *Ibid.,* II (1955), p. 393.

are provided for feast days. Thus a morning and evening psalm could be given for each day of the week to be sung either in antiphonal or responsorial form.

Finally, could we sing to Christ present with us during the Benediction of the Blessed Sacrament more beautiful praises than those which He Himself used during His mortal life? All the psalms of praise and thanksgiving are perfectly suitable. The office for the feast of Corpus Christi also gives us a choice of psalms which can easily be applied to the Eucharist.

The Melody of the Psalms

A psalm is not truly one unless it is sung. Moreover, in the missions, there is no real prayer which does not engage the whole person, body and soul. For our Christians, a prayer which is only murmured is not worthy of the name. In China, when two Christians meet in a deserted church, they do not, as do Westerners, go and kneel, one behind a pillar on the right and the other behind that on the left; they kneel together to chant the official prayer. That is why a simple recitation of the psalms does not satisfy their liturgical requirements. They must be sung. What melodies should be used? The words can be adapted to the Gregorian modes of the *Liber Usualis*. That is the solution adopted by the Congregation of the *Petits Frères* founded in China by Pere Lebbe. However, these modes, giving an equal value to each syllable without taking the accent into account, do not satisfy the ear; moreover, these abstract airs do not awaken echoes in the popular ear.[24]

The ideal would be to adapt the inspired texts to the best musical productions of the national folklore, either religious, if they exist, or even secular. In this case, care must be taken that these airs do not bring with them pagan, profane or even vulgar, memories. That was the method used by Mr. Chiang Wen Yeh for setting the Chinese psalms to music.[25] In Japan, a former missionary in China, Father Sturm, has adapted a certain number of the psalms to the Japanese mode.[26] Where nothing else has been tried, the masterpieces of Père Gelineau so perfectly suited to the French genius, will provide elements which can be used for an original work adapted to the country. Even as they are, the melodic themes chosen by Père Gelineau may be found pleasing in very different latitudes. At least, that is what I found to be the case in China and the Philippines, each time I have played his records.

24. See in *Missi*, December, 1955, p. 36, an example of secular music converted to a carol.
25. See the following paragraph.
26. Fr. G. Sturm, Catholic Church, Misuzawa, Iwateken, Japan.

We are perhaps confronted with a supra-temporal and supra-continental art, employing the groups of intervals which are natural to the human ear in all ages and in every civilization.[27]

The musical themes of the negro Spirituals, more colorful while remaining intensely religious, are equally suited to the text of the psalms. The catechists who followed the Summer Course of the Confraternity of Christian Doctrine at Manila in 1956 learned enthusiastically to sing some psalms to these tunes and are now teaching them to the children in their classes. These are provisional solutions, whose aim is to create a taste for the psalms and to encourage original work from indigenous artists in each country. We may add that for those countries where liturgical dances are the custom, the psalms provide choreographic themes for paraliturgies.

A reader of the liturgical magazine, *Worship,* complained to the editor: "I enjoy your articles called 'It can be done,' but when are you going to publish one called 'It has been done?'" Not to deserve the same reproach, I will here mention a work of which the Church in China has the right to be proud. In 1947 the Chinese pagan composer, Mr. Chiang Wen Yeh, discovered by chance the Catholic translation of the psalms published by the Biblical Institute, O.F.M., of Pekin. These sacred texts were a revelation to him. "I have at last found my path," he said. He set to work with enthusiasm; a specialist in ancient music, manuscripts of which he found in the National Library of Pekin, he adapted tunes inspired by folklore and from the religious repertory of the temples and pagodas to the text of the psalms. When Father Allegra, the head of the Biblical Institute, expressed his embarrassment regarding a suitable remuneration, the author reassured him, saying: "I want to do this in honour of the Spirit of Heaven (God) and for the glory of Chinese music." Thus, since 1947, China has had its "Gélineau" who has attempted to unite the inspired prayer to the finest creations of Chinese musical genius. Mgr. Julius Van Nuffel, head of the interdiocesan Institute of Religious Music at Malines, compares his "Psalm 150" to the music of Handel, "whom the Chinese composer surpasses however by the loftiness of his liturgical temperament." The composer has now set all one hundred and fifty psalms to music. In 1948, two editions had already appeared, containing thirty-seven psalm melodies, the *Magnificat,* the *Regina Coeli,* the *Ave Maria.* His works were beginning to reach the parishes and the wireless and were appreciated by the non-Christian public. The communist invasion stopped

27. Cf. Didier Rimaud, "Erneuernung des Psalmengesangs in Frankreich," in *Liturgisches Jahrbuch,* 4, Band, 1954, p. 251.

the publication of other psalms and hindered the diffusion of those already issued. But the work awaits better times.

Conclusion

The success of the psalm revival depends above all on the enthusiasm of the missionary. If he himself loves the psalms, he will easily kindle his flock. Do not let us wait to begin the movement until heaven sends each mission a Gelineau or a Chiang Wen Yeh. Let us set to work ourselves. No doubt our musical productions will not go down to posterity, but they will have started a movement, created an atmosphere of sympathy for the psalms which will make possible the birth of more perfect work. They will hasten the day when this divine book united to the finest creations of human civilization will become again what its Author wishes it to be: the book of canticles for the people of God journeying to the Promised Land.

CHAPTER TEN

The Celebration of the Liturgical Feasts

JOHANNES HOFINGER, S.J.

"The most effective form of preaching the Gospel is the celebration of a feast."[1] This general statement of Jungmann's has a special relevance to the missionary apostolate, and the messengers of the Christian faith have always been to some degree aware of this fact and have tried to put it into practice. If a detailed history of the missionary apostolate is ever written — there is none as yet[2] — it will indicate how missionaries in all centuries have striven to celebrate the great Christian feasts in a fitting way and how these celebrations have been one of the most effective means of evangelization.

True, the missionary value of Christian feasts has not always been fully understood or used by all; moreover, every method of celebration that has been adopted does not have the same value. And also, while recognizing what missionaries have already done in this field, we may be allowed to say that it would be possible to put the celebration of Christian feasts more clearly and more intensively at the service of

---

1. Jungmann, "Catechestics," *Lumen Vitae,* Brussels.
2. The science of missiology, which has flourished so greatly during the last decades, ought to undertake this important task. But a good general work on the subject cannot be undertaken until the necessary profound specialized studies have been made. And, in spite of the praiseworthy zeal that has inspired the research and publications of this science, such studies are not yet very numerous, though we should mention in this connection the excellent work of F. X. Bürkler, S.M.B., *Die Sonn-und-Festtagsfeier in der katholischen Chinamission,* Rome 1942. This evident lack of studies of the history and laws of missionary evangelization is not unrelated to the fact that the science of missiology, in spite of its missionary zeal, has often been conceived of in a way not entirely missionary-minded. In any case, catechesis and pastoral work in the missions have never been among its favorite subjects.

missionary work in general and of the work of evangelization in particular. We shall find this to be true if we study first the missionary value of evangelization proper to Christian feasts, and then seek to discover how this value might be increased and made more fully available to the faithful by an appropriate form of celebration and by the preaching of the word of God (sermon and catechesis).

The Value of Christian Feasts in the Work of Evangelization

Like every festival that is celebrated with a certain amount of pomp, the Christian feasts celebrated in the missions always draw an appreciable number of curious bystanders. This is true primarily of the part of the ceremonies held outside the church itself, that is, processions and paraliturgies. The special decoration of the church for feasts serves to attract unbelievers to enter, especially if care is taken to vary such decoration and to offer new things to be looked at according to the season, for example, a crêche at Christmas time, or some representation of the Passion and triumph of our Savior at Easter time. The Mass itself always attracts a number of pagans, and it would certainly attract many more if it were celebrated in great part in the language of the country, for the meaning of the ceremonies would thus be made clear, to a certain degree at least, even to uninitiated spectators.[3] The immediate effects of any feast, of course, vary in different regions. Generally speaking, they are more perceptible among simpler and more primitive peoples, where this first spontaneous contact with the Christian religion and with its life can become the starting point of a growing attentiveness to Christianity, and so of a future conversion.

But the evangelizing value of Christian feasts does not consist chiefly in the food that they furnish for the simple curiosity of those outside the Church, and neither does it consist in the satisfaction, much more precious, that they give to souls seeking the sanctity and the spiritual wealth contained in Christian worship. We do not deny these immediate missionary effects; they must indeed be taken into consideration and utilized in missionary work. But we should look further for the specific evangelizing value proper of Christian feasts; we should look for it where the missionary Church of the first centuries found the unique value of her solemnities, of the ancient Paschal celebration, for example: not in the immediate impression produced on unbelievers — who in any case were excluded — but in the teaching given to the Christians them-

---

3. It would be a mistake to desire a greater use of the vernacular in worship in the missions chiefly for the purpose of making the ceremonies intelligible to the unbelieving visitor, even a friendly one. The principle reason is, rather, to facilitate the understanding and participation of the Christians themselves.

selves, in the formative influence of the feast, in its radiation, through the faithful themselves, into missionary work properly so-called. And therefore what can be said of the missionary effectiveness of Christian feasts applies equally to countries in which no pagan would attend out of curiosity, where there are neither pagans, nor the merely curious, but congregations of Christians who should draw from participation in the feasts of the Church the joy of their faith and the awareness of their mission among religiously indifferent neo-pagans.

Here we are at the heart of the question. Our feasts do not manifest aspects of Christianity selected at random, but its fundamental values. In reality, only values can be celebrated. Purely theoretic truths and actions that are not lived as values can be explained or affirmed, but they can never be celebrated. It has never occured to any mathematician, however enthusiastic, to celebrate the feast of a mathematical formula, even of the Pythagorean theorem. It would be far more possible to celebrate Pythagoras himself, his merits as a philosopher and a mathematician, his outstanding personality. A Christian feast is essentially *a profession of faith of the community celebrating its special Christian values.* For such a festival, the value of Christianity appears to the average Christian in a vital way. What has seemed a sterile formula as given in the academic teaching of religion or in the catechism, now comes alive and becomes a value of *his* life. This is the time to celebrate with joy the unmerited happiness of being able to be a Christian.

A Christian feast thus achieves in a supereminent way an aspect of the work of evangelization which is most important in the missions: it brings out the values of Christianity in a shining and appealing way, so that Christianity is no longer considered and practiced primarily as a painful duty, but is lived as a free gift and a sacred commission.

Moreover, the feasts of the Church do not bring out the values of Christianity indiscriminately. When the feasts of the liturgical year are properly celebrated it is the *essential truths and values of Christianity* that shine out, clearly indicating its content and its essential elements, that is: our wonderful vocation to enter the kingdom of God by our union with the Son of God Who is the gift of the Father's love, given to us as our Brother, our Master, our divine Head; our redemption from sin to lead a new divine life in Christ; the gifts of the Savior, above all the Holy Spirit and the Eucharist; our expectation of the future consummation of God's plan for the redemption of mankind and the final triumph of the Lord, on the day of His return in power and glory.

So the great feasts of the liturgical year exemplify in a remarkable way what we have called *catechetical concentration.* The themes of the great feasts are interwoven with one another, but the whole year brings out one all-inclusive theme: the Mystery of Christ which includes the whole history of salvation, continually renewed and realized in the Church. Thus it might be said that the general theme of the liturgical year is our sanctifying participation in the Mystery of Christ, a theme that is progressively developed in the great feasts and the liturgical seasons. The development of this theme does not prevent the celebration of important feasts which bear little relation to the course of the liturgical year, for example, the Annunciation or the feast of St. Joseph, which occur towards the end of Lent. Even those feasts that obviously disturb the logic of the calendar are notable for their catechetical concentration. The theme of each is presented in such a way that it becomes interwoven into the general theme of the whole year, developing and deepening it. In these feasts also we are celebrating the Mystery of Christ, we are developing and realizing His life in us by celebrating it.[4]

Every Christian feast is thus truly *Christocentric*. Whatever its special message, it proclaims the generous love of the Father, revealed to us and given to us in Christ. The joyful gratitude of the new people of God for this incomprehensible gift of the Father, Christ Himself, for our own incorporation into Christ and His mystery — this is the final meaning of all Christian celebrations.

Thus the feasts of the Christian year have the same fundamental theme as does Christian preaching and teaching: Christ, our way and our leader to the Father.[5] It is a remarkable fact that the liturgical year develops this theme *in the same order* as that of the bible-narrative catechesis given in the first grades of school. Even though the liturgy knows nothing of academic methods of teaching, nevertheless the course of the liturgical year follows, in its broad outlines, the course of the history of salvation. This is of the very essence of the liturgy, and important with regard to its value in evangelization. Thus the message of the liturgical year is the Good News of what the love of God has done and still wills to do for us throughout all the chief stages of the history of salvation.[6]

But liturgical celebrations are not confined to history alone. In a

4. See the excellent study of J. A. Jungmann, S.J., *Das Christusgeheimnis im Kirchenjahr,* in the collection, *Gewordene Liturgie,* Innsbruck, 1941, pp. 2, 95.
5. J. A. Jungmann, S.J., *Christus als Mittelpunkt religiöser Erziehung,* Fribourg, 1939. J. Hofinger, S.J., "Our Message" in *Lumen Vitae,* 1950, pp. 264-280.
6. Up to the present time, we have too little recognized the necessity of bringing out the historical character of our religion even in systematic catechesis, and, as much as possible, in the arrangement of the material to be taught. On this subject, see J. Hofinger, S.J., *The Art of Teaching Christian Doctrine,* Notre Dame, 1957, pp. 74-83.

Christian feast, the far-off past becomes the immediate "here and now," bringing happiness, grace and courage. And this precisely constitutes the "mystery" of the great Christian feasts, placing them above any mere commemoration, making them vital for life here and now, rich experiences, fruitful, efficacious. Thus we can — though in another sense — fully apply to them the axiom of Catholic teaching on the sacraments: "dant quod significant:" they *cause us to participate in the mystery that is celebrated*. This is common Catholic teaching, independent of the various theories proposed on the meaning and nature of Christian celebrations, and it seems to us that to introduce in an exaggerated way the opinions of any special school of theology into our preaching and teaching concerning our feasts in no way serves the cause of Christian preaching in general or the liturgical movement.

Since the course of the liturgical year follows the great lines of the course of the history of salvation, the religious teaching given in the first years of school can easily be connected directly with the liturgical year, as modern catechetical theory so strongly recommends, a recommendation that has already born fruit. The climactic points of the liturgy can thus become the climactic points of catechetical teaching and of religious practice.[7] The liturgical year also provides an excellent plan for teaching the people generally, for it is actually *"the classic program designed for all,* the program that constantly recurs, and continually enriches souls by each new period of the year, so that they become at home in its spiritual world."[8] If the instruction of adults also is related to this program, it will gain a beneficial harmony between religious teaching and practice, and a true internal unity that is both flexible and fruitful. And this effect is particularly important in the missions, where millions of Christians can celebrate solemnly only the great feasts, often being deprived of Sunday Mass and preaching.[9]

So far, we have been discussing the value of Christian feasts as

7. See J. A. Jungmann, S.J., *Catechetics,* p. 62.
8. J. A. Jungmann, S.J., *Die Frohbotschaft und unsere Glaubensverkündigung,* Regensburg, 1936, p. 127. See the whole chapter "Die Predigt als Führung durchs Kirchenjahr," pp. 127-141.
9. This harmony between the liturgy and catechetical teaching is disturbed when the liturgical year is considered as beginning with Septuagesima, as, for example, in Pius Parsch, *The Liturgical Year,* Vol. I, (Collegeville). Parsch was naturally too practical to dare to arrange his whole work on the liturgical year in accordance with this idea. We do not believe that the historical and liturgical reasons invoked for it are sufficient. To make such a change does violence to the actual liturgy as we have it and uselessly offends the healthy religious sentiment of the people; it also seriously lessens the evangelizing value of the liturgical year. It is true that from the historical point of view, certain indications show that the liturgical year was not originally considered as forming a whole. Does it follow that the later development towards making it such a whole is not a real progress?

flowing from their content. But this value flows not only from what they proclaim, but also from the way in which they proclaim it. The proper celebration of a feast requires that the Christian community both accepts its message and *takes active part in celebrating it*. This is important from the missionary point of view: the more the community really celebrates — that is to say, is not content simply to hear exhortations or to play a merely passive role — the more we can hope to see our Christians spontaneously and joyfully bearing witness to Christian ideals in their daily lives, and so winning their unbelieving neighbors. For from active community participation is born both personal religious experience and effective practice. Here we meet an essential element of religious pedagogy: to make use of the principle of vital experience and personal activity.

Moreover, by its very nature, a religious feast celebrated by the whole community enables the feebler souls to share in the faith and fervor of the stronger. The many tiny flames which each by itself, could hardly be seen, when united together make a bright light. Have we no need of such light in the missions? And further, because they speak to our people's hearts, great feasts are powerful means of fostering *community spirit*. During the ceremonies, the members of a small community in one lonely station feel themselves united with one another in the solemn profession of the same faith, and they realize also that this particular community is sustained by the great fellowship of all the saints in heaven and on earth, celebrating with them this same feast, professing the same ideals, and that it is thanks to this same profession of faith that so many millions of their brethren in Christ have attained to the fullness of life in the triumphant Church.

Here we see another value of our feasts: they allow us *to experience the Church*, to realize that it is our spiritual homeland, our mother, the kingdom of God to come, which calls not only for our wonder and admiration but also for our ready obedience and courageous collaboration. At the same time, each feast evokes this final state of the kingdom of God, a state which our feasts here below in some way prefigure and celebrate: they are the meeting of the pilgrim Church and the Church already arrived at the goal. In her feasts, the Church reveals herself; here she manifests her hierarchic structure and her sacramental life. The Christian in the missions has great need for this profound experience of the Church and of finding in it an oasis in the desert of his pagan environment. This pure love of the Church, solidly founded, will also nourish his missionary zeal. A Catholic does not go to work for a formless Christianity. When he devotes himself to any kind of missionary activity in his environment, he does it for the visible Church whose incomparable religious values he has discovered from his own religious experience.

How Can These Values Be Fully Brought Out?

It is true enough that everything we have just said about the evangelizing value of the great feasts of the Christian year is true rather *potentially* than in actual realization. Realistic-minded people might even add that in the missions only a modest degree of realization has so far been achieved. This is certainly true. But it is equally true of our use of the evangelizing power of Holy Scripture or catechesis. The treasure is there, but it must be made use of. The question is not whether we have done so fully in the past, but how we can do so more fully in the future.

To make full use of the incomparable missionary treasure contained in our Christian feasts, two things must be assured: the proper organization of the celebration itself, and the proper exposition of the message of the feast in the sermon and catechetical teaching. Celebration and instruction should harmonize with one another and so bring to light, as well as make use of, the values of which we have been speaking. For both purposes, we must first of all understand clearly the true meaning of Christian feasts. By insisting, as our present subject demands, on the evangelizing value of these celebrations, we run the danger of seeming to believe that the primary and essential purpose of the feasts of the Church is to carry on the work of evangelization. And, obviously, this would be a gross error.

The primary purpose of all our feasts is Christian worship itself, the grateful homage of the Christian community to God, its introduction into His design, the communication of the divine life by which the Father responds to the adoration of His people. In the final analysis, the cult of our feasts does not exist for the sake of the work of evangelization; this work ought, rather, to place itself at the service of a celebration of divine worship that is as perfect as possible. Our feasts are essentially *far more than an especially imposing and solemn form of catechetical teaching* or an exceptionally favorable occasion for explaining Christian doctrine and making it loved. Their final purpose is not our knowledge of the divine mysteries that are being celebrated, but our profound faith in these mysteries and our personal participation in them. Knowledge is always a necessary means, but never an end in itself. Like religious instruction itself, the proclamation of the word which prepares for and accompanies the celebration of the Church's feasts, has primarily in view Christian life itself and, in this case, the perfect carrying out of the solemn worship in which the life and prayer of the community reach their climax. In any case, this is the way it should be. The nearer we arrive at this ideal, the greater will be the value of the feasts. Have we missionaries always taken account of this fact?

Keeping this central truth in mind, then, let us ask how we can most effectively work to realize the ideal. Here we can, of course, only make some suggestions called for by the situation in the missions.

In organizing the celebration of feasts, the missionary's first thought must be how to make it possible *for as many of his Christians as possible to take part,* especially in the case of the major feasts.

In missionary China, and also in other places, the great feasts are usually considered in practice to be four: Christmas, Easter, Pentecost and the Assumption. These feasts divide the year fairly evenly, although the space between the Assumption and Christmas is a little long. In North China, both Pentecost and the Assumption fall during the season of work in the fields, a season hardly favorable to a thoughtful celebration or to the participation of many of the Christians who live in distant stations. Yet the feast of the Assumption does offer to the peasant the great advantage of an interval of rest in the midst of his intense and continuous labors, an interval that comes just before the particularly strenuous time of the autumn harvest. The mystery of this feast, bringing before us the glorious consummation to which we aspire, is most appropriate to this time of year. These four great feasts, in fact, actually complete one another most perfectly and together celebrate the whole saving reality of Christianity: the Incarnation, the Redemption, the fruits of the Redemption, the final purpose of the Redemption. But in our teaching, we need to be on guard against seeming to put these four feasts on the same level, or, still worse, to talk about four cycles. The formulas of the catechism should also prevent such a misconception, although the present official catechism used in the Chinese missions is not at all satisfactory on this point. Easter and Christmas should always be shown to be the two great feasts of the liturgical year, both in our teaching and in the way in which the ceremonies are arranged. "They are the two pillars"[10] of the year. And also, should we not in practice give more importance than at present to the feast of All Saints? Coming at a favorable time of year, this feast has an especially rich content — Christian life — Christian fulfillment in heaven — the heavenly harvest festival coming at the end of the autumn harvesting.

Among our arrangements for great feasts, we need to see to it that the Christians who come from far away can spend the previous night at the station where the feast is to be celebrated, for this is the only way

10. On this subject, see Jungmann, *Die Frohbotschaft* . . . , p. 128 ff.

in which they can fully take part. The care of their lodging and food should fall, not on the missionary himself, but on the Christians of the station, who can thus be given a special opportunity to practice fraternal charity, hospitality and Christian social spirit, which in itself is a means of active participation in the feast. Obviously, these great feasts are not the only ones that can be celebrated with solemnity, even though we must give them an especially privileged place.

In certain missions, the priest is accustomed to celebrate almost all the feasts in the chief station of his district, the only one adapted to the carrying out of solemn ceremonies. But it would be better in itself, in more important districts, to consider the use of various outlying stations for the celebration of feasts of a certain importance, while still holding the great feasts at the chief station, especially if this is central and includes a much larger number of the faithful than any other. Where two missionaries live together — something desirable in itself — one of them could almost always preside over the ceremonies in the principal station, while the other celebrated the feast in one or other of the chief outlying stations. In any case, feasts of the second rank should be celebrated in those outlying stations that can assure the participation of a sufficient number, and all the Christians in the district, or at least the great majority, should be given the opportunity, in the course of several years, to celebrate at least once all the major feasts of the liturgical year.

Next, we need *to present and to celebrate each feast according to its importance in the structure of the liturgical year and its wealth of grace.* This does not necessarily coincide with the rank given it by the rubrics nor with the personal taste of the missionary himself. And, in this connection, *our preparation* for and celebration of the great feasts of Christmas and Easter themselves should include so far as possible the liturgical seasons that precede and follow them. Thus from the pastoral missionary point of view, it is to be regretted that some priests insist more on the celebration of the month of March as the month of St. Joseph than on the celebration of Lent; and the same holds true for the months of May and June. The question is not whether these devotions can be profitably used in the whole pastoral program of missionary work — they certainly can be[11] — but whether it is allowable to give less emphasis to the celebration, pastorally far more important, of the seasons of Advent, Lent and Eastertide. What a great part is played by these holy seasons in the life of the missionary Church! Where is the special expectation of Advent more fitting than in the missions where

11. See J. Hofinger, S.J., "Mensis S. Joseph," in *Collectanea Commissionis Synodalis,* Peking, 1942, 142-9.

the majority of the people have not yet entered the messianic kingdom? And do we have no need in the missions of the austere season of Lent as the special time of serious reflection, of spiritual renewal, so as to appear to the eyes of the unbelieving truly as "the city set on a mountain" and to win them to Christ by holiness of our life? And the Easter season is called to fill us with joy and gratitude for the glory of Christ and for His redeeming work, to increase in us our awareness of the grace of Baptism, and to make us true heralds of the Good News who, like the Apostles of old, "cannot keep silent" (Acts 4, 20) concerning the great things that we have experienced. In order the better to celebrate these holy seasons, we should emphasize them more in the community prayers, in the services held in the absence of a priest, and in the community evening prayer. Hymns and readings also could contribute a great deal.[12]

The great feasts can be celebrated by the missionary himself only in the more important stations. In this way many Christians from the smaller outlying stations are also given the opportunity to assist at divine service in a station not too far from their own. But these are only a minority; the greater number are not free to travel and cannot leave home to take part in the celebration of even the greatest feasts. What can be done for them? First of all, the missionary can see to it that *the services to be held in his absence will have on these great feasts as solemn a character as is possible* with no priest and no Eucharist. Here again singing can play a great part, though of course not even the most beautiful chant could ever make up to a Christian for the lack of the Sacrifice and the Eucharistic banquet.

In addition to arranging for services to be held in his absence on great feasts, the missionary can visit his outlying stations as soon as possible after the feast itself for a special celebration. Such a visit ought to take on a certain quality of solemnity even if it takes place on a feria, and the celebration should be centered in the mystery of the feast itself. To bring this about, it is most desirable, as we mentioned earlier, that the missionary be able to use on these occasions the actual Proper of the Mass of the feast. This would show that we Christians cannot live without our feasts, and that we cannot celebrate them rightly without a priest and the Eucharist. Missionary bishops could quite easily obtain the necessary authorization from Rome; similar permissions have been liberally granted in the past, for privileges that have nothing like the same pastoral importance: for example, the permission to use the votive Mass of the Sacred Heart on the First Friday of the month.

---

12. See J. Hofinger, S.J., "Keeping Sunday in the Missionary's Absence," in *Lumen Vitae*, 1953, 114-118. See also the following chapter of this book.

It is hardly necessary to say that any real feast must be *centered in the celebration of the Eucharistic Sacrifice*, not only in theory but in practice. In this, the people judge according to what they see and hear, and the priest will preach in vain about the Mass as the central element in the celebration of a feast if he celebrates Benediction in the afternoon with more solemnity than Mass in the morning,[13] as we have already mentioned in the chapter on the celebration of the Mass.

If the Mass is thus made the most solemn event of the day, the celebration will accord with the nature of Christian worship. But we must not confuse *real religious solemnity* with *profane or semiprofane pomp* and circumstance. True religious solemnity fosters the interior dispositions favorable to prayer, causes true Christian joy, gives a presentiment of the greatness of God, but worldly pomp tends rather to conceal the deficiencies of our interior dispositions by noisy and colorful stage-setting. Such pomp is destructive of the true spirit of Christian feasts and is radically opposed to them. But solemn celebrations that are as elevating, majestic and edifying as circumstances permit help our Christians to live their feasts more intensely and to profit from their evangelizing values. Although pomp and true religious solemnity are fundamentally different, in actual practice they exist side by side and are sometimes difficult to distinguish. The missionary often feels torn between his desire to adapt the celebrations to the needs of his people and to let them celebrate the feasts in their own way, and his zeal for the house of God which urges him to protect the purity of divine worship. But he needs to beware of making any decisions on the basis of his own tastes and Western ideas. Christian worship should be truly elevating and yet at the same time have the quality of spontaneity proper to the children of God who are celebrating a feast in the joy of their heavenly Father; and this cannot be brought about by holding to any foreign mode. These questions need to be decided in a truly priestly spirit, according to actual circumstances. Again, distinction should be made between the different parts of the sanctuary. For example, on great feasts we need not condemn as worldly a rather boisterous procession into the Church, provided that it retains a religious character and leaves aside anything that jars with this character. In the church, worldly music should be silent, especially during the celebration of the Eucharist.

---

13. If by reason of circumstances, the principal ceremony has to be held in the afternoon or evening, we can now, thank God, take advantage of the permission for evening Mass. In the missions, as elsewhere, the pastoral potentialities of evening Mass have not as yet been fully exploited; there has not yet been time to discover them. But we should be on the watch to find them out and make use of them.

The problem of liturgical adaptation has also another aspect. The Eucharistic Sacrifice becomes the true center of Christian worship, experimentally speaking, only to the extent to which we succeed in making the Mass comprehensible and familiar to our Christian people, in the setting of the active participation of the community in the ceremonies. Here we see *the importance of the privilege concerning the use of the mother tongue for the singing during High Mass*.[14] The development of popular liturgical singing is the quickest and surest way of obtaining the active and intelligent participation of the people in the ceremonies of the Mass; the communal singing makes worship a solemn prayer and a confession of faith full of joy vividly felt.

If we could not make the people understand the ceremonies of the Mass, we should be tempted to take refuge in paraliturgies and seek some substitute. For example, in certain missions conducted by Germans, the custom has been established of a ceremony anticipating the feast of Christmas. A statue of the Infant Jesus is received by the community and carried into the church. The midnight festivities may suffer from such ceremonies; they should play only a preparatory part, and not be made too prominent. We must, however, recognize the need for presenting the mystery to the senses, not only in paintings, but in scenes from the Bible or simple "mystery plays." Such presentations both instruct our Christians and arouse the curiosity of pagans, and, in the past, we have made too little use of liturgical drama in the work of evangelization or in that of celebrating feast days.[15]

If we succeed in capturing the soul of our people, then our feasts will sooner or later produce popular customs, especially in the countries in which an important segment of the whole population has become Christian. The formation of such customs is greatly to be desired, since they permeate the life of the people with Christianity. Truly living religious customs possess great evangelizing value, in virtue both of their content and of their effective elements. But while he is aware of their value, the missionary has to remember that a real custom cannot be made up or brought into existence at will; nor can it be an imitation

---

14. Several missionary bishops have obtained this privilege during recent years. It seems important to obtain the permission, as in Germany, not only to make use of the language of the people, but to replace the text of the Proper with appropriate hymns. See Fisher, "Das 'Deutsche Hochamt' " in *Lit. Jahr.*, 1953, pp. 41-53; J. Wagner, "Gestaltung des Deutschen Hochamtes," in Arnold B. Fisher, *Die Messe in der Glaubensverkündigung*, Fribourg, 1950, pp. 321-328. On the recommendation of the 3rd International Liturgical Congress at Lugano, see *Worship*, Collegeville, 1954.
15. See J. Hofinger, S.J., "Missionkatechetische Bedeutung und Gestaltung des religiösen Schauspieles," in *Zeit. f. Miss.*, 1953, pp. 320-324.

of the custom of a different people. The missionary can only make suggestions; the custom must be born of the people themselves.

After the question of the organization of feasts, we need to consider the *preaching* to be given. For a feast that is celebrated in an ideal way would be so clear and understandable as to need only a minimum of preaching, while preaching can make the best celebration more intelligible and fruitful for Christian life.

The most important feasts offer the missionary an excellent opportunity to proclaim the word of God. In most cases, he will find a numerous and well-disposed audience, one that many of his colleagues in Christian countries might well envy. Some of his hearers have come from a distance: their spiritual hunger has caused them to take a long journey, and now they wish to be nourished. If the feast is being celebrated in one of the larger outlying stations, the community feels itself honored; the Christians feel that it is a privilege and a source of encouragement to have such a solemnity held in their midst. How eagerly the missionary should take such an opportunity! As he knows very well, the center of any Christian feast is not preaching but the worship of God, above all the Eucharistic Sacrifice, and so his preaching will be at the service of the feast, and thus fulfill a most important and sacred role. Again, the missionary will not content himself with a brief sermon during the main service. In our opinion, a complete missionary celebration requires *at least three or four sermons*: the first to be given on the eve of the feast as an introduction; the second during the Mass; the third during the services held in the afternoon; the fourth on the day after the feast, during the Mass. Obviously, considering the wide variety of conditions in different missions, no rule can be laid down in this matter. But it is precisely this great variety of circumstances that imposes on us the task of seeking for the spirit that should animate our preaching on feast days, according to the word of the Lord: "It is the spirit that gives life" (John 6, 63).

The sermons that accompany each feast should form a whole, not in the sense of following a rigorously logical plan such as would be appropriate for a series of scientific addresses, but a living unity that is quite apparent, one that arises quite naturally from preaching aware of its function. The mystery of the feast itself will then constitute the center of all our preaching and give it unity.

Of the four sermons recommended above, *the first* which must also serve as the "instruction on confession" is, if not the most important, certainly *the most difficult to give,* for it has to fulfill a double task and the time available is usually very limited. This sermon should preferably be given, when possible, in the late afternoon or early evening before the feast, before the adults' confessions. (The missionary should previously have heard the confessions of the children, having prepared them beforehand by a short talk addressed especially to them.) This introductory sermon should first of all introduce the spiritual atmosphere of the feast; if it takes account of the capacity and the concrete needs of those who hear it, it will greatly facilitate their religious understanding of the feast and intensify their active participation. The art of giving such an introduction consists entirely in knowing how to put in a few words the meaning of the feast and its importance in Christian life in such a way as to bring it home to everyone.

And this introductory sermon should also prepare the people for confession. In the missions, thanks be to God, almost all those present at a feast receive the sacraments. But we want to reduce any mechanical religious practice to a minimum; and this is the purpose of giving some preparation for confession especially in stations that we visit only rarely. It is not that Christians in the missions lack the knowledge necessary for making an ordinary confession; taken as a whole, they are in no way inferior in this respect to the faithful in Christian countries. Nonetheless we need to help them make a good confession, and if we give them some preparation on the occasion of each visit, we shall in time see most abundant fruits. This is also the best occasion for inculcating Christian morals. But the most important aspect of this preparation is neither such teaching nor the help we may give towards their examination of conscience. It is much more important to help our Christians toward true repentance by suggesting the motives that flow from the feast itself. Thus we avoid the danger of monotony otherwise unavoidable in such preparation. The content of the feast can also determine the help that we give in making their examination of conscience, help which should, obviously, not take the place of personal thought, but rather stimulate it and make it truly personal.

The most important sermon is the second, that given during the Mass. Concerned especially with the mystery of the feast, it should show the faithful what they are celebrating with gratitude, what they are carrying out with joy. Let us here proclaim, as well as our weakness allows, the great things that the love of God has done for us and mysteriously accomplishes within us. The ideal feast day sermon is thus "mystagogic," introducing its hearers more deeply into the mysteries of divine love which are the mysteries of our Christian life. For the catechetical success of this feast day preaching, we must make the great works of God in the history of salvation understood and loved in relation to the particular subject of the feast.

With the simple people of the missions, and even elsewhere, this preaching should not try to penetrate all at once into the depths of the mystery. It is only when the basic ideas of the Redemption have been clearly grasped by the faithful, that we can try to go further and show how this redeeming action of God embraces our own time and this very hour in which we are celebrating the feast. We might make a comparison here with good catechetical teaching methods. Modern catechesis does not omit a simple and beautiful narrative drawn from Holy Scripture, nor does it omit or neglect to give a clear explanation, well adapted to the needs of the hearers, of the doctrine which the narrative contains, and to show its application to Christian life. In the same way, feast day preaching should avoid, on the one hand, giving the impression that Christian feasts are simple commemorations of blessings already given by God, nor, on the other hand, should it neglect the historical element. Thus, for example, a good Christmas sermon might take as its starting point the wonderful mystery of the moment in which the eternal Word of God was made flesh, when the true Son of God became a true man among men, one of us. And then it might go on to show how this wonderful mystery here and now permeates our Christian life, how it is accomplished in our midst.

Such a method of feast day preaching brings out the *Christian values* that are to be celebrated, and, by the very nature of things, leads us always to speak of the *Eucharistic Sacrifice.* It is precisely our solemn "Eucharist," our communal feast of thanksgiving, by which we thank the heavenly Father for all these wonderful things that His love has done for us and in us.

This shows the sense in which our preaching, in particular the principal sermon of the feast, ought to be *liturgical;* it should above all be concerned with the mystery of the feast, discovering and proclaiming its meaning, but without losing itself in any exegesis of the text. In so doing, it can bring up one or other liturgical text or dwell on some special characteristic of the day's liturgy. But let us beware of introducing into our preaching that superannuated analytic method which we have succeeded in banishing from our catechetical teaching.

All our great feasts are so rich! In a brief half hour — and no feast day sermon should last much longer, even in the missions —we cannot explain more than a part. The missionary can use the *sermon given during the afternoon service* to dwell on some other aspects. In the morning sermon, he should bring out especially the chief idea of the mystery, while in the afternoon he can develop the more important related themes. For example, on the feast of St. Joseph, the meaning, value and proper carrying out of Christian work might form the subject of the afternoon sermon. Sometimes, again, some spontaneous connection may arise between the sermon and the Benediction that follows it. Thus we might point out on Christmas afternoon that Benediction of the Most Blessed Sacrament is our "adoration of the shepherds"; like the shepherds of Bethlehem, we have come to adore the Lord. In the midnight Mass, we were above all concerned with thanking the heavenly Father for the Savior and Brother that He has given us, His only Son. Now we turn to Christ Himself. We thank Him, we adore Him, we promise to be faithful to Him in our pagan environment. Or, again, some special ceremony may determine the subject of the afternoon sermon: for example, on the feast of Christ the King, the meaning of the consecration of Christ the King might be very profitably brought out. For such consecrations have no value unless the people grasp their importance and the effect that they should have on Christian life, and unless they make them with full interior consent.

The sermon on the Mass of the following day is of special importance when the missionary celebrates the feast in an outlying station. On the morning after the feast, the missionary gathers the community together once more; the sermon during this Mass will be the conclusion of the whole festivity, and it should deal above all with the effects the feast should have in Christian living. Without wishing to separate too greatly dogma and morals in our preaching, for they are fundamentally united, nevertheless one sermon should deal especially with the mystery of the feast; but the closing instruction should rather emphasize the relationship of the feast to Christian life, to its concrete tasks and duties, and do so in a positive way, showing concrete purposes, giving encouragement, arousing zeal. If there is anything that is blameworthy and needs to be corrected, this should be done in the preliminary instruction on confession, since this has as its special purpose to foster reflection, purification, renewal.

In the missions, our preaching ought certainly to have *an unmistakable missionary character*. On ordinary days, as well as on feast days, in the catechesis or in the sermons, we should speak of our missionary vocation among the people in the missions. "In season and out of season" (2 Tim. 4, 2), let us always return to it, sometimes directly and sometimes indirectly, when we are expounding the religious reasons for our missionary attitude. No Christian truth and no Christian feast of any importance is without a wealth of missionary matter. Of all the sermons on feasts, that of the closing ceremony is the one which will insist the most strongly on this "centrum censeo" of our missionary preaching. The Christian feast is both a grace and a mission. After each celebration our Christians should have regained their consciousness of their quality as God's heralds sent to their own people and to the pagan masses.

If the missionary is inspired by the spirit of the liturgy in his feast day sermons, his preaching will take on another desirable quality: it will be remarkable for its *catechetical concentration.* The Church always considers and celebrates the mysteries with regard to the very center of the redemptive reality and in view of the whole of Christian doctrine. In the Christmas mystery, for example, she celebrates with the coming of the Savior, His divine origin, the majesty and greatness of His person, and she does so without isolating this aspect from that of His work and His mission; in this respect, the classic collect of the Vigil and that of the third Christmas Mass are characteristic. At Easter, the ceremonies present in an impressive way the Savior's victory and His paschal triumph, but do not separate them from His Person which has achieved the victory; the paschal hymns of the Church celebrate the Savior Himself. This concentration, characteristic of the Church's feasts, accords with the catechetical function which they should carry out in the missions. Innumerable Christians are rarely able during the year, even on Sundays, to assist at Mass and hear a sermon. From time to time, however, they may take part in a Christian feast celebrated in their own station or a neighboring one. Out of consideration for these forsaken children of the vast missionary regions, the missionary should try to fashion his sermons on these feasts so that they contain the greatest possible amount of doctrinal nourishment, in other words, that they should be remarkable for catechetical concentration.

The preaching cycle for feast days and especially for great feasts, should, therefore, offer in some way a summary of Christian doctrine, taking as the starting point each time the mystery which is being celebrated. But any overloading of these expositions must be entirely avoided; here also the saying applies: *"non multa sed multum."* And besides, we should talk as simply and practically as possible in an obvious sequence of ideas, for a well-thought-out order allows our hearers to understand, assimilate and more easily retain what is said.[16]

---

16. See Appendix B. for examples of outlines of such sermons.

PART THREE

COMMUNAL WORSHIP IN THE ABSENCE
OF A PRIEST

CHAPTER ELEVEN

Communal Worship in the Absence of a Priest: Its Importance and Its Structure

Johannes Hofinger, s.j.

Because of the lack of priests in most mission countries, each missionary has to take charge of several small outlying stations in addition to his central one. In China, for example, one missionary is frequently responsible for some twenty to thirty small Christian communities, and obviously can visit many of them only a few times a year. The Christians in these small stations can only occasionally make the long journey to the central station, perhaps for great feast days. Sometimes when Mass is celebrated at an outlying station not too far away from their own, the more fervent Christians who are able to do so take the opportunity to attend, but the others are left to themselves, without a priest and without the Eucharistic Sacrifice.

From the beginning, missionaries have attached great importance to the assembling of the Christians of such communities to carry out some form of public worship and to receive some religious instruction, even when the priest is not present himself. The letters of St. Francis Xavier speak of this subject frequently, but from the catechetical rather than the liturgical aspect. Sunday meetings without a priest for prayer and catechetical instruction constituted, from the first years of his apostolate, a salient feature of his missionary method.[1] The history of such meetings goes back even further; historical research would do well to study the origin and the structure of such priestless services in the missions

---

1. See, for example, his famous letter of January 15, 1544, a year and a half after his arrival in the Indies, in which he tells his colleagues in Rome about his method of evangelization: Schurhammer-Wicki, *Epistolae S. Francisci Xaverii,* Rome, 1944, I, 166. In a later Instruction (Feb., 1548), he inculcates the necessity of Sunday communal worship with prayer and catechesis: Schurhammer-Wicki, op. cit. I, 427.

as indicated in the various extant documents.[2] But today public worship in the absence of a priest has taken on an unusual importance, and the pastoral concern of missionaries is alert to the question of its organization and arrangement. We shall, therefore, speak first of the importance of such worship in the missions, and then outline the principles that should guide its arrangement.

The service to be held on Sunday morning is by far the most important, and it is this that we have above all in mind, without, nevertheless, underestimating the other services of this kind, especially public evening prayer, already customary in many places.

The Function and the Importance of this Communal Worship

Since the particular situation in the missions today obviously calls for the immediate and effective organization of community services that can be held in the absence of a priest, we might be tempted to think of such services as being merely temporary emergency measures. It is important, therefore, first of all to study their permanent missionary value.

Even in normal times of expanding missionary activity, public worship without a priest has a very important function, first of all from *the aspect of religious instruction*. During the period of relative peace and prosperity that characterized the first decade of this century, the mission school assumed the major part of the heavy burden of the religious instruction of Christian youth. In China and elsewhere, the missions offered the majority of Christian children the opportunity to attend a mission school, even if this was only a "prayer-school" in which they learned the catechism and their prayers, and also some elementary notions of reading and writing. The religious teaching certainly left a great deal to be desired, but we hoped to be able to supply the deficiencies by means of a renewal of catechetical teaching. And, actually, the catechetical movement has already borne fruit in many places and causes us to foresee great progress in the future.

Nevertheless, the catechetical problem has not yet been solved, even so far as the children are concerned. The modern science of catechetics itself shows that no teaching of religion can be adequate unless it is complemented by practice, by the exercise of Christian worship. How-

2. With regard to the Chinese Missions of the earlier and later periods, cf. X. Bürkler, *Die Sonntags-und Festfeier in der katholischen Chinamission,"* Rome, 1942. Bürkler's basic work is concerned primarily with "priestly" Sunday services and offers only scanty material on "priestless" worship. The first regulations that go directly into details for the time of the persecution of 1644 are presented in the "Ordonnances de la Sainte Église," publ. by H. Verhaeren in *Monumenta Serica,* 1939, 451-477.

ever good it may be, the school can only be a school; the communication of a full and vital religious life can only be given in the actual practice of religion carried on at home and in church. The school will always emphasize the rational element; this is its special function and it is quite right to do so, as long as its teaching is complemented by the religious living of the family and the Christian community. But in actual practice, for the millions of Christian children in mission countries and in small and isolated villages, the public worship that can be carried on without a priest is the only kind that counts. It follows, therefore, that if these services are really to fulfill their catechetical function, they must be carried out in such a way that the children, at least the older ones, also get something from them. It might be said that the religious education of children is better taken care of by the religious life of the family than by communal worship. This can be true, certainly. But pastoral experience goes to show that, in the missions, community worship is needed for a vital family religious life; where community worship is neglected, family religious life declines.

But it is quite true that the public worship carried out in the priest's absence needs to take care of the instruction of adults, especially of neophytes, even more than of children. The more Christianity makes progress and prospers in any region, the more numerous are the new Christians who have been baptized as adults after having received, let us hope, a solid course of instruction before Baptism. But this instruction cannot possibly include all the developed teaching ordinarily given to those who attend a Christian school as children. Missionary experience clearly shows that these new Christians have great need of continued spiritual direction and instruction after Baptism. Without this, the Church always finds that many fall away. Does not public worship in the absence of a priest have a most important function here? How is it possible to reach, to instruct, and to maintain the fervor of all the neophytes in our outlying stations in any other way than by the public worship held in their own village? It is this that must, week by week, furnish them with instruction, direction and encouragement.

And even for the old Christians, confirmed in the faith and well-instructed as they may be, communal worship still has a great catechetical value. Consider those communities that see their priest and hear his preaching only occasionally during the year: can this be sufficient to maintain their zeal against the assaults of pagan unbelief, of pagan ways of life? Can we be astonished if, under such conditions, even the greatest Christian truths begin to seem dim to these people, and are finally altogether forgotten. In such a situation, it is communal Christian worship that can take the place of the preaching of the missionary, preserve the awareness of Christian truth, and give the instruction and the encouragement necessary to lead a truly Christian life in a pagan environment. The mere recitation of the catechism, which is carried out in many places at the time of Sunday worship, does not actually fulfill the catechetical function of this worship. As we have seen earlier, readings from Holy Scripture itself have the greatest catechetical value, and these should be restored to a place of honor. And the catechetical value of the prayers used in such worship depends on the extent to which they reflect Christian doctrine in the spirit of the praying Church and make use of language and sentiments that are simple, popular and unsentimental.

In normal times, therefore, for the Christians of isolated stations, the Sunday service without a priest is *the form of worship that chiefly counts from a catechetical point of view*. Obviously, from the aspect of sacramental reality, such a form of worship cannot be compared with the Mass. But as things are, the regular "liturgy of the word" is more important for religious teaching than the celebration of the Mass, since this is, alas, so rare.

From the pastoral aspect also, public worship without a priest is of the greatest value. Christians of the outlying stations are certainly dispensed from the duty of assisting at Sunday Mass, by reason of the distance between their homes and the central station. But are they thereby dispensed from the duty of *Christian prayer?* We do not mean to propose a problem in casuistry, to decide the degree to which, and the conditions under which, Christians who are dispensed from attending Mass by reason of distance might be under the obligation of taking part in common family and community prayer. But we do mean to say unequivocally that a living and thriving Christianity is unthinkable without fervent prayer, and in the missions even more than elsewhere, true Christianity lives by Christian prayer. In a pagan environment, Christianity must have special powers of resistance and also powers of active radiation, if it is to fulfill its mission of bringing light to the unbelieving. And experience has proved to us that the faithful carrying out of a well designed form of public worship is the best means of keeping alive and of reviving the spirit of Christian prayer both in communities and in families. Without it, it is quite exceptional to find families or individual Christians that live a life of really Christian prayer.

Community worship also helps *to form the prayer life of the Christian community,* or at least it could and should do so. In the missions, is not both private and family prayer in danger of giving too much space to the prayer of petition and of losing itself among secondary devotions?

Should not the community worship exercise an educational function in this regard, should it not make up for the lack of Christian praise and thanksgiving so often not to be found to a sufficient extent in the prayer of so many individuals and families?

Sunday services without a priest have *to substitute for the celebration of the Eucharist* for millions of Christians in the missions. Such services cannot, of course, actually replace the incomparable homage that we render to the heavenly Father with Christ in the Mass. Nevertheless, even in such a celebration the Christian community can render to God a most fitting homage, one that also is presented to the Father by Christ. And by their very desire to take part in the Eucharistic Sacrifice of the Church — a desire that should be explicitly expressed in a well-designed Sunday service without a priest — these poor Christians do what they can; their homage prepares them for the next Mass that they will take part in, and each of these Mass-less Sunday celebrations serves to remind them of the sublimity of the Eucharistic Sacrifice and causes them to desire it.

Without some Sunday service regularly celebrated, any true *sanctification of Sunday* is impossible. Experience in the missions proves this to be true even more clearly than in Christian countries. In the Chinese missions, for example, before the coming of communism, it was customary for the Christians, even in stations with no resident priest, to assemble four times on Sunday for religious services; and the purpose of the missionaries in organizing such frequent services was, among other things, precisely the sanctification of Sunday.

It is not always equally possible to bring about abstention from servile work, but the principle of assistance at communal worship must always be held to firmly. This was, in fact, the practice and the idea of the early Church, which had as yet no prescriptions forbidding servile work on Sundays; what made Sunday the day of the Lord was above all communal worship. And this corresponds to present-day missionary practice, at least according to our experience in the Chinese missions. At the beginning of the summer, for example, the season for harvesting the wheat, Christians are allowed to continue with their work in the fields for four successive Sundays, and, at the season of the autumn harvest, for six. But the people are not dispensed from the obligation of Sunday worship; they come together at least for divine service in the morning. If this is neglected, they run the danger of forgetting their Christian vocation even on Sunday, and of returning to pagan practices.

And let us take note, finally, of the *unifying value* of communal worship. Our Christians have frequent need of such comfort; their sense of community needs a religious foundation and means of expression. They must find all this in a fitting and regular Sunday celebration of the whole community rather than in assisting very occasionally at the service held in the central station.

It is clear, then, that so long as the missions include a great number of outlying stations which cannot be provided with Mass every Sunday — and we look forward to no change in this respect during the foreseeable future — they must, for every reason, concern themselves with the question of the public worship that can be held without a priest in these small communities, with perfecting its structure and increasing its missionary effectiveness.

But, besides all this, it is clear that the missions are today entering on a new period, one that makes such services *even more necessary than before*. We are not thinking primarily of the danger of communism[3] now threatening more than one missionary region. For even if this particular danger were to be averted, thanks to a kind dispensation of divine Providence, *mission schools and their catechetical apostolate would still be constantly threatened*. We are living in a period of the emancipation of colonial peoples. Even the non-communistic governments among these peoples gives evidence of totalitarian and antiforeign tendencies that could become dangerous at any moment to mission schools. These newly formed nations, proud of their recently won independence, desire to take in hand the education of future generations. At the present time, they are still making use of the missions and their schools, especially for education on the secondary level. But will not notions imported from Europe, according to which the school is an agent of the State, be propagated here as well? Already the progressive introduction of universal education on the primary level has meant trouble for the schools of small missionary stations. Up to the present time such communities have had, perhaps, a small mission school, primitive certainly, but far better than nothing. The pagans in the same villages had nothing at all. But this situation has changed. The new State has established an official school alongside of the mission school, and requires that its program be followed. To do so is not impossible for the better organized schools of the main stations, but it leads to the disappearance of the schools in the smaller stations which were often only "prayer-schools" and little more.

Some might answer: if this is the case, then we can teach religion to Christian children outside of school. If only this were as easy to do as

3. See chapter III on the urgency of the liturgical renewal, pp. 34-37.

it is to say! It is obvious, then, that present circumstances urge us to make as full use as possible, above all in the smaller stations, of all the means capable of promoting religious instruction among the young and among those who are not in school. And among these means does not community worship take the first place?

In the face of the communist danger itself, the immediate and determined effort to organize forms of worship to be held without a priest is a most pressing need. Without losing time in making conjectures about possible future victories of communism, let us fortify ourselves beforehand, profiting from the experiences of the missions that have already passed under its sway. These experiences are everywhere the same: everywhere our enemies use the same ideas and the same methods of procedure; everywhere there is the same life-and-death combat between atheistic communism and the Catholic missions.

The first victim of these new governments is always the mission school, and most especially the primary school. Catholic children are obliged to attend the communist school. Can we imagine what this purposeful and refined antireligious propaganda means to the children thus handed over to its influence day after day? In the great majority of cases, above all in country districts, it is impossible to give the children anything like regular religious instruction outside of divine service. Our enemies do not willingly attack public worship properly so called; they wish to give the impression that they are not persecuting religion and are allowing freedom of worship. The celebration of services by a priest is easily interfered with: foreign missionaries are driven out, and native priests are forbidden to travel, and so are prevented from visiting their distant stations. But it is much more difficult for our enemies to touch public worship without a priest. They can doubtless confiscate our churches and the other possessions of the mission; this has already been done in many places. But such worship can easily be carried out in private houses and, if necessary, by each family. In the midst of persecution, when the mission school has been destroyed and all priestly aid is lacking either to give instruction or to administer the sacraments, this form of worship can give our Christians, and especially our Christian youth, the necessary religious teaching, can keep them united, can inspire them by common prayer with the strength necessary to resist firmly. To fulfill this task in times of persecution, these forms of divine worship must have been arranged beforehand and have become familiar to the people. Once the persecution has begun, it is too late, as we have learned from the persecution in the Far East.

But, some might say, to make any arrangements in view of a persecution to come would create a psychosis of fear among our Christians, and would prematurely weaken their resistance. Obviously, we must not disturb our people by any useless discussion of future events. To make sure of the future, let us content ourselves with doing what we ought to do in any case, even if there were no communist threat. Let us therefore give to divine worship held in the absence of a priest the importance and the attention that it demands, as we should have done long ago in normal times.

The Structure of these Sunday Services

Services to be held without a priest both allow and require a much fuller *adaptation to the temperament of the people concerned* than does worship celebrated by the priest. To fulfill their catechetical and pastoral function, these services should be truly "popular." Their structure will, therefore, vary in different missions; but certain principles will hold good everywhere. Let us apply these principles first of all to the Sunday service, and afterwards speak briefly of other forms of public worship.

We are speaking here of the "principal Sunday service" in outlying stations. The Christians in such places, as we have said, are accustomed to coming together several times on Sunday, and this is certainly not true of the Chinese missions only. But they are quite aware of the fact that only the service on Sunday morning, in which they carry out the "Sunday prayer" (Chu -jih -cking), is obligatory. More than in the case of the other services, then, it is desirable that this service be given *very clear direction by a properly qualified authority of the Church.* Here we have a veritable liturgical service, at least in the sense in which the word is applied to the prayers recited at certain fixed times by religious. Here we have the worship of a Christian community, organized by the Church and carried out at its command. We should, therefore, strive by every means to make the faithful understand clearly that it is the Church who calls them to this celebration, who herself gives them the readings and puts on their lips the various prayers; that they themselves are coming together for this service as an ecclesiastical community. Also from this viewpoint, it is desirable that the celebration have more than a mere leader, such as is needed for recitation of the rosary in the family or in church — almost anyone who has come to the age of reason can do this. But the case of this main Sunday service, some ecclesiastical direction should be manifest; the services should be conducted by a leader of the Christian community who has been designated as such by ecclesiastical authority. In a community where several leaders are appointed, as in the Chinese missions, they take turns in directing the communal services. Concerning the establishment of a permanent diaconate in this connection, we shall deal in Chapter XXII with the various aspects of this question.

In any case, the Sunday service needs suitable direction, if only for technical reasons, since, in view of its function, it ought to be more substantial and not consist only of the common recitation of a "Sunday prayer," which is always the same, and of litanies.[4] This necessitates *practical liturgical training* especially in the art of leading a congregation in prayer in a reverent and intelligent way, both for catechists and for carefully selected students who can receive their formation in the principal stations. It is from these that will come the "prayer-leaders" of our small communities.

The Structure and Development of the Sunday Service

The following are given only as being some principles that hold good almost everywhere and are flexible enough to allow for the necessary adaptation to local circumstances.

The external form of the ceremonies should be *very simple,* so that the service can be celebrated by any small community with a few Christian families, or even, if necessary, by one family alone. And if these ceremonies were given in a diocesan prayer book made sufficiently available, completely isolated Christians also could make use of them to carry out their "Sunday devotions."

But this simplicity should not exclude *the necessary variety.* This is required first of all in each particular service, both as to content and as to external form. Therefore there should be no long series of prayers, even though these might contain very elevated thoughts, for their effectiveness is greatly lessened by the fact that the congregation recites them one after the other, too often in a merely routine fashion. Even in a very simple ceremony it is easy to have alternating prayers, readings, and responses. Furthermore, these services should vary from Sunday to Sunday. This is obvious in the case of the readings; but it is also desirable for the prayers, although the requirement of simplicity imposes

---

4. This chapter cannot go into the details of missionary usage, even in relation to one mission. Concerning China, Bürkler, *Op. cit.,* p. 105 ff, gives various concrete facts. The Chinese missions directed by the Jesuits had adopted another form. Their "Sunday Prayer" is usually the pivot of the ceremonies; it varies according to the four Sundays of the month and according to the litanies added. In certain places, the litany of the Holy Name of Jesus is always recited; in other places the litanies vary on each Sunday of the month: of the Holy Name, of the Sacred Heart, of Loretto, and of St. Joseph. The Litany of the Saints is not used, although this would correspond especially well to the meaning of the Sunday service. On feast days the "Sunday Prayer" is replaced by a prayer connected with the feast, and thus a little of the needed variety is provided.

rather strict limits. Too much variety not only complicates the service, but makes it lack popular appeal, for the people like a good deal of uniformity in their prayers.

The plan of the Sunday service should also be *capable of development*, since these ceremonies will be held under many different circumstances. In the missions, quite a large congregation may find itself obliged to celebrate Sunday worship without a priest. If the plan of the service is left open to some possibility of development, such a congregation could then include more chants. Many small congregations who do not dare to sing every Sunday — though we should in time teach them a few hymns suitable for congregational singing — would like to celebrate a great feast by some appropriate song. Unceasing adaptation to the special place and to the season will help to preserve the people from routine. Popular devotions that are repeated unvaryingly over and over again are naturally subject to the psychological laws of habit; we should not be shocked at this fact, but take the necessary countermeasures. One thing is certain: a stereotyped Sunday service will be of little use to us in the present situation in the missions.

The basic plan of the service should distinguish very clearly between *the liturgy of the word and the liturgy of prayer* in accordance with the best tradition and with the internal laws of Christian worship.[5] Is not the worship of God the response of God's people to His call? In this way, the catechetical values of the service and its prayer values will both be fully gained. In joining together in this way the readings and the prayers, we are making use of *the structure of the Mass itself,* and so fostering the people's understanding of the Mass: God speaks to His people; they respond to Him by their prayer, which reaches its climax in the giving of thanks. And in this way the great difference between worship without a priest and the sacrifice of the Mass is made clear; without a priest, the true offering of thanksgiving is lacking; we have to content ourselves with thoughts and words of gratitude.

The service should be about half an hour long, the time necessary for the celebration of Mass. It is better to shorten the other exercises of devotion on Sunday than to speed up the morning service. This is the only one that has the quality of obligation and so it should adequately satisfy the Christian's needs for instruction, encouragement and prayer.

---

5. On the question of the structure of the celebration of Christian worship, see J. A. Jungmann, S.J., *Die liturgische Feier. Grundsätzliches und Geschichtliches über die Formgesetze der Liturgie,* Regensburg, 1939. Eng. trans., *Liturgical Worship,* New York, 1941. The principles developed by Jungmann hold good in great part for community worship without a priest, though obviously it cannot be concluded by the priestly prayer.

Following the principles just laid out, we arrive at the following outline:

Basic outline for the celebration of Sunday worship

	Opening prayer or appropriate hymn.
	First reading: Epistle of the Mass of the day.
Liturgy of	Psalm used as interpolated chant, or a prayer.
the word	Second reading: Gospel of the Mass of the day.
	Psalm used as a responsory, or a prayer.
	Third reading: catechesis.
	The Apostles' Creed.

	Prayer of petition (General prayer — Oratio Fidelium —hymn).
Liturgy of	Prayer of thanksgiving with the Sanctus and the Pater
prayer	Noster.
	(Commemoration of the day).
	Final hymn.

To be fully effective, this "Sunday service" should not be confused with any other exercises of devotion. Where the Christians are accustomed to recite their morning prayers together on Sunday, these prayers should be separated by a pause from the "Sunday service." It would be better also to put off to some other time the recitation of the Rosary, the Way of the Cross, and the recitation of the catechism. If the recitation of the catechism must be associated with the main service, the best place for it would be after the Gospel, instead of the responsory, or immediately after the catechetical instruction. In any case, this recitation should not be considered to be a mere exercise of memory; it is a community profession of faith, to be spoken in a dignified way. The *Way of the Cross* is the best devotion to be connected with the Sunday service. It should then represent the renewal of the sacrifice of the cross which takes place at Mass. Its place would be during the "liturgy of prayer," the second part of the service. We do not recommend this inclusion; but if it must be done, care should be taken to adapt it to the function that it should fulfill in this service: to bring out the soteriological significance; together with the sufferings of Christ, to show the glory of His resurrection. In any case, the celebration should culminate quite naturally in the community prayer of thanksgiving, and go up to the Father through Christ. Every Sunday thus should remind us of the grandeur of our membership in the Church and fill us with gratitude to God. The profound significance of the ceremonies is more important than any set plan; this plan, together with its different elements, are all at the service of this ultimate meaning.

The Different Parts of the Sunday Service

The liturgy of the word has primarily a catechetical function; the readings, therefore, have the most important place. As to the number of readings, it would be best to have three: the Epistle and Gospel of the Mass, and a catechetical reading instead of a sermon. The possibility of including a fourth reading from the Old Testament, to be given before the Epistle, should also be studied. The Old Testament is used too little in communal worship although it contains many magnificent texts, rich in teaching values. If the most desirable reform of the lectionary of the Roman Missal ever comes about and a reading from the Old Testament is then prescribed or allowed, this could be used also for these Sunday services without a priest. As there seems to be good hope of such a redaction of the lectionary with at least the facultative grant of a reading from the Old Testament, it might be better not to be too eager for any new ruling in this matter; for it might well be that, precisely by means of some experimentation in these priestless services, we could furnish Mother Church with good grounds for prescribing some reading from the Old Testament during the Mass.

The length of the ceremony would offer no difficulty so far as a fourth reading is concerned, for even with one, the service as outlined in our plan would take not much more than half an hour. More to be feared would be the possibility of the peoples' being unduly wearied by four readings, of which the last, the catechetical instruction, should last for some time. But experience will show us how far this is a danger; the conditions in various missions, for example the fact that some peoples really enjoy listening, may reveal great differences. In any case, the personal feeling of the missionary himself, often more inclined than his people to demand a short service, should not be the decisive factor.

Some have asked whether, for catechetical reasons, the readings of the Mass of the day should not be replaced by other extracts from the Epistles and Gospels.[6] It would certainly be easy to find readings that complemented one another more perfectly and that were richer in

---

6. There exists no actual prohibition against reading to the people during the Mass pericopes other than those of the Missal. Catechetical reasons might even recommend it; and one could further refer to the authority of Cardinals Faulhaber and Innitzer, and of Bishop Keppler. See Heinz Schürmann, Eine dreijährige Perikopenordnung für Sonn-und Festtage, in *Liturgisches Jahrbuch,* 1952, 59. By this means, would not the Latin reading of the celebrant, which is not the private spiritual reading of the priest, but above all meant for the people, be still further deprived of its full significance?

teaching values than are the present readings of the Mass. Do not liturgists concede the fact that our lectionary gives rise to certain wishes for reform and is in urgent need of renewal? But in spite of the deficiencies of our present lectionary, we should vote for the use of *the readings of the Mass* in our Sunday service without a priest rather than for a special lectionary, and this for the following reasons. First of all, for a social reason: it seems most desirable to pattern the Sunday service of isolated communities on the Holy Sacrifice of the Mass, and thus to strengthen these Christians in the sense of their union with the whole Church. This is why we should read precisely the Epistle and the Gospel that the Church is having read on this very day to the millions of Catholics who have the happiness of taking part in the Mass. Furthermore, the missionary visits some of his more important outlying stations fairly frequently; if the services held without him do not use the readings of the Missal, a certain disorder would result.

From a new arrangement of the lectionary of the Missal, we also await the bringing of *more unity of theme into the readings* of the individual Masses. This unity, required from a catechetical point of view especially in mission countries, now does not exist between the Epistle and Gospel of the Sundays after Epiphany and after Pentecost, as we have pointed out in a previous chapter. As things are, we should try to assure that the other two readings in the Sunday services, that is, the reading from the Old Testament and the catechetical instruction, should form a connected whole at least with the Gospel of the day. We do not ask for any strictly systematic unity, like that of a textbook, but for the flexible unity of a work of art. And these readings, to be inserted in the lectionary for these Sunday services, should be at once substantial and easy to understand.

The *catechetical reading,* recommended in our outline as the third of the readings, should be very carefully composed in view of its important function in the missions of giving the Christians the motherly teaching of the Church to take the place of the living word. The question is not of giving the people private spiritual reading, but the teaching of the Church to her members: the bishop speaking to his Christians whom he cannot visit personally each Sunday. He gives them the book that contains his catechetical instructions: it is a book to be used in worship. This catechetical reading should be neither a mere commentary on the Gospel nor a learned explanation of some chapter of the catechism. Taking the Gospel as its starting point, and eventually the Epistle as well, it should give an exposition of some important point of our religion in a popular and vital way, always in relation to the Christian life and to the concrete situation of the Christians in the particular mission.

In choosing the subjects for these catechetical instructions, any over-systematization should be avoided; on the contrary, the course of the liturgical year, its content and its atmosphere, should be taken into account. All the main truths of the faith should be adequately covered in the course of the year. This is most important in the formation of our catechumens, for who can guarantee that in the future we shall be able to give them any detailed and adequate instruction for Baptism? A catechumen who assists faithfully and attentively at these services for a year should from this fact alone be aware of all the essential truths of the faith, in such a way that in case of necessity, the instruction for Baptism could simply sum up and fill out the teachings that had already been received. This was the practice in the ancient Church, as we pointed out in a previous chapter, and one that was most effective.

The catechetical reading in the Sunday service should also be a model of deep and yet popular exposition of Christian truth, one which would be capable of inspiring both missionaries and catechists. It would be desirable to have several yearly cycles of such instructions worked out by missionaries having a catechetical and kerygmatic formation. The same cycle could then be used in missionary regions having analogous pastoral conditions, having been approved by their bishops; and in each diocese, these instructions would be presented to the people by the local bishop. Obviously, such instructions would be preferable to the oral teaching given by ordinary catechists — provided of course, that the readers were sufficiently trained in reading printed texts aloud.

The question of the *chants or hymns* to be used offers more difficulties than that of the readings. In the community worship that we knew in China, there were no readings and no singing. But religious singing renders extraordinary services to worship. Does it not create a true atmosphere, a community of spirit? Is it not the real expression of awakened faith, of a prayer that is lifted to heaven? Wherever there has previously been no singing in communal worship, we must demand very little at the beginning. And the small number in many of these priestless congregations makes this necessary also. But certainly at least one hymn could be found or composed which would be appreciated by the faithful and willingly sung by all present, and which would conform to the spirit of the Sunday service.[7] The development of sacred chant which might come about in the future would depend obviously on the taste of the

---

7. It would be enough, to begin with, to have a verse and response sung first at the beginning and then at the end of the office. With time, on great feasts, an appropriate hymn could be included with three verses: one sung at the beginning and one at the end, and the second perhaps between the prayer of petition and that of thanksgiving.

natives and on the cooperation of the mission school. The school of formation for catechists ought to foster a good formation in religious music, in the sense of the intensive cultivation of popular sacred singing.[8] Whatever the use to be made of them in the Sunday service, the hymns should be rich in meaning, easy to sing, and appealing.[9] In this connection it would be a most rewarding task to make *the psalms* at home in the missions and used in common worship (see Chapter IX), including these priestless services.

For the psalms and also for the prayers recited in common, or at least for a part of them, we should recommend the *responsorial method.* This method of recitation not only combats the danger of routine, but it eases the burden on the memory. This second advantage was not important in the past. The peoples in missionary countries were usually endowed with excellent memories, and also, in the mission schools of the old style which were primarily schools for learning the catechism, there was time to have the students confide to memory the treasure of Christian prayer. If only the prayers had been explained as well as they were drilled in! But at the present time the mission schools, obliged to adapt themselves to modern school programs, welcome anything that will get rid of memory work and allow more time to be given to the necessary explanations.

The various prayers recommended in our outline do not need to be justified at length. The *Apostles' Creed* concludes, as at Mass, the liturgy of the word. It should never be omitted in any Sunday service in the missions; it should be understood as an enthusiastic "yes" to the free invitation of God, and should be recited with a certain solemnity. Is it not the Sunday renewal of the baptismal vows, and so the ideal transition from the liturgy of the word to the worship of prayer?[10]

After the Symbol, at the beginning of the "liturgy of prayer" comes the "General Prayer." This should be inspired by the old *Oratio Fidelium.* In certain places where this striking part of the ancient Mass liturgy has already been reintroduced, in the form of a prayer to be recited by the congregation during the offertory, the same form could easily be inserted in the Sunday service. The communal *prayer of thanksgiving* that follows ought to be connected with the "general prayer" by

8. See J. Kellner, S.J., "Singing during Divine Worship," *Lumen Vitae,* 1955, pp. 355-362.
9. In any small community in which reasonably well-executed singing is not possible, at least at the beginning, the singing could perhaps be replaced, at least to begin with, by a prayer said together on a tone of solemn *recitatif.*
10. On the importance of the Apostles' Creed, see J. Hofinger, S.J., "The Apostles' Creed is a Real Prayer," in *Lumen Vitae,* IX, 1954, pp. 247-254.

a hymn or a psalm, and should issue naturally into the *Sanctus,* sung or recited solemnly by the congregation. In the place of the Eucharistic Sacrifice and Communion, there should be a beautiful prayer expressing *the desire to participate in the Holy Sacrifice,* a prayer which would end with the common recitation of the *Our Father.*

Dogmatic, liturgical, catechetical and ascetical reasons all argue in favor of a prayer expressing the desire of the congregation to participate in the Sacrifice of the Church and in sacramental Communion. From the aspect of dogma, this formally expressed desire is called for, since, in view of the impossibility of the sacramental participation required in itself, the desire must take its place. Liturgically speaking, "spiritual" Mass and Communion — we do not wish in any way to aid in propagating these unsuitable expressions! — have here their place, for the congregation itself should, in such a situation, possess, entertain and therefore express the desire to take part in the sacramental worship of the Church. The Sunday service without a priest is not a kind of accessory to sacerdotal community worship with the Sacrifice and Communion; it must take its place, and therefore be essentially referred to this sacerdotal worship. From the ascetical point of view, this formal desire helps each member of the congregation to take part more fully in the fruits of sacramental worship. And, finally, catechetical considerations enter also. The marked relationship with the Sacrifice and Communion brings out the central position belonging to the celebration of the Sacrifice in Christian worship. At the same time, any confusion is avoided between the two kinds of celebration, even though the service without a priest has, to the extent suitable to its own function, the same structure and the same forms as the Mass celebrated by the priest.[11]

After the "spiritual Communion," a brief commemoration of *the liturgical season* might very well be included, so that the congregation can nourish their souls during the week to come with the special blessings of the liturgical season. For great feasts, a special formula for the prayer of thanksgiving might be worked out.

It is hardly necessary to note that the new order of Sunday service should not be left to the good pleasure of each missionary. This is the business of the bishop of the diocese. Since among all the community services without a priest, the Sunday morning service holds by far the

---

11. The missionaries of former times clearly recognized the necessity of bringing out in some way the connection of the Sunday service without a priest with the Mass itself. According to the Synod of Ningpo, in 1933, the Christians should, on Sunday, in stations deprived of Mass, recite the prayers of the Mass as if they were present at a celebration. Formerly the Christians of this missionary diocese in South China had, on such occasions, to recite prayers that clearly had little relation to the Mass. See Bürkler, *Sonntagsfeier in der Chinamission,* p. 105.

most important place, and since its adaptation to the present missionary situation constitutes an urgent problem, its reform needs to be undertaken first of all. If this is carried out as it should be, then a new ordering of the other celebrations to be held without a priest will follow of itself.

Other Exercises of Worship to be Held in the Absence of the Priest

Community evening prayer, in use in many missions, certainly deserves to be widely spread; missionaries who have tried it appreciate its value.[12] On this subject, we should not be influenced by any too hasty comparison with Christian countries in which the pastoral conditions are quite different. Obviously it would be impossible to bring about communal daily evening prayer in most modern city parishes — although devotional exercises are held in many places on several evenings of the week, and at least moderately well attended. But in a rural population in the missions, where the whole community lives according to the same rhythm and pattern of daily life, community daily evening prayer is not at all an impossible ideal. And while we may exhort our people to family prayer, let us not forget that community evening prayer possesses *missionary values* which cannot be gained so completely by family prayer.

First of all, in the pagan environment of the missions, this evening community prayer strengthens the feeling of community and of sharing the same life and activity as one's fellow Christians, above all if care is taken to avoid any routine recitation and to procure a real raising of hearts and minds to God. Furthermore, here Christians can find a daily opportunity to talk with one another, to learn about one another, to feel themselves to be a large family in which they share one another's joys and sorrows. This evening prayer also makes it easy to exercise some definite control over the religious life of a Christian community. The fact that each individual takes part in this exercise and the way in which he does so directly indicates the degree of his religious fervor. And let us, finally, take note of the fact that community prayer constitutes for many Christians an important aid, one that is often actually necessary; for, however much we may insist on family prayer in common, many families abandon the practice after trying it for a while, above all the neophytes.[13]

---

12. J. Hofinger, S.J., "Zur Frage des gemeinsamen Morgen- und Abendgebetes," in *Neue Zeit. f. Miss.* 9, 1953, pp. 122-133.
13. This is what we believe to have been observed in China: in the communities in which the community evening prayer was practiced faithfully during the rest of the year, each family of its own accord assumed the function of the community at the time of harvesting. In spite of their great fatigue, quite a long evening prayer was carried out in each family. And in such communities, it was even

Community evening prayer is also the means of promoting catechetical instruction and training in prayer, if the various prayers are arranged according to the spirit of the liturgy and if some spiritual reading is included. The function of *an appropriate daily reading* seems to have escaped the notice of many people. A true attitude of prayer is one that first listens to God, that allows itself to be fructified by the divine word by attentively listening to His word. The prayer that breaks out after such listening is then at the same time the response of the Christian heart to the invitation of the Father. If God has too little part in prayer, if He is given no longer any time in which to speak to His children, Christian prayer easily degenerates into meaningless repetition like that of the pagans (Matt. 6, 7). Should not anything like this be carefully avoided in the missions?

The catechetical importance of a reading is particularly striking. Suppose that our Christians, during their evening prayer, were to listen attentively each day, or at least, on certain days of the week, to some spiritual reading that was brief and well-chosen. Their elementary Christian instruction would thereby be assured. The fundamental truths of Christianity could here be presented to them continually under different aspects. Even the negligent or indifferent Christians who only attended from time to time would profit at least to a certain extent from this basic teaching. And this was the incomparable method that the Church of former times used for the instruction of her children.

What should be read? Should we not try some kind of *lectio continua,* continuous reading of Holy Scripture, as was done with great profit in the ancient Church — obviously, with some adaptations corresponding to modern conditions? As we have seen, it is not so easy to give to the reading of the Old Testament the place in the Sunday service that belongs to it. But the reading of Scripture during daily evening prayer would allow the Old Testament to be given its due importance. A lectionary, carefully worked out for this special purpose and presented to Christian communities by their bishop, would need to include the parts of Scripture most profitable for the instruction of the faithful. We do not need to follow the order of the canon of the Scriptures, but rather to adapt the reading to the course of the liturgical year, as does the Church in the Breviary. It would be desirable to spread out the course of reading over two or three years so as to have all the main parts of

---

quite easy to lead the more fervent families to carry out a short family prayer besides the community prayer. But in the best-run missions that had no communal prayer, every effort to keep their families faithful to the practice of family prayer seemed to be only partially successful. It would be well worth the trouble to find out whether the results of this experience could be generalized.

Holy Scripture included without making any single reading too long. A good title for each reading, followed by a phrase introducing its essential ideas and one or two explanatory remarks, would greatly increase the effectiveness of these readings.[14]

The inclusion of such a reading would not unduly prolong, as might be feared, this community evening prayer. The reading should last at the most for some seven to ten minutes, and there is nothing to prevent the customary prayers from being somewhat shortened, so that the whole service would last not more than a good quarter of an hour. In any case, a community evening prayer service should not be too short, for people will not take the trouble to come to church for a few minutes only, and if it is very short, it will be all over before the late-comers arrive. And, in view of the lack of any notion of punctuality so common in the missions, we can never hope to have the faithful arriving nearly at the same time. The recitation of the rosary before the regular prayers would be desirable from this point of view; we should even gently urge the faithful to assist at it.

Morning community prayer should follow the same principles. It is only under the most favorable circumstances that the whole community can take part on work days. Every experienced missionary is aware of this fact and is on guard against insisting too greatly on attendance, lest both he and his Christians lose heart. Even in the family, common morning prayer is much more difficult to carry out than evening prayer.

But on Sunday morning, at least, the whole community ought to take part in the community prayer. This should come before the celebration of Mass, or, in the absence of the missionary, before the Sunday service. Sometimes, however, it is not to be followed by the Mass or Sunday service, and its structure depends upon which place it is to take. If morning prayer is to precede the Eucharistic Sacrifice, it should be short and not go on during the Mass itself, as was too often the case in China. It should rather form a whole with the Mass and help the Christians to understand that the Eucharistic Sacrifice is our real morning prayer, our homage and offering *par excellence,* the opening of the Christian day which fills it with the idea of abnegation in union with Christ's sacrifice. In any case, such morning prayer should seem above all to be an anticipation and extension of the Fore-Mass. The same considerations apply to a certain extent to the common morning prayer preceding Sunday service without a priest.

If the morning prayer is followed by no other service, it ought to be

14. See, for example, Rudolf Grafe, *Lektorenbuch für die Schul-und Gemeinde-Messfeier,* 3rd ed., Paderborn, 1953.

longer. A brief reading, for example on the saint of the day, might well be included. Above all, it should have its climax in self-offering in spiritual union with the Eucharistic Sacrifice of the Church.

We should think also of composing a short but substantial form of morning prayer, to be carefully explained to our Christians and recommended to them as an *indispensable minimum* when they do not take part in any community prayer. It should include first of all the *Apostles' Creed,* in which we profess our faith, give thanks for the grace of our vocation, and renew our baptismal promise to live according to this faith. An *Our Father,* accompanied by a concise formula of self-offering and of union with the sacrifice of Christ would also express our response for the grace of our divine adoption. In conclusion, a *Hail Mary* would proclaim our devotion to the mother of the Savior. Who could deny that these few prayers include the essential desires of the Christian heart at the beginning of a new day? If we could only lead our Christians to recite faithfully and devotedly this short form of morning prayer!

The Rosary and the Way of the Cross hold a place of honor among communal services everywhere in the missions. History teaches us that Christian people resort spontaneously to the Rosary in times of distress and persecution, and it would be easy to give striking proofs of this fact from present-day persecutions. Precisely because we deeply appreciate these two prayers and recognize their unfailing popularity, we should seek to include them in our whole pastoral program, resolutely and methodically. But we should not consider them to be universal panaceas, capable of taking the place of everything else — even the Mass cannot do this. Nor let us believe that the fervent praying of the Rosary and of the Way of the Cross will suffice to safeguard the treasure of the faith in times of persecution and to transmit it to the rising generation. Our catechetical problem is not so easily solved. Nevertheless, these prayers render great services, and could render still more if one or more minor adaptations were made. The Rosary is recited in the missions in two ways, each of which has its reason for existing: simple recitation, in which the Mysteries are simply mentioned; solemn recitation, in which the mention of each Mystery is accompanied by a short meditation, sometimes in the form of a hymn. This second method in itself is obviously preferable, both from the catechetical aspect and from that of prayer. Let us strive to give these meditations on the Rosary a dogmatic content and a truly appealing Christian character, as these marvelous Mysteries should have. For the Way of the Cross, let us also insist on bringing out the dogmatic content and the idea of the glory of the resurrection to which the Stations bring us nearer like stages on a road. It is not necessary to add a fifteenth station — although such a development is not excluded — but to project, from the very first station, the light of the Easter victory of Christ on the sufferings of the Savior and on our own.

The composition of services to be held in the absence of a priest, adapted to the needs of our times, is one of the most urgent problems of missionary pastoral care. Would that many of our missionary bishops might soon devote themselves to this work, the difficulties of which do not in any way lessen its importance! We cannot of course expect a perfect solution all at once: this will require a certain amount of experience and as it were a time of apprenticeship. But we can hope for courageous attempts answering without delay to the chief needs of the present time. Far better a useful experience that is gained in time, than a wonderful accomplishment that comes too late.

CHAPTER TWELVE

Suggested Text for the Sunday Service

JOSEF KELLNER, S.J.

We are presenting here a basic plan, and the complete text for one "ordinary" Sunday. The basic plan follows in its broad outlines the pattern of the Fore-Mass, which, as late as the time of St. Augustine, could be held as an independent liturgical function. Omitting some less important elements of the opening rites, which have enriched them but also, perhaps, made them less clear, this pattern consists of: reading, chant, prayer (prayer of the people and prayer of the priest); and this, according to J. S. Jungmann, is the *fundamental liturgical pattern* ("liturgical ground-plan") to be found in various forms in our liturgy. To this pattern, we have added an opening prayer or entrance hymn (which serves the same function as the singing of the Introit). And, since there is no priest, there is no distinction to be made here between the prayer of the people and that of the priest. Although, strictly speaking, the Collect is a priestly prayer, we include it since it may be recited by lay people, religious, for example, when they recite the Divine Office in choir. But in the Thanksgiving we have not followed the pattern of the Preface of the Mass, since this is exclusively the priest's prerogative. The "General Prayer," the Thanksgiving, the Commemoration of the Mass and the Our Father, all together form a separate unit, to be distinguished as the "Liturgy of Prayer" from the "Liturgy of the Word" consisting mainly of readings.

Three readings are suggested: the Epistle (or another more appropriate selection when the Epistle does not bring out the theme of the day), the Gospel, and the Instruction which takes the place of the sermon.

The chants suggested might be replaced by hymns already familiar to the congregation, of appropriate content and music. It is, of course,

146

always possible simply to recite the texts, but our aim should always be progressively to form the congregation in singing.

As to physical posture, the congregation should stand to begin with, sit during the first and third readings, stand for the Creed, kneel during the General Prayer, and stand during the rest of the service.

The Leader's part, as indicated both in the basic plan and the complete example, includes three separate functions: that of prayer leader, reader, and chant leader. These may be divided up among three persons, or two, if circumstances permit — the great differences in personnel and capacity existing between different communities in the missions make great flexibility necessary. But for practical reasons it is advisable whenever possible to provide two chant leaders. And in trying out any such services, it is always wise to proceed slowly, and, for the first attempts at least, to rehearse a special group among the congregation ahead of time: school children, or the group of catechists.

Various additions and modifications to the usual scheme might be suggested for special occasions: for example, a ceremony at the Crib for Christmas, making use of texts taken from the Christmas Masses; or, again, the adoration of the Cross on Good Friday, and the renewal of the baptismal promises on Easter Sunday, using translations of the text given in the restored Holy Week Ordo.

BASIC PLAN

Introductory words: Varying according to the day and circumstances.

The Liturgy of the Word

Opening Prayer

Leader—Lord Jesus, Thou hast said: where two or three are gathered together in My name, there am I in their midst. We pray Thee, then, be in our midst so that, free of all division and discord, united in Thee, our Leader, we may worthily carry out this sacred service.

All—Lord, have mercy on us; Christ, have mercy on us; Lord, have mercy on us.

L—Lord Jesus, Thou art the way, the truth and the life. We pray Thee, then, purify us by Thy word and sanctify us by Thy truth that we may ever more fully know and love Thee and the Father Who sent Thee, and so attain true life.

A—Lord, have mercy on us; Christ, have mercy on us; Lord, have mercy on us.

L—Lord Jesus, Thou hast called us, Thy people, out of darkness into the glorious light of Thy kingdom; We pray Thee, then, that we may adore the Father in spirit and in truth, and obtain His blessing.

A—Lord, have mercy on us; Christ, have mercy on us; Lord, have mercy on us.

Note. Instead of this opening prayer, the service may begin with a hymn, sung by all, especially on feast days and solemn celebrations. This opening hymn should give the atmosphere of the day's feast, and vary accordingly.

First Reading: The Epistle of the day's Mass, or another reading from Scripture suitable to the theme of the day.

First Responsory: Varying according to the time and circumstances. To begin with, and on days with no marked character (such as the Sundays after Epiphany and after Pentecost), the same refrain might be used for all the Responsories: Praise be to Thee, O Jesus Christ, King of eternal glory!

Second Reading: The Gospel of the day.

Second Responsory: Varying according to the time and circumstances.

Third Reading: Instruction on the Sunday or the feast (see p. 137, above).

The Apostles' Creed.

The Liturgy of Prayer

General Prayer: as in the text suggested for a community Mass, nos. 1-11, up to the "pause" inclusive (pp. 60-61). An addition introducing the theme of the day in prayer-form is provided in the following example of a complete text.[1] In order to avoid routine, this General Prayer could be varied by using other formulae of intercessory prayer, for example, the petitions of the Litany of the Saints beginning with "We sinners," the *Deprecatio Gelasii,*[2] or the Good Friday prayers. But this should always lead up to the following:

Hymn of Supplication

L—Lamb of God, Who takest away the sins of the world,
A—Protect us, O Lord.
L—Lamb of God, Who takest away the sins of the world,
A—Protect us, O Lord.
L—Lamb of God, Who takest away the sins of the world,
A—Have mercy on us.

Collect of the Day: taken from the Missal. The leader introduces it by saying: Let us pray, and then reads it. It is concluded by the Amen of the whole congregation.

Thanksgiving: (Modifications of this general formula might be made

1. Josef Goldbrunner proposed that this be done also during the Mass. See *Lit. Jahrbuch* 5 (1955) 245.
2. See J. A. Jungmann, *The Mass of the Roman Rite,* Benziger, New York, 1951, vol. I, p. 336 f.

for special feasts, bringing out the special blessings for which we wish to give thanks on this particular occasion.)

L—Let us all arise, and with holy joy raise our hearts and our voices to God, saying: Thanks be to Thee, O Father, through Thy Son, in the Holy Spirit.

A—Thanks be to Thee . . .

L—O Lord, holy Father, Who hast created heaven and earth and all things therein; Who dost preserve them by Thy power and Thy goodness; Who dost give them to us in abundance for our welfare, to aid us in Thy worship and in our sanctification — gladly do we thank Thee!

A—Thanks be to Thee . . .

L—O Lord, holy Father, Who, when we were children of wrath, sinners deprived of salvation, far away from Thy presence, didst have mercy on us and send us from heaven Thine only-begotten Son to save us from sin and death, to bring us divine life and everlasting happiness — gladly do we thank Thee!

A—Thanks be to Thee . . .

L—O Lord, holy Father, Who didst give Thine eternal Son to be made flesh for us in the womb of the immaculate Virgin Mary, to die on the Cross for our sins, to rise from the dead for our glorification, going before us into heaven to be with Thee always as our Brother and our Leader, our Mediator and our Lord — gladly do we thank Thee!

A—Thanks be to Thee . . .

L—O Lord, holy Father, we thank Thee for all the blessings Thou dost give us through Thy Church, the Bride of Christ and His Mystical Body, in whom He lives and works on earth until the end of time. We thank Thee that by Baptism we were made members of this Body, sharing in the treasures of the Redemption as Thy chosen people. We thank Thee that in the Church Thou dost teach us the way of salvation and give us Thine overflowing grace in the sacraments. We thank Thee that in her community we look forward in hope to the everlasting joys of heaven.

A—Thanks be to Thee . . .

L—O Lord, holy Father, Whose Son will come one day in glory to judge the living and the dead, to give an imperishable beauty to heaven and earth and lead us, Thy children, into Thine eternal kingdom — gladly do we thank Thee!

A—Thanks be to Thee . . .

L—O Lord, holy Father, Who dost continually bless us with the innumerable gifts of Thy love; never can we thank Thee worthily.

We unite ourselves then, here and now, with all Thy holy Church in heaven and on earth to celebrate Thy glory and to praise Thee with gladness, saying:

Hymn of Praise

L—Holy,
A—Holy, holy is the Lord God of the heavenly hosts.
Heaven and earth are filled with Thy glory.
Hosanna in the highest!

Commemoration of the Holy Sacrifice (invariable)

L—Lord and Father, this is the hour in which Thy Church assembles to renew in Holy Mass the sacrifice of our redemption, when our High Priest, Jesus Christ, changes bread and wine, the offerings of the community, into His Body and Blood to give Thee an adoration, a thanksgiving, a reparation worthy of Thy majesty. Here today we have no priest with whom we can celebrate this priceless Sacrifice. Look, then, on our desires, regard favorably the wish of our hearts, and grant that we may share in this Sacrifice of praise.
A—Amen.
L—Lord and Father, since the bread and wine which Thy priests are offering to Thee all over the world are symbols of the lives, the love, the works and the sufferings of Thy faithful, dedicated to Thee; accept, we pray, also our lives and our love, our works and our sufferings. Unite them with the Sacrifice of Christ and His Holy Church, so that we may be Thine in happiness and distress, in life and in death.
A—Amen.
L—Lord and Father, Who hast willed that the Flesh and Blood of Thy Son should be the Food of His life in us; behold we, Thy children, are hungry for this heavenly Bread, but there is no one here to give it to us. Grant us then, we pray, that we may share spiritually in Thy banquet and nourish our souls for life everlasting.
A—Amen.

Final Prayer (invariable)

L—O Lord Jesus Christ, Thou hast promised Thy Church to be with her until the end of time. We believe that Thou art present here with us as our Mediator with the Father. Lead us before His throne and make our prayers and our thanksgiving pleasing to Him, in virtue of the prayer that Thou Thyself didst teach us: Our Father . . .

A—(slowly and devoutly) Who art in heaven . . . but deliver us from evil. Amen.

Final Exhortation: this should relate the worship that has been offered by the people to their daily life: a kind of *lectio brevis,* varying according to the theme of the day. A general formula might be John 15, 9-10, 12, 17.

Prayer for Blessing (invariable)

L—May the grace of Jesus Christ and the love of God and the community of the Holy Spirit be with us and go with us everywhere, so that we may walk according to our vocation and carry out the will of God in our work and our rest, in our thoughts, words and deeds.

A—May the blessing of almighty God, of the Fa + ther, and of the Son + and of the Holy + Spirit descend upon us and remain unto life everlasting. Amen.

Concluding Hymn. This should be sung by the whole congregation and vary according to the season and circumstances. A chant fitting for all occasions would be the *Christus Vincit.*

COMPLETE SERVICE FOR THE FOURTEENTH SUNDAY AFTER PENTECOST

(We are giving an example of the celebration for an ordinary Sunday. The responsories, especially the refrains to be recited or sung by the congregation, are to be considered as a kind of common formula to be used on other Sundays throughout the year. This is to be recommended particularly whenever the congregation is not yet familiar with this type of celebration.)

Introductory words

L—Today is the fourteenth Sunday after Pentecost, when the Church would have us remember especially the loving care given us by our Father in heaven.

Liturgy of the Word

Opening Prayer or Opening Hymn: Holy God.

First Reading: Gal. 5, 16-24, or a reading on the same theme from the Old Testament: Deut. 4, 32-40, which should be introduced as follows:

L—Like a wise and loving father, God cared for His chosen people with kindness and firmness during their journey across the desert to the Promised Land. His fatherly care is far greater for us, members of

His Church, the chosen people of the New Covenant, as we journey to our eternal home. Moses writes to the Israelites: . . .

First Responsory

L—Praise be to Jesus Christ, King of eternal glory. (This refrain, which could also be used in the second chant, is intended to bring out as strongly as possible the idea that Sunday is the day of the Lord, the day of Christ, on which the Church assembles to meet her glorified Lord.)
A—Praise be . . .
L—The Lord is my shepherd,
 I shall not want,
 He gives me rest in green pastures.
A—Praise be . . .
L—He leads me to waters of peace,
 He refreshes my soul.
A—Praise be . . .
L—He guides me by right paths,
 for His name's sake.
A—Praise be . . .
L—Though I walk through a death-dark valley,
 I fear no harm.
A—Praise be . . .
L—Yes, goodness and mercy will follow me
 all the days of my life.
A—Praise be . . .

Second Reading: The Gospel of the Sunday.

Second Responsory

L—In Thee, O Lord, do I trust, my fate is in Thy hands.
A—In Thee . . .
L—Happy the nation whose God is the Lord,
 the people He chose for His heritage.
A—In Thee . . .
L—The Lord looks down from heaven,
 He sees all the children of men.
A—In Thee . . .
L—Our soul awaits the Lord,
 He is our help and our shield.
A—In Thee . . .

L—In Him our heart rejoices,
  we put our trust in His holy name.
A—In Thee . . .
L—Let Thy mercy, O Lord, be upon us,
  to the measure of our hope in Thee.
A—In Thee . . .

Third Reading: Instruction for the Sunday on true confidence in divine Providence.

The Apostles' Creed, as in the basic plan.

The Liturgy of Prayer

The General Prayer: as in the basic plan, but with the following additions.

L—Let us ask the Lord to fill us with great trust in His providence.
A—We pray Thee, hear us.
L—Let us ask the Lord that we may neither be proud in prosperity, nor discouraged and despairing in adversity.
A—We pray Thee, hear us.
L—Let us ask the Lord that we may see His fatherly hand even in suffering and the cross.
A—We pray Thee, hear us.
L—And let us ask the Lord our God to grant us the grace to console and help our brothers in their misfortunes as instruments of His loving Providence.
A—We pray Thee, hear us.
Chant of Supplication: as in the basic plan.
Prayer of the Day: Collect for the Fourteenth Sunday after Pentecost.
Prayer of Thanksgiving, Hymn of Praise, Commemoration and *Final Prayer,* as in the basic plan.
Final exhortation: John 15, 9, 10, 12, 17. (This also might be used as a text for other Sundays.)
Prayer for Blessing and *Closing chant* as in the basic plan.

PART FOUR

Music and Art in Christian Worship

CHAPTER THIRTEEN

Music in the Missions: Its Importance

JOSEF KELLNER, S.J.

Music has always been a most valuable, if not an indispensable, aid to the missionary: the missionary history of every century bears witness to its services. The work of the Benedictine monks in Europe at the beginning of the Middle Ages, of the sons of St. Francis of Assisi during the centuries that followed (sequences and *laudi*), of the Jesuits in China and Paraguay at the beginning of the modern era, are only a few examples. Quite recently, the encyclical of Pius XII, *Musicae Sacrae Disciplina*, of December 25, 1955, gives directives on this subject, teaching that music should not only "effectively arouse and inspire the people to profess the faith and cultivate piety," but that it also "is a welcome and important help to the Church in carrying out its apostolic ministry more effectively."[1] And even before the appearance of this important encyclical, missionary literature all over the world concerned itself with the use of music in the missions, thanks largely to recent discoveries in ethnology which allow us to understand more clearly the attitude of non-Western peoples toward music. We have discovered with some astonishment that music is a more essential factor in the life of many of the peoples in missionary countries than it seems to be in ours. This fact brings out more clearly than ever before the great importance of music for the missionary and for his work.

The Place of Music in the East and in the West

The average man of modern Western culture places music in the

1. *Musicae Sacrae Disciplina*, Acta Ap. Sedis, vol. 48 (1956). N.C.W.C. trans., Nos. 28 and 29.

category of "beauty." To him, it answers to an aesthetic feeling, or, if you wish, to an aesthetic need; it is an occupation that offers an agreeable method of relaxation and a noble form of enjoyment, superior, certainly, to the pleasures of the gourmet, but one that remains merely a "feast for the ear," an agreeable decoration added to one's existence. Even the music of the Church, or as we say "serious music" — an oratorio, a symphony — gives us no more than an intense aesthetic experience. People can be found with particularly sensitive natures who are so profoundly moved by the *Messiah* of Handel, *St. Matthew's Passion* of Bach, or the *Ninth Symphony* of Beethoven or of Bruckner that they feel its echoes in their moral life and realize that they have changed for the better when they have returned from the realm of music to ordinary living. But such people seem unusual; and, generally speaking, we find both strange and Utopian the phrase of Plato that the quality of a State corresponds to the quality of its music.[2]

Music and morality have, according to our present-day ideas, little to do with one another. But for Plato, the philosophy of music — this term fits his thought better than does "aesthetics" — is at the very heart of morality. He treats music in its ethnic effects. He says, for example, that the Dorian mode (on our modern keyboard: E to E) strengthens the will, the Lydian mode (C to C) has a weakening and paralyzing influence. Nor was this the teaching of one thinker alone, but the conviction of all those who ruled the destinies of his nation. Plato's appeal that the State take charge of the musical education of youth found an echo: in Arcadia, all the young men up to the age of thirty were instructed in the most important branches of music at the expense of the State; in the other States, training in instrumental music was declared obligatory.[3] The reason for all this is to be found in the basic attitude of the Greeks toward music, *an attitude essentially different from our own*. In ancient Greece, music was taken seriously in a way quite different from anything that we are aware of today. It was not an occupation on the margin of human life, but something that engaged the whole person, something rooted in the hearts of the people and even a matter of public concern. And for the Greeks, music was something the State could no more neglect than the athletic training of youth or the solemn festivals, at once national and religious, celebrated at Olympia, Delphi and Corinth.

But what seems surprising to us is to find that, as modern ethnic psychology clearly proves, the same profound esteem for music is to be

2. See Fritz Högler, *Geschichte der Musik von der Antike bis zur Wiener Klassik,* Vienna, 1951, p. 29.
3. Högler, *op. cit.,* p. 29 ff.

found today in almost all the peoples who have not been formed by Western civilization. We find this to be true in China, in Japan, in Oceania, in Africa, in India, among the American Indians, in Central America. . . . Let us consult, for example, the most ancient traditions of China, those that go back to the times of the mythical emperors and founders of the State.

"According to the legend, Huang ti, one of the five mythical emperors of ancient China, had first of all to harmonize music with the cosmos. He had a bamboo reed cut a foot long, according to the unit measure of that time and all the musical instruments were tuned to the pitch of this flute. And all the later dynasties took great care to rediscover the fundamental "right" pitch (huang tshung); and the length of the reed was also the unit of weights and measures. The note changed at various times, because, when a dynasty fell, the pitch that it had been using was declared to be false; the defeat was attributed to the fact that its standards of measurement were not right, were not in harmony with the universe."[4] The normative pitch, then, concerned not only the verification of weights and measures, but was bound up with the philosophical and moral ideas of the Chinese people: and thus the conception of music in ancient China took on a cosmic value. The five tones of Chinese music: Kung, shang, kio, chi, yu, correspond to the seasons, to the ages of human life, to the various movements of the soul. There exist whole lists of these correspondences, for example:

Kung	Shang	Kio	Chi	Yu
the whole of life	manhood	childhood	youth	old age
the whole year	autumn	spring	summer	winter
the center	west	east	south	north
earth	metal	wood	fire	water
yellow	white	blue/gray	red	black
thoughts	care	anger	joy	fear
knowledge	sense of duty	sense of kindness	politeness	fidelity
sweet	harsh	sour	bitter	salty
Saturn	Venus	Jupiter	Mars	Mercury

The series could be continued indefinitely; each of the tones can be the fundamental note of a whole gamut that receives from it its cosmological significance. "The melodies having *kung* for the dominant note give good thoughts and are good on all occasions; the melodies

4. Fritz Bose, in *Atlantikbuch der Musik*, published by Fr. Hamel and Martin Hürlimann, Zürich/Fribourg in Br., 8th ed., p. 803.

having *kio* as the dominant note should be played to children, for they give a warlike feeling and promise long life. The melodies in *chi* radiate joy and win love; the melodies in *yu* awaken fear; the melodies in *shang*, sadness, for they correspond to autumn and to white, the color of mourning."[5] This cosmic ideology still endures to a certain extent among the Chinese people.

Singing now occupies an important place in the program of education being carried out in communist China: in the schools, in indoctrination courses and "brain-washings," in meetings, even in the prisons, the people must sing. The American missionary Mark Tennien, of Maryknoll, who spent months in the prison of Schumkai in the province of Kuangshi with Chinese prisoners, reports that the prison regulations prescribed singing for four hours a day; a boy who neglected to learn the communist songs was put in chains for a month.[6]

To understand the importance thus given to singing, we must realize that for these men music is not only an agreeable means of passing the time — in communist prisons, the authorities are not interested in providing amusements for the prisoners; music is a living expression of the whole man, possessing a formative power that reaches even the profound depths of the soul which for the most part escape the direct influence of thought and will. No difference exists between this fundamental attitude to be found in modern China and that of ancient Greece.

When we realize this fundamental place given to music in the life of both the individual and society, we see the life of peoples different from ourselves in a new light. We realize that, while in the countries formed by Western civilization, music has received an amazing technical development that we do not find in other civilizations, it is outside of Western civilization that music possesses, in public and private life, an influence and power that is considered almost supernatural, magical, divine. This non-Western music usually seems to us so simple, so lacking in complexity, that we can hardly understand its power, and at one time we were inclined to reject it all as being "primitive."

But when a missionary asks his negro Christians to sing him some of their native wedding songs and receives the answer: "But, Father, no wedding is being celebrated now, how can we sing any wedding songs?," or when the natives show their joy at the visit of a European by repeating a short melody of three or four notes with the same words, for instance: "Hurrah, the white man is here!" — while singing and dancing for hours on end — is this primitive? Does not the same thing

5. Bose, *op. cit.*, p. 804 ff.
6. Mark Tennien, *No Secret is Safe*, N. Y., 1952, p. 119 and 124.

exist in countries with a very high degree of civilization? Cultivated Chinese, for example, can be interested for hours in the national musical plays whose plot is insignificant; people walking along the streets stop and listen for hours to storytellers recounting tales known by everyone and delivered in a monotonous sing-song. Traveling singers who chant their poems to a simple melody can always find an untiring audience, in India and in Africa as well. "Hindus celebrate a feast in which the holy writings of Hinduism are recited from one end to the other without interruption for seven days and seven nights. In the villages where these chants take place, groups of singers relieve one another and the auditors scarcely take time for eating a few mouthfuls and snatching a short sleep. Inspired by this celebration, the Christians in several villages have already, during a celebration lasting three days and three nights, sung poems composed on Biblical themes; this attempt aroused the enthusiasm of the audience and acted like a very effective retreat."[7] I myself have recently witnessed the way in which the Filippinos, a few days before Easter during their "Pabasa," sang for twenty-four hours an epic poem in Tagalog that begins with the history of creation and, after some scenes from the Old Testament, describes the life of Christ, especially His passion, death, resurrection and ascension, and His return at the Last Judgment. These some three thousand strophes of four lines each are sung on three or four melodies and thus offer, from the musical point of view, no more variety than does the *Dies irae* of the Mass of the Dead. Is this primitive? Connoisseurs today are too prudent to use this term. A very sensitive musical temperament is affected by even the faintest impression and can take pleasure in it for a long time, as is shown in the life of some of our great masters. One note on a violin, the unvarying song of a bird can, under certain circumstances, move the very depths of the soul. We do not mean to say that a Bach or a Beethoven is concealed in every non-Westerner — the melody that moves these people is often only a musical sketch with a superior spiritual content, as in our liturgical recitatifs like the Pater — but the examples we have cited confirm one fact: all the peoples to whom we rightly attribute a gift, a preference and a great love for music — the Mongols, the Chinese, the Japanese, the peoples of Oceania, the Malays, the Hindus, the Negroes, the Indians, etc. — feel that the very essence of their being is bound up with music; it is an inseparable aspect of their life and their soul. Father Wilhelm Schmidt, S.V.D., has said of

7. Stephen Fuchs, S.V.D., in *Zeitschrift für Missionswissenschaft und Religionswissenschaft,* 1952, p. 132.

the black races: "Among these peoples, music springs from their soul. To take away this music from them would be to mutilate their soul."[8] What the research of scientists teaches us on this subject is confirmed a hundredfold by the experience of every missionary.

The missionary, then, who is called to win men, to win souls — would he not be committing a sin of omission with disastrous results if he were to neglect this fact? Let us briefly consider its implications in our missionary work.

Implications

The tasks and the methods of the missionary can in some ways be compared to the aims and the practices of those who attempt to propagate ideas of the scientific, political or cultural orders; like them, he can make use of legitimate modern methods of propaganda, of music in particular. But the missionary is more than a propagandist: he, like his predecessors and the Apostles themselves, is the messenger of God, who brings to men the Good News of the love of God for us and the means of responding to that love; he is the pastor of souls who "leads the sheep that are not yet of his flock" to incorporate them into the flock, the community of Christ; he is the minister of worship who is continually seeking those who will adore the heavenly Father in spirit and in truth. Teacher of truth, guide of the community, priest who offers sacrifice at the altar: the missionary has always been and must continue to be all this. And in order, as priest, leader and teacher even more than as propagandist, to reach the most intimate depths of souls, he must realize that among the peoples whose whole life is permeated with music, he can and should use this music as an aid to him in his apostolate.

The missionary is a teacher. His teaching is not addressed only to the minds of his hearers; the truths that he is preaching are not abstract verities, remote from practical life. On the contrary, they are decisive, they are ordered to revolutionize the life of the catechumen, to transform his thoughts, feelings, will, his very unconsciousness for "the Kingdom of heaven is like the leaven that a woman took and put in three measures of meal until the whole was leavened" (Matt. 13, 33). It is the whole man that must be gained for Christ. Knowledge alone is of little avail; through sacred music, the universe of the faith moves us, animates us, marks itself on our memory, arouses a holy enthusiasm, disposes us to sacrifice.

8. Johannes Beckman, *Die Katholische Kirche im neuen Afrika*, Einsiedeln/Köln, 1947, p. 136.

The people with whom the messenger of the faith has to deal have little taste, in general, for abstract expositions, but they become easily interested in what is told them in concrete language, in music that is agreeable to them. In spite of certain awkwardnesses and imperfections, the catechism chants were and are a valuable aid in the missions (and they can always be improved where this is necessary).

"These hymns, which are often sung in the language of the people, are memorized with almost no effort or labor. The mind grasps the words and the music. They are frequently repeated and completely understood. Hence even boys and girls, learning these sacred hymns at a tender age, are greatly helped by them to know, appreciate and memorize the truths of the faith. Therefore they also serve as a sort of catechism. These religious hymns bring pure and chaste joy to young people and adults during times of recreation. They give a kind of religious grandeur to their more solemn assemblies and gatherings. They bring pious joy, sweet consolation and spiritual progress to Christian families." These words of Pius XII are particularly applicable in mission countries. The apostle of the faith often meets with innumerable difficulties in striving to communicate his own enthusiasm. Perhaps he does not have an adequate grasp of the native language; perhaps he has not yet become sufficiently familiar with the customs, the mentality, the way of life of his Christians and his catechumens to be able to find the best points of contact for the Gospel message; or perhaps he has charge of so vast a region that it is only rarely that he can personally visit some of his communities. And yet he is sent, like his Master and Lord, to cast fire into the hearts of men, and he can desire nothing else but that it be everywhere enkindled. In this task, what words and writings cannot carry out, the singing of hymns can accomplish. It arouses a true joy that makes difficult things easy, an enthusiasm that does away with many obstacles. Here the religious life draws a new power and a new nourishment: the doctrinal content of sacred hymns exercises a constant influence; it helps to complete a religious formation that may be deficient, both of new Christians and old.

What power of attraction there is in a song! We find the proof of this in the Crusaders with their hymns in honor of the Holy Cross, in the Flagellantes with their stirrings songs, the Reformers with their religious battle songs. With his one hymn, *Ein feste Burg,* Luther made many more converts than with all his sermons and his ninety-five theses posted at Wittenburg.

The missionary is a guide. The Christian community in a mission country often includes a large proportion of neophytes. They have joined the Catholic faith either by families or individually. They may have had no great difficulty in accepting the teachings of the faith, particularly if those who converted them knew how to help them grasp it easily. In their first fervor of love and gratitude, in their confidence in divine grace, they took the firm resolution of observing the Christian moral law. But in passing over to Christianity, they built up a wall between themselves and their environment. They can no longer take part in the sacrifices, the fertility rites, the magic ceremonies and the calling up of spirits, in many of the marriage and funeral rites of their people. They now find themselves, as it were, beings of a different order, who, as long as they remain in the minority, will be considered by their compatriots as dissidents, despisers of the national culture. And this arouses in their relations and acquaintances, especially in small villages, feelings of aversion, often of real hatred, and is almost always the cause of an isolation from which the new Christians suffer intensely.

They feel themselves rejected by their own community and, from a social point of view, living in a vacuum. We must, therefore, give them a new spiritual homeland, awaken in them a consciousness of belonging to the family of God which will make up to them a thousandfold for the earthly advantages that they have had to sacrifice. The brief and appealing exposition of the mysteries of our faith, the repeated reminder of the fatherhood of God and the communion of saints in the Church of Christ brings strength and comfort in moments of struggle or discouragement. Yet the most profound Christian convictions cannot completely eliminate the feeling of a void, the sensation of having been uprooted. The new community to which the neophyte objectively belongs by virtue of Baptism must be experienced from within; a new feeling of community must be born in his soul. How can this be brought about more easily than by means of songs and hymns? Singing together is not only the expression of the community, it gives it a new awareness of itself; it creates precisely the sense of community.

How many groups of young people who have come together as isolated individuals, have gained a real sense of "belonging" to a community, thanks to singing together? Every real community needs singing. It is a means of uniting men gathered together for work, for war, or for worship, for every solemn occasion in human life. Many manifestations of social life are inconceivable without music. But the Christian in missionary countries has a far greater need than do we of this community-building power of music. Thanks to singing,[9] the new family of God which is the Church becomes a reality to him, an experienced fact, an intimate unforgettable experience. If in the missions we wish

9. Scouts and other youth organizations prove the community-building effectiveness of singing.

to form not only individual Christians, but a Church, a community, which will bind them together and give them the courage, enthusiasm and fervor of belonging together in one great whole, then singing is absolutely indispensable. To spread it is a duty imposed on the enlightened guide of the Christian community in the midst of a non-Christian and hostile environment. If the history of pastoral care in the missions is ever written, we shall be able to see the profound influence that music has had, or should have had, in the community formation of new Christians. And pastors should strive with care and with zeal to cultivate such music in the family and the school, in the teaching of catechumens and, above all, in divine worship.

The missionary is the minister of the liturgy. It is as the priest and leader of those who adore the Father in spirit and in truth, that he feels most keenly, perhaps, the necessity for music. Christian worship should be a celebration that is at once the expression and the source of the religious life of the Christian community, the solemn assembly of the baptized, in which each person renews his strength and his enthusiasm, his courage and his hope to support the burdens of daily life. Without singing that comes from the heart and returns to it, above all without community singing, worship cannot be a "celebration." Wherever men pray to God together and offer Him sacrifice, music and singing also arise; many people have even thought that the very origin of music is to be found in worship.[10] And, certainly, singing has been associated with Christian worship since its beginnings.

The Savior Himself sang the Hallel (Psalms 112-117 and 135) at the Last Supper: "After the psalms had been sung, they set out for Mount Olivet" (Matt. 26, 30). In several Epistles, St. Paul urges his hearers to sing together: ". . . speaking to one another in psalms and hymns and spiritual songs" (Eph. 15, 19; cf. Col. 3, 16). It even seems that he quotes an ancient Christian hymn in the fourteenth verse of his letter to the Ephesians. About the year 112, when the governor of Bithynia and Pontus, Pliny the Younger, sent to the emperor Trajan a report concerning the Christians in his province, this conscientious official and exquisite writer described Christian worship in these words: "They have the custom of assembling on certain specified days before the sun rises and to sing a hymn in honor of Christ as their God."[11] In the missionary Church of the first centuries, Christian community sing-

---

10. Bose, *op. cit.,* p. 790.
11. "Quod essent soliti stato die ante lucem convenire carmenque Christo quasi deo dicere secum invicem." C. Plinius Minor, *Epistolarum Liber* 10, 96, ed. Schuster Lipsiae, 1933, by Conradus Kirch, S.J., *Enchiridion Fontium Historiae Ecclesiasticae Antiquae* 7, n. 30.

ing, not the sensuous blatant music of the pagan temple feasts, was the language of the Christian soul in the presence of God. And the Church has always continued her singing. ". . . when the Catholic Church sent preachers of the Gospel into lands not yet illumined by the light of faith, she took care to bring into those countries, along with the sacred liturgical rites, musical compositions, among which were the Gregorian melodies."[12] For hundreds of years, the Eucharistic Sacrifice was a celebration in which all took part by singing. Music is a necessary element of public worship.

The individual person, in the presence of God, can do without song; it is enough for him either to express his gratitude, his praise, his desires in words, or to open his heart to God in silence and humility. But it is not the same with a community. Community worship requires order, a set method of procedure and discipline that yet does not stifle the inner fervor of each participant. It is here, more than anywhere else, that congregational singing can fulfill its religious mission. Does not history tell us that a considerable diminution in the number of faithful present at solemn public worship took place during the era when external participation in the liturgy, especially by means of singing, began to decline? An intimate bond exists between the two facts. It was as an effective strategical means that the Reformers tried in every way to cultivate the community singing of their hymns.

But we can still observe today the lack of community singing in Catholic worship, and its deplorable effects. In some parts of the Philippines that suffer from a lack of priests, the sects gain a remarkable number of converts among the Catholics. And why? In the religious services of these sects, the people can express their hearts by singing hymns, while in their own Church, even when a priest does visit them, they have not been given the same outlet.

The Christians of mission countries love music; and they have need of it, they are hungry for it. Song is to their hearts what vitamins are to our bodies. Let us, then, strive to procure for them what they need, so that they may not suffer and perish by being deprived of it. They so rarely have the opportunity of celebrating the Holy Sacrifice with a priest that the coming of the priest is a great feast day for them. Can they not somehow proclaim their joy? The rare celebration of the holy mysteries loses something of its value if only preaching, reading and prayer accompany the sacred rites.

If we consider the fact that the Sunday of innumerable Christians in the missions is a Sunday without a priest and without a Mass, we

12. *Musicae Sacrae Disciplina,* N.C.W.C. trans. N. 71.

can understand the necessity of filling this void with a form of community worship in which community singing will play a greater part than even in the Mass. Let us think of the attraction of the Protestant service though it is one with no Eucharist — as ours must be in communities with no priest. In these little stations, there are no splendid vestments for feast days, no sacred ministers to carry out the ceremonies with special solemnity; it may not even be possible to decorate the poor little mission church. There remains nothing but singing to inspire and encourage the assembled faithful, to fill their hearts with joy and enthusiasm, to make them happy in their faith and filled with legitimate pride in it. A Sunday celebration with no singing necessarily becomes dull and insipid; it loses its attractiveness; instead of a real celebration, it becomes a mere obligation which people have little enthusiasm about fulfilling.

The missionary who is conscious of his threefold function as teacher, guide and priest must, therefore, take great care to foster sacred music, above all community singing, whatever his own tastes and inclinations may be. To promote sacred music is to exercise a real apostolate, as Pius XII has clearly stated: "All those who use the art they possess to compose such musical compositions, to teach them or to perform them by singing or using musical instruments, undoubtedly exercise in many and various ways *a true and genuine apostolate*."[13] These words, which in their context refer primarily to artistic singing, to the activity of choirs and of associations for sacred music, apply even more fully to those who work to promote community singing which expresses more directly the religious sentiments of the faithful than does the artistic singing of specially trained choirs. In speaking directly to the bishops of the Church, the Pope says of community singing: "We can do no less than urge you, venerable brethren, to foster and promote diligently popular religious singing of this kind in the diocese entrusted to you. . . . Those in charge of the religious instruction of boys and girls should not neglect the proper use of these effective aids. Those in charge of Catholic youth should make prudent use of them in the highly important work entrusted to them."[14] Concerning mission countries, the encyclical says particularly: "Many of the peoples entrusted to the ministry of the missionaries take great delight in music and beautify ceremonies dedicated to the worship of idols with religious singing. It is not prudent, then, for the heralds of Christ, the true God, to minimize or neglect entirely this effective help in their apostolate."

13. *Op. cit.*, N. 38.
14. *Op. cit.*, Nos. 66 and 67.

The place of music in the life of the missions is thus clearly indicated: music is not an aesthetic pleasure to embellish some of the leisure hours of the missionary, nor a merely marginal employment for him outside of his essential work, it is a "powerful aid to the Catholic apostolate that cannot be disdained or neglected."

CHAPTER FOURTEEN

Music in the Missions: Its Qualities

Josef Kellner, s.j.

The attitude of the East towards music, so different from that of modern Western culture, must necessarily influence our missionary apostolate. But another factor also must be taken into consideration, and that is the special genius of the music of missionary countries.

Two Worlds of Music

Modern Europe enjoys a high level of musical culture, the history of which contains a long series of famous names and immortal works of art. But this wealth does not prove that our musical universe is the only one there is. The sciences of ethnology and of comparative music both reveal the fact that outside our Western culture are musical treasures of an entirely different order, a music that is beautiful, elevating, appealing, though quite unlike our own. Without possessing all the means of expression discovered by our European music, this music is very rich and varied. Moreover, the music of all the various extra-European civilizations possesses common characteristics that distinguish it as a whole from our modern Western music, so that we can speak — at least since about a thousand years ago — of two different worlds of music.

During the first millenium, the problem of transferring European music to non-European peoples would have been much easier to solve, since at that time European music was still based on melody, as non-European music is today (insofar as it is as yet untouched by the introduction of European civilization in certain circles). But toward the end of the first millenium, the West broke away from what had, up

1. K. G. Fellerer, in *Missionswissenschaft und Religionswissenschaft*, Münster, 1947/48, p. 100.

to that time, been the characteristic principle of the music of the whole world.[1] The turning point in the development of European music at that time is to be found in its orientation toward so-called functional harmonics, i.e. that kind of polyphony which brings succeeding chords into internal relationship. The fixing of the rhythm into determinate measures, the replacing of the modes of the music of the Middle Ages, modes originating in Greek music, by the two invariable modes, major and minor, the development of the diatonic scale into the exuberant chromatic scale and finally into modern atonality — all this has been the work of the last ten centuries.

The music of non-European civilizations is quite different. There is no harmony, in our sense of the word. Its chords — inasmuch as it includes the use of several voices — are independent of one another. The melodic line of the fundamental voice has a fixed correspondence with the other voices, which remain always a fourth or a fifth higher or lower. The same musical picture that we find in the *Organum* of the *musica enchiriadis* in the Flanders of the tenth century is to be met with also in Oriental music, for example in Chinese compositions for instrumental music.

In many cases, however, Oriental music is strictly linear, a unison homophony, or accompanied only on the octave. The melodies often resist any attempts to introduce harmony, as do many Gregorian chants. (Where, for example, can be found a satisfactory harmonization of the hymn, *Ave Maris Stella?*)

In its concept of rhythm also, the music of the East differs from that of the modern West. To metered rhythm, felt to be constraining, it prefers a free rhythm that is more adaptable to the cadences of speech. Yet the music of India, of Indonesia and of Africa, as of some American Indians, shows a very highly developed sense of rhythm; examples of simultaneous polyrhythm (different rhythms superimposed on one another) are to be found here and there.

The rich coloring produced by the use of a chromatic scale, with its possibilities of modulations by semitones, is quite foreign to the genius of non-European music, which in general, holds to a diatonic scale (apart from certain "sliding" notes or even micro-intervals in South India). Or it completely avoids half tones (in the ancient Chinese five-tone scale, as also that used in Java, in Bali, in the South Seas); or uses only the half-tone intervals proper to a scale (in Japan); and even these with great reserve (modern Chinese music does so only in a descending passage). The ascending half tone, above all the leading tone, too easily blends into the tonic: they sing *A - C - C* rather than *A - B - C.*

But the greatest cleavage between the Eastern world of music and our own lies in their use of systems of tones and intervals that are completely different from those to which we are accustomed. According to the "cent" system proposed by Alexander John Ellis,[2] our tempered scale is made up of whole tones of 200 "cents" and half tones of 100 "cents," the Slendro scale of Java and Bali has only 5 tone-intervals to the 234-240 "cents," while the Palog scale goes up to 7 intervals to the 156-210, 171 respectively. Such eighth and three-quarter tones sound false to the European ear; and, similarly, our intervals seem impure to the Javanese, for example, and our music will always be a closed book to him unless he has been introduced to it from early youth.[3]

Influences

But missionary countries present a very varied picture, musically speaking; countries whose music has remained purely oriental are now rare. There are places in the East and Southeast, where European music has completely supplanted the native. But generally in these non-European countries, the two worlds of music exist side by side.

This fact is due, first of all, to the missions. The apostle of the faith, arriving from a foreign country, naturally tried to make use of the beneficent powers of music. And so he turned to the hymn books of his home diocese, chose melodies from them, and had the texts translated into the native language. Thanks to the children in the mission schools, the teachers and catechists, the other Christians little by little learned these foreign melodies, which then were sung in church, more or less well and more or less modified by the taste of the people. And when the great feasts or a special procession attracted curious pagans, they also became familiar with the hymns of the Church. Candidates for the priesthood at the seminary of the mission extended their knowledge of European music by taking part in polyphonic singing or in studying instrumental music.

European music has penetrated into foreign cultures also by means of the great centers of formation, the schools and universities of the West to which an increasing number of students from Asia, Africa, Oceania, etc., come eagerly to pursue their education. And even in their native universities and other institutes, they are introduced to our music; and music professors come to these countries from Europe to run music schools and to instruct private students.

Colonization, trade and world travel are the third way in which our

2. "Cent = 1/100 of an equal semitone." *The Sensations of Tone,* by Helmholtz, tr. by A. S. Ellis, Peter Smith, N. Y., 6th ed., p. 446.
3. Fellerer, *op. cit.*, p. 202.

Western music has penetrated into other civilizations. In all the ports, in all the centers of trade and administration, in the great centers of employment to which the natives flock to seek work on the farms, the factories, the mines run by Europeans or Americans, everywhere Western music is heard: the music of the movies, jazz, dances, marches pervade the atmosphere. This is not religious music, certainly, but it is a music that accustoms these peoples to the harmony, the rhythm and the chromatic coloring of the West. The radio and records play an important part. And when the miner, the seasonal fieldworker, the factory hand returns to his native village, these impressions stay with him. And besides, record players are now so widely distributed that the large American firms send their salesmen and establish stores even in the heart of Africa.

The effects of this development have not been delayed. The European tempered scale has more and more come to supplant other systems. The ancient Chinese scale of eight tones, with its intervals of 261 degrees and its absence of an octave, has given way to the European intervals, or at least now limits itself more or less strictly to five tones: fa #, sol #, la #, do #, re #. In India and in Japan, the ancient classical music of the country hardly interests anyone outside of circles of music lovers. The Slendro and Pelog scales are little by little being replaced by our Western scales, and, in many places in Africa, above all in the cities, the native music seems to be disappearing. Thus when the two musical worlds meet each other head-on, our Western music proves itself the stronger.

But, on the other hand, we must recognize the fact that in many mission countries a renewal of interest in native music is now taking place, not only among ethnologists and musicologists, but also among the people themselves. Significant from this point of view was the first Congress for native music in Southeast Asia, which took place in Manila in 1955; such Congresses are to be held periodically. The end of the period of colonization and the founding of new states has centered the people's attention on their native culture, its language, music, architecture, sculpture, etc. Native people have become the more proud of these values as Western civilization has been losing prestige since the two world wars. What is European now seldom arouses any unmixed admiration. And so there is coming to be less of a trend toward European culture and music in or outside of church, and more love and enthusiasm for the native art.

Effects in Christian Worship

Attempts to give native music a place in Catholic worship have been welcomed by many missionaries. More and more do they recognize the value of such attempts and devote themselves to the work of encouraging them. If in former times, they were content to have European hymns sung to texts translated into the native language, now they realize that this is not enough; the melody, the music itself must be born of the native culture or at least have taken root in it. To attain this end, various methods have been used.

Sometimes appropriate native melodies were given religious words, or again, on the occasion of liturgical feasts, local musicians performed already existing pieces of music without any words. Those of pagan origin were not excluded. It is interesting to compare various experiences along these lines. In the missions of Sienhsien, Kinghsien and Yungnien (North China), musicians played on their traditional instruments, such as violins with two strings, flutes, flutes of Pan (made up of thirteen flutes of different lengths), chimes formed of little gongs, tambourines, etc., some of the music which, according to tradition, was to resound at the imperial sacrifices of Pekin. Even today, these pieces are played by musicians from Buddhist temples and by Catholics during Catholic worship, and nobody is scandalized. Both Christians and pagans find this music a true expression of religious joy. On the other hand, the remarkable musical adaptation of the Psalms by a Tchang Wen Yeh did not meet with the unanimous approbation of his compatriots, because it was in great part inspired by songs on a merely human level, love songs and wedding songs.

But in Kivu in the Belgian Congo, when Father de Gester composed religious texts to go with native melodies and wanted to have them sung in church, he came up against the resolute opposition of his Christians. "Everyone will laugh," they said.[4] Obviously, they felt that the new words did not fit the spirit of the melodies; in spite of the religious words, these tunes would distract people from divine worship and awaken in the hearers thoughts and feelings unsuitable to men who are praying to God. This is fundamentally the same attitude that led European and American bishops to forbid the playing in church of opera or concert music, such as the Ave Maria from Verdi's *Othello*, or the Wedding March from *Lohengrin*.[5] Music to be used in church should lead to, not away from, the altar and God.

Here and there further steps have been taken toward the use of native music; European missionaries have often set themselves, with great courage and sympathy, to understanding more fully the musical genius

4. Beckmann, *Die katholische Kirche im neuen Afrika,* Einsiedeln, Köln, 1947, p. 236.
5. See *Time,* Pacific ed., vol. LXVI, n. 17, p. 16.

of their Christians and to seeking inspiration in it for new compositions, new music. In Africa, for example, Father Alphonse Walshap, MSC., (now dead, alas,) composed a Mass called the Bantu or Congo Mass, using motifs of the Nkundo Bantus, which had a great success. It was widely sung not only in the Belgian Congo and throughout East Africa, but also in Belgium and France; it was played over the radio and recorded.[6] In India, where the poems and compositions in Hindustani of Father Proksch, S.V.D., are spreading more and more widely, the native art has found a determined promoter in the person of Cardinal Gracias, Archbishop of Bombay, as was shown at the Marian Congress held in Bombay in December, 1954. In New Guinea, the natives sing with enthusiasm the hymns that Fathers J. Küppers, S.V.D., and Hubert Hubers, S.V.D., have composed under the inspiration of the music of the country. Sometimes a successful work is born from the collaboration of foreigners and natives, like the "Mass of the Pirogue Riders" sung for the first time in the new cathedral of Brazzaville (French Equatorial Africa) and broadcasted.[7] But, obviously, the final step on the road to a church music which is the authentic expression of the genius of any people must be music composed by native artists who are at once permeated with the spirit of Christianity and thoroughly aware of the soul and the musical language of their own people. But such artists must be born; we can only fit ourselves to contribute to their later formation and ask God for them in prayer, for they are a blessing from heaven. They must find in the foreign missionary their best friend and helper. The Holy Father exhorts bishops to send to the Institute of Sacred Music in Rome the talented artists of the future to assure their formation.[8] And already, here and there, the genius of native music is timidly producing some fruit. In the Congo, Paul N'goi and Joseph Kiwele are becoming known for promising compositions; and, in Dahomey, the poet-composer Jopke. In the apostolic vicariate of Rabaul (New Guinea), native catechists have composed hymns inspired by the "lili" formerly sung by women at funeral wakes: the choir answers by an unvarying refrain to the chant of the soloist, as in the ancient responsorial chant of the church.

In India, the episcopate tends to favor and to promote officially the classical musical tradition. The first Plenary Council of India, in 1950, expressly recommended the "ragas" for liturgical functions and also permitted the discrete use of native musical instruments to accompany

6. See *Nouvelle Revue de science missionnaire,* Beckenried, Switzerland, 1953, p. 313.
7. *Die Katholischen Missionen,* Fribourg in Brisgau, 1952, p. 11.
8. *Musicae Sacrae Disciplina,* N.C.W.C. trans. N. 76.

the chant of the Church.[9] Since their chords and tonality are completely different from those of Indian music, European instruments like the organ and the harmonium are useless for accompaniment.

The highest ecclesiastical authorities in Rome themselves recommend native liturgical music. The *Motu proprio* of St. Pius X said: ". . . every nation is permitted to admit into its ecclesiastical compositions those special forms which may be said to constitute its native music," but "still these forms must be subordinated in such a manner to the general characteristics of sacred music that nobody of any nation may receive an impression other than good on hearing it."[10] At the time of the preparations for the missionary exposition at the Vatican in 1950, Cardinal Celso Constantini, then Secretary of Propaganda, showed himself very much in favor of all authentic native art, and gave this directive to all missionaries: *Omnis lingua confitebitur Domino* (every tongue shall praise the Lord).[11] Msgr. Saverio Paventi of the congregation of Propaganda wrote along the same lines: "In every mission country, hymns in the language of the people are to be heard, because every people prays more willingly in its own language and sings according to its own tastes. The messenger of the Gospel should, then, strive to have native melodies used for liturgical worship, even in the chant that accompanies the Holy Sacrifice."[12] Pius XII clearly points out to missionaries: "The preachers of the Gospel in pagan lands should sedulously and willingly promote in the course of their apostolic ministry the love for religious song which is cherished by the men entrusted to their care. In this way, these people, whose (pagan) religious music is frequently admired even in civilized countries, can have Christian sacred hymns in which the truths of the faith, the life of Christ the Lord and the praises of the Blessed Virgin Mary and the Saints can be sung in a language and in melodies familiar to them."[13]

9. *Acta et Decreta Primi Concilii Plenarii Indiae,* n. 352-354.
10. *Tra le sollecitudini,* Nov. 22, 1903. Trans. of the White List of the Society of St. Gregory of America, N. Y., 1954.
11. *Die kath. Miss.* 1950, p. 168.
12. In *La Chiesa Missionaria,* Rome, 1949, p. 431.
13. *Musicae Sacrae Disciplina,* N.C.W.C. trans, N. 70. In this connection, the Third International Congress of Sacred Music, held in Paris in January, 1958, ended its list of suggestions which "constitute a code based on the 1955 encyclical *Musicae Sacrae Disciplina"* with the following pertinent suggestions: "1. That, in countries where they do not already exist, an association of church musicians be formed, with the approbation of the hierarchy, to foster the compositions of indigenous Church music and to afford mutual cooperation and encouragement to musicians and composers. 2. That an international association of sacred music be formed, under the sponsorship of the Holy See, to consolidate the work being done throughout the world in this most important field." The recommendations given had already "warned against imposing foreign music and hymns on people

The results of such efforts can be observed in reports from many parts of the world. The very first attempts of Father Walshap were enthusiastically received by the native people; his "Mass of the Congo" has been accepted and is widely used to a quite remarkable extent, in spite of opposition from certain quarters. When the "Mass of the Pirogue Riders" was sung, "All those who took part in the ceremony were profoundly impressed and some showed their approval with great enthusiasm."[14] When the Christians of Rabaul sang for the first time in their own fashion the praises of the divine Infant of Bethlehem, the missionary was forced to interrupt his sermon several times, for the faithful continued to sing this hymn over and over again, the first hymn that they had ever sung that really came from their hearts.[15] The Kanaka hymns that Father Küppers taught to the faithful in New Guinea were sung even by the pagans who had come to the service. Whereas before a veritable uproar had reigned in the church filled with some fifteen hundred Christians and pagans, now those present avoid all unnecessary noise while the schola of six boys' voices begin the hymn which is then take up by all the people. The faithful are so enthusiastic about these hymns that, at the time of the Corpus Christi procession, they themselves replaced the customary prayers by singing: they wanted only to sing and to keep on singing.[16] The same reaction is to be found among peoples with an ancient culture of their own. Con Merberini, for example, writes: "When I was able to present my Chinese seminarians with a little Marian hymn composed in pure Chinese style with a Chinese text, the first time they sang it, these good young men were so moved, that they were not able to continue to the end."[17]

It is true that European hymns are also sung with pleasure; but they do not arouse anything like the enthusiasm to which these examples give witness — examples that are by no means unique.

Gregorian Chant — the Bridge

But however great may be the desire of the missionary to see his Christians united more intimately in the Church by means of their own

---

in mission countries and urged that missioners strive to develop a native music and hymnody in their various mission areas." (From the report on this Congress given in The Boston Pilot, Jan. 25, quoting from the N.C.W.C. News Service. See also Paul Brünner, "The Liturgical Adaptation of Indigenous Music," in Mission Bulletin, Hongkong, 9, 1957, 668-669, which is a report on this same Congress particularly from the missionary viewpoint.)

14. *Die kath. Miss.*, 1952, p. 11.
15. *Op. cit.*, 1950, p. 168.
16. *Op. cit.*, 1953, p. 146.
17. *Op. cit.*, 1950, p. 168.

Christian music, such truly indigenous art cannot be manufactured to order; it must grow up little by little in an environment that has become to some extent Christian. This cannot happen all at once; but what is to be done in the meantime? The European hymns that once tried to fill this gap no longer seem sufficiently suitable, and this for several reasons. Today we have a greater awareness of the difference between European and non-European music; we see more clearly how essential it is not to hamper the work of evangelization by even the most gorgeous heirlooms from our past and our particular civilization; we understand better the desire of non-Europeans, both ancient and new, to develop their own genius in the bosom of the Church. And we realize that we must strive in all honesty to eliminate "Europeanism" or "Americanism" wherever this constitutes a hindrance rather than an aid to our apostolate.

What, then, can we do? Sacred music is just as essential to the solemn celebration of the liturgy in mission countries as everywhere else. But let us remember the fact that our own sacred music was born at a time when the musical universe had not yet been divided into two separate hemispheres. This music — which is our very own but which nonetheless often seems strange to us — is the Gregorian chant. "The oldest liturgical melodies and the way in which they were sung in the primitive church as they are today in Oriental liturgies, without fixed scales or 'time' in the European sense, have the deepest kinship with non-European music. Thus we can say that Gregorian chant, freed from the harmonic and accentual misinterpretations unfortunately introduced into it by the development of Western music, is particularly qualified to serve as the bridge between the music of the West and that of the East in the missions outside of Europe. But Gregorian chant must be rendered in accordance with its nature, as a pure melody without accompaniment, which, in any case, is unsuitable."[18] In fact, it is because of all the elements in genuine Gregorian music which seem strange to our Western musical sense: its monody and lack of accompaniment, its free rhythm, its diatonic and eloquent melodies, its unusual modes, and, finally, its various forms of responsorial, litany-like singing — it is because of all these elements and to the extent to which it contains them that plain-chant is akin to the non-European musical world. And herein lies the unique function of the chant and its outstanding missionary value.

Different mission countries all over the world have experienced this fact. Once when Father Küppers had sung his colleagues one of his hymns in the native style, another Father got up, opened his book of plain-chant and sang a phrase that remarkably resembled the Kanaka

18. Fellerer, *op. cit.*, 110.

melody just sung; the same thing happened with the second hymn; it was like "a first degree of kinship," said the report. The former Chinese statesman, later the titular abbot Dom Pierre Celestin Lou, finds that "the literary Chinese language is marvellously suited to Gregorian plain-chant."[19] G. Schauffhauser also states that "the two worlds of Gregorian chant and Chinese vocal music are not far from one another; the law of the five-tone gamut with no half-tone intervals that dominates in Chinese music appears here and there in some Gregorian chant also. . . . Furthermore, the Mixolydian and Lydian modes of plain-chant have many of the qualities of later Chinese music."[20]

Anyone who has heard the prayers chanted by Chinese Christian communities recognizes their Gregorian-like character, recalling some Tract melodies or the tone of the Pater Noster in Requiem Masses. It is not astonishing, then, that the Chinese Christians, particularly those who have been to mission schools, know a good number of Gregorian melodies: several Masses, the Requiem, some hymns, some antiphons, etc. And this has come about although, without taking into account Chinese musical taste, they have been given mainly chants such as the *Missa de Angelis*, the *Adoro Te*, the *Salve Mater misericordiae* which approach more nearly to modern European music and are very much favored in the missionaries' own homelands.

On the other hand, it is by means of plain-chant that we Europeans can best come to understand most non-European music, for example that of South India, which is very like Gregorian in its tonality, its melodies and its spiritual quality. One can say much the same of the Hindustani music of North India. Thus, for example, the Dorian mode corresponds to the *karasharaprya* of Karnatic music, and to the *kapi* of Hindustani music. Thus anyone who realizes how far removed from this is our modern European music, will appreciate the enormous missionary effectiveness of plain-chant as a bridge between the one and the other.

The mission of Madagascar is famous for the care with which it has cultivated plain-chant, particularly in the centres at Fianarantsoa and Tananarive. The reason for this is to be found not only in the zeal of the missionaries, but also in the inclination to plain-chant shown by the natives. J. Vanackene, S.J., who directs a boys' choir at Fianarantsoa relates: "The little singers are eager to hear records of plain-chant. 'Father,' a small boy of thirteen said to me, 'Please play us again the

19. Dom Pierre Celestin Lou Tseng-Tsiang, *Souvenirs et Pensées*, Paris, 1948.
20. G. Schauffhauser, in *Neue Zeitschrift für Missionswissenschaft*, Beckenried, 1948, p. 214.

Ascendit Deus for the Ascension sung by the Benedictines of Solesmes!'
But, I said, you have heard it several times already, haven't you? 'Just
once more, Father, it is so beautiful!' "[21] Missionaries in other parts of
Africa have had similar experiences. "Plain-chant is more in accord,
as practical experience shows, with the art and the musical sensibility
of the black races than is the European music of imported hymns."[22]

The insistence of the Popes that the people should be taught the
undying melodies of Gregorian plain-chant has often been more faithfully
and enthusiastically echoed and more effectively obeyed in the missions
than in Christian countries. "In the majority of missions that have gone
beyond the first stages, the chants of the Mass are taught not only to
children but to adults, so that the whole community can take part in
the Sunday celebration of the Holy Sacrifice. Whoever has heard
hundreds of negro Christians singing the *Mass of the Angels* or some
other plain-chant Mass together must recognize the fact that liturgical
education has done more even in Africa than in many old parishes
in Europe."[23]

This is the reason why a number of hymnbooks in the missions
contain more plain-chant than does the average European diocesan
collection issued at the same period. For example, the little book *Cantus
sacri (King keue tchaiyao)* of the mission of Sienhsien, published in
1940, contains three plain-chant Masses besides the Requiem, and more
than twenty plain-chant motets. *Sacred songs,* issued in Shanghai in
1935, contains about the same, together with the Propers for the principal
feasts and a number of other chants, in all more than half of the four
hundred and four selections in the book. And besides the Latin chants,
many hymns in the native languages use plain-chant melodies. For
example, the hymnbook for the Belgian Congo entitled *Tukembila,*
published by J. van de Casteele, S.J., includes nineteen plain-chant
melodies with texts in the native language.

Difficulties

But the composition of texts in the language of the people for use
in worship often meets with difficulties that do not exist in Europe.
In the so-called tone-languages like those of the Far East and of Africa,
the melody of spoken language plays a great part in its meaning. The
Chinese word *ma* means *mother,* or *hemp,* or *horse,* or *scold,* according
to which of the four "tones" of the language is used. These "tones"
influence both poetry and music. Although it is not necessary, for ex-

21. *Chine Madagascar,* 1954, p. 148.
22. Beckmann, *op. cit.,* p. 272.
23. *Ibid.*

ample, only to use words in Tchy-sheng (the low tone) to go with low notes in a melody, yet the variation of the different "tones" in the course of a poem and their relationship with the melody is regulated by fixed laws that cannot be ignored. In the African tongues which are also tone-languages, similar laws must be presumed to exist that limit the freedom of the translator or adapter.

The indigenous music of the African missions presents special difficulties: the melody, which usually has little variety, is covered by the rhythm (especially of the drum). The need for movement is felt so intensely by the negroes that they cannot possibly imagine singing without dancing. "In Africa, music is very closely related to poetry and to the dance. The fact that the native melodies cannot be separated either from the rhythm, which is a dance rhythm, nor from the words, presents one of the greatest difficulties in the use of native music by missionaries."[24] To overcome this difficulty, Father van de Casteele, S.J., recommends that popular religious singing be cultivated according to this principle: create new melodies, but do so in conformity with the technique and characteristics of native music and in accordance with the religious solemn character of true sacred music.[25] And would it not also be possible to satisfy, even in church, the intense need of the Negro for movement by some determined rhythmical gestures? Perhaps in attempting to carry out this extremely delicate task, we could use some of the suggestions given in the work of Thomas Ohm, O.S.B., on prayer-gestures?[26]

Again, certain tone patterns often constitute another problem for sacred music: various determined intervals or successive sounds are related to ideas and feelings that "have nothing to do with music as such, but are rooted in our experience of cosmic and religious life."[27] To take an example from my own experience, in Vienna the warning signal of a fire brigade is a fanfare on a horn — a short G before a longer C; and even after twenty years away from Vienna, this same sound pattern arouses in me feelings of excitement. Thus such "patterns" constitute either an aid or an obstacle in the composition of sacred music; in any case, we must take account of them in order to avoid embarrassing mistakes.

And let us, finally, take note of the difficulty of ascertaining the laws proper to those non-European languages that have not yet codified

24. *Op. cit.*, p. 238.
25. Van de Casteele, S.J., "La place du cantique dans la musique religieuse indigène," in *Revue du Clergé Africain*, 1949.
26. Th. Ohm, O.S.B., *Die Gebetsgebärden der Völker und das Christentum*, Leiden, 1948, especially, pp. 145-149, as well as chap. I, pp. 6, and chapter 2.
27. Fellerer, *op. cit.*, p. 103.

their rules. Here the translator must become a scientific discoverer of the native language who works out these rules from what is done by the people. Every language, every missionary region, of course, presents its own special difficulties and also opportunities. It is only by cultivating both love and understanding of the national genius of his people, of their language and their culture, together with patience, imagination, pastoral intelligence and prudence, that the missionary can find a true solution for these problems.

CHAPTER FIFTEEN

Music in the Missions: Its Function in Worship

Josef Kellner, s.j.

The special importance and the specific qualities of music in missionary countries result from the particular characteristics of the various peoples and their environment. And, in turn, these characteristics affect the carrying out of the function of music in Christian worship and in the work of evangelization.

"Sacred music, being a complementary part of the solemn liturgy participates in the general scope of the liturgy, which is the glory of God and the sanctification and edification of the faithful. It contributes to the decorum and the splendor of the ecclesiastical ceremonies, and since its principal office is to clothe with suitable melody the liturgical text proposed for the understanding of the faithful, its proper aim is to add greater efficacy to the text, in order that through it the faithful may be the more easily moved to devotion and better disposed for the reception of the fruits of grace belonging to the celebration of the most holy mysteries." From these words of St. Pius X,[1] it necessarily follows that liturgical music should express in a living manner the sentiments of the faithful for the celebration of Christian worship. Otherwise, how can it honor God and develop the religious life of the participants?

"To honor" is, according to St. Thomas, "to give external expression to our acknowledgment of the excellence of another."[2] When I express in a sensible manner my intimate conviction of the perfection, the virtue,

1. Motu proprio, *Tra le sollecitudini,* Nov. 22, 1903, Trans. of the *White List of the Society of St. Gregory of America,* New York, 1954, p. 7. The same teaching is given in the encyclical *Musicae Sacrae Disciplina.*
2. *Summa Theologica,* IIa, IIae, Q. 103, Art. 1. "Honor testificationem importat excellentiae alicujus."

the merit of another person, then I "honor" him. Thus the great task of sacred music is to provide the means whereby all the assembled faithful can sing their intimate conviction of the omnipotence, the love, the mercy and the perfection of God. The function of the art of music is to lend its language to adoration, gratitude, love, joy, all the religious sentiments of the community, so that it can express them. Without excluding aesthetic pleasure, nevertheless the interior satisfaction that this connotes is not indispensable to divine worship.

People have different ways of expressing themselves; this is true even of abstract language, and far more so of the language of the heart, the language of music. Even in Europe, or America there are many parishes in which music in the grand style, for instance a Palestrina Mass, would be entirely out of place; far from providing a means of expression for the community at prayer, it would seem to them nothing but a great confusion of sound. If this is true in countries with a Western civilization, how much more in countries with quite different cultures? It is necessary, therefore, particularly in the missions, to take into account the people's affinities to the music used in worship, affinities which cannot be commandeered or even suggested. When these are lacking, the music will lack authenticity, it will remain a purely external activity, without a soul, which has, therefore, no value as the expression of the people's hearts to God; it is incapable of promoting the glory of God. Sacred music must be different among different communities of the faithful; it must be the true expression of this or that congregation at prayer.

Sacred music must, according to the will of the Church, also be impressive; it must "speak" to the congregation present, proclaiming the greatness and goodness of God; it must give power, color and vitality to the sacred texts, so that the word and the grace of God may more easily find their way into the hearts of the faithful, more deeply take root there, and bear more abundant fruit. In this way, sacred music aids the sanctification and the edification of the faithful.

Like Westerners, the peoples of mission lands are not equally impressed by, or open to, different kinds of music. Just as we often find ourselves cut off from any appreciation of an alien kind of music, so it frequently happens that non-Europeans, though of great musical perceptiveness, can arrive only with difficulty, if at all, at an understanding of our music. One might say that their receiving station is set up for a different wave length. It frequently happens that even cultivated Chinese friends, after listening to a Bach fugue or a Beethoven symphony ask, "What does it mean?" Our music is a strange world to non-Europeans; they do not know how to take it. Thus European hymns often do not appeal to Oriental peoples, and such hymns cannot be imposed without great difficulty and without running the risk of giving a merely technical formation and an imitation that is entirely external. To the Oriental mentality, our music lacks impressiveness as well as expressiveness. This is, of course, true especially of the regions that have been least touched by Western influences, but it holds good also for countries of an ancient culture in which there still reigns an attachment to their rich ancestral heritage. Efforts to try to impose European melodies on these Christians are a Sisyphian task, not seldom unsuccessful. Father Walshap, a missionary in the Congo, writes: "When we have imported European melodies, with a few exceptions, it has been a fiasco. Good will cannot take the place of understanding, of sympathy, of the same sense of rhythm. The effects are deplorable, even grotesque. We have brought it about that these people, who in their own songs never go off-key, never lag, never abandon the rhythm, now in our churches, scream and lag behind in most miserable ways and show no sense of rhythm at all."[3] Such results are most unfortunate; to avoid them we must be attentive to the personal requirements and the concrete tasks that our missionary work imposes on us in the domain of singing and of music generally.

Formation of the Missionary

"The herald of the Gospel and the messenger of Jesus Christ is an apostle. His office does not demand that he transplant European civilization and culture, and no other, to foreign soil, there to take root and propagate itself. His task in dealing with these peoples, who sometimes boast of a very old and highly developed culture of their own, is to teach and form them so that they are ready to accept willingly, and in a practical manner, the principles of Christian life and morality; principles, I might add, that fit into any culture, provided it be good and sound . . . and which give that culture greater force in safeguarding human dignity and in gaining human happiness."[4]

In connection with our subject, this signifies that the missionary, who has left his homeland to spread the kingdom of God in a strange land, must be resolved to "leave his country, his family and the house of his father," his civilization with all the good things that belong to it, and, therefore — to the extent to which it is required by his apostolic ministry — his music also. He must learn to judge not according to his own personal conceptions or preferences in music, nor according to those of his own culture and country, but according to the needs of his Christians. He should strive, therefore, to acquire as profound a knowledge as possible of the musical universe of his Christians, to appreciate it at its

3. *Die kath. Miss.*, 1950, p. 167.
4. Encyclical *Evangelii praecones*, June 2, 1951, N.C.W.C. trans., N. 60.

just value, and, so far as he can, to make it his own. His own musical sense, the product of European or American training, should not prevent him from showing understanding of, and respect and sympathy for their music. And, for the same reason, he should apply himself to the cultivation of Gregorian chant. All this may demand sacrifices; but what true missionary would hesitate where the kingdom of God is concerned.

Music is a language, and, as there are regions where European languages are not understood, so there are countries in which European music is a "strange language," little understood or not at all, conveying little if anything. Its missionary value is thus diminished or even destroyed. It is, then, the task of the apostle of Christ to render the musical language of another country fruitful for the extension of the kingdom of God.

Like the liturgy itself, the music which is its most valuable ally has a pastoral aspect, and this is particularly true in missionary countries. Certainly it is not within the power of many missionaries to create an "indigenous" sacred music, and no one needs to try to be a "musician" in order to carry out an effective apostolic work in this field. But every missionary should *show a pastoral interest in the cultivation of music,* above all of liturgical music. He should have at heart the work of making his Christian communities into *singing communities.* A community that sings will always be one that is living and active; a community that is asleep, even figuratively speaking, is usually one that is silent. "I cannot conceive of an active participation in the Holy Sacrifice, or a devout celebration of the Mass, without singing, the singing of all the congregation," said His Excellency, Bishop Weskamp of Berlin, at the liturgical study session at Lugano in 1953.[5]

Anyone who understands the importance of sacred music will never give over completely to anyone else the charge of the singing. During the liturgical services, Benedictions, processions, he will be taking part himself, rather than keeping silent or "making good use of the time" by reciting his Breviary. For *the example of the missionary* here carries great weight. He will keep himself informed as to what hymns are being sung, more to give a "negative norm" than to impose his own program. He will find out what is being sung during the Sunday services held without a priest. He will not feel himself in danger of losing his dignity if he learns a new hymn with the community or the school children. And he will take care to explain the doctrinal content of the hymns or chants; it can be most profitable to take the text of a hymn as the material of his preaching. The faithful should be able to see that the missionary attaches great importance to all aspects of liturgical singing.

5. *Liturgisches Jahrbuch,* 3, 953, p. 179.

Budding talents are to be encouraged and recommended to the Ordinary for special formation, so that the praise of God may be sounded according to the special genius of his people. "If, among the students in a seminary or religious house of study, anyone shows remarkable facility in or liking for this art, the authorities of the seminary or house of study should not neglect to inform you about it. Then you may avail yourself of the opportunity to cultivate these gifts further. . . . "6 The missionary will also encourage profane music by recommending its cultivation as a good means of recreation on Sundays and feast days. In former times, we thought we were doing the right thing when we exhorted our Christians to come to church at least five times on Sunday. But today we recognize the fact that every exaggeration harms the life of the community.

Since music has such an important function in the missionary's pastoral work, the necessary *preparation* and *training* must be given him during his years of formation. The ordinances of the Church concerning the training of future priests are very clear on this point. St. Pius X stated: "Let all the candidates for the priesthood, not only in seminaries but also in religious houses, be formed, from their earliest years, in Gregorian chant and in sacred music. Since the training of their voices demands less effort, it is easy to teach young people to sing truly; any faults that exist can more easily be eliminated or diminished; but later on, in adult life, it is almost impossible to remedy them. The study of the chant and of music should begin in the first year of the primary school and be continued in the secondary. In this way, those who are called to receive Holy Orders, initiated into the chant without, so to say, their having realized it, may be able, in the course of their theological studies, without effort or difficulty, to be formed in the higher discipline that can rightly be called 'aesthetic,' of Gregorian chant and religious music, in the art of polyphony and of playing the organ, of which the clergy have an absolute need."7

The regulations concerning this seminary training in music are *quite detailed:* "Church music must be included in the obligatory subjects; all candidates for the priesthood, therefore, must be given instruction in it from the first year of their studies in the humanities to the end of their course in theology. The material to be studied during each year must be presented to the Ordinary by the professors and approved by him. The time to be spent on the subject of church music should be

6. *Musicae Sacrae Disciplina,* N.C.W.C. trans. N. 76.
7. Apostolic Constitution, *Divini Cultus Sanctitatem,* Dec. 20, 1928. *Acta Ap. Sed.* 21 (1929) White List Trans., p. 19.

regulated according to the Apostolic Constitution, *Divini Cultus Sancti-tatem,*[8] and must be added to the general curriculum. In the fall vacations, more time can be given to practice and rehearsals for individual students, for special groups and for the whole student body; study weeks can be held for the philosophers and the theologians in which the major questions concerning church music can be more thoroughly discussed. The students must take an examination in church music each year just as in their other subjects. Each seminary should have a qualified teacher of church music who is a regular member of the faculty."[9]

These prescriptions take on an *additional importance* for future missionaries and for the seminaries in which they are trained. In the missions, a knowledge of phonetics, of musical theory, of how to read music, ability to play some instrument, etc. are also most valuable. But the professor of sacred music must from the very beginning take into account the special needs of the missions. Without insisting on the history of music, on polyphony, the organ, etc., as much as he might with future priests who are to work in Europe, he should particularly form the future missionaries in plain-chant, which will give them as it were the instinct for sacred music and allow them to form sane judgments on native music, to which in most cases plain-chant alone offers the key. In the missions, the violin or the flute will eventually replace the organ or harmonium. An initiation into musical pedagogy, above all one ordered to the teaching of communal singing, will spare the missionary many future difficulties. And, furthermore, he cannot begin too soon the basic study of Oriental music in general and of the special music of the field of his future work, for, once he is out in the missions, both time and energy will usually be lacking for any profound study; at that time he can more easily develop the knowledge that he has already acquired. "To free oneself from the European conception of music, there is an essential requirement that must be observed from the time of taking up the study of non-European music. It is not enough to study this music from a musical point of view only, by means of records, tape-recordings, etc.; it is necessary also to know its inner structure, its relationships with the movements both of the body and the soul, with the manifestations of life and of nature."[10] In this connection also, while the seminarian is studying the native languages of his

8. "For the proper training of the secular and regular clergy, a brief but frequent, even daily, lecture or practice in the chant and Church music should be held in seminaries and other houses of study." *Acta Ap. Sed.,* op. cit. 37.
9. *Acta Ap. Sed.* 41 (1949), p. 618 ff.
10. *Fellerer,* op. cit., p. 105.

future field of activity, he would do well to study the words of the hymns sung in his mission, and even to learn them by heart.

Our *various lay helpers* in the missions will show greater zeal if we give them an appropriate musical formation. Then they will not only have learned a dozen or so chants and hymns, but they will realize their responsibilities with regard to sacred music, and they will strive to live up to these requirements. The office of choirmaster and leader takes on a great importance in view of the community services that must be held without a priest and therefore depend entirely on the laity. In ancient times, the chant-master was named by the bishop, and our present Pontifical contains a chapter *De officio psalmistae*. Even today, the choirmaster carries out an ecclesiastical task, and the man who holds this office, therefore, has a missionary apostolate and carries out a liturgical function. He should strive to avoid any of the human peculiarities or secular vanity sometimes to be found among opera singers or concert hall soloists; he should learn to think, feel and live with the Church. His office requires a good liturgical formation, a training in good taste, a true and sure voice and the ability to teach others so that he can instruct and direct children and adults in liturgical singing. He needs also to understand the religious and musical content of what is to be sung, as well as to know by heart a sufficient number of chants. Special courses in vacation time would allow these choirmasters to review and to complete the knowledge acquired during their time of formation, as is often done for the catechism, the Bible and the liturgy. Again, competitions in singing with some small prizes would stimulate their zeal.

Concrete Objectives

To allow the community to take part in liturgical singing, the first thing that is needed is a *hymnbook* that can be put into the hands of the Christians, wherever they are able to read. A number of missions are already working toward diocesan hymnbooks. To compose these is a great responsibility: such books have a determining influence on the worship of a whole region, as well as on individual piety, and this for a long time. This task obviously should be entrusted only to those who give evidence of real talent and a sound formation in this field.

What kind of hymns should we expect to find in a hymnbook for the missions? The concrete needs of the Church in the particular area must be taken into account, using as a basis hymns that are already in use, retaining the good but leaving out the less good. The general principle should be adopted of giving the first place to plain-chant and to native hymns (to the extent to which these exist); European hymns should be quite secondary. These last actually occupy too great a place in mission hymnbooks; it is the task of future authors to reduce their number, first of all rejecting the worthless. A European hymn only deserves to be inserted in a mission hymnbook if it appeals to the Christians of the mission, if it possesses real religious value both literary and musical, and furthermore, if it is already widely known, as for example, the *Adeste Fideles,* the *O sanctissima, Holy God, we praise Thy Name.*

The preference should be given, therefore, to *indigenous liturgical music.* Is this not what is done in the different countries of the West? When in one missionary country, for example in China, French melodies are sung in one place, German in another, Italian or Spanish in others, this is understandable, humanly speaking, but it is certainly not ideal. By doing this, the Church and her priests give grounds for xenophobia even among people of good will.

And furthermore these European hymns are not indispensable, even where a sufficient number of native hymns does not yet exist. In worship we can make use of *Gregorian chant,* which, to all its other advantages, adds that of being free from the reproach of coming from a particular foreign nation. Taken as a whole, it is neither German, nor English, nor American, but Catholic. This quality of universality "is possessed by the Gregorian chant to the highest degree. For this reason, it is the proper chant of the Roman Church" said St. Pius X.[11] Pius XII speaks in the same sense: "It is the duty of all those to whom Christ the Lord has entrusted the task of guarding and dispensing the Church's riches to preserve this precious treasure of Gregorian chant diligently and to impart it generously to the Christian people. Hence what Our predecessor, St. Pius X, who is rightly called the renewer of Gregorian chant, and Pius XI have wisely ordained and taught, We also, in view of the outstanding qualities which genuine Gregorian chant possesses, will and prescribe to be done. In the performance of the sacred liturgical rites, this same Gregorian chant should be most widely used and great care should be taken that it be performed properly, worthily and reverently."[12] Missionaries in particular are exhorted to remember that "from the beginning, when the Catholic Church sent preachers of the Gospel into lands not yet illumined by the light of faith, it took care to bring into those countries, along with the sacred liturgical rites, musical compositions, among which were the Gregorian melodies."[13] It is well-known how zealously the messengers of the Gospel have always

11. Motu proprio, *Tra le sollicitudini,* White List trans.
12. *Musicae Sacrae Disciplina,* N.C.W.C. trans. N. 44.
13. *op. cit.*

carried out this papal directive.[14] Community singing of plain-chant is more widely practiced in mission countries than in many Western regions; and this is the more remarkable since the Latin texts present the greatest difficulties to the Christians in many missions, far greater than to any Westerner.

If we wish really to familiarize the Christians in the missions with the Gregorian melodies, outside of the Missa Cantata which is still bound up with Latin, we cannot avoid the question of *plain-chant with vernacular texts*. This question is being discussed with considerable violence in musical circles both in Europe and America; here we speak of it only from the missionary point of view. One thing is quite clear; the intimate association of the words and the melody in many Gregorian chants certainly militates against any indiscriminating translation into other languages. The delicate play of the accents of the melody and of the text, which sometimes coincide so as to reinforce one another and sometimes occur separately so as to create a certain "tension," the expressive character of the melody which often weaves a marvelous embroidery upon a single word, the wonderful harmony of each of its parts which yet do not lose their organic unity, the whole musical "interpretation" of the text, and many other values are imperiled as soon as the Latin is replaced by another language. These considerations, which are not of the aesthetic order alone, certainly have their weight.[15] It would be difficult for any translation, even if it were the work of a great master, to retain all these qualities.

Let us not forget, however, that this loss of quality is accepted without hesitation in another and much more important domain: that of Holy Scripture. Into how many languages has it been translated? It is needless to insist on the similarities between the two cases. Is it not better to make the word of God available to the faithful in spite of a certain loss (the translated text no longer possesses the great privilege of being inspired!) than to preserve it un-understood in the original text? The same reasoning holds good for plain-chant, although with certain reservations.

The Latin text of the chants is generally just as incomprehensible to the Christians in the missions as is the Hebrew text of the psalms to the average European; frequently he cannot even pronounce the words exactly,[16] still less understand them. One cannot but be filled with

14. See the preceding chapter.
15. See the fine study of Urbanus Bomm in *Liturgisches Jahrbuch* 4 (1954), pp. 44-53.
16. It is sad that in spite of a great deal of trouble and many practices, our Christians in China do not sing *kyrie eleison*, but *Tschi-li-ai ai-lai-i-saun*, and not Amen, but *Ja-mong*, or *Ja-men*, etc. And the Chinese are not the only Christians who thus involuntarily mutilate Latin!

amazement when one thinks of the number of hours that the missionary — ordinarily overloaded with work — must devote to preparing a high Mass for a feast.[17] It is easy, then, to understand the desire that we expressed earlier,[18] begging our Mother the Church considerably to reduce the amount of Latin in her liturgy for the spiritual welfare of her children in the missions — and, a little also, for the love of the beautiful Latin language.

This desire does not run counter to the encyclical *Musicae Sacrae Disciplina,* which once more inculcates the use of Latin in the solemn celebration of the liturgy. This encyclical confirms the exceptions made up to the present time (for example, the "German High Mass") and only insists that these not be extended to other cases and other regions without the special authorization of the Holy See.[19] Furthermore, the encyclical contains very thought-provoking phrases: "What we have written thus far applies primarily to those nations where the Catholic religion is already firmly established. In mission lands it will not be possible to accomplish all these things until the number of Christians has grown sufficiently, large church buildings have been erected, the children of Christians properly attend schools established by the Church and, finally, until there is an adequate number of sacred ministers."[20] In other words, Rome understands very well the special difficulties of the missions, and requests along these lines might well be granted.

On the hypothesis of a less rigorous use of Latin, the missions would not abandon the Gregorian melodies which alone are capable of enabling our musical sensibilities to unite with those of non-Europeans. Plain-chant, even with a non-Latin text, always constitutes a means of access to the music of other peoples, and at the same time forms a bond between the various nations and races in the one Church; it will remain a most powerful bond uniting the whole *Una Catholica,* a symbol of the spirit of Pentecost which does not stifle the national genius of each people, but preserves it, enobles it, increases it beyond the narrow limits of one country in the vast domain of the universal Church. Thanks to these common melodies, whatever the diversity of tongues, the Catholic sense of the faithful will remain strong and watchful. The Gregorian melodies, even clothed with another language, will play the

---

17. The responses of the congregation in the Missa cantata call for some simplification. The simplest high Mass with plain-chant requires four different melodies for *Et cum spiritu tuo,* two for *Amen,* without mentioning the ferial tone and the solemn or more solemn tone for the Preface that influences the preceding responses.
18. See chapter 1, 3 and 4.
19. *Musicae Sacrae Disciplina,* N.C.W.C. trans. N. 47.
20. *op. cit.,* N. 50.

role of the second language of the Church, a kind of "musical Esperanto" enabling a stranger to take part in the worship of any community by knowing and understanding its singing.

It belongs to ecclesiastical authority to determine the extent to which the language of the people can replace Latin. In any case, we are inclined to understand in this sense the words of the Pope concerning exceptions to the law of Latin: " . . . where it is licit to use these exceptions, local Ordinaries and other pastors should take great care that the faithful from their earliest years should learn at least the easier and more frequently used Gregorian melodies, and should know how to employ them in the sacred liturgical rites, so that in this way also the unity and the universality of the Church may shine forth more powerfully every day."[21] Only, "where, according to old or immemorial custom, some popular hymns are sung in the language of the people after the sacred words of the liturgy have been sung in Latin during the solemn Eucharistic Sacrifice . . . (otherwise) the law by which it is forbidden to sing the liturgical words themselves in the language of the people remains in force."[22]

This same encyclical *strongly recommends the Gregorian melodies to missionaries,* when it exhorts the messenger of the Gospel to introduce into the missions both native music and the liturgical chants, and among these, Gregorian melodies (*Gregorianos modos*) "so that the people who are to be converted might be more easily led to accept the truths of the Christian religion by the attractiveness of these melodies."[23] Gregorian melodies with good translations or free adaptations of the original Latin text can satisfy, to a great extent, the needs of the missionary Church, especially where there are not yet enough indigenous hymns, or if it is necessary to fill the place left by the removal of unsatisfactory European hymns.

But when one takes the risk — and it is necessary to do so in the missions — of giving a different linguistic setting to the pearls of plainchant, there are certain *reserves and conditions* to be observed if our boldness is not to become mere temerity.

The first condition is *an outstanding knowledge of the language* into which the text is to be translated. Long familiarity with the language of daily speech is not a sufficient preparation for this difficult work. One must also know the sacred language of the people, the language of the poets and that of the people's songs, and be permeated with the genius of the national tongue; one must know how to distinguish shades

21. *op. cit.,* N. 46.
22. *op. cit.,* N. 47.
23. *op. cit.,* N. 71.

of meaning, so as to use a style that is neither too elevated — and so difficult for the people to understand — nor too common — that is, trivial and lacking in religious character. To exactness, good translating must unite dignity, beauty and appeal.

A second condition is *an intimate familiarity with Gregorian chant,* its melody, its rhythm, its manner of interpretation, its suppleness and its potentialities of adaptation. Antiphons, for example, often use the same melody for different texts and always with a new charm. The good translator must know how to make use of this quality, and yet not to abuse it so as to do violence to the melody. He will also make full use of the flexibility of Gregorian chant. The rules for psalmody in Hebrew (cutting the last notes of unstressed syllables) is a classic example of this. Should we be stricter with plain-chant than it is itself?

The third condition is that the translator be allowed a *certain flexibility.* With each difficulty that arises, he should ask himself in which direction he should seek the solution: in the text itself by a new choice of words, renouncing too literal a translation so as to expand the original text or compress it; or in the melody, by drawing out a musical phrase to fit the length of the text or by giving to two syllables in the vernacular version two notes that go with one syllable in the Latin? What relationship should he establish between the rhythm of the melody and that of the text? These are some of the questions that can only be adequately answered by someone with refined sensibilities both in the field of language and in that of music.

And, finally, a *good choice* must be made of the Latin texts to be translated. The responses and the "acclamations" of the Mass, such as *Amen, Et cum spiritu tuo, Habemus ad Dominum, Dignum et justum est, Deo gratias,* etc. as well as the *Kyrie eleison* do not need to be translated if they are explained in the course of catechism lessons or on other occasions, though it is necessary to take care that these formulas do not come to lack real meaning to the faithful. But even the *Agnus Dei,* and perhaps also the *Sanctus* with the *Benedictus,*[24] are more difficult to understand in Latin, even if the explanation is given aloud or in an interlinear translation. The need of vernacular texts is felt most urgently in the long chants, especially the *Gloria* and the *Credo.* The chants of the Proper that presume a trained schola are often omitted in mission countries (as is also frequently the case in Europe and America); if this practice spreads, at least we in the missions can refer to the encyclical *Musicae Sacrae Disciplina.* Thus a whole group of chants is eliminated, the translation of which is beset with many difficulties. There

---

24. We hope that some day these two chants will again be united, at least for compositions to be sung in unison.

remain the psalms, hymns and antiphons, the melodies of which, being simpler and more syllabic, can more easily be adapted to the language of the people. If the above conditions are observed, it is possible to reduce to a considerable extent the inconveniences inherent in any translation.

The example of Europe and of America, where some Gregorian chant in the vulgar tongue is already in use, shows that it is possible to go ahead on this road. In Germany and Austria, this practice is now well-established in official diocesan hymnbooks. In the missions, we already possess a book of Christian hymns for the Congo, entitled *Tukembila*. In 1953, the Chinese Jesuit, Joseph Yang, published a little book: *Hymni et Cantus sacri (King kene ye yao)*; with seventy-three hymns, about sixty of which are adaptations of liturgical chants with the original Gregorian melodies. This work was fairly well received even among Chinese of a most exquisite literary sense. Attempts along the same lines exist in other missions as well, for example in the dioceses of Japan. Translation, above all translation of the liturgical chants is a delicate affair; foreign missionaries who do not have the help of those born to the language cannot possibly solve the problem in a satisfactory way. We must, therefore, content ourselves with temporary solutions until from among the native Christians themselves there arise persons capable of producing definitive ones.

As to the question of the *number of chants,* a manual for use in the missions can include a good deal less than one for Europe or America; we need to be less anxious about the quantity than about satisfying real needs. As to the quality, the encyclical of Pius XII is quite clear on this point: religious hymns "must be in full conformity with the doctrine of the Christian faith. They must also express and explain that doctrine accurately. Likewise they must use plain language and simple melody and must be free from violent and vain excess of words. Despite the fact that they are short and easy, they should manifest a religious dignity and seriousness."[25] A good hymn is doctrinally rich, though not overladen; it is elevated and ardent, but not sentimental, so that it can be sung reverently by men, women and children alike.

Again, the choice of hymns should be made *on the basis of a certain hierarchy:* God, Christ, the cycle of His life, should predominate over hymns to the saints. Let us learn from the book of psalms, the book of the hymns of the Church herself, not to reduce too greatly the number of songs of praise, of gratitude, of confidence, of petition, etc.

When it is impossible to have a book actually printed, we can make

25. *Musicae Sacrae Disciplina,* N.C.W.C. trans. N. 63.

use of one of *the many simpler and cheaper means of reproduction.*
This is a good way of preparing for the later publication of a book, and
for getting new hymns widely known. Finally, when a hymnal is to
be printed, it can be combined with the official prayer book, as is done
in many dioceses in Europe.

This discussion has been centered on the question of *congregational
singing.* In the missions, the opportunities for cultivating *artistic singing*
are less numerous than in Europe or the United States: the congregations
often have few members, the missionaries and his aids have no time for
choir practices, polyphonic music is quite foreign to native Christians.
Nevertheless here and there in the missions, choral societies and children's
scholas do exist; in the seminaries, the art of music is frequently cultivated
with diligence and with success. To all these lovers of more perfect
music, the encyclical *Musicae Sacrae Disciplina* gives excellent directives.

The cultivation of liturgical chant will assure great advantages to
the missionary's pastoral ministry; to neglect it, on the other hand, will
be seriously harmful to this ministry, in Christian countries, and even
more in the missions. But the individual efforts of missionaries cannot
prosper unless their ecclesiastical superiors appreciate this work at its
real value. Thus Pius XII ends his encyclical, addressing the bishops:
"Moved by paternal solicitude, We have dealt with this matter at
some length. We are entirely confident that you, venerable brethren,
will diligently apply all of your pastoral solicitude to this sacred subject
which contributes so much to the more worthy and magnificent conduct
of divine worship."[26] We hope and pray that every missionary may
make his own the deep understanding of the important role of sacred
music in the worship of the Church and in her missionary work inculcated by Pius XII in this encyclical!

26. *op. cit.*, N. 80.

CHAPTER SIXTEEN

The Liturgical Arts in the Missions

JOHANNES HOFINGER, S.J.

In the German edition of this book, a special chapter on sacred art was not included, the editors contenting themselves with a brief mention of the subject in connection with the education of future missionaries. We felt ourselves justified in not treating sacred art *ex professo,* in spite of its missionary importance, for two reasons. The first was the fact that here and there the opinion still exists, in the missions as in home countries, that the liturgical renewal is primarily concerned with promoting the beauty of liturgical ceremonies. To dissipate this misunderstanding, it seemed wise to reduce to a minimum any discussion of the liturgical arts, since, while they could and should be handmaids to the liturgical renewal, they are not its primary concern. And our second reason was that for a fully effective discussion of this subject, good illustrations would be needed, but to include them would put the price of the book out of the reach of the missionaries for whom it is primarily written. And we were the more reconciled to omitting such a chapter, since we know that this subject involves various delicate questions which should not be touched on unless it is absolutely necessary.

Nevertheless, we now feel obliged to include a chapter on the liturgical arts in this English edition. Any study of the liturgical renewal obviously requires such a chapter in order to be at all complete. And — a far more compelling reason — present trends in missionary countries, as we now realize, categorically demand the reorientation and renewal of the liturgical arts, as they do of liturgical music. In order to clarify our discussion, it should be noted that we are not attempting to deal with the whole field of Christian art, but only with art in the service of public Christian worship; that is, with liturgical art as such.

196

Since it is above all the particular situation in the missions today which has determined our addition of this chapter, it seems best to begin with an examination of this situation.

What is the Condition of the Liturgical Arts in the Missions Today?

The answer to such a general question will, obviously, not be the same everywhere. But it can hardly be denied that even in the missionary countries that possess their own ancient and lofty traditions of religious art, a fairly low standard of Christian art is to be found, and that *very little has been done in the way of genuine adaptation* of indigenous tradition to Christian uses. This fact was emphasized recently by a competent authority in the field of sacred art, Msgr. Jérôme Malenfant, O.F.M.Cap., Apostolic Prefect of Gorakhpur, and Director of the Commission on Christian Art established by the Bishops' Conference of India. Msgr. Malenfant recently published a very significant article on "The Adaptation of the Liturgical Arts in India"[1], at the beginning of which he honestly answers our question:

"What is it that we wish to know concerning Christian art in India? What it actually is, or what it could be? I will answer mainly the second question, since the answer to the first is somewhat deceiving and I should prefer to pass over it. It would be better, in fact, to dissipate at one blow any illusions, however consoling they may be, that certain expositions in the Vatican and elsewhere and certain too optimistic articles or reports may have generated. True indigenous Christian art is, in India as in all missionary countries, as yet only a feeble seedling just beginning to bear its first flowers. Certainly, we can have great hopes for it, but up to the present, it has not had time to develop fully. We do possess in various countries a certain number of works of indigenous Christian art. But let us be honest, and recognize the fact that these are not always the work of native Christian artists; the majority has been done on command, for exhibition to foreigners. Such works of art are very rarely to be found in mission countries themselves, and still more rarely are they admitted into our churches. The native clergy, and Christians, and the majority of missionaries are often ignorant of their existence or else they categorically reject them."[2]

In explaining the chief reasons for this deplorable situation, Msgr. Malenfant first emphasizes the fact that converts from paganism often believe that they must not only abandon their pagan religion but also their traditional culture which they see to be so permeated with paganism.

1. Jérôme Malenfant, "L'Adaptation des Arts liturgiques en Inde," *Rhythmes du Monde,* 1957, 255-256.
2. *Op. cit.,* p. 255 ff.

"To this first difficulty is added the fact that certain colonizers, in pretending to 'civilize' the peoples of the East, brought in a flood of their own inferior productions, while they themselves made every effort to reproduce their own homes in these 'new' countries. In turn, the native peoples came to believe that to make themselves respected they must faithfully imitate the Westerners' way of life. So it came about quite naturally that clergy and faithful alike acted in the same way in the churches, and, in the domain of the liturgical arts as in that of 'objects of devotion,' the preference was given to products of European art.

"The majority of the missionaries, alas, allowed themselves to follow this same trend. Ignoring or neglecting the clear and repeated directives of the Holy See, they did not realize the fact that to implant the Christian faith in a country does not in any way mean to introduce the culture and customs of the West. This is the second reason why, in India as elsewhere, the local art has found no place in our churches."[3]

Msgr. Malenfant is aware, of course, of the promising efforts toward the development of indigenous sacred arts made in various missions. He himself mentions and recognizes the work done by modern Indian painters such as Angelo da Fonseca and Angela Trinidade. But he rightly points out the fact that these efforts are a first modest beginning, and also that it is only in rare cases that their products are intended for liturgical use.[4]

From Msgr. Malenfant's words, it is quite evident that he does not intend what he says to apply only to India, a country particularly rich in non-Christian religious art, but also to mission territories generally. And anyone who knows the situation from experience will hardly be tempted to oppose these statements. True enough, Msgr. Malenfant is speaking only of indigenous Christian art. But is the situation with regard to imported art in any better case? Can we say that this foreign art makes up by its high quality for what it lacks in suitability to the people's native genius and needs?

3. Op. cit., p. 258.
4. For more detailed information, Msgr. Malenfant refers to: L. Van den Bosche, "Les Arts en pays de missions," Coll. *Les Questions missionaires,* ed. Abbaye St.-Andre-Bruges (Belgium); P. J. Donoghue, S.M.A., "The Use of Native Culture in Missionary Work in Africa," *Worldmission,* 1956, 370-373. The hopeful aspect of promising Christian art in mission countries is given by Sepp Schüller in his books: *Christliche Kunst aus fernen Ländern,* Düsseldorf, 1939; *Neue christliche Malerei in Japan,* Freiburg, 1939; *Neue christliche Malerei in China,* Düsseldorf, 1940. Valuable material has also been published by *Liturgical Arts,* especially the fasc. on India, Nov. 1953, with contributions by Dayakishor, Leon Eberhard, Joseph Pereira, H. Heras, S.J., Angela Trinidade, and an introduction by His Eminence, Valerian Cardinal Gracias.

A sincere examination of the present situation forces us to admit at once that *imported Christian art* is, generally speaking, *of a very low artistic quality;* in fact, all too often it is positively unworthy to be called art at all in any sense of the word. This is especially true of the "art objects" produced in Western factories and sent out to the missions. An enormous amount of rubbish has been brought in, even from countries that have a great Christian tradition.

But even where the imported Christian art is of a relatively high standard and has been accepted by the people, it cannot be considered as being the genuine expression of their own mentality and way of life; and we should not deceive ourselves into thinking that it can become so. It always remains foreign, unnatural, even though the people are so accustomed to it that they believe they like it. The truth of this statement may be seen from the fact that even among mission peoples who are undoubtedly gifted in the field of art generally, there are extremely few Christian artists able to produce good work in Western styles. Even the Christian élite among these peoples, then, can at the best only accept and, perhaps, appreciate our Western art; they cannot create it themselves. Or again, we find educated Christians, not excluding seminarians and priests, often showing a remarkable lack of taste with regard to Western Christian art — for example, when seminarians choose pictures for their ordination cards, or when priests select sacred pictures, statues, and liturgical furnishings for their chapels. Nor can the lack of artistic training be held entirely responsible. This lack of taste results also from the fact that Western art is in no way the genuine expression of their own personal experience; they have no "feel" for what is good in it, and are therefore attracted simply to what shines the brightest and appeals most immediately to the senses.

This general picture of the condition of Christian art in missionary countries is not a consoling one. Certainly we missionaries of today are aware of our deficiencies in this field far more clearly than were our predecessors of a generation ago. And, in the era when colonialism was taken for granted, the question of the fostering of sacred art at once indigenous and truly Christian was not as vital as it is in our present era of independence, with its emphasis on native cultures. In the age of colonial imperialism, even the inferior products of the art of the Western conquerors were unquestioningly accepted as real art and admired as such, though they were not understood. This is no longer true. And today we have to reckon, not only with the new political situation and its cultural repercussions, but also with the new spirit in the arts themselves, valuing sincerity so highly, detesting and fighting so pitilessly against empty forms and soulless imitations.

All this makes an *examination and a reorientation of our attitude to the liturgical arts* in particular absolutely necessary. To neglect this demand of our times must sooner or later involve us in great difficulties in the carrying out of our missionary apostolate. The individual missionary, especially if he is working out in the "brush," the jungle, or is completely absorbed in the pastoral care of "old" Christians, may not yet be aware of its urgency. But this does not prove that it does not exist, and is becoming daily more pressing.

The Demands of the Liturgy Itself

What the present political and cultural developments in nearly all mission countries demand is, therefore, the cultivation of a religious art that is at once truly indigenous and truly Christian, together with the setting up of stricter standards of artistic quality for art objects in Western idioms that are sent from the home countries or produced in the missions. But we also should realize the fact that the liturgy itself lays down these same requirements.

Since liturgy is *"corporate"* worship, it requires the use, not only of men's souls, but of their bodies and material things as well. And since it is *worship,* it necessarily tends to attract to its service the most beautiful and skillful human making, since only the best can even begin to express man's reverence towards the infinite majesty of God, his gratitude for God's countless and priceless gifts. Even in non-Christian cults, this immanent tendency of corporate worship to make use of human arts has always been evident, and has effected at all times, among all peoples of any degree of culture, a deeply rooted *connubium* of religion and the arts. And this should be even more true of the liturgy of the Church, since it is the purest and loftiest idea of God's majesty that she communicates to her children, since she considers the visible world as "the work of His hands," and calls us, as God's beloved children, to praise Him for the grandeur and goodness that He manifests in this visible creation.

This does not mean, of course, that we Christians cannot do without great art in our worship. Christian worship is, finally, our filial adoration in spirit and in truth (John 4, 24), and as such is essentially independent of art — in the sense that it can be carried out perfectly in the extreme poverty of a missionary outstation and be lacking in a magnificent service carried out in a beautiful cathedral. Yet a truly Christian attitude makes us ready and eager to bring the service of the arts to aid our filial worship. Under any circumstances, genuine Christian reverence requires that we eliminate all insincere and unworthy rubbish from the service of the liturgy. And the true missionary spirit impels us to avail ourselves of all the natural gifts of the people among whom we are laboring, so that these too may take their place in the one great worship which the Word Incarnate offers to His Father in the Church. But this means that the liturgical arts must accord with the mentality and needs of each people.

This accord is required also for the development of truly active and personal participation by our faithful in the sacred mysteries, for the more the forms used in corporate worship are familiar to the people, are the genuine expression of their particular mentality, the easier it is for them to take their personal active part. Whatever makes the worshipping congregation feel more "at home" in carrying out a liturgical celebration, facilitates true participation. Moreover, we of the Latin rite have a special need to stress and to cultivate truly indigenous liturgical arts. Since, for weighty reasons, the possibilities of adapting the liturgical language and the rite itself to the mentalities of the various missionary peoples are quite restricted, the liturgical arts need to compensate in a special way for this rigidity. This may be one of the reasons why the ecclesiastical authorities favored indigenous liturgical arts even in periods when liturgical legislation itself was extremely cautious about any adaptation of the liturgical language and rite. For we can certainly say that if the cultivation of indigenous liturgical arts has been lacking in the missions, it is not the result of any unfavorable legislation, but of quite different causes.

In addition to this requirement of suitability to the particular culture of the worshipping congregation, true liturgical art must have other essential qualities, all derived, like that of suitability, from this one fundamental requirement: *liturgical art is functional.* Liturgical art can never be an end in itself: it is essentially a means. It exists for the service of worship. It is carrying out its proper function insofar as it really aids and fittingly expresses the genuine Christian worship of the community. As soon as this essential and unique task is neglected or forgotten, the arts become a hindrance to the liturgy and need to be reoriented toward their proper goal. Among various recent writers, J. A. Jungmann in particular has repeatedly pointed out what a great service rightly oriented art can render to Christian worship, and, equally, what a grave danger it can be when it goes astray. "Admittedly the arts do also constitute a danger for the liturgy. In art there seems to be a kind of centrifugal force, a tendency to break loose from the holy and humble service of divine worship and to become an end in itself. It is necessary, therefore, to return to the living principles of its proper use."[5] The harm that can be done by disoriented liturgical art is, obviously, all the greater in countries where external conditions have produced some kind of hypertrophy of sacred art — but this is hardly the case in the missions. On the other hand, it is especially important in the missions that whatever liturgical art is available should fully carry out its proper function. And this function is, specifically, to *profess and to proclaim* the Good News of salvation, just as the liturgy itself is our profession of faith and our proclamation of it in worship. This particular "proclaiming" is, above all, directed toward the faithful and carried out by them in prayer; it is not primarily a missionary proclamation to those outside the Church. It must, therefore, be intelligible to the praying community, and it must be the fitting and living expression of their faith. It must be the sacred art *of the community* and *for the community*.[6] This means, obviously, that the liturgical art used in any given church or chapel needs to accord with the particular genius of the national culture and its arts; but it also means that it should fit *the needs of the concrete congregation* for which it is intended. Especially in the missions, the concrete circumstances of a given community may necessitate variations from the general idiom of the national culture.

Like the liturgy itself, again, the liturgical arts are not called upon to proclaim simply something about the Christian faith, but "the" faith, the central mystery of our religion, the mystery of Christ that we proclaim and celebrate and re-enact in our Christian liturgy. Genuine liturgical art, therefore, needs concentration on the essentials of the Christian religion. This concentration does not necessitate of itself a high level of artistic talent or achievement. With the necessary religious understanding and good will, it can be assured without any great expense —that perennial missionary problem.

And yet such concentration is of the utmost missionary importance, both directly and indirectly. Indirectly, it assists greatly in the Christian formation of our faithful; directly, it communicates to nonbelievers a true notion of the Christian religion. It is both understandable and tolerable that our sanctuaries in the missions should be distinguished more for their poverty than for their wealth of art, but that they should so frequently exhibit an undeniable lack of religious concentration is deplorable. The great majority acquaint a visiting nonbeliever with many Christian devotions, but they seldom proclaim with sufficient

5. *Public Worship,* translated by Clifford Howell, S.J., Liturgical Press, Collegeville, Minn., pp. 6 ff. See also Jungmann's booklet on Liturgical Worship, New York, 1941, and "Church Art," *Worship,* 1955, 68-82.
6. J. A. Jungmann, *op. cit.,* p. 72.

emphasis "the" Christian mystery and its unequaled greatness — either to strangers or to the faithful. This lack of true Christian concentration in the liturgical arts certainly is connected closely with the same deficiency in our preaching. And so we can hope that the return to the necessary concentration in preaching, so characteristic of the renewal of both Christian preaching and Christian art in the home countries, will be fully effective in the missions also. This concentration will bring it about that the altar itself is given more importance than the altar furnishings and altarpiece; the baptistry than the statues of saints, etc. It will, above all, unite us with the Christ of glory, through Whom, in Whom and with Whom all our Christian worship rises up to the Father.

How May the Desired Progress in the Liturgical Arts be Promoted?

It is not enough, obviously, to deplore the poor condition of sacred art in the missions nor to point out what the liturgical arts should be and, alas, are not at the present time. We must also try to indicate what can and should be done here and now in order to improve. The following suggestions, as we well know, are not exhaustive or complete, but they do at least deal with points that are of special importance at the present time.

Let us do everything in our power to stop both *the importing and the producing of rubbish*. How can this be done? In relation to the *imports* from his home country, the poor missionary finds himself frequently in a very difficult situation. In his poverty, he is most grateful for the generous help of his benefactors and he cannot, in fact, do without it. But, as experience shows, mission-minded generosity is not necessarily combined with good taste and a real understanding of the situation in the missions. But this difficulty might be reduced to a bearable minimum if the mission bureaus of the various missionary Societies were to possess this good taste and understanding, and help us influence our benefactors in the right direction. As a rule, it is much more helpful (and economical), rather than to send ready made objects of art to the missions, to give the money to have them made in the missions. This procedure favors the development of the liturgical arts in the missions, it makes it possible for the missionary to get what is really suited to his needs. Moreover, for the amount of money which, in his home country, could buy only mass produced objects of poor taste and poor workmanship, he could not infrequently in the missions obtain quite good products of indigenous craftsmanship.

Concerning the *production* in the missions of objects of liturgical art, we must admit that up to the present time it has imitated to a great extent the bad taste of the imported rubbish; this is true not only of manufactured articles, but also to a shameful degree of handmade products as well. In the missions, as in the home countries, there are not a few orphanages and convents making a living by producing religious articles. In general, such work shows considerable technical skill combined with poor taste. But these centers could do much to develop indigenous liturgical arts if their leaders and directors had the necessary artistic and liturgical training. Would it not be possible for the diocesan commissions for sacred arts, which in the missions as elsewhere are supposed to be established and really functioning in every diocese, to insist effectively on a better artistic formation of these directors and teachers?

But in this field, as in others, the kind and the quality of the products depend above all on the taste and the demands of the customers. Let us, then, *promote the production of true and worthy sacred art through a better formation of the most important customers* in this field, the missionaries themselves.

Very little has been done in the past about a better aesthetic formation of future missionaries. The instruction of the Holy Office *De Arta Sacra*[7] asks for the solid formation of future priests in the field of sacred art. Missionaries, both foreign and indigenous, need such formation even more than do priests in the home countries. But it would not require a lengthy special course in sacred art: the necessary theory could be included in the liturgical courses or given in some condensed lectures, perhaps in the latter part of the summer vacations (which in the missions are mainly spent in the seminary). More important than special lectures on sacred art is the formation of really good taste. The missionary may never have the opportunity to buy a work of great art; he has to learn how to make good use of what is available. He does not need to know names and dates in history of art, but he does need to possess the educated good taste by which he can manifest in his very poverty both religious reverence and human cultivation. And, obviously, the essential prerequisite for this education in good taste is training in order and cleanliness.

Such education must begin long before the time of the major seminary. Everything that the students see about them in the seminary, and especially in its chapel, from the time they begin their formation, the way they design and celebrate festivities, etc., should aid and not hinder this education. And we need not only to show them many works of art, at least in good reproductions, but also to indicate why a given

7. *Acta Ap. Sed.* 1952, pp. 542-546.

work of art is beautiful and why another is not. Moreover here, as in the field of sacred music, we need to awaken the students in the home countries to appreciate the art of traditions other than their own, and to give them some awareness of the universal criteria of all true art, and the special criteria of Christian liturgical art.

The studies known as "the humanities" should, of course, assist greatly in this formation, provided that together with the letter we manage to communicate the true humanistic spirit. And, if we thoroughly imbue the students with the spirit of the liturgy itself, this will prove of even greater assistance. In the liturgy, we not only learn how to pray, but we are given an effective training in good taste and the true sense of beauty. There is no doubt that one of the major causes of the lack of good taste to be found among the pious faithful and even the clergy is the neglect of the liturgy and its spirit.

It may seem strange at first glance that the native clergy in mission countries are often found to be quite reserved about, or even strongly opposed to, the use of indigenous forms and techniques in liturgical art, especially in painting. One reason for this opposition is the proper feeling that first attempts along these lines are generally immature products showing more good will than artistic perfection. In this case the opposition comes from good taste and a real sense of fitness, although it may be that such opponents expect too much from what must be beginnings. And another cause of opposition along the same lines may come from people of trained taste who feel that native styles and techniques are being wrongly used, or have not been truly Christianized and so carry the wrong connotations, as can so easily happen in the case of liturgical music also when a Western artist attempts to use indigenous Eastern materials. But there are many other cases in which the opposition comes simply from insufficient education in the field of art; such people simply do not recognize the poor quality of the Westernized Christian art in their mission, and they treasure it because they are used to it. The only way of solving this particular problem is by improving the education both in art and in liturgy given in the seminaries, and throughout the whole educational system as well.

But we also need a better training for Christian artists. There have as yet been very few Christian artists in the missions, either native or foreign. In many places, there are no first-class artists and, perhaps, none even of second rank, only a few dilettantes, some untrained enthusiasts, and a group of skillful artisans. As in the case of indigenous sacred music, we cannot command or produce true artists at will. But we can and should at least give a better formation than at present to the aspiring talents we possess. They should be encouraged and enabled to study the artistic traditions and the modern trends in their own country; they should be able to receive training and inspiration from the leading native artists of their country. But if they desire to produce work that will be truly liturgical art, they need to be, as a necessary prerequisite, thoroughly imbued with the spirit of the liturgy and to study the special function of their particular art in relation to the whole work of Christian worship. Thus, and thus only, can liturgical artists succeed in truly serving the worshiping Church.

The recommendation is often made today that laymen also should be encouraged to go out to mission countries to aid in the missionary apostolate. Might not this field of liturgical art be one in which lay missionaries could be especially useful and carry out a greatly needed work? A layman, who was himself a trained and practicing artist, would be in a much better position in many cases than a priest or religious to make the right contacts with native artists and native trends in art, and to lead them to the service of Christian worship. But it goes without saying that such an artist-missionary would need himself to be imbued with the spirit of liturgy, or he would do more harm than good.

In addition to the elimination of junk, and to the better formation of customers and artists alike, we also need *a more effective guidance* on the part of the ecclesiastical authorities. As we have already mentioned, the instruction of the Holy Office concerning sacred art (June 30, 1952) requires the formation of a special commission on sacred art in each diocese. The instruction supposes that, in addition to these diocesan commissions, there exist metropolitan commissions outstanding for the special qualifications of their members. In the missions, this would mean the establishment of a special commission of sacred art on the national level in each country. How important their task would be may be seen from the article by Msgr. Malenfant, referred to above, who is himself the director of such a commission in India.

"In January, 1950, the Plenary Council of Bangalore, basing its action on the pontifical directives and making them explicit so far as was possible, indicated courageously the path that should be followed in working toward a prudent renewal and reorientation of the liturgical arts in India. Drawing their inspiration from a resolution of the same council, the permanent Conference of the Indian Hierarchy instituted, at its meeting in October, 1953, a Commission of Christian Indian Art.

"The role of this Commission consists in sounding out the opinion of the Indian clergy and faithful; in striving to orient it gradually in the direction desired by the Holy See and by our bishops; in studying, with the aid of persons competent in this field and in consultation with Indian priests and with foreigners working in the missions, what it is actually possible and desirable to do here and now, while always preparing for the future. We endeavor to guide and encourage artists, to foster new talents, and, above all, to awaken the interest of the clergy of tomorrow in our Indian seminaries and houses of study, and also to arouse the interest of the most influential section of the Catholic public by means of circulars, talks, scholarly journals, exhibitions. We are as yet poorly supplied both as to personnel and means. But a certain changing of opinion and some perceptible progress can be noticed from year to year."[8]

If everyone working in this field could say as much, how bright the future would be for the order and beauty of the houses of God all over the world and for the integrity and fullness of the worship offered to the Father through Christ by His children of all races and nations!

---

8. Malenfant, *op. cit.*, p. 266.

PART FIVE

The Administration of the Sacraments

CHAPTER SEVENTEEN

The Celebration of the Baptismal Rites

JOHANNES SEFFER, S.J.

It is said of certain Christian communities in the missions that they are aware of only one sacrament, that of Baptism. This obvious exaggeration nevertheless brings out the fact that, in isolated places where the people see their priest but seldom and are not too thoroughly instructed in Christian doctrine, many have a great esteem for Baptism and are proud of having received it. It is Baptism that unites them with the Church and separates them from their pagan surroundings. Yet it must be said that, apart from the Mass itself, no liturgical action needs more adaptation to modern conditions than does the Rite of Baptism. Baptism lays the foundation of the Christian life and is truly the cornerstone of the Church's liturgy; thus the teaching given by Baptism should be that of the basic Christian message. This sacrament, which is in a special way the sacrament of the missions, should be the visible sign of the great love of God Who adopts us as His children in Christ; at the same time, it should commit us to a progressively more perfect Christian life, the response of our grateful love to the divine invitation. It is, therefore, desirable above all that the Rite for the Baptism of Adults be better adapted to present needs, without excluding the possibility of some reform in that for the Baptism of Children as well.

All through the ages, the Church has always been concerned with giving the greatest possible degrees of effectiveness to the Baptismal initiation. She teaches that the degree of grace received depends in part on the dispositions of the candidate, and she therefore desires to arouse in him those interior attitudes which will allow the fullest scope to these "opera operantis." The ceremonies accompanying the essential rite of Baptism were, therefore, designed to awaken the understanding in

211

the candidate of the grace given by Baptism, and arouse his will so as to ensure the most fruitful possible reception of it. And by means of these ceremonies the Church desired also to strengthen and direct the candidate's will so that the reception of the sacrament would be the true beginning of a wholly new Christlike life. It is obviously necessary, then, that the ceremonies of Baptism be so arranged as not only not to hinder the work of God, but as to carry out fully once more their function as the sign of the grace of Baptism itself.

But what is the state of affairs today? An enquiry among missionary circles would certainly show great discontent with regard to the present baptismal ceremonies. In the face of the danger to our missions presented on the one hand by Protestant revivalism and the easy victories of the various eschatological sects with their forceful baptismal symbolism, and on the other by the alluring manifestations of expanding materialism making use of all the modern means of mass communication, we must re-examine our apostolic methods, and especially the liturgy itself. The privileges that Rome has already granted to many countries in Europe and America are a pledge of the Church's motherly understanding of the needs of her missionaries.

The Chief Difficulties

The greatest difficulty, without any doubt, is *the exclusive use of Latin as the liturgical language.* If we strictly observe the rubrics forbidding any explanation of the ceremonies while they are going on, we cannot help the catechumens' being simply bored by the rite instead of being filled with happiness and rejoicing by the mystery of their rebirth to the life of God. To prove the truth of this statement, it is quite sufficient to look at the expressions on the faces of those present at a Baptism — the candidates themselves, the godparents, relations, friends, who in reverent boredom go through the formalities. Instead of being the wonderful initiation that it should be, Baptism too often becomes a mere ceremony that people have performed over them because it is customary. There is no true dialogue between the minister and the recipient of Baptism, but rather a monologue, incomprehensible to those present, in which the priest generally asks the questions and gives the answers. How can Baptism conferred in this way seem to be what it is: the conferring of a share in the life of the God of truth and love? In our days also, God wishes to reveal Himself to us in and through the liturgy. It should be truly a "locutio Dei attestans," God speaking to men, and this presupposes that the hearers are really listening to Him. But in Baptism as it is today, the people do not hear enough, or if they do, they understand hardly anything of what God is saying to them.

A second difficulty is the *length of the ceremonies*. A missionary, especially when he visits his isolated communities, must be economical with his time, and therefore usually prefers, where this is allowable, to use the shorter rite for the Baptism of Children, thus losing a valuable pastoral opportunity. Actually the ceremonies at the beginning of the rite were not designed as part of the rite of the sacrament itself; they were meant to mark progressive stages in the catechumenate in preparation for Baptism. These have been added on to the essential rite; and the result is that the whole is not only far too long, but poorly proportioned and, therefore, hard to explain. These preliminary ceremonies take far too great a place in the whole, to the detriment of the essentials that occupy only a short length of time at the end.[1] It would be most desirable, therefore, to effect some shortening of the ceremonies so as to bring out the essential structure.[2]

Proposals for Reform

The principles of a sound reform are the same for any of the rites of the liturgy, whether it be that of the Mass or of one of the sacraments. In this domain above all we owe a deep and filial respect to our holy Mother, the Church, a respect which should cause us to approach the ceremonies of her age-old past with prudence and discernment. The principles that would allow a healthy and lasting reform to be made consist above all in rearranging, in revising and in giving a better mutual proportion to the existing ceremonies and prayers.

The proposals that we would respectfully bring forward, therefore, for a reform of the Rite for the Baptism of Adults fall under two headings. The first, without any doubt, is *the use of the mother tongue*. It seems to be an absolute necessity that the candidate should understand the prayers and the rites that concern him. The various expedients used to get around this major difficulty are only somewhat better than

1. The lack of proportion between the essential rite and the preliminary ceremonies has been clearly presented by A. Stenzel in *Lit. Jarhbuch* 3, 1953, p. 316 ff. In this article is also to be found a good description of the main lines of the historical causes for this state of affairs; these were at once the progressive devaluation and the final downfall of the catechumenate.
2. When Baptism is to be administered at the Easter Vigil, the preliminary ceremonies may be carried out on Good Friday morning, according to the Instruction, *De Ordine Hebdomadae Sanctae instaurato rite peragendo*, n. 14. Since these ceremonies are thus permitted to be separated from Baptism, why not give them back their early significance as the entrance to, and progressive stages in, the catechumenate, as we are proposing in this chapter?

nothing; the solution of giving everyone present an explanatory booklet is hardly practicable in countries where many people are still illiterate. The use of Latin is, in fact, such a great obstacle to Baptism's once more becoming a true initiation into the Christian life, that any effective reform must do something to remedy it. The missionary should be given back the opportunity to speak to his people through these wonderful baptismal prayers, allowing them to explain in their own unequaled fashion the doctrine of this great sacrament. The sacramental formula itself, to which is attached the *ex opere operato* power of the sacrament, could well be retained in Latin, so as to signify that Baptism is the great sacrament of unity, incorporating the neophyte into the one and indivisible body of Christ: "One Lord, one faith, one Baptism, one God and Father of all" (Eph. 4, 5).[3]

The second proposal is the *distribution of the preliminary ceremonies over the whole period of the catechumenate*.[4] As things are, these ceremonies seem to be mere additions, out of proportion to the central rite. Why, then could they not be again separated from this central rite, and so regain their true value as the liturgical steps in a progressive initiation? This would, furthermore, give a new interest to the catechumenate, which has to such a great extent now lost its original significance. In many missions, it has become primarily a catechism course for adults; the systematic course of instruction by itself is often discouraging to the Oriental mentality, which needs to be attracted more by reasons appealing to the heart than arguments addressed to the mind. What would be better, then, than to give them also the liturgical means by which their religious personality could be formed at the same time? A progressive liturgical initiation would support and sustain the personal efforts of our catechumens who so often become disheartened in the face of the length and dryness of the formation now given. The missionary is often tempted to shorten the trial and to admit such people to Baptism too early, at the risk of having them soon turn into apostates. The solution to the present problem would be to mark their progressive initiation by giving the exorcisms at set intervals over a period of several months, while allowing a sufficiently long time to elapse before allowing the candidates to be baptized. In certain missions, in China for example, there already exists a paraliturgy in which the catechumens, after several months of faithful attendance at the catechism classes and at the religious

3. This desire for the use of the vernacular in the baptismal rites has already been granted in the *Collectio Rituum* for the dioceses of the United States, in that for all the dioceses of Germany, in the new French ritual, etc. See chapter XXIV, p. 282 ff., on this whole question.
4. See A. Stenzel, *Lit. Jahrbuch* 3, 1953, p. 316 ff.

exercises of the Christian community, make a solemn promise to continue their way to God and to enter the Church by receiving Baptism. But it would seem far better to revive the successive stages of the catechumenate as the various exorcisms in the baptismal liturgy would easily allow them to be reconstructed.

The First Step: Solemn Admission to the Catechumenate

Corresponding to the first exorcism in the present ritual for the Baptism of Adults, there could be reintroduced a solemn ceremony of admission to the catechumenate. In the early Church, the first step towards admission into the Christian community was the official reception by the Church into the catechumenate. This initiation gave the right to take part in certain Christian assemblies and in the so-called "Mass of the catechumens." It would be easy to revive such a ceremony, and it would show the newcomer that he was being welcomed and taken charge of by his new family. As things are, too often he feels himself to be an outsider with whom the authorities are concerned only as a new member of an organization, and he is ill at ease during the liturgical mysteries into which he has not been properly initiated and at which he is allowed to be present too soon. Many leave the catechumenate who might not have done so if they had been welcomed in a more solemn and progressive way. It is too easy today for people to enter the Church as if it were a public hall, and this is why they also leave the catechumenate as if it were a mere course of lectures open to anyone. And, furthermore, we should not forget that the pagans who come to us have a ritual idea of religion and are looking for some formal introduction above all into liturgical worship. Let us then give them the opportunity to take part as soon as possible in ceremonies made especially for them.

This solemn reception could take place two or three months after the arrival of the candidate. He would thus have time to prove the seriousness of his intentions and to prove his good will by faithfully following the catechism course. The Gelasian sacramentary of the fifth and sixth centuries could serve as a starting point for such a ceremony. After an *introductory dialogue* which would be not only an enquiry about the candidate himself and his intentions, but also an exhortation on the obligations resulting from the new state to which he is pledging himself, there might come a ceremony in which the candidate places his clasped hands in the hands of the priest, as is done by a newly ordained priest when he promises obedience to his bishop. The symbolism is clear: it signifies the first self-commitment of the catechumen to the Church and his being taken charge of by her. More meaningful even than the handclasp which expresses more particularly friendship and confidence, this handing over of one's joined hands is the medieval gesture of the vassal taking oath to serve his lord, who in turn engages himself to protect him. This liturgical gesture, which the Christian will frequently make thereafter when he recollects himself and prays, would then always remind him of his first commitment to God and His Church.

The *imposition of hands* which should follow would signify the gesture of the authority of the Church, taking the candidate in charge and assuring him of her maternal protection against the attacks of the devil and of the world. This benevolent taking charge by the Church would be manifested also in the wonderful gift that She gives the new candidate, the gift of the "Good News." This would be symbolized by the *handing to the candidate of the book of the Sacred Scriptures;* the godparent could have a New Testament or at least the Gospels ready to be solemnly presented by the priest.[5] This could be accompanied by the *rite of insufflation* recalling the breath of life received by Adam on the day of his creation and signifying the gift of the Spirit of Christ enabling the candidate to understand the Scriptures. If the rite of *giving the blessed salt* should be retained, it should certainly be placed here. For it is by judging people and events according to the norms of Sacred Scripture that the candidate is to make a new criterion for living, a criterion which will give to everything in his life the Christian flavor of the true salt of Wisdom.

To prolong the good influence of this first initiation, one or other of the foregoing rites could be repeated during the months that follow. The solemn reading of the Gospel during the catechism lessons would be a useful reminder of the reception of the Scriptures, and it would be easy for the priest to give his blessing in the form of the imposition of hands. To sum up, this ceremony would without any doubt help the catechumen to feel himself from the very beginning a member of the Christian family, not indeed a perfect member as yet, but a child already living in the maternal womb of the Church.

The Second Step: the Calling

The second step would be the selection of the candidates who are to be directly prepared for Baptism. This would correspond to the ancient rite of inscribing the initiates on the list of the "Chosen," preceding the intensive course of preparing for Baptism. By this ceremony, the catechumens become "Chosen," *illuminandi, competenti,* or "postulants." In other words, they have taken a definitive step in their

---

5. The solemn rite of former times, as it is described by J. Pascher, *Die Liturgie der Sakramente,* Münster, 1951, p. 46 ff, would be quite impractical for the missions and even for the average parish in America or Europe.

journey towards the new land of promise. To revive this ceremony today would have the advantage of arousing the fervor of the catechumens before beginning the last stage preceding baptism. Lent would be the ideal time for this preparatory retreat, but where the candidates are too numerous to be baptized all together during the Easter Vigil, one group could be prepared during Lent and the others divided into groups to be baptized on the feasts of Pentecost, Christmas and Epiphany, as in former days. The norms of selection would remain as they are in the majority of missions: besides the ability to recite the principal Christian prayers, and the understanding of essential doctrine, there should also be inquiry into the life of the postulant and his practice of his religion; only on this basis can a proper choice of candidates be made. The emphasis should be on the privilege of being "called," bringing with it the right to be officially a catechumen of the Church, and to be admitted to various liturgical ceremonies. And this would undoubtedly awaken a greater generosity in the candidate's response to divine grace.

The ceremony would begin with *the solemn reception at the door of the church* of the candidates accompanied by their godparents. There would be a public questioning on the intentions of those seeking admission and of their knowledge of the prayers and of some important doctrines. The imposition of the sign of the cross would follow, imitating the imposition of the *sphragis*. When the priest has made the sign of the cross on the candidate's forehead, this might be repeated by his godparents. The *Ephpheta* would conclude this part of the ceremony. (As it exists today, this ceremony is anachronistic by reason of the multiplicity of signings made by the priest. These correspond to a custom that has disappeared: the bishop who was administering Baptism was assisted by priests and deacons who all signed the candidate after the Bishop himself, as at ordinations today when the priests present impose their hands on the candidates' heads after the Bishop has done so.) The imposition of the sign of the cross might be accompanied by an imprecatory prayer corresponding to the responses given by the candidate. To the assertion that he desires henceforth to renounce Satan, the world, and sin, the priest would explain to him the obligations that he was now assuming and would officially entrust him to his godparents, asking them truly to take charge of their protégé.

The solemn "traditio" of the Apostles' Creed and of the Our Father would mark the climax of the ceremony. This would symbolize the maternal role of the Church whom Christ has entrusted to transmit His message of life. A final exhortation would encourage the "Chosen" to make progress in the knowledge and the service of God, and the whole ceremony could be concluded by a hymn of thanksgiving.

In the time that followed before Baptism, one or other blessing or the imposition of the cross could be repeated over the candidates. During the retreat immediately preparatory to Baptism, it might be suggested to the candidates that they make an extra-sacramental confession for which they should be carefully prepared in order to arouse in them true contrition for their sins; this, together with a sincere desire to receive Baptism could have most salutary effects. This prebaptismal confession, if it were repeated on occasion, would also accustom the catechumens to a procedure which would then be less difficult for them after Baptism.

The Final Step: Administration of Holy Baptism

The third and final step would obviously be the administration of Baptism itself. As we said earlier, this should take place on the great feasts, preferably at Easter. Care should be taken to make this as solemn a community celebration as possible. After *the entrance in procession* into the church, the ceremony of *making the baptismal promises* would follow the public renunciation of Satan, his works and pomps. This would mark the definitive and total commitment of the candidates to their new Leader and new family. This self-donation would be confirmed by the anointing with *the oil of catechumens* recalling the strengthening anointing once given to athletes before their struggles. Immediately afterwards, *the administration of Baptism* would take place, with the greatest possible solemnity and reverence. The *anointing with holy Chrism* and the *clothing with the baptismal* robe would follow as in the present rite. These ceremonies could be brought out more fully than when, as at present, they come at the end of a rite already too lengthy. The anointing should be a real anointing, and the robe a real garment and not some kind of cloth. The *giving of the lighted candle* to the neophyte would regain its full meaning if the ceremony were held during the Easter Vigil, which is without any doubt the special feast of Baptism. If for any reason the ceremony has to take place at some other feast, it would seem desirable to repeat the blessing of the baptismal water with formulas recalling those of Holy Saturday, for they contain such a wonderful catechesis on baptism that it would be a great loss to omit them.

We can regret the fact that for various reasons of convenience and modesty, any real baptismal immersion has given place to ablution, for it is far more difficult to explain the mystery of death and resurrection in Christ from the symbolism of the present practice. Might it not be hoped that in this regard the Church might grant a certain liberty here to the missions? It would not be difficult to administer Baptism by immersion as it is carried out by various Baptist sects in warm climates. There is nothing really inconvenient about it, and modesty is completely safeguarded. But in any case, as things are, let us at least make it a real baptismal ablution, and take care that the lifegiving waters really flow over the head of the candidate.

The Baptism of Children

Today in the missions we use three different forms of the rite for the Baptism of children. *Solemn Baptism* conferred by the missionary could have a catechetical value similar to that of the Baptism of an adult, if only the ceremonies were carried out in the language of the people in the presence of the community, and the present rites were simplified along the lines we have suggested for the Baptism of adults. The existing rites could be simplified and, above all, rearranged so as to bring out their essential structure, and at the end of the ceremonies an admonition to the godparents could be added. This would explain to them in simple language the obligations flowing from the sacrament and the vocation conferred of living henceforth as a Christian, as well as the responsibilities of the Church towards her new child. This talk would also show them the seriousness of the responsibilities undertaken by godparents to watch over the religious and moral formation of their godchildren.

Simple Baptism in danger of death poses no problems of adaptation, for the Church has here already made all possible concessions.

Simple Baptism where there is no danger of death is relatively frequent in isolated communities which the priest can visit only seldom in the course of a year. In practice, it is administered by the leader of the Christian community or by the catechist who has been duly instructed in how to do so. Would it not be possible, according to the judgment of the Ordinary or the local hierarchy to determine a certain degree of solemnity that might be used in these cases? For example, after an introductory prayer, the renunciation of Satan and the baptismal promises might be recited by the godparents, since this should be required even for simple baptism. Then Baptism could be conferred in the language of the people, if need be, and the ceremony concluded with a final prayer.

The reforms that are to be desired in solemn Baptism would have a normal repercussion on the "supplying of the ceremonies" for children baptized *extra formam* in danger of death, which is of frequent occurrence in the missions especially. The problem which now shocks any missionary with a living sense of the liturgy is that of having to repeat over a little Christian the ceremonies which make sense only for a pagan, a child of wrath. Nothing seems more out of keeping than to carry out these exorcisms on a child of God. If one can understand the imposition of the sign of the cross and of the salt, one is completely puzzled by the need to recite the various imprecatory prayers to drive away the devil who has already been driven out by the sacrament. It is, therefore, greatly to be hoped that this supplying of the ceremonies be adapted to the very special case of a baptized baby. And if these ceremonies were adapted to the reality and were no longer simply the more or less formalistic ritual complement to the sacrament already given, they also would have a real catechetical value for the Christian community.

CHAPTER EIGHTEEN

Instruction in the Sacrament of Baptism

Johannes Seffer, s.j.

"Go into the whole world and preach the Gospel to every creature. He who believes and is baptized shall be saved, he who does not believe shall be condemned" (Mark 16, 15-16). From these words, it is clear that, together with the announcement of the Good News for salvation in Christ, the conferring of Christ's life in Baptism is a climax of missionary activity. It should assure the final breaking away from error and sin of those who were pagans, and their introduction into the new life in Christ. Consequently, it is of the utmost importance that they should take this crucial step in a way befitting its character. The final preparation of our catechumens for Baptism, therefore, should call forth our best efforts as educators and witnesses to God's love.

The question here is not merely one of instruction designed to give a clear concept of the sacrament, but of an effective initiation into the divine mystery which it signifies. In order that this basic change, this conversion, should not be a chance and ineffectual event, but the true beginning of a whole new life, when our converts receive the Sacrament of Baptism the *metanoia* should already have begun. For this, a merely theoretical course is entirely insufficient. Clear concepts enlivened by grace assist the act of faith, but the liturgy is indispensable if this basic response of faith to God's message and God's love is to become the formative principle of a new way of life. Rightly lived, the liturgy of the sacraments itself is the best introduction into the life that they give us. Celebrated with reverence and fitting splendor, it not only unfolds a clear concept of the mystery represented, but also gives the inspiration imparted by grace that is required for transforming one's life. The liturgy goes beyond a simple explanation, and creates a space enfolding not only the intellect, but the feelings and the will awakened by an understanding of the symbolic rites and the accompanying prayers. This liturgical experience corresponds to the "audio-visual" methods advocated today to make real, and give a vital understanding of, abstract concepts. But too often we tend, in our instruction on the ceremonies of Baptism, to concern ourselves only with teaching our catechumens how to go through them properly, excusing ourselves on the grounds that these ceremonies cannot be easily explained. Rather than making doctrine visible and comprehensible, we say, these ceremonies conceal it. But this is not true. It is quite possible to explain the significance of the main ceremonies in such a way that they themselves will once more serve the purpose for which they were designed by the Church, illuminating the great themes of baptismal instruction in their own way, from a new aspect. As an aid in giving such explanations, the following suggestions may prove of value.

To lead our catechumens into the mystery of Baptism, we must present the Christian message in all its purity and power. Baptism is eminently the sacrament of man's salvation through becoming "Christened," binding us to the Father, through Christ, in the Spirit, making us new men, and introducing us into the glorious vocation of becoming "other Christs." This *Christian vocation* is presented in the liturgy of Baptism as being the invitation to die with the crucified Christ and to rise again from the grave to divine life with Christ. These two *motifs* are repeated in all the main ceremonies. The first of these is the entrance into the Church, signifying the approach to the Christian Mystery, to the Church, to the Mystical Body of Christ, to the new family of the children of God. The second is the signing with the cross and the various exorcisms, signifying the freeing of the soul from the life of slavery to sin, and its commitment to God, the Author of true life. The third is the climax of the rite, the washing, plunging the soul into the death and resurrection of the Redeemer, the new birth to divine life, the life of God's children. The baptismal formula, finally, signifies the free and unconditional consecration of the candidate to the Most Holy Trinity. We can order the various accompanying ceremonies around these three main ones, and show how everything brings out the central theme of death to sin and rebirth to divine life.

Entering into the Church

Entering into the Church is the first symbol to be given a detailed explanation. It is carried out in three stages: the first is the welcome at the threshold of the church, the second is the entering into the church building, the third, the entrance into the baptistry from whence the neophyte is to come out to take part in the assembly of the children of God.

It is easy to show our catechumens how these various entrances are more and more urgent calls to separate ourselves from, that is, to die to, the life of sin, going through death to the life of the risen Christ. This "passing through" is one of the great themes of Holy Scripture. The candidate presents himself at the threshold of the Church like Noah before the ark that was to save him. Like him, he has been chosen from amongst a multitude by the grace of the Lord who has sent his angel, the priest, to draw him out of perdition. He has been invited by the new Moses to come out of the country of slavery; he is, as the parable says, the invited guest at the royal wedding feast who has accepted the divine invitation. This first step toward Life presupposes the abandonment of a pagan life, of once cherished habits, and perhaps, of both family and social relationships. But if he must leave a world that is dear to him, it is in order to find the promised land, paradise regained.

He should, then, answer joyfully to the calling of his name, singing in his heart the mercies of the Lord. Another prodigal son who has decided to return to his Father, he should generously leave behind his life of sin in order to come back to his Father's house. He should be truly converted and turn his back once and for all on the night of sin, as did the wise virgins on the threshold of the wedding feast.

The admission into the church symbolizes a journey that is a testing. A time of probation separated the exorcisms from one another in the early Church and allowed the authorities to make sure of the sincerity of each conversion. After choosing His elect, God arranges for a time of trial in order to strengthen, by means of successive victories over temptation, the faith, hope and love of His friends. The death to the "old man" in Baptism must be continued by lifelong mortification. It is only by journeying across the desert of Sinai that the chosen people attained the promised land: it is in the midst of temptations and trials that the new chosen people of God must journey with Christ towards heaven. Let the candidate take courage and know that he is not alone in his troubles: Christ says to him: "Fear not . . . for it has pleased the Father to give you the kingdom" (Luke 12, 32).

The entrance into the baptistry opens out into the banquet hall to which the candidate will be admitted after he has put on the wedding garment. This last door that the initiate is to cross is the gate of Christ's sheepfold, the entrance into the promised land across the new Jordan. It is the entrance into the tomb where Christ awaits His chosen one in order to cause him to die to sin, which opens out on the joy of Easter. At the time of taking this last step, how the candidate should strive to intensify in his soul a profound contrition for all the sins of his past life and a desire to be intimately united with the living Christ!

The signings with the cross, connected with the various exorcisms, are the second group of rites to be explained at length. Here again we find the same motifs of death and resurrection with Christ. These signings are the symbol of the character or *sphragis,* the seal of Christ, which the sacrament will stamp upon the soul of the baptized. No other rite so well serves the purpose of striking the senses in such a way as to awaken the spirit as does this, the *signatio,* one of the most ancient of them all. Originally it consisted simply of the sign of the cross made on the forehead of the candidate, but it has been developed in a most meaningful way. Let us open the Gothic missal of the sixth century at the rubric *ad christianum faciendum,* and read the ancient text which has enriched the Roman ritual: "Receive the seal of Christ, hear the divine words, be enlightened by the Word of the Lord, for today you are recognized (confessed) by Christ. I mark you on the forehead in the name of the Father, of the Son, and of the Holy Spirit, so that you may become Christian. I mark you on the eyes, so that you may see the brightness of God. I mark you on the ears, so that you may hear the voice of the Lord. I mark you on the nostrils, so that you may breathe in the fragrance of Christ . . . on the lips so that you may speak the words of life . . . on the heart, so that you may believe in the undivided Trinity . . . on the shoulders, so that you may bear the yoke of the service of Christ. I sign your whole being, in the name of the Father and of the Son and of the Holy Spirit, so that you may have eternal life and live forever and ever."

These several signs of the cross are first of all the sign of death, the mark of Jesus crucified for our sins. From the very beginning of his initiation, the catechumen should undertake some mortification and should share in the death of Christ by crucifying the "old man" with his vices; it is to help him in this journey through death that the Church, on several occasions, gives him the aid of her exorcisms. The cross on the forehead is to extinguish in his soul the spirit of pride and revolt, with its utopian dreams of an existence lived without God. It is to arm him against error, against being ruled by worldly prejudices — in brief, against all the temptations of the mind. The sign on the ears is to silence the importunate noises of the world and the tumult of false teaching. The Christian should learn henceforth how to make his silence Christian, to find in it the peace in which God dwells. The sign on the heart is to extinguish disordered affections and any unworthy love that goes against God, the sign on the shoulders to deliver the candidate from the yoke of slavery to the devil.

These signs of the cross are signs of death with Christ, but they are also the mark of the risen members of the risen Christ, the symbol of assimilation to the Priest Who is eternally living and glorious. The sacramental "character" is not actually given until the moment of Baptism, but it is signified in advance by the imposition of these signs of the cross. By it the Lord causes us to participate in His priesthood, as Scheeben so well says: "The baptismal character constitutes above all the fundamental consecration of the Christian and, in consequence, his participation in the priestly power of Christ. It effects in the soul of the baptized a consecration analogous to that given to the humanity of Christ by the hypostatic union." Thanks to this character, the new Christian becomes truly capable of taking active part in the sacrifice of the Mass as a co-offerer, and fruitfully to receive the other sacraments. It is, properly speaking, because of this baptismal character, symbolized by the imposition of the *sphragis*, that we can say with St. Paul, "We are the body of Christ, member for member" (1 Cor. 12, 27).

Our catechumens should respond to this Mystery of death and of life, on the one hand, by a great desire for mortification and, on the other, by an eager welcome to the new life which is to be given them in Christ. If they foster these desires while the exorcisms are being given them, they will not be wearied by the repetition of the sign of the cross and of the exorcisms, but rather aided to enter more profoundly into this Mystery of death and life. The other rites of the exorcisms need only a word of explanation: the grace of the Lord must penetrate the whole being of the candidate as salt penetrates food, and as healing oil penetrates a wound. The imposition of hands obviously signifies the taking possession of the new Christian by Christ, his Leader, and by the Church, his mother.

It is, finally, in the *essential rite of the baptismal washing* that we find in all its power the symbol of death and resurrection in Christ. It is quite easy to show how this washing is the symbol of purification. The sacrament washes away sin as the water washes the forehead of the baptized. But we need also to bring out the Gospel idea of death and rebirth: "Unless a man be born again of water and the Spirit, he cannot enter into the kingdom of God" (John 3, 5); "Do you not know that all we who have been baptized into Christ Jesus have been baptized into his death" (Rom. 6, 3).

In most mission countries, water is easily recognized as an image of death. Floods are of relatively frequent occurence and they leave devastation behind them. It is not difficult to cause our people to share the feelings of the Jews when they hear the story of the Flood or of the destruction of the Egyptian army in the Red Sea. The description, dramatized if need be, of baptism by immersion as this was practiced in the early Church, also helps people to understand better how the candidate at Baptism goes down into death with Christ. Often the catechumen, having taken off his garments, went down into a font shaped like a sarcophagus and was literally buried in the water. But even more than a sign of death, water is the sign of life. In the countries in which water is scarce, it is obviously the bringer of fertility and freshness; in many mission lands, a real resurrection of nature is to be seen as soon as the first rains begin. It is easy, then to make the people recognize the baptismal water as the symbol of life, to understand that here a new birth takes place by the power of the Holy Spirit, so that the candidate becomes the adopted child of God.

And here we should show how the reality of Baptism is superior to human adoption which can only give the child a legal title to the goods of those who adopt him, whereas Baptism causes us really to participate in the life of God.

The anointing with perfumed oil, the clothing with the baptismal robe and the carrying of the lighted candle all enrich the symbolism of this new life. We cannot insist too much on this idea of rebirth, of a new beginning, of return to original purity. By Baptism, man truly rises to a wholly new life in Christ. At the solemn moment of the baptismal washing, then, the candidate should do his utmost to make an act of faith in his Savior, to promise wholeheartedly to change his way of life and henceforth to imitate his Lord, offering himself unreservedly, with great generosity, to Christ and to His Church.

We should also explain how this resurrection in Christ is carried out *in the name of the Father, the Son and the Spirit*. From the very beginning, let us give the fundamental teaching on the mystery of the Trinity. Baptism engages the new Christian in a life of entirely new relationships with the three divine Persons, causing him to enter into the current of the life of the Trinity. Consecrated to the service and the glory of the Father whose adopted child he has become, the neophyte becomes a member of Christ, his older brother, and the temple of the Spirit Who comes to live in his soul as the God who transforms. He should, therefore, give himself wholly to the Blessed Trinity by a consecration that is of a higher and entirely different order from any self-offering to the Blessed Virgin or to the Saints.

And, finally, we should stress the radical transformation that should follow this death and resurrection in Christ. The Bible narratives of the lives of great converts, such as Abraham and Moses, well indicate the obligations that our baptismal vocation brings with it. And other comparisons can be useful, such as that of a little beggar boy, abandoned by his parents and living a miserable life, who, by a wonderful opportunity, becomes the friend of the king's son, who brings him to his father's palace. The king adopts this little beggar as his own son and makes him a prince. We can describe the blessings of his new life, so different from his previous misery, and the feelings of joy and gratitude that fill his heart. Henceforth he should devote himself to imitating his elder brother, living and acting as he does, sharing his interests and his concerns. He would not dream of returning to his miserable past life, but would do everything in his power to deserve the confidence and love of his royal father. It is easy to draw the moral from this story; are we not the adopted children of God (Col. 3, 1)? On the day of our Baptism, then, we undertake a great adventure, that of imitating Christ by daily mortification of our passions in order henceforth to live a truly Christian life (Rom. 6, 1).

If we prepare our candidates for their Baptism along these lines, the reception of the sacrament will not be merely the conclusion of a longer or shorter period of instruction, but primarily the starting point of a new commitment in Christ. What a wonderful life opens out to the neophyte, a life of companionship with the well-beloved Son of God, Who has made Himself the model for our thinking and acting, as we journey towards the Father, with the efficacious aid of the Spirit living in our hearts!

To summarize, then, in order that Baptism will not seem to be merely a happy accident in our converts' lives, an event that quickly becomes something past, the memory and influence of which are soon dimmed, we should prepare them for it by means of a real initiation. And this should be centered on the mystery of death to sin and resurrection to the very life of Jesus Christ.

And after Baptism, *every Sunday* should recall to our minds the wonderful fact of our passing through the waters of Baptism to become members of the family of God's children, living in the promised land. The *holy water* with which the new Christian signs himself at the threshold of the church should be a reminder of his rebirth in the baptismal water. Every sign of the cross should be a renewal of the mark received at Baptism, impressing the Christian "character" more deeply on his soul. The singing or recitation of the *Credo* at the Mass should be a means of renewing his baptismal engagement to the three divine Persons. And, finally, let us give all possible solemnity to *the ceremony of the renewal of the Baptismal promises* during the Easter vigil. For any renewal of the *ex opere operato* grace received at Baptism depends to a great extent on the way in which this ceremony is explained and prepared for.

When we are initiating our Christians into the *other sacraments,* let us not forget to show their relationship to Baptism. Confirmation causes the expansion and growth of the grace of Baptism, assimilating us, thanks to the character given by the sacrament, to Christ as King, Priest, and Prophet. Communion nourishes with the bread of the Sacrifice the divine life received at Baptism. At the Sunday Mass, the Christian is reminded of his privilege of being a co-offerer, which gives him the strict obligation actively to participate in Christ's sacrifice of thanksgiving. A well made Confession is the renewal of the initial purification of Baptism, a new death to sin and a new resurrection to Christ's life. And Extreme Unction, finally, develops the grace received at Baptism and makes still more beautiful the white robe received when we came up from the life-giving waters. In brief, the sacramental stream which, like the rivers of paradise, renders fruitful the soul during our whole life on earth, has its source in the mystery of Baptism.

More than ever before, the world has need of truly great and strong ideals; in the face of modern "mystiques" that promise a better world as the result of human efforts alone, let us strive to give our catechumens *the joyful conviction of being truly risen from the dead with Christ,* new men, dead to sin, vivified by the Spirit, henceforth engaged in the most glorious of adventures. There is no greater ideal than that of living the life of Christ in our thoughts, our desires, our actions, of bringing Christ into our world today. This conviction of being a ransomed people journeying toward the promised land, will make our Christians true missionaries, eager to have their brothers share their blessings. They will be aware of their duty to be leaders and to exercise their priesthood by a fervent liturgical life. Our task is, then, to proclaim this wonderful news, the news of the salvation given by Baptism, and to prepare the ground so that the liturgy of Baptism itself may announce the wonders of this salvation in all their truth and beauty and power. There is no doubt that, if we do so, our efforts will be rewarded by new and magnificent fruits of Christian living.

CHAPTER NINETEEN

The Celebration of Christian Marriage

JOSEF KELLNER, S.J.

A wedding is a great occasion in the life of the bride and groom, and also in that of the whole community to which they belong. This is true among nearly all peoples, and consequently of our Christians in the missions as well. Even though, as often happens, the newly married couple do not immediately establish their own home but go to live with the parents of the bride or groom, nevertheless the marriage is still the foundation of a new family, of an *ecclesiola,* a Church in miniature. Here we shall discuss the liturgical aspect of marriage, and mention its juridical, dogmatic, social, economic aspects only to the extent to which these bear on our considerations of the liturgical solemnity.

The events of this great day are ineffaceably impressed on the memory of the young people who come together to the altar; if we can take advantage of this natural fact, and sow good seed in the earth already prepared for it, we shall find that it will bear fruit a hundredfold, that it will be a priceless spiritual dowry for the new life of bride and groom. Moreover the special circumstances surrounding marriages in mission countries indicate a need for special liturgical solemnity. For in addition to everything else, we ordinarily need to take into account the lack of time for sufficient preliminary instruction, the non-Christian ideas about marriage and family life often current among our people, and also the customary atmosphere of community festivity which surrounds weddings in these countries.

Preparatory instruction

Every entrance into a new state of life, if it is to be well carried out, demands sufficient preparation and instruction, and this is true above

229

all of the state of marriage and parenthood. Today wise pastors and teachers of youth attach more and more importance to the serious preparation of young people for marriage. Courses are arranged in which the instruction given to engaged couples by the priest is supplemented by competent teachers of biology, hygiene, psychology, sociology, child care, home economics, etc. Special retreats are held for engaged couples — very well attended in Holland and elsewhere — which give the young people the opportunity to see the world in the light of their religion before they enter on their new lives. But in the missions, the chronic lack of priests greatly reduces the possibility of giving such preparation. A catechist, a teacher (perhaps a missionary Sister for the girls) initiates the young candidates for marriage into their new duties. The missionary must usually content himself with giving a brief summary[1] that he completes in the confessional. Often he does well if he can make sure that the young couple, and especially the bride, are freely choosing the state of marriage and to marry this particular person.

Yet some preparation is especially needed in the missions. The children of long-time Christians, especially if they have attended a mission school, are comparable to the young Christian people in home countries. But what can be said of the new Christians whose catechumenate lasted only a few weeks or months; new Christians who received no Christian formation in their own homes; the children of long-time Christians who have not been able to attend a mission school, wholly or entirely illiterate, and so incapable of completing their Christian formation by reading — how can these young people be properly prepared for Christian marriage and family life? Some teaching on the duties of their state, given by the missionary perhaps during his annual official visit, is not enough. We must take advantage, then, of the festive atmosphere of the wedding itself to give the needed instruction, in and also by means of, the liturgical ceremony itself.

The place for formal instruction is, obviously, the allocution ordinarily given by the priest at the beginning of the ceremony. This should not have, at least primarily, the sense of a congratulatory address (which belongs after the marriage), but should rather strive to recall the thoughts of those present, especially of the bride and groom, from the agitation of the preceding days to the silence of the house of God and the presence of God, and to enlighten them on the great step which they are about to take.

This allocution could be compared to the *allocutio* pronounced by

1. Sometimes the priest does not feel that he should deal with some of these aspects at all, since his people think that these are subjects "that a priest does not talk about."

the bishop at the beginning of the ordination of deacons (as at the other ordinations) *Prevehendi, filii dilectissimi, ad Leviticum ordinem, cogitate magnopere ad quantum gradum Ecclesiae ascenditis.* . . . The bride and groom will be ready to open their hearts to the words which their pastor, standing by the altar and clad in feast-day vestments, addresses to them in the presence of the assembled community. Would it be too much to ask that this allocution be preceded by an appropriate reading of the inspired word of God (for example, Gen. 2, 18-25; Tobias 7, 1-8; St. John 21, 11), or of the teaching of the Church (for example, an extract from the encyclical *On Christian Marriage*) which would reinforce the words of the priest. If such readings and talks were varied, in the course of several weddings in the same community the most important points concerning Christian marriage could be covered for the instruction of the newly married — and of those long married as well.

Erroneous ideas

The average person does not get most of his ideas on marriage and family life from his or her own observations, but in the main blindly accepts the way in which his whole society regards them. This point of view is not only expressed in conversation but still more in customs and ways of acting. When, for example, in conformity with custom, it is the parents or representatives of the family who decide on a marriage without asking the consent of those concerned, one can hardly talk about a free choice of husband or wife. Wherever this custom persists, openly or secretly, of buying the bride, there persists also the materialistic idea that the wife is the property, the possession, the merchandise, or the slave and servant of the man and his family. Such a conception is certainly remote from the Christian idea of the value of the personality of the woman. And is not the kind of moral double standard equally unchristian which severely condemns prenuptial sexual experience for a girl, but forgives indulgently, with a mild smile the same sin committed by a young man?

Again, in the missions and elsewhere, we often find that the current notions of good and evil, of "what is done" and "what is not done," are quite different from those of the Church. In mission territories, we can sometimes observe more sensitivity or even prudery than in Western countries, and sometimes more natural frankness, even to the point of shamelessness. But even when a pagan culture recognizes the fact that marriage is in some way bound up with religion, the people may, nonetheless, be quite ignorant of the special sanctity of Christian marriage, unaware that it is the image of the mystery of the union between

Christ and His Church. In many places, under Western influence, a neopagan materialism has lately influenced the people's ideas on sexual life. All these various notions about marriage and family life have their effect on our young people, for they are current even in the Christian section of the population. Many generations of Christianity must succeed one another before any notions that are so rooted in a people's mentality can be changed for something better.[2]

The messenger of the faith, therefore, must work patiently and untiringly to form the mentality of his Christians according to the spirit of Christ, and he must take every possible opportunity to do so. During his allocutions at weddings, in particular, he must bring out the grandeur of Christian marriage in all its aspects. In the face of pagan and neopagan materialism, he must emphasize the supernatural dignity of the sacrament, the religious vocation and the missionary significance of the command "Increase and multiply"; he must present the task of the Christian family to be the seedbed of the Church, the original cell for the growth of the kingdom of God, and show that a truly Christian family life offers a happiness which is more full and lasting than the apparent joys of the world. He should teach them that Christ is the founder and the sustainer of Christian communal life, and that it is at the altar, in partaking in Christ's sacrifice, that the Catholic begins and nourishes his married life. When the young couple establish their own home, the pastor should advise them from the very beginning to give a religious consecration to their family life by praying together, by attending the services of the Church together, by celebrating the Christian feasts in the family[3] and being faithful to Christian customs.[4]

The Participation of the Community

In the West, a marriage is the concern of the families concerned, of their relations and friends; in small villages almost everybody takes part in the festivities. The Oriental is still more inclined to share his

---

2. Europe had been Christianized for a long time when the ancient Germanic family system still prevailed and the marriage contract was made between the bridegroom and the father of the bride, her guardian, not with the bride herself. (See V. Thalhofer and L. Eisenhofer, *Handbuch de kath. Liturgik* II, Freiburg, 1933, 412).
3. *Around the Year with the Trapp Family*, by Maria Augusta Trapp, N. Y., 1955; *The Year of the Lord, a Handbook of Christian Feasts and Customs*, by Francis X. Weiser, S.J., N. Y., 1958 (a combined re-edition of the author's previous books: *The Christmas Book, The Easter Book, The Holy Day Book*).
4. On the wedding day, if the parents of the bridal couple are Christians, the formation of the wedding procession might be preceded by the giving of the parents' blessing, as is the custom in certain Christian countries. In the same way, the *Benedictio domus et thalami* (*Rit. Rom.* tit. VIII, cap. vi) might terminate the procession from the church to the new home.

joy with the whole community, the wedding feast of Cana being a good example of this fact. In a pagan village, the litttle group of Christians ordinarily carry on their lives more or less shut off from their neighbors, but when there is a Christian wedding, the whole village takes part. The Christian families, in particular, take an active part in the celebration and all come to church who can possibly do so. Must we, then, keep them from taking any active part in the liturgical ceremony itself? Must we treat them as mute spectators who are present merely out of curiosity, like pagans? Certainly not. Let us give them an active part to take by means of communal prayer, singing, and above all, the community Mass offered for the bride and groom.

It would be fitting also, that at the time of the actual marriage the whole community be called to witness and to watch over the new marriage bond being contracted. In the *Collectio Rituum* for the United States and in that for Germany, the priest after receiving the mutual consent of the bride and groom, addresses the congregation in these words: "I call upon all of you here present to be witnesses of this holy union which I have now blessed. 'What God has joined together, let not man put asunder.' "[5] But at least in the priest's own allocution, he should remind the community of its responsibility toward the success of the new home, a responsibility which means not only avoiding anything that would disturb the peace of the young couple, but also of doing whatever is needed to help them by word and deed.

Festal Atmosphere

"An intense state of soul tends to create external symbols in which it expresses itself, and this very form of expression reacts on the state of soul that caused it, increasing its intensity and duration, and giving a clear perception of it."[6] This fundamental law of natural psychic life is the more active the closer men are to natural impressions and the more removed they are from the world of abstract thought. It prevails more especially in the lives of young people than in the aged, more among people who have little or no intellectual formation than among those with a great degree of it, more among the Orientals than Occi-

---

5. *Collectio Rituum pro omnibus Germaniae Diocesibus,* pars I, tit. iv, n. 7; *Collectio Rituum ad instar appendicis Ritualis Romani, pro Diocesibus Statuum Foederatorum Americae Septentrionalis,* Tit. IV, cap. i, n. 4. Both these Rituals also provide a special opportunity for the congregation to pray for the bridal couple: after the giving of the ring and the singing or reciting of Psalm 127, followed by responses and a prayer, the priest extends his hands over the couple and asks that the blessings of married life may be theirs; after each group of petitions, the whole congregation answers: Amen.
6. A. Willwoll, S.J., in *Studia Missionaria,* vol. I, Rome, 1943, p. 829.

dentals. Oriental peoples particularly use any occasion to organize a festival. They know how to give to a day or an event a festal atmosphere by music and dancing, by dramatic representations, by a feast, a procession or a "program," as they say in the Philippines.

If we compare this healthy gaiety of the Oriental mentality with the simple Roman *Ritus celebrandi matrimonium* which consists only of the giving and receiving of the consent of bride and groom, of the *confirmatio* of the bond by the priest and of the blessing of the ring(s), one cannot help but feel some dismay. No singing, no music, hardly any symbolic actions other than those of clasping hands and putting on the ring(s). Is this all? one cannot help asking. How impressive is the marriage ceremony in the Greek Church, how rich in singing and in symbolic action, in the ceremony of the placing of the veil on the bride's head and the presentation of the nuptial crown! The Latin rite is the more barren by contrast with similar ceremonies, for example those of the ordination of priests or of the consecration of virgins. These have beautiful prayers, moving chants and symbolic rites which make the whole an unforgettable event. The marriage ceremony also in ancient times had a much fuller ceremonial, still continued in some few places and, in part, related to the nuptial blessing during the Mass. Thus, according to a Roman custom, a veil was put over both bride and groom, and both of them were given crowns; these customs had been taken over from pre-Christian times. In many countries, there was added the ceremony of the ring placed on the finger of the bride by the bridegroom as a symbol of the fidelity that she henceforth owed to him.[7] The *velatio nuptialis,* which was suppressed in the Roman Ritual of 1614, the prototype of our present Roman Ritual, still exists in some places, for example in the archdiocese of Manila in the Philippines, having been taken over from the rite of Toledo in Spain.

The impression of too stark a simplicity corresponding so poorly to the needs of mission peoples, disappears if, in conformity with the rubrics of the Roman Ritual,[8] the Nuptial Mass with its solemn blessing follows immediately after the marriage ceremony; it is precisely the Nuptial Mass and the blessing that are called *solemnizatio matrimonii.* And in fact it is the Holy Sacrifice itself, celebrated as a community Mass with hymns and prayers, in which the bride and groom take part in the sacred banquet, in which the priest extends his hands over them in blessing, that gives to the hearts of those present the sense of a solemn

7. J. A. Jungmann, S.J., *Public Worship,* Collegeville 1958, p. 87.
8. *Rit. Rom,* tit. VII, cap. ii, n. 4. Cf. *The Roman Ritual in Latin and English,* trans, and ed. by Rev. Philip Weller, Bruce, Milwaukee, Vol. I, p. 465 and 467.

religious act. The missionary, then, should never omit the Nuptial Mass except in case of necessity.

To answer the need of his Christians for greater solemnity in the marriage ceremony, the missionary can also use various obvious means such as the addition of flowers, lights, wearing the cope, etc. One remark in the Ritual deserves our special attention in the missions. "Let it be observed that wherever it is the practice to employ other laudable customs and ceremonies at weddings, it is fitting to maintain them."[9] The way always followed by the Church for the celebration of marriage could not be better described. The fact of contracting marriage is of decisive importance both for the individuals concerned and for the community to which they belong. And so the Church has always taken into consideration, in establishing her marriage liturgy, customs of the various peoples and nations in her fold. From this adaptiveness comes the marriage ceremonial in the Roman Ritual and it explains also the various forms still in use in the Catholic Church.[10]

Thus it is evident that the present rite is only a basic form which the Ordinaries of each place can fill out by fittingly adding various local usages. The new ritual for the dioceses of Germany (1950) is an example. The dioceses of the Philippine Islands, again, have a still richer ceremony. It includes the holding of a veil over the bridal couple during the nuptial blessing in the Mass, while a cord or ribbon in the form of a figure 8, a symbolic yoke, is placed over the shoulders of the married couple as a sign of the marriage union. The marriage ceremony itself begins with an exhortation; then comes the scrutiny of the impediments to the marriage, in which the people take part; after the mutual consent of the bride and groom and the *confirmatio,* the priest blesses the rings and the "pledges," pieces of money which the groom, before putting the ring on the finger of his bride, lets fall in her open hand as a sign of his promise to provide for her subsistence. Then, after various prayers of blessing, the marriage contract is signed before the priest.

It is particularly surprising that the marriage ceremony includes no singing, although the chant has such a part in all other solemn liturgical actions.[11] The various "wedding marches" taken from operas and concert music, too often heard on these occasions, are foreign to the spirit of the Church and forbidden, very rightly, by the bishops. But

9. *Rit. Rom,* tit. VII, cap. ii, n. 6; Weller, op. cit. p. 465 and 467.
10. Joseph Pascher, *Die Liturgie der Sakramente,* Münster, 1951, p. 259 ff.
11. Baptism and Confirmation are only apparent exceptions to this rule; the liturgy of the Easter Vigil, during which these sacraments were originally administered, is not lacking in chants.

does not their use reveal a real need calling for some positive satisfaction, a void to be filled by truly appropriate Christian music? Among all peoples, but especially in the Orient, the period of life preceding a wedding is filled with singing; and it would be difficult to find any people who celebrate weddings without some singing and music. Why, then, should music, the language of the heart, be forbidden to Catholic bridal couples on this great day? The natural expression of solemn and festive joy is singing.

One obvious possibility is to sing the psalms provided in various rituals (for example, Psalm 127 in the German, the American and the Philippine). This could be sung in the responsorial form, with the whole congregation singing, between the verses of the psalm itself sung by the choir or a chanter, the refrain: "May the Lord bless you from Sion, He who made heaven and earth."

In any case, it is most desirable that some hymn be sung by the whole congregation during the entrance and the exit of the bridal couple. If we had such hymns, the various profane "wedding marches" would automatically disappear from the house of God. And then the wish of the Church expressed in the Introit of the Nuptial Mass would be more fully accomplished both for the bridal couple and the whole congregation: "Lord, cause them to bless Thee more fully."

CHAPTER TWENTY

The Missionary Value of the Liturgy of the Sick and of the Dead

JOHANNES HOFINGER, S.J.

The motherly care of the Church for her children shines out most clearly in the liturgy for the sick and for the dead. According to my own experience in the Chinese missions, it was customary to send for the priest whenever any Christian fell seriously ill, even if the priest were far away and could not be reached, or come to the sick person's help, without a great deal of trouble. But no sacrifice seemed too great, and in spite of the difficulties involved, fewer Christians actually died without the aid of the Last Sacraments in the missions than in some less fervent communities in Christian countries.

Missionaries everywhere have done a great deal to make every Christian understand the value of the last sacraments, but work still needs to be done in convincing Christian communities of their obligation to care for their sick and to see to it that the priest is sent for in time of need. This duty is the more urgent in regard to isolated Christians who live in pagan families, and so have a special need for, and claim on, the affectionate attention of the whole Christian community to which they belong.

Thus, in the spirit of the liturgical renewal, we should strengthen the already existing appreciation for the liturgy of the sick, and should strive to intensify the fraternal interest of the whole community in obtaining care for its sick members. For such interest is one aspect of true participation in the sacramental life of the Church: the reception of any sacrament is in some way the concern of the whole community, and each individual has a part to take in the development of the sacramental life of the whole community.

In more than one mission, until recently, because of the great distances

237

involved, it simply was not possible to administer the last sacraments to every Christian. Happily for us, the age of the renewal of the liturgy comes at the same time as the age of modernization of means of transport, and it is particularly in mission countries that an extraordinary development of means of travel has taken place. Appreciation for the last sacraments will certainly be resourceful in finding means whereby to assure to a greater number of Christians the last comforts of religion.

The importance of the last sacraments for the salvation of the soul is obviously great, first of all because it is obligatory to receive them at the hour of death, and then because they have assured eternal salvation to innumerable Christians. But in addition to these motives, let us make our Christian communities understand that the reception of the last sacraments is the fitting conclusion of their sacramental life with Christ, the final sacramental preparation for our eternal union with Him, thanks to which the sacramental symbols will give place to the unveiled glory of our perfection in Christ. In the missions, even more than in Christian countries, we need fully-formed Christians who are not only preoccupied with assuring their eternal salvation, but who live in the joy of their awareness of their incomparable vocation.

Where the missionary encounters superstitious and pagan methods of healing, medicine men, quacks, who hover around new Christians, he can exercise an effective counter-influence by pointing out the healing power of Extreme Unction. Inculcating the practice of true Christian abandonment to the will of Divine Providence will shut out any too material notions of this sacrament.[1]

The long journey that must be made by the missionary, and the rarity of his visits create in the sick person a state of mind most favorable to the ministrations of the priest. The more the sick person realizes the eagerness of the priest to come to help him, the more he will be inclined to accept this help. The sick person and his family are, then, from the beginning, favorably disposed and receptive, and we should make use of these good dispositions in the carrying out of the rites. Here the desire to carry out the liturgy in the language of the country seems to be completely justified: is it not simply a question of allowing the sick person and his family to follow the rites? As everyone knows, Rome has desired for a long time, for the missions, versions of the Ritual in the languages of the people and has been urging this work for some fifteen years, while reserving to itself the right to control such versions and give them final approbation. Hence it is greatly to be desired that

---

1. Eugen Walter, *Die Herrlichkeit des christlichen Sterbens,* Fribourg en Brisgau, 1940, p. 46-49.

many bishops, realizing the pastoral importance of a vernacular ritual, request this concession for their dioceses.

And there are other reasons also. In the majority of cases, the priest must administer during one visit both the last sacraments and the papal blessing for the hour of death. The sick person is often exhausted. If the priest has to say everything first in Latin, the liturgy of the sick is unduly lengthened and loses much of its persuasive power. Even when the priest does not say the prayers twice, in Latin and then in the vernacular, and even if he uses the abbreviations authorized by the Ritual, the ceremony is often too lengthy by reason of the consecutive administration of several sacraments. We need, therefore, especially in the missions, a rite which will coordinate the different elements of the various ceremonies. Then Holy Viaticum could once again take its rightful place after Extreme Unction as the crown and conclusion of the whole, without separating Extreme Unction and the absolution *in articulo mortis* from the Sacrament of Penance. Or the Absolution might be given after Holy Viaticum.[2]

Without wishing to underestimate the papal blessing which confers a plenary indulgence at the moment of death and is a sign of the fatherly affection of the Vicar of Christ, we believe nonetheless that emphasis should be placed upon the sacraments properly so called. They also bring about the purification of the Christian soul for its meeting with Christ. And, in reference to the remission of the temporal punishment due to sin, we should stresss primarily the effectiveness of Extreme Unction, exhorting our people to receive it with contrition and abandonment to God. For it is precisely by this sacrament that Christ wills to take away everything that could still hinder our definitive union with Him.

Obviously, it is in rare cases only that the missionary can remain in the vicinity of the sick person to be able to minister to him up to the moment of death. His priestly duties call him to some other part of his territory. The Christian community, then, must take over, and stand by the sick person in death. The leaders of the Christian community, the catechist and the Sister above all, should be present. A good translation of the prayers for the dying or a popular adaptation of them with a few short exhortations would make it easy for them

---

2.   The absolution might also be given after Holy Viaticum. An example of such a unified rite is to be found in the *Collectio Rituum ad instar Appendicis Ritualis Romanae pro omnibus Germaniae Diocesibus*, I, Tit. III, cap. 4; and in the *Collectio Rituum* for the United States, Tit. III, cap. 4: *Ritus continuus infirmum muniendi sacramentis extremis*, in which the repetition of the Confiteor is eliminated.

to carry out their duty to their dying brother and to help him make a good death. In these prayers for the dying, concluding with the prayer for the newly departed soul, the liturgy of the sick passes over into the liturgy of the dead.

The Liturgy of the Dead

Missionaries generally feel, and rightly, that it is better to make sure of administering the sacraments to the dying than to be present at the funerals of members of their flock. The great distances involved and the great dearth of priests make it impossible for missionaries to come back to celebrate the funeral and burial services. The liturgy of the dead is, therefore, practically non-existent in the missions, being often reduced to a Mass for the dead celebrated by the missionary on his next visit which may take place several weeks or even months after the day of death.

It would, of course, be a mistake to make a principle out of the absence of a priest at Christian funerals. But there is some question of granting concessions to actually existing circumstances which we have to accept whether we wish to or not. Nevertheless, modern facilities for travel as well as the undoubted growth in the number of native priests resulting in the division of each district into smaller sectors, may already have made it possible for more missionaries to celebrate the funeral rites, and will certainly do so to an increasing degree in the future. Pastoral care should, then, make use of this development, even though, at the present time, the presence of the priest is not always possible. In any case, the ordering of the funeral rites, with or without a priest, certainly should claim the attention of every missionary.

The great importance of the liturgy of the dead in missionary work flows first of all from the fact that Christian burial is an aspect of Christian worship accessible to pagans, one which is carried out for the most part *in the presence of many pagans*. This alone is a cogent reason why the funeral rites, whether they are celebrated by a priest or not, should be dignified, understandable, and deeply moving. Any Christian service, even the service for the dead, is of course primarily directed to those who have been baptized. Nevertheless it can be carried out in such a way that the pagans are impressed in a truly religious way and gain from it a first and most valuable contact with the Christian religion. This opportunity is the more favorable since, in the presence of death or at the grave of a dear friend, everyone tends seriously to reflect upon the meaning of life. The liturgy of the dead brings out clearly and beautifully those great Christian truths which give a purpose and value to our existence. Unbelievers, who come to attend the ceremony only for social reasons, do not like to be spoken to directly. They would "close up" if they felt themselves directly addressed. They will submit much more easily to the objective and persuasive influence of the sacred liturgy itself as it manifests simply and profoundly what Christians think about life and how their faith is victorious over death itself.

Nevertheless, we do not wish to insist too much on the direct influence of the liturgy of the dead on non-Christians. Its chief function is to *fill the faithful themselves with the true Christian spirit,* to make them real apostles. Our Christians, living continually in a pagan atmosphere, are in no way immunized against the pagan culture of this world. We shall not triumph over paganism, and still less over the neo-paganism that is flooding even missionary territories, with people who are leading only more or less Christian lives. We need Christians who are truly transformed by their new life in Christ, who, strong in the hope of glory, know how to direct their present life toward that to come. Only thus can they become the leaven of their pagan surroundings. Everything, then, that can serve to reinforce this fundamental attitude toward life and death, and to diminish the effect of the pagan atmosphere, has great missionary value. This is certainly true of the liturgy of the dead. And it is therefore necessary to celebrate it in such a way as to bring out its fundamental structure and meaning, and not to allow it to be reduced to a service simply to help the dead person, a service pre-occupied almost entirely with the thought of Purgatory and of the duty of the living to show fraternal charity toward the souls of the departed.

We should also take into account the fact that the pagan religions of the majority of our people in missionary countries hold funeral cere-monies that are often extremely colorful. *For apologetic reasons alone,* we should not let them think that our religion is lacking in piety for the dead. Of course this does not mean that our practice should try to adapt itself to the noisy and often very primitive characteristics of pagan funerals. Here the missionary finds himself faced with a difficult prob-lem, but he cannot content himself with the thought that one Mass is of incomparable value to the departed soul, and that therefore it is unnecessary to do anything to make Christian funerals seem more im-pressive. On the contrary, we need to find ways of providing ceremonies that are truly moving and filled with the true Christian spirit.

In order to work toward solutions of this problem, we need in many cases a deep knowledge of our people's customs, and an acute awareness of the distinction between pagan superstitions and civil usages (as is seen from the controversy on the rites in China). Much patience is needed also in order to eliminate what is unChristian in our people's customary ways of acting — moaning, official "weepers," sacrifices and dances, meals for the dead, etc. — and to substitute new Christian customs instead. And further, we must strive to recognize those special qualities of our people's culture that are "sound and pure" (Pius XII), for "the Catholics in every country are above all citizens of the great family of God and of His kingdom, but they do not renounce for all that their citizenship in their earthly homeland."[3] If in Europe it is rightly required that "the singing, the decoration of the church and other expressions of social life which surround a burial should express our faith in the Resurrection," obviously this is even more necessary in a missionary country.[4]

Since it is so essential to have a liturgy of the dead in the missions which will be marked by a careful adaptation to the feelings and customs of the people and at the same time bring the mystery of death into the full light of Christ and so triumph over the sadness of death by Christ's life, it may be useful to indicate certain *indispensable qualities of truly Christian funeral services*. In thus making a comparison between Christian and pagan customs, we are, of course, aware of the fact that pagan usages are not always equally characteristic, just as Christian ceremonies are not always equally Christian.

A truly Christian ceremony is entirely religious, that is to say, *oriented to God*. Its proper theme is not man, but God, the Master of life and death, the just Judge, the Merciful, the unfailing Source of eternal life and joy. The death itself is the actual beginning of the ceremonies, and the dead person himself is never forgotten. But the rite should raise our thoughts from man to God. It should not glorify the departed, but rather God, thus becoming a form of worship. Even in matters that are not part of the liturgy properly speaking, Christian funerals should learn from the liturgy. They should be theocentric, as is the whole worship of the Church, unlike pagan funerals which do not go further than the thought of the dead person himself, paying him a respect surrounded by more or less religious activity.

Thus, precisely because of this theocentricity, a Christian funeral is not merely a ceremony of mourning. This does not prevent true Christians from feeling great pain at the death of someone dear to them, yet, in spite of this fact, *the fundamental tone is not sadness, but hope based on faith*, together with the eager desire for our union with God in eternal blessedness, a union which will know no separation. This is, precisely, the salvation which we Christians await from our Savior, Jesus

3. Encyclical *Evangelii praecones,* June 2, 1951.
4. *Der Seelsorger,* Vienna, XXII (1952), 411. An extract from *Lex Orandi* No. 12: *Le mystère de la mort et sa célébration,* Paris, Ed. du Cerf, 1951.

Christ. The man who truly believes in Him and in His redemption, cannot sorrow like those who have no hope.[5] Thus a Christian funeral should be a moving expression of homage to Christ Who has conquered death and opened to us the gates of eternal life; and so be really "Christian." As a result, we obviously cannot allow unrestrained expressions of grief as do the pagans who are thinking only of death.

Since pagan funerals have no power to give true consolation, they endeavor by all their trappings to deceive people about the seriousness of death. We need, then, to give our ceremonies the *seriousness and dignity* befitting the mystery of death understood in the light of Christian faith. We should *avoid all the pomp* which, far from disclosing this mystery, serves rather to obscure it more completely and to turn our minds from the great truths that are to be celebrated. Thus in China, for instance, we should not show the same concern as do non-Christians for elaborate and costly caskets, which are a luxury completely out of place and not suitable for Christians.

In the question of who is to take charge of the funeral arrangements, we should take into consideration the fact that Christian funerals are much more *the concern of the whole Christian community* than of the family of the departed, above all in the liturgical service itself. The sense of the community should predominate. Every missionary knows how the vitality of his parish is augmented by fellowship in joy and in sorrow. Thus, in the liturgy of the dead properly so called, the liturgical action belongs indisputably to the Church, and it should be celebrated in such a way as to bring out the motherly care of the Church for her dead children. In this connection, we might note that in Christian funerals, even outside of the liturgy in the strict sense, the Christian community, "the Church," should be made visible to non-Christians even more clearly than on other occasions. It is, therefore, not a matter of indifference that our fellowship in Christian worship should be expressed here in a way that is concrete and striking.

Since it is funerals that are, more than any other ceremonies, celebrated in the presence of non-Christians, we should take care to use the *language of the country* to as great an extent as possible. Those outside the Church should not receive from their first contact with our worship the impression of useless unintelligibility. It is very easy to obtain from Rome the permission to use the language of the country in the missions; Rome is waiting to have editions of the ritual in the language of the people submitted to her for approbation. And perhaps it should be emphasized here that the funeral rites can, more easily

5. I Thess. 4, 13.

than other services, be adapted to different circumstances; we should, therefore, find a form that answers the needs and the concrete possibilities of each missionary region.

Here we must distinguish between the liturgy celebrated by a priest and *the ceremonies that the Christian community carries out in his absence*. The presence of the priest at funerals is still very rare, and it is, therefore, the more necessary to give attention to the way in which funerals are to be celebrated without him. Here, even more than in other services held without a priest, it is urgent not to leave what is to be done to some pious improvisation, but to have it laid down by the bishop for his whole diocese, along the lines of the liturgical renewal. Two things to be insisted upon are: the intense active participation of the faithful, and the suitable carrying out of the ceremonies. It is also essential to make sure of the appropriate directing of each ceremony.

To correspond fully to pastoral needs, the diocesan regulations concerning funerals in the absence of a priest should actually propose and recommend two forms of celebration. It would not suffice to develop the burial service itself in order to make it into a moving and impressive ceremony; another form of funeral service without a priest should be developed as well, which would have the character of *an hour of Christian meditation and prayer,* corresponding to some degree to the Office of the Dead. This service should take place in the home of the deceased or in the church, as circumstances dictate. Attempts along these lines have been made in various missions; for example, in China a translation of the Office of the Dead has been in use for a long time. During such an hour of prayer, it has been found that the Christians of a community realize their fellowship and feel more at ease than at the funeral itself. To bear full fruit, this service should be more than a prayer for the dead; without losing sight of the original reason for the ceremony, it should be an hour of real meditation, which will awaken in the whole community a realization of the great and consoling truths of the faith which come to mind of themselves at the time of the death of one of their brothers. There is little fear that, in the missions where Christian communities have so few members, such ceremonies would occur too frequently; for the same reason, everyone knows everyone else, and the death of one member is felt profoundly by all the others.

The structure of this prayer hour, while it should resemble the Office of the Dead, should not be a simple translation of it. For example, the readings should be different; the book of Job does not give us the full Christian response nor all the consolations of Christianity. We need to put the emphasis on Christ Himself, on His resurrection and our own.

The actual funeral ceremony which is the richest in meaning and the most fruitful is, without doubt, the Mass for the Dead. He who sees the Mass as the representation of the Redemption of Christ and our participation in the Mystery of His death and resurrection understands why this is so. In the missions, where the priest can seldom assist at funerals, the Mass of the Dead becomes "the" Christian ceremony for the deceased. Just as in the Chinese missions, so the people of other mission territories place a high value on the Mass of the Dead. But this esteem, in the concrete forms it takes, has its pastoral drawbacks. The majority of Masses said by the missionary have to be offered as Masses for the Dead. The faithful insist upon it. In order to do this, many missionaries make use of the privilege that allows them to say the Mass of the Dead on minor feasts. And so it comes about that the majority of the rare Masses that the missionary celebrates in small communities are nearly all Masses of the Dead. When after Easter, for example, he goes to his distant stations to proclaim the Paschal victory of Christ, certainly a Mass for the Dead is not in order. And so also for Christmas time. The faithful must be made to realize that it is not the liturgical color that gives value to the Holy Sacrifice. They must come to see the Mass, however great its value for the dead, as the incomparable sacrifice of praise and thanksgiving of the New Covenant, and to realize that, the more we celebrate it in a spirit of adoration and gratitude, the more it will become a source of blessings for our dead and for ourselves.

PART SIX

Factors in the Liturgical Renewal
in the Missions

CHAPTER TWENTY-ONE

Should We Work Towards Permanent Deacons in the Missions?

JOHANNES HOFINGER, S.J.

There has been a great deal of discussion in recent years on the advisability of restoring the diaconate as a permanent state with its own functions in the Church. Laymen especially, but distinguished clerical leaders as well, are interested in this question, primarily in connection with the pastoral situation in central and western Europe.[1] The discussion has often been complicated and rendered less fruitful by the fact that some people — though not the most prominent among the advocates for a permanent diaconate — have turned this question into a discussion for or against *married* Deacons. But the gist of the question is simply this: In the Latin rite at the present time, the diaconate, like the subdiaconate and the minor orders, is merely a step on the road to the priesthood. A man does not become a deacon in order to remain a deacon and to carry out the functions of the diaconate as his permanent life work, but rather to take the last step on the long road to the priesthood. But in earlier times, in fact for more than a thousand years, in the Roman rite as well as the Oriental rites, the diaconate was considered and carried out as an Order which, aside from any later promotion to the priesthood, was conferred primarily to be a permanent

---

1. Concerning German material on this question, especially the articles of Josef Hornef, see J. Hofinger, "Ist in der Mission ein eigener Stand der Diakone anzustreben?" in *Zeitschr. f. Missionswissenschaft* (Münster, 1957, p. 201-213, W. Schamoni, *Familienväter als geweihte Diakone*, Paderborn, 1953. Regarding an eventual restoration of the Minor Orders, see: W. Croce, "Die niederen Weihen in ihrer hierarchischen Wertung," in *Zeitschr. f. Kath. Theol.*, 1948, 257-314. Y. Congar, *Jalons pour une Théologie du laicat*, Paris, 1953. (This section is omitted in the English Trans. pub. by the Newman Press.)

and often lifelong function in the Church. This is still today the unquestioned practice in Oriental rites, both those in union with the Holy See and those outside.

The question, then, is, precisely, should we recommend, in view of the urgent pastoral needs of our times, the restoration to the diaconate of the permanence and special functions which belonged to it in the ancient Church. This would mean that candidates would be allowed to receive this order who wished to remain deacons all their lives and to serve the Church by preaching the word of God, by administering the sacraments of Baptism and the Eucharist, and by carrying out various peripheral activities. In this whole discussion, it is always taken for granted that, if a permanent diaconate were to be restored, the Church would allow those who renounced once and for all the possibility of future promotion to the priesthood to be married or even to get married after their ordination to the diaconate.

It would be erroneous to consider this whole question as a chimera produced by some unbalanced "progressive" people in central and western Europe, a question deserving no serious consideration. The Holy Father certainly considers it worth solid and prudent study. As he said in his discourse to the Second World Congress for the Lay Apostolate, October 5, 1957, "We know that some thinking is being done concerning the introduction of a diaconate conceived as an ecclesiastical function independent of the priesthood. The idea, at least today, is not yet ripe." Yet he considers it possible that — obviously as the fruit of sound study of the question — "the idea should some day ripen" (N.C.W.C. Press trans.). The whole problem is, as is well-known, being opened up for discussion by competent people in Rome, and is considered to be in the process of ripening. Yet it is quite possible that some experts who would unequivocally admit the usefulness of permanent deacons in Europe, would shrink from the notion of trying out such deacons in the missions.

How the missions have become increasingly involved in this discussion

As early as 1948, the missiologist August Tellkamp, S.V.D. mentioned the restoration of a really functional diaconate as an eventual remedy against what he called "missionary asphyxia," that is, the slow suffocation of the missionary apostolate as a result of the missionaries becoming overburdened with "parish" activities.[2] In 1955, Joseph Hornef, the foremost lay advocate of this restoration, published an article that

2. A. Tellkamp, S.V.D., *Die Gefahr der Erstickung für die katholische Welt-mission*, Münster, 1950, p. 62.

received a great deal of attention, in which he tried to substantiate the request with reasons of a missionary nature.[3] Although Dr. Hornef, a judge in Fulda in West Germany, has no actual missionary experience, he has nevertheless discovered and presented in a fairly adequate way the missionary aspect of this question.

But what is the attitude of experienced missionaries themselves? The fact that many distinguished missionaries have, on the whole, a favorable attitude, was brought out at the International Congress of Pastoral Liturgy at Assisi, September, 1956. His Excellency, William van Bekkum, S.V.D., Apostolic Vicar of Ruteng in Flores, spoke for the missions. In his great speech on "The Liturgical Renewal in the Service of the Missionary Apostolate" which was received by the Congress with more than ordinary enthusiasm, Bishop van Bekkum dealt at some length with the problem we are now discussing, finally summing up the desire of missionaries as follows: "It is to be wished that the lower degrees of Holy Orders might be restored in a form corresponding to present-day conditions, and that the Church's commission (for pastoral helpers, catechists, etc.) should be bestowed in a liturgical ceremony conducted by the Bishop or a priest, also that the revival of the diaconate be considered for work such as preaching, distributing Holy Communion and baptizing, in regions short of priests."[4] This was the first time that a missionary bishop had spoken out so clearly and urgently for the restoration of the diaconate, and at such a large and illustrious gathering. Bishop van Bekkum's words have a special importance in view of the fact that he had been requested by the organizing committee not so much to give his own personal wishes as to present an objective picture of the missions today and their needs.

In the days immediately preceding the Congress itself, this same question was discussed in a special meeting of the missionaries who were to take part in the Congress.[5] Here also the request, as formulated afterwards by Bishop van Bekkum at the Congress, met with the understanding and agreement of the missionaries present, although they did not intend to give any special emphasis to this point above others. Also characteristic of the growing interest of many missionaries in, and their positive attitude towards, this question is an article on "Married Deacons in the Missions" recently published by the Assistant General of the Mill Hill Missionaries.[6]

3. J. Hornef, "Erneuerung des Weihediakonates in den Missionen?" in *Die kath. Missionen,* 1953, 42-44.
4. *The Assisi Papers,* Liturgical Press, Collegeville, Minn., 1957, p. 111.
5. On the International Congress of Pastoral Liturgy at Assisi and the preceding meeting of missionaries, see Appendix 1.
6. John de Reeper, M.H.F., Married Deacons in the Missions, in *Worldmission,* Fall, 1957, pp. 33-41.

But these various signs of growing interest in no way prove that the majority of missionaries are as yet in favor of a restoration of the diaconate in mission territories. Many missionaries, in fact, are positively against it, as we have discovered ourselves in the course of traveling through many mission countries in the last few years. In particular the idea of recommending *married* deacons for the missionary apostolate seems to many missionaries a real cause of scandal, and only goes to prove to them how little the wishes of European liturgists are related to the particular situation and needs of the missions. This strong resistance of many missionaries obviously indicates that a restoration of the diaconate would meet with many special difficulties in the missions, and that these special difficulties should be carefully considered. Only by an unbiased examination of the reasons for and against such a step can we arrive at a solution which will do justice to the real needs and potentialities of the missions.

Advantages of a permanent diaconate in the missions

At the International Congress of Pastoral Liturgy in Assisi, the speaker for the missions stressed particularly the valuable services that could be rendered by deacons in distributing Holy Communion to the faithful. "In the missions, it is often difficult to arrange *the distribution of Holy Communion* in such a way that it becomes a real sacrificial banquet." This is particularly true "when on the occasion of a great feast, thousands of the faithful wish to receive Communion, and only one or two priests are available to distribute It. On such occasions, the course of the Eucharistic celebration is greatly disturbed and the duration of the Mass is unduly lengthened."[7]

The objection might be made that such cases do occur far more frequently in the missions than in home countries, but that even in the missions they are rather exceptional, and therefore could hardly justify such a radical change in ecclesiastical discipline as the use of married deacons in the service of the Blessed Sacrament. In answer to this, Bishop van Bekkum pointed out in the same speech that deacons would also be of assistance in many ordinary circumstances. "In the missions it quite often happens that one priest has to care for some twenty stations." He himself can celebrate Sundays and feast days in only one of these stations at a time. The long distances between stations frequently make it impossible for him to say Mass in different stations on the same Sunday. Even though the recently granted privilege of

7. Most Rev. William van Bekkum, S.V.D., *The Liturgical Renewal in the Service of the Missions,* in *The Assisi Papers,* The Liturgical Press, Collegeville, Minn., p. 95-112.

evening Mass makes binating much more possible in the missions, there still remain some twenty stations with no Sunday service conducted by a priest, no Mass and Communion. Would it not, therefore, be of great pastoral benefit to the faithful if there were deacons stationed in some of the more important outposts? Then the faithful of the other smaller stations would also profit since, at least occasionally, they might find it possible to come to a station with a deacon near their own, and the deacon himself might be able to go and conduct the Sunday services in some small stations when he had carried out those in his own.

Deacons could also be of great assistance in bringing Holy Communion to the sick, and, in exceptional cases, even by administering Viaticum. Because of the great distances involved and the still greater dearth of priests in most mission districts, the sick who live outside the central station can receive Communion only very infrequently. They are happy if they can at least receive the last sacraments in time. And in cases of sudden collapse or accident, even this is frequently impossible. Thus one of the important duties of a missionary deacon would be to take care of the sick in his district, and to call the priest whenever the illness took a turn for the worse. Cases would also occur in which it would be too late to call the priest. Then, if the sick man had good will, the deacon could not only help him to prepare for a good death, but even without Confession, could give him Holy Viaticum after due preparation.

These Eucharistic functions of a deacon would be of even greater pastoral importance in the missions than in home countries. But there are other important missionary functions waiting to be carried out by permanent professional deacons, especially that of *conducting Sunday services without a priest* — whether or not they could eventually distribute Holy Communion as well. We have already discussed the enormous missionary importance of such services earlier in this book (Chapter XI), and it is obvious that they could be celebrated much more effectively if they were directed by a well-trained deacon. He could not only have charge of the priestless services in his own station, but could also train the faithful in the minor stations around his own, and from time to time direct the services in these small communities. There is little doubt that if deacons were entrusted with the care of the Sunday services in large priestless communities and if lectors were named for the small stations, that the urgent question of Sunday services in the absence of a priest could be most effectively solved.

But professional deacons could also be of great assistance in carrying out the sacred liturgy itself in such a way as more perfectly to satisfy the people's needs. Liturgical ceremonies in the missions today give evidence of two shortcomings in particular: they are not sufficiently solemn, and they are not sufficiently intelligible. The lack of true liturgical solemnity is often the occasion for the growth of unliturgical pomp; the lack of intelligibility interferes with the catechetical and pastoral effectiveness of the liturgy, and, besides, it prevents many missionaries from working towards any better celebration of the liturgy, for "whatever we do, the people will not understand it." By means of an assisting deacon, a much more solemn celebration of Mass would be possible. And he could become the link desired between the priest and the people, and the ideal interpreter whose help is so much needed in the Roman rite. It can be taken for granted that if the professional diaconate is restored, the Church would also be prepared to make the necessary changes in the rubrics so that the deacon would fully carry out his liturgical functions of serving and assisting: serving the priest by uniting him with his flock, assisting the faithful to understand and to participate as they should in the sacred action of the priest.

Another valuable service that could be rendered by permanent deacons is that of *administering Baptism*. Because of the dearth of missionaries, many — and in some missions, the majority — of babies are given private Baptism by the catechist or Sister employed by the mission. The missionary then supplies the baptismal ceremonies when he makes his next visit, it may be some months later. But would it not be much better if as many children as possible received Baptism with the due ceremonies? This desire is the more understandable in these times when the Church is encouraging missionary bishops to work out vernacular rituals so that the wonderful ceremonies of Baptism will gain in catechetical value. It cannot be denied that to "supply the ceremonies" after the sacrament has been privately administered is not ideal. And the desire to confer the sacrament properly to as many children as possible will be even greater in the event that Rome allows a new arrangement of the baptismal liturgy, for which the prospects at present seem quite favorable.

The dearth of priests again is the main reason why in the majority of missions — obviously contrary to the natural desires of the people themselves — the liturgy of the sacrament of Matrimony and of Christian funerals has not been developed to any extent. Here too, the aid of professional deacons could help us achieve a solution which would satisfy the needs of the people much more perfectly. Nearly all the peoples in mission territories attach such great, and, in the final analysis, religious importance to weddings and to funerals, and it is obvious that the Church should always be visibly represented and should consecrate these celebrations in a fitting liturgical function.

The *professional preaching of God's word* is also part of the deacon's liturgical domain, or, at least, is very closely related to it. By the diaconate, he is in a special way ordained to the ministry of the Word. Like the priest, he is to proclaim the word of God, and primarily in the course of liturgical services. In the missions, one of his classic functions would, therefore, be to conduct the Sunday services without a priest, and through his ministry these would be elevated to the dignity of liturgical services strictly so called.

But by reason of his sacramental ordination and the mandate given him by the Church, his preaching outside of liturgical functions would also gain an especially sacred and ecclesiastical character. The professional preaching of God's word which is given in the name of the Church and which is addressed to the faithful, more especially to the assembled community of the faithful, is fundamentally a function of public worship, carried out in the name and by the authority of the Church herself. It is, therefore, obviously desirable that he who thus proclaims God's word be initiated into his sacred function by ordination. In the fact of his being ordained, both the sacred character of his preaching activity and his being commissioned by the Church to preach would be clearly evident. The fact that we have lost our Christian sensitivity to such sacred requirements to the extent that we have is one of the sorry characteristics of our overmechanized age. If the man who proclaims God's word in the name of the Church to His people were an ordained deacon, and not simply an appointed catechist, then the sacred character of that word would once more be easily perceived by all the faithful.

To a far greater extent than in home countries, the priest needs many assistants who devote their whole lives completely to the preaching of the Gospel. It is true that we already have numerous catechists, and, wherever they have been carefully selected and thoroughly trained, they carry out a splendid work for the missionary apostolate. But it is also true that professional deacons could carry out the same work still more perfectly by reason of the power of the sacrament of Orders and because of a more complete ascetical and professional training. A restoration of the diaconate in the missions would force us to stress quality more than quantity in the training of these ordained catechists and, ultimately, to do the same in the selection and training of ordinary catechists.

Professional deacons, finally, would also find in the missions many important tasks to be carried out in the field of *ecclesiastical charity and administration,* and, by their work along these lines, could effectively free the priest for the missionary activities which by their nature require a priestly missionary and leader. In the ancient Church, administrative and charitable service was considered to be the special domain of deacons, and up to the high Middle Ages, the first assistant to the Pope in ecclesiastical administration was the Archdeacon of the Roman Church, whose functions were roughly those of the present Cardinal Secretary of State.[8]

And it would be a wonderful thing if the sacred diaconal character of those entrusted to carry out the administration and charitable work of the Church would remind the faithful that these functions are "sacred" tasks of the Church to be carried out accordingly. In former times it was much easier to carry them out in such a way, since both administration and charity had a much more personal note, a quieter tempo, and a more religious quality even in externals and methods. In the missions especially the sacred character of these activities needs to be brought out, for it is only activities that are carried out with an evident and genuine religious spirit that really help to open up the hearts of the people to the coming of God's kingdom.

All these considerations clearly go to recommend the restoration of the professional diaconate in the missions. But there are also several weighty reasons against it.

Disadvantages of Married Deacons in the Missions

When we are considering the disadvantages of the restoration of the diaconate, we use the expression "married" deacons which we have avoided previously. Here it seems necessary to use it, since this term brings up the most serious objection. Would not the use of married deacons inevitably give the impression that, even in the Latin rite, the Church is becoming more ready to soften the strict law of priestly celibacy? "Today married deacons, tomorrow married priests" — the possibility and even the probability of such a misunderstanding on the part of the faithful and even some priests cannot be denied when we consider the concrete situation in many mission territories today.

In order to weigh this objection fairly, we must realize the fact that frequently in the missions celibacy involves a far greater sacrifice for a native priest — especially if he is not a religious — than it does for the average priest in home countries. We do not need here to go into a discussion of the various causes of this fact; missionary experts will,

8. Even in the 19th century, Cardinal Antonelli, the famous Cardinal Secretary of State to Pius IX, was only a deacon. At the present time, all the so-called Cardinal Deacons are at least ordained priests. But in former times they were actually deacons. This fact brings out the importance of the work done by deacons in the Roman Church.

we believe, agree that it is true, not so much in "the missions in general," but in many particular missions with their concrete situations. And, obviously, great difficulties encountered in observing celibacy arouse the desire to obtain some mitigation.

The danger of misinterpretation is all the greater by reason of the fact that to begin to use married deacons at the present time, without any previous preparation of the people's minds, would appear to be such a revolutionary change. In many home countries also, the idea of having married deacons serving in the ordinary parish would seem absolutely inconceivable to the majority of the faithful, although in other countries, where the liturgical renewal and its constructive ideals have already formed to some extent the mentality of the ordinary faithful, there might be little or no opposition. But are we in the missions as advanced as these latter countries?

Another objection often made is that the restoration of a professional diaconate would, at least in the missions, *not bring about the freeing of priests* for the work of the missionary priesthood as such, because the use of married deacons would diminish to a considerable extent the number of priestly vocations. But this objection appears to us to be much less serious than the first we have mentioned.

Let us grant that if the possibility existed of serving the Church as a married deacon, here and there some diminution in the number of priestly vocations might result. But let us avoid making generalizations and not state that this would be the effect everywhere in "the" missions. For wherever, in the appeal for vocations and in the training of future priests, the real motives, ideals and specific values of the priesthood are operative, and not an unacknowledged but all too effective hope of rising to a higher social level, there we would not need to fear any disastrous emigration of candidates for the priesthood to the seminary for deacons. Some few certainly, would go and apply for the diaconate, but the majority would be those who felt themselves unable to make the sacrifice of an unmarried life. Would not such seminarians, if they became priests, be more of a hazard to the Church than a help? As priests, they would almost certainly fail, whereas as married deacons they might render excellent service. For it is simply not true that the call to an unmarried life necessarily goes along with the possession of all the other qualities needed for an effective missionary apostolate.

Furthermore, could it not be said that, here and there, in order to live up to the urgent directives of Rome at least by having an impressive number of seminarians, there has been somewhat too much concern with the quantity of priestly vocations and not so much concern for the necessary quality? In the missions, even more than in home countries, we need to examine vocations for the priesthood very carefully. Seminary life alone does not give sufficient guarantee; very well-behaved seminarians have been known more than once to have failed disastrously in their later priestly life when they were on their own and deprived of the safeguards of the seminary. Several missionary Bishops, therefore, now test their candidates by a special year of service in the missionary apostolate, after they have finished their theological studies and have received the diaconate. These bishops say that this is the only way in which they can hope to make sure that the candidates are actually equal to the severe requirements of priestly life in the missions.

And, finally, we should not overlook the possibility that a certain diminution in the number of priestly vocations at the time of the introduction of a married diaconate might well, in a relatively short time, be more than compensated for by the abundant vocations coming from the families of married deacons, provided that we were able to give these deacons a good formation and to continue to conserve and deepen their missionary spirit during all the years following their ordination.

From the *viewpoint of finances,* certainly, the restoration of a professional diaconate would mean a noteworthy additional expenditure. This restoration can only produce its fruits if the candidates for the diaconate are carefully selected and thoroughly trained for their special apostolate. This training would require a preliminary high school formation and would need some years of special training on the college level. After their formation, the deacons would need, obviously, to be paid a salary sufficient to enable them to raise a good Christian family on their own social level. When we take into consideration the low wages frequently paid to catechists, we must stress the fact that a restoration of the diaconate would require quite a drastic change in the wage scale of missionary personnel, first of all, with regard to the deacons themselves and, in consequence, to the other helpers in the missionary apostolate. We are well aware of the fact that it is much easier to lay down the requirements for the formation and remuneration of professional deacons than to carry them out. And therefore the decisive question is this: In the missions today, are we sufficiently advanced to be ready and able to fulfill these requirements?

It might, perhaps, be thought that one way of avoiding the difficult question of adequate salaries would be to suggest the employment of *part-time deacons* in the missions. But we would not dare to propose this solution, at least not unless the majority of the deacons in a mission were to be full-time deacons. For a part-time deacon would spend less time in the service of the Church than would the full-time catechists and teachers in the missions who, usually, receive very modest compensation. And what could be the formation of such part-time deacons? If they were not given a solid, and therefore, necessarily fairly long and specialized formation, they would be on the same level as, or even below the ordinary catechists, whose formation, thank God, in many missions, indicates a most promising progress. Part-time deacons without the necessary formation would not be honored by the faithful, and the abuse might well arise of considering such a diaconate as a kind of ecclesiastical distinction given for special service in the lay apostolate.

The case is quite different with the Minor Orders. They should not, obviously, become ecclesiastical distinctions given to lay Catholics as rewards of merit. But the functions of these Orders, by their very nature, do not require full-time service.

The question has often been raised whether, in the missions, the faithful would in any case accept married deacons and give them the necessary confidence. It is true that the faithful in the missions are very proud of the celibacy of their priests. In a pagan environment, they appreciate fully this special characteristic of the Catholic priest that distinguishes him even in the eyes of unprejudiced pagans. But deacons are not priests. Although they would render the priest very valuable services and share to some extent in his pastoral duties, they could never claim the same religious confidence from the people as does the priest. But the respect and confidence that they could rightly demand would, I believe, be given them without difficulty if they were properly presented to the faithful by the Bishop, and given due respect and honor by their priestly colleagues.

After all these considerations, many missionaries may feel that since there are so many "buts" and "ifs" in the whole question, at least at the present time, no general recommendation for a restoration of the diaconate is desirable or even possible, and that this is certainly true in relation to the missions, even if Rome were to grant all the necessary permissions. Thus the idea is not yet ripe for any realization. The word of the Holy Father on this question also, as we saw earlier, was, "not yet ripe." But let us take this prudent judgment of the Pope's in the sense in which it was meant. It does not mean that we should not pursue this question any further but should rather concentrate all our attention on what is already "ripe," or what we can cause to "ripen" almost immediately. We need both the energetic and realistic work of planning and carrying out our apostolate here and now, *and* wise long-range planning for the future. Both are needed, and they must be pursued together. In laying down the following principles, we have tried to consider both aspects and harmoniously to combine them.

Some leading principles for the present and the future

1. We should not let our friends in the various home countries receive the impression that an opportune restoration of the professional diaconate is primarily a missionary concern, in which missionaries should take the initiative. On the contrary, the pastoral condition of *some home countries would seem, at the present time, to be "riper" for such a restoration* than that of the majority of missions. But when these countries have taken the initiative, then a well-prepared for and properly adapted restoration of the diaconate might be of great help to the mission apostolate also.

2. Although in principle, one would welcome professional deacons in the missions, one would certainly, here above all, plead that *progress be made to this end by easy stages.* It does not seem desirable to begin at once with restoring the diaconate. *The first step would be the opportune restoration of the Minor Orders,* especially of the lectorate to be conferred on catechists. This was also the explicit request of the missionaries assembled at the Congress of Pastoral Liturgy at Assisi. The formulation of this request both in the pre-Congress meeting of missionaries and in the Congress itself was the result of the personal initiative of Bishop van Bekkum. And even before Rome makes the necessary arrangements for the highly recommended and immediately feasible restoration of the lectorate, the ecclesiastical commission of professional helpers in the missionary apostolate (catechists, etc.) could and should be conferred by means of a special "liturgical" function, for example, by the imposition of hands and blessing given by the Bishop or the priest. And even this restoration of the lectorate would make it desirable that the catechists who are to be ordained lectors should receive a more complete ascetical and professional training than do the majority as things are.

3. An eventual restoration of the diaconate might be accomplished gradually by *beginning in those missions that are the best prepared for it.* In many home countries, the important and undeniable fact is frequently overlooked that in the field of the liturgy, as in everything else, "the missions" are not a homogeneous unit. Furthermore, Rome itself would probably prefer to grant the necessary permissions by regions, as has been the procedure in the case of vernacular rituals, and in allowing the use of the vernacular in the sacramental liturgy, with different solutions for different places according to their varying pastoral needs.

4. Even when and where the soil is sufficiently prepared for the restoration of the diaconate, we should take care *not to exaggerate the liturgical and missionary importance* of this particular request. A well-prepared and gradual restoration of the various orders, including that

of the diaconate, does seem to be desirable, and, at a developed stage, would make significant contributions toward freeing priest missionaries for their most urgent and specific priestly work. But it must be made clear that the so-called "missionary asphyxia" — which others name, perhaps better, "convert-saturation" — is not a phenomenon to be found only in Africa,[9] and that it is one which must be dealt with at once by much more comprehensive and effective measures.

At the present moment particularly, we should carefully avoid anything which would foster the impression that the liturgical renewal so urgently needed in the missions is a movement for getting "married deacons." Since, in the majority of missions, we are only at the beginning in relation to the liturgical renewal, there is a special danger that some immature elements — some of whom may even consider themselves to be our friends — may take some "spicy" or newsworthy point of quite secondary importance out of our whole program and present it to others as being "the" aim of the liturgical renewal. The worst possible service that one could render to the true aims of the liturgical renewal would be to present it as a movement which is primarily concerned with having the priest celebrate Mass facing the congregation, the employment of married deacons, and doing away with Latin in the liturgy.

9. In this connection, see the very enlightening article on the "Convert Saturation Point in Taiwan," by Ivar McGrath in *Mission Bulletin,* Hongkong, 1958, p. 6-14. Another striking example of the same problem is to be found in the famous Chota Nagpur Mission in India. There, as in so many other places, the missionary is so taken up by the necessary pastoral care of the faithful that any vigorous extension of his strictly missionary activity would exceed his moral and physical strength.

CHAPTER TWENTY-TWO

Centers of Liturgical Renewal

JOSEF KELLNER, S.J.

The liturgy, rightly understood and carried out, offers tremendous possibilities for the fruitfulness of our apostolate in newly Christianized regions, but it also presents, as we have seen, a series of problems as yet unsolved. The task of the missionary as a pioneer of the faith and his task as a celebrant of the worship of the Church do not constitute two spheres of activity that are opposed to one another, or that can only coexist peacefully at best. These tasks are not related to one another solely through the recitation of the Breviary which the messenger of the Gospel offers for the souls entrusted to him, and through the celebration of Holy Mass which gives his Christians the opportunity to fulfill their religious duties. On the contrary, as we have seen throughout this book, the liturgy, in fulfilling its primordial role as adoration of the Father in spirit and in truth, can also become a most powerful force for the deepening of every aspect of Christian life in the missions — but only on condition of adaptation and renewal.

Everyone knows that today no such renewal can be made except under the direction of the Roman ecclesiastical authorities. But whose business is it to draw the attention of these authorities to the needs, the difficulties, the desires of the present time, or to make a start by gathering together the necessary facts and information? The development of the liturgical renewal in the Church, even during the last ten or twenty years, shows us that *the attitude of the Ordinaries is a decisive factor.* The Motu Proprio, *In cotidianis precibus,* introducing the new translation of the psalms, says that desires for a new translation were expressed not only by learned authors in scholarly books and reviews, but "came to us from many sacred ministers, from bishops and also from several cardinals of the Holy Roman Church." It was also the bishops who asked for the restoration of the Easter Vigil, who concerned themselves with making reports on its success, who asked for the extension of the experiment, and who finally obtained the renewal of the whole of Holy Week. The decree, *Maxima redemptionis mysteria*,[1] making effective the renewal of Holy Week, emphasizes the role of the episcopate: "the same Ordinaries having repeated the requests in which they asked that, following the example of the Easter Vigil, the liturgical renewal be extended to all the days of Holy Week. . . . "

"Bishops should watch over the future progress of the liturgy and direct it with firmness," is one statement made in a letter from the Secretariat of State addressed to Cardinal Bertram of Breslau in 1943.[2] These words had at that time a rather negative sense, but the encyclical *Mediator Dei,* which appeared five years later, clearly showed that, in the eyes of Rome, the episcopate is the first to be called to promote the liturgical renewal and to favor its healthy development. "We earnestly exhort you, Venerable Brethren, that after errors and falsehoods have been removed, and anything that is contrary to truth or moderation has been condemned, you promote a deeper knowledge among the people of the sacred liturgy so that they may more readily and easily follow the sacred rites and take part in them with true Christian dispositions."[3] And the Holy Father calls for similar initiatives in his encyclical *Musicae Sacrae Disciplina.*

The interest that Rome brings to healthy and pastorally effective liturgical progress comes from its understanding of, and complying with, well-founded desires, especially for mission countries. A classic example is the problem of the language in the liturgy. To mention only one instance, in 1954 the three Vicars Apostolic of the Island of Flores in Indonesia obtained the permission to use in their districts the principle of the "High Mass sung in the language of the people," a permission already granted to the dioceses of Germany; and this permission was expressly confirmed in the encyclical *Musicae Sacrae Disciplina.* Rome had already gone still further. As early as 1941-1942, several legations and apostolic nuntiatures had been invited to translate, with certain restrictions, the ritual into the language of each country and to try out these translations for a period of ten years before going to Rome to obtain definitive approbation. This invitation given to China, India, Indo-China, Indonesia, Japan, New Guinea and Africa,[4] was renewed

1. March 24, 1945.
2. December 24, 1955.
3. *Mediator Dei* (N.C.W.C. Trans. n. 186).
4. See the article "History of Vernacular Usage," *Worship*, XXVIII, 1953, p. 391-395, especially the concluding paragraphs.

in the same form in 1949, and, it appears, was then addressed to all the legations and nunciatures of missionary countries.[5] In the eyes of Rome, the bishops of the Church are truly a leading Council, exercising a decisive influence on all important resolutions.

The International Congress of Assisi (September, 1956) became a landmark in the liturgical renewal of the Church. Its president was the prefect of the Sacred Congregation of Rites; the speakers and lecturers were almost exclusively bishops and abbots; many missionary bishops were among the participants; the conclusion of this illustrious meeting was a talk delivered by the Holy Father himself. None of the preceding liturgical congresses could boast of such an honor.

In Germany and in Austria, since the episcopate has taken the lead in the liturgical renewal, it has gained in extension, in depth, in continuity and in fruitfulness. To it are due a common fund of chants and hymns, excellent diocesan prayer books and hymnals, unified regulations concerning community Mass, a ritual which, besides a wide use of the language of the people, provides various improvements in the rites themselves, as for example, in the liturgy of the sick and the marriage ceremony. The hour might seem to have come in which a similar development would extend to the whole Church. And the bishops of mission countries, who know well the needs and circumstances of their flocks, will be able to gather its ripening fruits for their faithful.

The liturgical renewal is a great pastoral duty,[6] not the only one, obviously, but one among many. Even in small dioceses, this task is too great for one man, and therefore Pius XII hoped that in each diocese a *liturgical commission* would be set up to study the various problems and to find means of solving them.[7]

In missionary countries, such liturgical commissions are even more necessary than in others. All the questions relating to Christian worship, questions of which this book has given only a glimpse, require expert treatment. Missionaries themselves, the majority of whom are too pressed for time and too lacking in the means necessary to devote themselves to profound studies, will gratefully accept any help along these lines. And work will not be lacking! How many dioceses possess a manual of prayers and a hymnbook that corresponds to the wishes of the Church, to the needs of the present time and of each ecclesiastical district? Who is concerned with unifying the way in which community Mass is celebrated? Who will suggest to the faithful the texts and the

---

5. See *The American Ecclesiastical Review*, CXXV, 1951, p. 334.
6. St. Pius X had said already: *Inter pastoralis officii sollicitudines proculdubio praecipua."*
7. *Mediator Dei* (N.C.W.C. Trans. n. 169).

appropriate directives for celebrating Sundays and feast days in communities with no priest? Who will search for fruitful solutions of all the problems of a pastoral-minded liturgy? Who will make a liturgical library generally available to all? Who will organize courses in the liturgy and study-weeks for priests and laity? Who will take care of good Catholic radio and television services? Who will inform the workers in the Lord's vineyard of the positive results that are being obtained in the liturgical life of the Church today and point out to them the information that is especially useful in their field of action?[8] So many questions, so many urgent problems! For all these and many other needs — let us consider only the liturgical formation of future priests and mission helpers — a diocesan liturgical commission would render priceless service to the higher authorities. In many cases also, it could coincide, in whole or part, with the commission on sacred music prescribed by St. Pius X.

The work of the diocesan liturgical commission would necessitate — for "liturgical weeks," for example — places in which the liturgy could be carried out not only "according to the circumstances" (which are often rather poor), but in its fulness and its splendor. There have long existed missionary abbeys and convents of contemplative orders that feel themselves closely connected with the missionary vocation of the Church, from the monasteries of the Middle Ages that gave us an Augustine of Canterbury or a Boniface, to the abbeys of today with overflowing missionary activity, such as St. Odile and other orders and congregations. (Nor should we forget, in this connection, the Carmelites, who gave us St. Thérèse of the Child Jesus, patroness of the missions.) To them we owe centers of liturgical radiation such as Yenki (in Manchuria at the frontier of Siberia and Dorea; the Abbey has now been abolished by the communists), or Peramio and Ndanda in East Africa. True to the great traditions of their order, the monks here carry out the classic liturgy, high Mass, Vespers, Compline, etc. and strive with success to lead the Christians in their vicinity to take active part in their worship, and to open up to the people the religious values of worship by means of schools, teaching, writings, and practice.

Between the liturgical commissions of each diocese, such *interdiocesan liturgical centers* could establish the necessary connections within a

8. There is no need at the present time to found a new liturgical missionary magazine, those already existing for the purpose of aiding the work of evangelization are enough. Reviews such as *Worldmission, Mission Bulletin* (Hongkong), *Lumen Vitae, Clergy Monthly* (Kurseong, India), *Ephemerides Liturgicae*, etc., willingly open their columns to articles on worship in missionary countries, whenever any are offered to them.

country or a linguistic region. In the United States, St. John's Abbey in Collegeville, Minnesota, is a radiant center of the liturgical apostolate. In Europe, every country has such centers: in Germany, the Institute Liturgique of Trèves, working in close connection with the liturgical commission of the Episcopal Conference at Fulda; in Austria, the Institutum Liturgicum in Salzburg; in Italy, the Centro di Azione Liturgica; in France, the Centre de Pastorale Liturgique; in Belgium, the Centre interdiocesain d'action liturgique et paroissiale, etc.

To answer the needs of the work of evangelization in pagan countries, this work is not limited to the liturgical apostolate, it includes the catechetical and pastoral renewal as well. This is the case with the center *Lumen Vitae* in Brussels, publishing a review in French and in English; other centers are in Mayidi (Africa), in Poona (India), in Quebec (Canada), in Rio de Janeiro and Sao Paulo (Brazil), in Athens (Greece), in Oslo (Norway), in Upsala (Sweden). The most recent foundation of this kind is the Institute for Mission Apologetics in Manila (the Philippines), where former missionaries from China, of different nationalities, all members of the Society of Jesus, study problems of pastoral practice, of the liturgy and of catechesis in the missions. The present book is one result of this teamwork. The Institute plans also to bring out a study of the catechetical renewal in the missions and a more complete manual for the celebration of Sunday worship in communities without a priest.

The work of the liturgical apostolate along the lines laid out by the encyclical *Mediator Dei* will produce, then, the fruits expected only to the degree to which all concerned — bishops with their seminaries and schools for catechists, religious with their convents, diocesan and interdiocesan centers with their various means of action — work together to achieve it.

CHAPTER TWENTY-THREE

The Liturgical Formation of Clergy and Faithful

JOHANNES HOFINGER, S.J.

Once the liturgical renewal has won over the missions and is taken for granted, then the liturgy itself will form both priests and people, filling them with its own spirit. But we are still a long way from this condition. First of all, there must be created an atmosphere, a state of mind, favorable to the liturgical renewal. Here the liturgical formation of future missionaries is obviously of primary importance. We shall, therefore, begin with a discussion of this question, although much of what we have to say concerning missionary seminaries holds good also, to a certain degree, of the liturgical education of missionaries, of catechists and of the faithful.

Liturgical Formation in Missionary Seminaries

The future clergy of the missions receive their priestly formation either in the great seminaries of their home countries or in seminaries in the missionary countries themselves. Generally speaking, foreign missionaries are ordained before coming to the missions, while native missionaries receive their formation in missionary seminaries, with the exception of a few specially gifted seminarians who are sent to complete their studies in Rome. The missionary priests sent by the various congregations to the missions often arrive without any adequate liturgical formation. And once they have arrived, there is no way of their making up for this lack. Thus it is that only a part of them have come to understand in the course of their priestly formation the possibilities inherent in any form of Christian worship properly presented and conducted. If our missionaries had come to the mission fields equipped with an adequate liturgical formation, the liturgical renewal would long since have won over the missions. It is for this reason that the present chapter, which is as important as any other in this book, is addressed to the seminaries of non-missionary countries as well as to the native seminaries in the missions.

We should, perhaps, ask ourselves first of all: What is the reason for the deficiencies in the liturgical education given in our seminaries? This question is the more important since even the seminaries most famous for their missionary zeal show no more than a minimal interest in the problems of worship in the missions. There is no question of any hostility or negligence; it is simply one of *misunderstanding*.

We are often told that an intensive concern for the liturgy is all very well, but that it has only a relative value for missionary seminaries, since these have the duty to form missionaries *totally devoted to the apostolate,* not monks vowed to the peaceful carrying out of the praise of God. Their spiritual life must be formed without any reliance on the consolations afforded by solemn services, since, in fulfilling the requirements of their missionary calling, they will have to leave all such services to their contemplative colleagues.

This objection needs to be met frankly and fully. First of all, it is certainly true that the ascetic and liturgical formation of future missionaries should not be the same as that of clerics in a contemplative order. In the life of a missionary, the liturgy has a vital role, but it is not the same role as in the life of a contemplative. The future missionary, then, should not receive the same formation as a contemplative, and we shall come back to this point later on. But does it follow that the practice of worship and the liturgical formation in missionary seminaries should be relegated to an order of secondary or tertiary importance? Does such an idea not involve the danger of a man-centered conception of the missionary vocation? The seminary certainly has the duty of inspiring future missionaries with the apostolic spirit and of preparing them for their future apostolate, but, as we brought out earlier, the missionary apostolate, in the spirit of Christ Himself, finds its culmination precisely in the worship given to the Father in the missions. If, therefore, we desire to form missionaries whose apostolate, like that of Christ, is centered in the service and the glory of the Father, then we must form them also for the liturgical apostolate: the final aim of their apostolate must be to win those who were formerly pagans to the true worship of the New Covenant. This worship, it is true, does not include only the celebration of the holy mysteries; but, according to Catholic doctrine, it is centered in the sacrifice of the New Covenant. The Eucharistic Sacrifice, then, is the most sublime act that we, the redeemed children of God, can carry out. Must not the future missionary begin very early to see his vocation in this authentically "Christian" sense? Should his seminary training not be ordered toward this primary aim? How can he appreciate the great catechetical and community building powers of the liturgy if nobody opens his eyes to their value and if nobody shows him how to make use of them? From his seminary training itself he ought to be able to distinguish between a form of celebration that really teaches and one that is merely commonplace, and to be capable of making the liturgy truly fruitful in catechetical values.

But liturgical formation is necessary not only because of the apostolic vocation of the future missionary; it is necessary also for *his own spiritual life*. In liturgical worship, the priest finds the indispensable means of perseveringly orienting himself and his work to God in the midst of his exhausting external activities. Without this repose in God, his apostolic activity becomes a kind of apostolic activism that is as dangerous for him as it is for the souls in his charge. An honest over-all view of the missionary life shows us the great extent to which the missionary today is exposed to the danger of exteriorization. We tend to lack that interior recollection, that contemplative zeal, of which we have an absolute need if we are to be the messengers of God. Who would dare to deny the missionary value of an intensification of the liturgical spirit? For only he who is initiated into the mysteries of God, and lives by them, can effectively proclaim them.

Thus it is clear that a true liturgical formation in the seminary is of the utmost importance in the training of a future apostle. In this age of St. Pius X, the great initiator of the pastoral-liturgical movement, and of Pius XII, the Pope of the encyclical, *Mediator Dei* and of the epoch-making new liturgical rulings, few directors of missionary seminaries could be found who would actually deny the importance of liturgical formation. It may be, however, that this very theoretical assent in not a few cases is still lacking in practical application. And this may well be the result primarily of the fact that there is still very little clear understanding of the scope and the special qualities of liturgical training in mission seminaries.

How might a liturgical formation be given to future missionaries?

Three elements seem to be the most important: adequate instruction in the liturgy, a fervent liturgical life, and the timely integration of liturgical training with the whole formation of the future missionary.

Education in the liturgy should include much more than a conscientious instruction in rubrics. Nobody denies that the missionary needs a solid knowledge of the letter of the rubrics, but, from the beginning, he should be clearly shown their "spirit." We should avoid both extremes: ritualism, on the one hand, and negligence on the other. A ritualistic priest is more concerned with the purification of his chalice than with that of souls, while a priest who is careless about the carrying out of the divine mysteries will be careless about his apostolate as well. He who dares to handle the Blessed Sacrament disrespectfully will have little care for immortal souls. A religious respect for the rubrics is, for every priest, a wonderful school of respect for religion itself. In the missions, however, any excess or rigidity as to the letter of the law would be wrong, would create internal tensions. One cannot act in the missions as if one were in a large and beautiful church in a Christian country. The seminarian, then, should begin to realize that the holy mysteries do not exist for the rubrics, but the rubrics for the holy mysteries, and these for men: as the theologians put it, *sacramenta propter homines.*

Future missionaries need, above all, good conferences on the nature and the spirit of the liturgy, on its role in the life of the Church, of every Christian, and, *a fortiori,* of every priest. They need also to be given conferences on its catechetical and pastoral value, on the various parts of Christian worship, and in particular on Holy Mass. So that they will understand the present structure of the liturgy, historical explanations are necessary, not for the sake of "archeologizing" but of penetrating, the meaning and the spirit of our liturgy today. Such liturgical conferences would enable the seminarians to respond with full awareness to the admonition given them by the bishop at their ordination: *Agnoscite quod agitis. Imitamini quod tractatis.*

We are sure, from our own experience in a missionary seminary, that such conferences on the liturgy are a powerful force in the priestly and apostolic formation of future missionaries. Since the liturgy is the worship of the Church, obviously an initiation into the liturgy is of its very nature a wonderful initiation into the spirit of Christian prayer. And how greatly this is needed! For is not the missionary apostolate in great measure an education in authentic Christian prayer? And only those who can communicate to neophytes this spirit of Christian prayer can form true Christians.

We must, let us say it again, begin with conferences on the *liturgy of today.* This is what the missionary must understand, celebrate, appreciate in its missionary significance, and love. Historical studies can help towards this end, and we should make use of them, for often the ancient form of the liturgy gives us more clearly and fully the spirit of the liturgy or enables us more perfectly to interpret the meaning of the various ceremonies. We need to learn from it. But we must not allow our admiration for the ancient liturgy to cool our enthusiasm for the liturgy of today.

And this applies also to the *liturgy of tomorrow*. It would be a great mistake to spend our time on liturgical projects for the future and to lose sight of the liturgical renewal that is so necessary here and now in the missions. Let us inculcate in future missionaries a respect for the liturgy of the Church as it is today, let us help them to carry it out as perfectly as possible. Let us show them the possibilities in the liturgical prescriptions, so that they may celebrate Christian worship with the greatest possible degree of apostolic effectiveness. When all this is taken care of, we may point out the catechetical and pastoral problems that demand one or other modification in our liturgy. We are even obliged to enlighten future missionaries as to such questions. Why? Considering the many prescriptions newly promulgated by recent Popes, it is clear that we are living in a period of liturgical transition. The Popes who are responsible for the Kingdom of God in our times have already made decisive modifications in the field of the liturgy. The last fifty years, from the reforms of St. Pius X to the recent decrees of Pius XII for a better celebration of Holy Week and the paschal liturgy, have produced more transformations in this field than all the five hundred years previous. And this process of reform is not yet finished. Why has Rome acted so suddenly, with so much energy, in a domain that has been so "set," we might wonder.

Even a superficial study of the reforming work of Pius X and Pius XII tells us the reason: pastoral considerations, and not historical, have urged them to carry out these reforms. If, then, these liturgical reforms are understood to correspond to the needs and problems of our priestly ministry, is it too much to ask that the clergy of today inform themselves on these problems and their relations with the liturgy? If the clergy of Christian or of missionary countries lack a realization of the needs of our times, they will welcome papal reforms only with skepticism, as has happened frequently since the decrees of Pius X on Holy Communion. At the best, such missionaries will accept the decrees of the Popes with silent docility, but they will not know how to make good use of them. Was this not what happened in many missions in connection with the Easter Vigil, with the relaxations of the Eucharistic fast, and with making pastoral use of the permissions for Evening Mass?

It should not be thought that Rome would be opposed to some discussion in seminaries of problems concerning eventual modifications of the liturgy. Some three years ago, I heard the conference given in the seminary of Linz by Rev. Joseph Löw, C.SS.R., Vice-Relator General of the historical section of the Sacred Congregation of Rites, on the occasion of the Austrian meeting of seminarians of 1953. Father Löw spoke with persuasive candor of the necessity for a thorough reform of the liturgy, of the fundamental principles that should govern such a reform, of the problems connected with the new liturgy of Holy Week, of the much needed reform of the Breviary, and of eventual modifications of the rite of the Mass. Toward the end of his talk, he even spoke of the delicate problem of the restoration of the diaconate as an independent order not necessarily leading to the priesthood. It was most encouraging to hear a man of the competence of Father Löw on these questions. And he obviously felt that he was not acting against the wishes of Rome in so doing, as was proved by the publication of his talk. In our own liturgical conferences, therefore, we do not need to act differently from the officials of the Pope. Obviously, we need to realize clearly that here, as elsewhere, "the tune makes the song"; everything that we say should breathe a loyal love of the Church, a profound respect for her authority, zeal for the salvation of souls and for a still more perfect worship. And, let us say it once more, we should never concern ourselves with the worship of the future in such a way as to neglect the worship of today or to minimize its value. The only purpose of concerning ourselves with the worship of the future is to help to lead the liturgy of today to its own perfection.

To carry out a program of liturgical teaching such as we have just outlined *would not mean a multiplication of class hours* that would overload the seminary curriculum. To form true apostoles, it is necessary to give the priority to dogma, to moral theology and to exegesis, that is, to the message that we have to teach. If these three branches of study are really well laid out, that is to say, in relation to the Christian life and to missionary teaching, without sterile formalism, then everything else can be concentrated in a relatively few number of hours. We know from experience that some sixty to eighty periods, that is to say, two or three hours a week during one year, are enough to initiate seminarians into the liturgy of the Church, about a third of this time being devoted to the study of the rubrics. It would be important here to hold the seminarians to the study of the rubrics and to liturgical research on their own account, and to indicate, by means of a final examination, that they had really profited from this study. But we should always keep to the principle that the more a seminary is characterized by a rich liturgical life, the less necessary is any lengthy instruction in rubrics. Here the principles are learned by practice. The part of the master of ceremonies is to see to it that all the seminarians gain experience in the celebration of the liturgy, and that everything is carried out in an orderly and dignified way.

The lack of suitable textbooks is a great difficulty. We know of none that answers the pastoral and liturgical needs of future missionaries. The best seems to us to be that of Anton Drexel, S.J.,[1] but even this does not fulfill the requirements of instruction in pastoral liturgy. Furthermore, it does not make good use of the history of the liturgy to further a deep understanding of the liturgy of today. Perhaps the book of J. Jungmann, S.J., *Public Worship*,[2] might be reworked for use in seminaries. This work would need to be oriented towards the liturgical problems of the missions, and, perhaps, to bring out more clearly the interdependence of the liturgy and Christian life, as well as specifically priestly spirituality. In every other respect, this book manifests the great qualities of Jungmann: concentration on essentials, solid historical foundations, the use of the experience of history to further an understanding of today's liturgy, the clarification of present problems. This book has the further advantage of being able to be arranged for classroom use.

If the instruction given in the liturgy is to be fruitful in the apostolic formation of future missionaries, it must have the collaboration of the *practical disciplines of pastoral theology and catechesis*. These also should bring out the pastoral and the catechetical values of Christian worship, and the professors who teach such courses should not leave these tasks to their colleagues, for questions of this kind need to be treated from both these aspects. And further, the future missionary needs to be initiated by actual practice into the art of liturgical preaching and of celebrating the liturgy so as to be catechetically fruitful. Have we as yet made sufficient use in this regard of the exercises in preaching and catechetical work customary in seminaries today? This work could be carried out in part even during the years of philosophy, since in many seminaries in the missions, the seminarians work as catechists for one or two years when they have completed their philosophy, and thus prove their aptitude. And they should also be capable — to a certain degree at least — of directing public worship in a mission in the absence of a priest, and of orienting the teaching of the catechism toward participation in worship. During this time of testing, they could begin to render great service in the liturgical training of Christians when they

1. A. Drexel, S.J., *Liturgia sacra. Compendium institutionum systematico-historicarum liturgiae ad usum auditorum theologiae ac sacerdotum*, Shanghai, 1949. This book can only be found at present in Bellarmine College, Bagnio-City, P. I.
2. Liturgical Press, Collegeville, Minn., 1958.

accompany the missionary in his work, but, obviously, only if they have already received the necessary formation in the seminary. This formation should also include a serious *training in liturgical music,* as we have already seen in our chapters devoted to sacred music, and at least some formation in good taste, religious aesthetics and sacred art, as we pointed out in our chapter on liturgical art.

The practice of the liturgical life is more important in the seminary than teaching about the liturgy. For the great need is not to familiarize seminarians with the rubrics, but to give them a priestly bearing and mentality, the fruits of living the liturgy rather than merely learning about it. The future priest must be taught the value of the liturgy by being drawn into an intensively liturgical life; that is, an integrated spiritual life, founded entirely on God and His worship, of which the culminating point is the celebration of the Holy Mysteries.

As to the amount of time to be spent in the seminary in liturgical worship, the question is not one of quantity, but of quality. *Non multa, sed multum.* In many missionary seminaries, it is true, the amount of time also is insufficient. This has been justified by the pretext of the "aliturgical" life of the missionary, for which the seminary life must prepare him. This rather strange idea does not correspond either with papal documents or with the missionary apostolate itself. But it has a basis in reality, in the fact that the missionary life demands that the apostle have a personal spiritual life (not an individualistic one!), in which he must depend more on his own resources and be less sustained by public community prayer than in a seminary or monastery. We should certainly take this fact into account in the priestly education of missionaries. And so we should have none of that "panliturgism" that seeks to live by the liturgy alone and to make use of other spiritual exercises, such as meditation and the examination of conscience, only so as not to come into conflict with the law of the Church. But at the present time this danger seems to threaten us less than that of trying to get along without the liturgy, to content ourselves only with the indispensable minimum.

We should render our seminarians a great service if we had them recite in choir the whole Office or a great part of it on great feast days, and on Sundays, Lauds and Vespers. During the week, they could well recite Prime and Compline together as morning and evening prayer. But if this community prayer is to be fruitful, obviously we must introduce the students into it in a practical way, in view above all of the difficulties that many of them have with Latin. We cannot overcome these difficulties simply by putting off the recitation of the Breviary until it becomes obligatory. The fact that courses in the liturgy are not given until towards the end of the years of theology is another difficulty. But since it is customary in most seminaries to give the students some special introduction into the spiritual life after they have entered the seminary, why not begin then to initiate them into an understanding of the liturgy?

A *high Mass,* with plain-chant properly rehearsed, is usually obligatory in missionary seminaries on Sundays and great feast days. This high Mass is not a "spectacle," nor an "imposing ceremony," but the Eucharistic feast, the high point of the day, and Communion finds its rightful place here. To have another "Communion" Mass not only overloads the progress with religious exercises, but is in danger of giving the mistaken impression that Communion requires a particularly "pious" kind of Mass, and that ceremony is opposed to piety.

Should we favor a daily high Mass in the seminary? Certainly not for seminaries having only twenty or thirty students. But we would not favor it for seminaries with hundreds of students either. The future missionary should not get the impression that only a high Mass is a complete communal Eucharistic celebration; this would have very regrettable repercussions on his future pastoral work. The present situation makes it necessary for us to give the predominant place to simpler forms of community worship. The seminary education should take account of this fact and familiarize the students with the simpler forms of celebration, and the resulting variety will be by no means displeasing to the seminarians.

The same motives of early formation for the apostolate should regulate *the religious exercises held in the afternoon,* in which could be included the forms of public prayer which the missionary will have to carry out later on with his Christians. There is no reason for separating unduly the prayer of the priest from that of his flock. It is he who should guide it; but this presupposes that he knows how to pray in the forms used by the people and that he finds himself really at ease in them. But let us always try to fill these more popular exercises with the spirit of the liturgy; to have them popular in their external form, but breathing the essential spirit of the praying Church.

Here we touch on a most important point. Our seminaries have to form those who will carry on the liturgical renewal of the future, and this presupposes that they will use in the missions those external forms of public prayer that are popular and easily comprehensible, allowing the people the maximum of active participation. Only by this means can Christian worship fulfill its liturgical and catechetical mission to the people. Thus, in giving public worship an "aristocratic" form, such as is suitable to our cathedrals and monasteries, we are not getting any nearer to our goal, but rather going further away from it. This should be taken into account in planning the liturgical education to be given in seminaries: *non seminario sed vitae missionali discamus.*

A professor of liturgy in a large theological seminary once told us that the active participation of seminarians in the "aristocratic" forms of liturgical worship carried out in cathedrals and seminaries does not succeed in awakening in future priests the desire for the greatest possible degree of active participation of the faithful in Christian worship. They attribute their own participation in these ceremonies — a participation which is quite distinct from that of the people — to their privileged situation as clerics, while they think that the passive role ordinarily adopted by the faithful attending such ceremonies is quite sufficient. This observation is fully confirmed by history. Seminarians participated intensively in the solemn offices of cathedrals and seminaries even during the centuries of liturgical "coldness," but no trace of a liturgical renewal resulted from it.

But neither teaching about the liturgy nor practice of it will, in the final analysis, bear fruit unless they are harmoniously *integrated into the complete training given by the mission seminary.* Obviously, this question of integration is meaningless if we are content with teaching rubrics. But if we are trying to inculcate a spirit and an attitude of soul, the whole training should harmonize with the spirit and promote the attitude of harmonious integration.

It is most desirable that common fundamentals be kept in mind in *all theological teaching.* We can fight successfully against every kind of formalism in the field of the liturgy and assure the primacy to the interior spirit if this attitude rules in the teaching of theology, above all in the teaching of dogma, morals, and exegesis.. The way in which canon law is taught is also important, but it is primarily in the teaching of dogmatic and moral theology that we can give to the future missionary the understanding of the theological foundations of Christian worship, in a way that no course in the liturgy can do. And the teaching of Holy Scripture? To give the future missionary a practical love for the Scriptures and to initiate him into the spirit of the Bible, is to open out to him the meaning of the liturgy. Everyone recognizes the interdependence of the efforts being made today in the liturgical, the kerygmatic and the biblical renewal, which all have this same basic end in view: the reawakening of Christian life and the Christian spirit so well expressed in the motto of Pius XI: *instaurare omnia in Christo.*

From this fact also flows the necessity for integrating the spirit of the liturgy with *all the ascetical teaching given* in the seminary. The rhythm of seminary life should synchronize with the rhythm of the liturgical year and be impregnated with it; this, through the liturgical celebration of feasts, fidelity to liturgical usages, the adaptation of the daily schedule to the liturgical season, frequent references in conferences on the spiritual life to the liturgy and the unfolding of the liturgical year — but all without falling into an unhealthy "panliturgism." The liturgy is not the only thing needed in the seminary or afterwards; it is not the whole of prayer, still less of the Christian life. And alongside of liturgical prayer in the strict sense, some more popular forms have every right to exist in the seminary, even in communal prayer.

But it is absolutely essential to hold that, while the external forms of prayer can vary according to circumstances, the spirit that animates them cannot. The spirit of all prayer must be that of the praying Church, that is, the liturgical spirit. We should, therefore, avoid those prayers born of an unhealthy subjectivism and individualism, foreign to the marvellous theocentrism and christocentrism of the liturgy, and those that are poor in dogmatic content while overcharged with emotion. For future apostles, the missionary importance of their training in prayer cannot be overestimated. Are they not called, finally, to make out of those who serve idols — pagans of the old style or the new — worshippers of the one true God?

There are many more fields that might be mentioned as needing to be correlated with a fully rounded liturgical education. Let us consider only one: the *spirit of community and of peace* necessary for contemplation. Everything that can contribute to awakening and to deepening the students' sense of Christian community, everything that can help them understand the *value of silence* and above all to observe it interiorly, will also contribute to their liturgical life. For are not the lack of the sense of community and the lack of the spirit of recollection among the great obstacles that prevent us from penetrating into the spirit of Christian worship?

But *what can be done to help those who already are missionaries?* During the time of their priestly formation, many missionaries have had no opportunity to study the meaning and purpose of the liturgical renewal. In more than one seminary, the students are even warned against this renewal as being something dangerous and perhaps semi-heretical. We need, then, to explain our aims in a positive way and to point out their immense importance for the missionary apostolate of the present. Our own observations, made in many fields of the missionary apostolate, show that for a large number of missionaries the liturgical renewal does not even exist! Many see it as a kind of promotion of better "staging" rather than a true renewal, thinking of it as being concerned with the multiplication of high Masses, with the use of Gothic vestments, and with the celebration of Mass facing the people. An explanation of our aims is therefore absolutely necessary, and this is the work essentially of specialized missionary reviews. We need also to discuss this vital question during conferences, congresses, and retreats; showing missionaries clearly and practically what they can do to improve the celebration of Christian worship and the advantages of so doing. For the liturgical renewal will never win over the missions unless it is presented in a truly missionary light. And to this end, we need *liturgical missionary centers,* a point that has been already discussed in the previous chapter.

The Liturgical Training of the Laity

In missionary countries, the priests are assisted in their ministry by many non-clerical elements: *religious, lay catechists, teachers in mission schools.* Theirs is a most important work, and our success depends in great measure on them. These assistants must be won over to the cause of the liturgical renewal and enlisted in its service.

The majority of the schools of formation for these assistants to the missionary, like the missionary seminaries themselves, do not give to liturgical education its due place in the whole training. Except for certain special questions, what has been said in connection with seminaries applies to these schools also. Their piety especially should be permeated with the spirit of the liturgy. *Religious,* above all, are aware of this need, as we have been able to prove. Yet in some religious congregations we meet the following arguments: the religious have grown up, ever since entering the novitiate, in a non-liturgical atmosphere; they are already overloaded with exercises of piety with quite a different spirit. And so there is nothing to be done, if those in charge of such congregations look upon any transformation and adaptation of their customs as a sin against the Holy Spirit! But, we might answer, did not the Pope write his encyclical *Mediator Dei* for these religious also? Should not the spirituality of religious be inspired by the breath of the Holy Spirit in His Church, and so not cut itself off from new currents, and still less consider the influence of the spirit of the praying Church to be a danger to their "religious spirit."

Let us, then, work to overcome these misunderstandings with a spirit of good will and sympathy, and the necessary transitions will be made. To bring this about, let us beware, first of all, of any mere external additions: this would only overload the spiritual program of these religious and, perhaps, disturb the unity of their spiritual life. It is the whole prayer life of religious that needs to be integrally oriented.

This integral orientation into the spirit of the liturgy can be brought about, first of all, by giving a beautiful and varied character to the community Mass in the motherhouse. The preference should be accorded to those forms of celebration that best help the religious to understand the meaning of the Mass, that enable them actively to participate in it, and that will be valuable to them in their future work. The use of a form of the Office that is relatively short, adapted to the needs of religious and carried out in the language of the country, will enable them to take part in their own way in the canonical hours. Some of the canonical hours have already been thus adapted in many congregations of women, but it seems, unfortunately, that these are not sufficiently known and used in the missions. The *sine qua non condicio* for any introduction of a Breviary should be, naturally, the abandonment of some other spiritual exercises that have been part of the program of daily prayer, so as not to overload the schedule and to produce a beneficial variety.

Next to religious, *catechists* are the missionary's chief assistants. They have a very important part in worship itself; it is they who direct it in the absence of the priest. And they can take over the work of rehearsing the chant with the people and of rehearsing the ceremonies with the altar boys and the choir. They should act as readers during the various services, and, besides, in their catechetical work with children and adults, they can aid in initiating these into Christian worship. They need, therefore, to receive a liturgical formation, but always according to the principle of Father Jungmann: "not a great deal of liturgical knowledge, but a great deal of liturgy." For them, specialized courses have less value. Everything that needs to be said about the liturgy can be included in teaching Christian doctrine and in giving religious formation. In our talks on the spiritual life, we need to come back constantly to the true spirit of the prayer of the Church, of Christian worship and of the celebration of feasts. And in connection with their catechetical work, we should show our catechetists both how to make use of divine worship to further a knowledge of doctrine, and how to lead the faithful by means of catechetical teaching to a truly Christian celebration of worship. The musical formation of catechists is also very important, as we have said already. And catechists already at work should be able to fill out their catechetical and liturgical knowledge by means of meetings and by "refresher" courses.

The faithful must be won over to a more intense participation, both interior and exterior, in divine worship. The first condition of success is the *unified effort* of all concerned, an effort *inspired by a great surge of missionary zeal.* To make a new ordinance concerning Christian worship is obviously not the business of a mere missionary, but that of the missionary Bishop, if not of the Holy See. But the Bishop will have obtained such an ordinance in vain if he is not seconded by a convinced clergy. And each missionary must always depend on the intelligent collaboration of his assistants.

In many cases, Christians in the missions may be somewhat conservative, especially those that are called *"old Christians,"* that is, those whose families have been Christians for generations. As compared with the new Christians, they represent the element of tradition, and it is most important that they be won over. Precisely because of this element of tradition, based on a solid faith, the missionary can accomplish nothing without the support of his Bishop. These "old Christians" have, generally, a very great respect for the hierarchy, that is, for the Bishops on up, and they will go on doing what they always have done if they suspect that their missionary is alone in his efforts, a solitary innovator.

But the best new liturgical prescriptions will be fruitless if the active participation of the faithful does not *come from within*. The first question is, therefore, how to create the *spiritual conditions* for this participation. To avoid formalism, catechesis must play a great part in this work. Opening the hearts of the faithful to the liturgical ideal is directly connected with the presenting of Christian principles. And in this work, the following points are of special importance: Christianity ought to bring out the primary necessity for self-giving. We need to awaken in the faithful the understanding of our living union with Christ in His Church and our wonderful participation in His death and in His life. We should continually remind our people that truly Christ-like devotion means the primacy of love, and requires a direct orientation to the Father; and that our mysterious union with Christ, the union that gives the Christian his value and dignity, has its source in Baptism and is intensified and developed by the sacrament; that our offering of ourselves to the heavenly Father finds its perfection here below, primarily in our interior, and secondarily in our exterior, participation in the sacrifice of Christ and of the Church.

Obviously, *some liturgical teaching* properly so-called is needed in order to instruct the Christian people in the profound meaning of the liturgy: the liturgy of the Mass, and also the liturgy of the sacraments, of which we have spoken already in previous chapters.

And, finally, the interdependence of an active participation in the worship of the Church and a no less intense participation in her missionary apostolate needs to be brought out more clearly than ever, so that the faithful may become fully aware of it. By Baptism and Confirmation, we are called to active participation in the holy Mysteries and at the same time we are sent out to work for the growth of the kingdom of God. The missionary apostolate of the laity — so necessary in the missions today — should receive its most powerful inspiration from a conscious participation in the worship of the Church, a participation which our lay apostles should always consider as being both the magnificent reward for their collaboration in the apostolate of Christ and as the invitation to still greater zeal.

CHAPTER XXIV

What We Desire and Request of the Church

JOHANNES HOFINGER, S.J.

In the course of our discussion, we have pointed out, again and again, the great values to be found in the liturgy in its present form. We have tried to offer suggestions as to how to make the fullest possible use of this treasure in our missionary work. Nor, we trust, have we left any doubt in our readers' minds that, in our opinion, the liturgical renewal must obviously be promoted on the basis of the principles governing the liturgy as it now exists.

To be sure, our discussion has at the same time brought out the fact that there still remain several urgent requests to be made to Mother Church if the liturgy is to regain that missionary effectiveness which it enjoyed in the early missionary Church, and which it certainly needs today.

It is in the interests of the missions that we shall now review, once again, these needs and requests, formulate them clearly, and justify them. We shall limit ourselves definitely to those questions which we have discussed over a period of years, first in missionary journals, and then, with the hearty agreement of the Bishops and specialists present, at the International Conference at Lugano (September, 1953).[1] We shall first present the desires of the missions and then, rather briefly, go into the best ways of requesting that these be satisfied.

1. We had previously dealt at length with these same questions in our contribution to *Messe in der Glaubensverkündigung*, Freiburg, 1950, esp. 230-238. We attempted to present the leading principles of liturgical accomodation to the missions in the article, "Liturgy and the Winning of the Nations," *Worldmission* 6, 1955, 25-34, 173-184.

Our Requests: Their Content, Justification, Prospects

Our requests fall naturally under three main headings: greater use of the vernacular in worship; the revision of the rites for the sake of clarity, simplicity and naturalness; a more flexible conformity in the place of strict uniformity. In each case, we shall first give an exact formulation of the proposal, then its justification from a missionary point of view, and, finally, a weighing of the possibilities that the request may be granted.

1. Greater freedom in the use of the vernacular

Exact formulation of the need

There is *absolutely no* question here of dispensing with Latin as the liturgical language of mission countries, nor of requesting any "Mass without Latin." Such excessive, vague and misconceived statements of the problem do great harm, and are most particularly to be avoided.

Rather, what we desire is that amount of vernacular in worship which seems necessary, under present circumstances, to assure to the worship of the Church its full missionary effectiveness and its quality as a fully developed congregational celebration. *Thus,* we ask for the use of the vernacular in the texts which the people themselves have to sing or say, as also in all those texts in which the celebrant or one of his assistants (deacon or lector) addresses himself directly to the people or to some one person among the people (as in the administration of the sacraments).

Reasons for this proposal

The main reasons for desiring this amount of vernacular are, first of all, *catechetical.* Only by this means can our Christians, slightly and inadequately educated as they are, attain an intelligible form of worship which, on the one hand, requires a minimum of accompanying commentary and, on the other, transmits Christian teachings and conduces to prayer.

A similar use of the vernacular also seems necessary if our worship in the missions is to prove as effective as possible in *forming the Christian community.* As we have already pointed out, a patriotic celebration carried out in a foreign language would not, even if it were clarified by translations and commentaries, have anything like the same effectiveness in uniting the people as members of their national community, as it would if it were carried out in their own language. The same would be even more true of a small, family-like community such as those to be found among the Christians in mission lands. Does not the same principle hold good for the celebrations proper to our people as members of a Christian community, of the "holy nation" of the Church?

It can hardly be doubted that the missionary situation throughout the world today requires as much freedom of adaptation as is possible, and this not merely in some departments of the Christian religion, but above all in its very core: its worship and ways of teaching — as far as these are susceptible of adaptation without harming their intrinsic nature. If we do not undertake such adaptation, we may, as we have been doing in the past, convert a few individuals of good will among the still unconverted peoples of the missionary territories, but any such thing as the conversion of the peoples themselves seems, humanly speaking, impossible. In this connection there are, it seems to us, three questions which should be given very serious consideration:

First, would the Christianization of the Roman Empire ever have been accomplished if the Church had not, from the very beginning and with an astonishing firmness, adapted the Hellenistic culture and the languages then predominant throughout the Roman world to its worship and its ways of teaching?

Second, does the condition of our missionary world today — we are referring principally to the territories of the great Eastern cultures — resemble more closely the missionary conditions of the ancient world where the Church found an already established culture, or the missionary conditions of the Middle Ages where there were peoples with no established culture, so that the Church, along with the Christian religion, transmitted the higher culture of the Mediterranean and felt no need greatly to concern herself with any problems of adaptation?

Third, has there ever been a case in all missionary history in which the Church succeeded in Christianizing a great people with a highly developed culture of their own except by adapting its worship and teaching to her worship and teaching methods, as she did in the early Christian period? In the eras of colonial imperialism, the authority of the Christian colonizers and the supposed pre-eminence of European culture made any form of adaptation seem more or less unnecessary. But the end of colonial imperialism has brought with it the end of the effectiveness of what might be called "colonial" missionary methods. Without something on the order of a missionary miracle, which we can hardly hope for, the Christianizing of the great Eastern cultures is as unthinkable without some adaptation to their needs as the Christianizing of the Roman Empire would have been without the adaptation practiced by the early Church.

In the missions today, as never before in recent times, we are confronted by enemies of the strongest kind. Christian worship, therefore, must be made, by every means at its command, a primary *source of Christian strength*. We must make Christian worship into the vital reality that it can and should be. But this requires that we bring to life everything that is dead — or lop it off. This is true, above all, of the liturgical readings which, though unquestionably designed for the people, are now presented to them in a foreign language by someone who turns his back on his audience. Nor can we maintain here that these readings are primarily for the benefit of "the Church" in the sense of the Universal Church, and are therefore read primarily to "Her," so that it does not matter whether the actual congregation present at Mass understands them or not.

This request for greater freedom in the use of the vernacular is also made *for the sake of worship itself*. This is a reason of particularly great significance in the missions and everywhere else as well. The fact that the very nature of Christian worship involves the close union of the people with the hierarchical celebrant in this homage paid by the redeemed children of God to their heavenly Father, obviously makes it desirable that the congregation be able to communicate with the priest and with their Father in heaven in their own language. And the Christians in the missions, above all, need to be given from the outset the opportunity to gain a sound understanding and deep experience of what Christian worship really is.

But there are, nevertheless, very weighty reasons for *the retention of Latin in the central action of the Sacrifice*. Here the priest is carrying out the sacred function peculiar to him as the ordained celebrant. He has received his power and authority to carry out this function, not from the congregation, but from Christ Himself. By the use of the Latin language here, the unmistakable and ineradicable difference between the ordained priesthood and the priesthood of the laity is made clear. It is easy, therefore, to see why Mother Church wishes to safeguard this, the very heart of the liturgical celebration, from any possible danger of corruption.

Nor is it difficult to understand why, in this era of excessive nationalism, the Church does not underestimate the value of the unity afforded by a universal liturgical language in the Roman Rite. But this question of unity, a question of vital importance to the Church, might be put in this way: in the domain of language, what actually binds the various individual communities throughout the world with the center of Catholic unity in Rome? Is it the not understood Latin heard by the Christian people, or is it the understood Latin which the priest has mastered in the course of his studies, which he uses in praying his Breviary in union with the hierarchy in Rome, and in his other priestly prayers? Does not a very serious danger exist at this time in that the undoubtedly powerful bond of unity to be found in a well-understood and continually cultivated common language is getting looser and looser, while the people in the Church still have to endure what is undeniably a liturgical burden, the use of a foreign tongue which the vast majority do not understand?

All this is not meant in any way to suggest that the Roman Church has not had very weighty reasons for adopting the Latin language for its worship and for retaining it through the centuries. In the first chapter of this book, we indicated how, historically, the development of the missions among the uncultured Germanic peoples almost of necessity brought about the use of supranational Latin as the language of the Church. The question remains, however, whether the reasons which promoted this development hold good to the same extent today. And it certainly seems significant that, even when the use of Latin in the liturgy had long been taken for granted in Middle Europe, the inclination still existed to make exceptions for the missions. This was shown not only in the evangelizing of the Slavic peoples by Sts. Cyril and Methodius, who won the right for far-reaching liturgical accomodations in spite of the strong opposition raised to the authorities in Rome by Germans, neighbors to the Slavs. Even in the high Middle Ages, when in Christian Europe only more or less heretical elements were calling for the use of the vernacular in worship, the great Franciscan missionary in the Far East, John of Montecorvino, the first Archbishop of Peking (Cambala), had the courage to celebrate the Mass using the Tartar language at the time when the Mongolian dynasty of the Yuan was ruling China. He nevertheless called special attention to the fact that, in so doing, he had carefully followed the Roman rite.[2]

Since the high Middle Ages, the attacks of heretics (Albigensians, Protestants, Jansenists) and obviously schismatic tendencies such as those appearing among the adherents of Gallicanism, strengthened the decision of the Church authorities to maintain Latin as the official language of the Church. Thus a solution which had been arrived at "de facto" gradually became something considered as "de jure." In the battle against those who favored innovations in dogma, the Council of Trent came out clearly in favor of the retention of Latin as the language of the Church. But with great foresight, it formulated this decision as follows: *Non expedire visum est Patribus ut (missa) vulgari passim lingua celebraretur* (Denziger 946). Clearly the decision was based on the circum-

2. A. van den Wyngart, O.F.M., *Sinica Franciscana* I (Quaracchi, 1929), 344-345. Also mentioned by N. Kowalsky: "Römische Entscheidungen über den Gebrauch der Landessprache bei der heiligen Messe in den Missionen," *Neue Zeitschr. f. Missionsw.* 9 (1953), 241.

stances of the time. Because of these, the general use of the vernacular was forbidden, but not in such a way as to exclude the possibility that circumstances might arise in the future which would call for and justify its use.[3]

At the same period, moreover, it was becoming increasingly clear that such exceptional circumstances were likely to occur above all in the missions. This, in fact, is the reason why the Jesuits in China obtained, as early as 1615, the privilege to celebrate the Roman liturgy (including the Breviary) in the Mandarin language. Unfortunately the missionaries of the time failed to take advantage of this permission, and it was not until the period from 1670 to 1675 that P. Buglio translated the Missal and the greater part of the Breviary into Chinese. But by then it was too late, and the privilege was not allowed to be used thereafter, although it has never officially been revoked.[4]

The severe attitude of Rome at that time is easy to understand in view of the difficulties caused by the Jansenists in France.[5] And, besides, the conflict that had broken out in China over Christians participating in the customary Chinese rites, had an unfortunate effect in this domain. Any kind of accommodation easily came to seem a mere party issue raised by the Jesuits. The Church, therefore, became unusually strict in the matter of the liturgical language, although as Nikolaus Kowalsky has demonstrated,[6] the authorities even at this time showed a sympathetic understanding of the special situation of the missions, and in this spirit granted a whole series of privileges. But in these, it was the missionary motive that predominated, and they were mainly a matter of quite special privileges mainly for the sake of work among the separated Christians of the Orient. In consequence, these privileges had virtually no influence on the missions generally. They had, moreover, come to an end by the beginning of the nineteenth century.

As time went on, less and less attention was paid to liturgical problems

---

3. On this important disciplinary decision of the Council of Trent, see H. Schmidt, *Liturgie et la langue vulgaire*, Le problème de la langue liturgique chez les premiers Réformateurs et au concile de Trente, Rome, 1950.
4. On this whole question of this highly important privilege, see S. Chen, *Historia tentaminum Missionariorum Societatis Jesu pro liturgia Sinica in saeculo XVII* (Rome, 1951). And on the same point: J. Jennes, C.I.C.M., "A propos de la liturgie chinoise," *Neue Zeitschr. f. Missionsw.*, 1946, 241-254.
5. Voisin had translated the Missal into French in 1660. As early as 1661, Alexander VII had decreed in the Bull *Ad aures nostros* against, not simply Voisin's translation, but any further translation of the kind, on pain of excommunication. So too, Clement XI, in the Bull *Unigenitus* ruled against the works of Quesnel, the Jansenist (see Denziger 1436); similarly, Pius VI, in 1786 against the Jansenist synod of Pistoia (Denziger 1566).
6. N. Kowalsky, *op. cit.*, 241-251.

in the missions. No longer did requests come from the missions themselves for the use of the vernacular. The conservative attitude was predominant. The problem of the liturgical language in the Roman rite became more and more a question which even the most progressive missionaries did not feel to be open to discussion. It is only in the light of this fact that we can understand why it was that when the subject of adaptation began to be increasingly stressed and discussed, no one dared to apply its basic principles to the field of the liturgy. To do so was felt to be tantamount to disloyalty to the Church. And even when, in Europe, problems of this nature once more began to be discussed respectfully but nonetheless openly, and even though it was quite clear that the Holy See recognized the question of the special treatment required by the missions, the conservative attitude still reigned throughout the mission world itself.

Typical of the attitude is the liturgical manual of Anton Drexel. It appeared two years after the publication of *Mediator Dei,* and in general, shows a thorough appreciation of this fundamental and epoch-making encyclical. As we have already indicated, this book of Drexel's seems to be the best we have on this subject in the missions. But when it deals with the question of language in the liturgy, so vital from a missionary viewpoint, it brusquely dismisses the very possibility of any discussion of this issue: "Etiam hic verba S. Augustina applicanda sunt: Si tota per orbem frequentat Ecclesia,, quin ita faciendum sit, disputare insolentissimae insaniae est."[7] ("Here too apply the words of St. Augustine: If the whole Church throughout the world does anything, it is nothing less than insolent stupidity to question whether this thing ought to be done.") And the author makes this statement even though he has just cited, a few lines earlier, the words from *Mediator Dei:* "In non paucis tamen ritibus vulgati sermonis usurpatio valde utilis apud populum existere potest."[8] ("Nevertheless, the use of the mother tongue in not a few of the rites may be of much advantage to the people.")

We missionaries can hardly be said to be very helpful when we answer an unmistakable invitation of the Holy Father in such a way as this. Is not a change of heart in order here? Being more papal than the Pope is hardly being loyal to the Papacy.

7. A. Drexel, *Liturgia Sacra,* Shanghai, 1949, 21.
8. The force of this basic principle was not lessened by the declaration of Pius XII in his address to the Congress on Pastoral Liturgy (Sept. 22, 1956) in which he stressed the fact that the Church "has serious reasons for retaining steadfastly in the Latin Rite the unconditional obligation of the celebrating priest to use the Latin language" (in the Mass). (*Acta Ap. Sed.* 48, 1956, 724; *The Assisi Papers,* Collegeville, Minn., p. 236.)

Prospects

As this brief historical review indicates, the prospects for the granting of any vernacular in the liturgy were not very bright even so short a time as twenty years ago — if at that time, any prospects should be said to have existed. The question was still taboo. But about 1940, there were clear signs of a notable change. At that time, there went forth from the authorities in Rome in charge of the missions an invitation to Bishops of various mission territories to prepare translations of the ritual into the various vernaculars. Only the words essential to the administration of each sacrament were to be retained in Latin. But, unfortunately, this invitation, which was intended as a friendly directive, was not understood, and did not get the positive response, the echo, that was expected. This was quite evidently the result of the altogether too conservative treatment of this question in the early training of the clergy. The Japanese mission to which the invitation was primarily directed still has no Japanese Ritual. The first mission field which, after the necessary preliminaries, took advantage in 1950 of the permission for an extensive use of the vernacular in the administration of the Sacraments was, to our knowledge, India (*Rituale parvum ad usum diocesium Hindicae linguae,* Indore, 1950, Sat-Prachar Press). In China before the war, little effort seemed to be made to get a Chinese Ritual. As things were then, the translation would have been made into the old classical Chinese, and, as a result, would hardly have been in a generally understood vernacular.

In any case, there is no doubt that the impulse toward unlocking the treasures hidden in the Latin of the Church came first from the mission authorities in Rome, and was barely understood in the missions themselves. The moving spirit in these efforts was the then Secretary of Propaganda, now Cardinal Celso Costantini. As early as 1940, he came out openly, in an article in *Osservatore Romano* which was very well received, for adaptation in the domain of liturgical languages: "The missionaries in the early Christian centuries gave the Church a firm foundation through the establishment of native clergies, and, in the liturgy, they made use of the various tongues as they found them, the Syro-Chaldaic, the Greek, the Latin, the Slavic, etc. We have tried to move the Orient with a foreign hierarchy and with Latin. But the Orient has not been moved."[9] Indeed, the Cardinal in a certain way plays up the contrast between the conservative attitude of the missions

9. "Noi abbiamo tentato di far passare l'Oriente attraverso una gerarchia estera e attraverso il latino, a l'Oriente non e passato." (*Osservatore Romano,* Jan. 25, 1950. The article presents a discourse which Msgr. Costantini had given on Bishop Franz Pallu shortly before, on Dec. 7.

themselves at that time and the attitude of the Church which was ready and willing to permit accommodations: "The missions, in and of themselves, are not the Church. They prepare the ground for the Church. We have not, in the far East, founded the Church, with its flexible structure that admits accommodations, but only 'foreign missions.' And Asia has not been converted."[10]

The decisive word here quite clearly has been spoken in *Mediator Dei:* Extensive use of the mother tongue ("in non paucis tamen ritibus") is expressly acknowledged as very useful ("valde utilis"), along with the retention of Latin as the basic liturgical language, although the granting of particular privileges is the exclusive privilege of the Holy See.[11] Moreover, in his encyclical *Musicae Sacrae Disciplina,* the Holy Father specifically points out that the missions can rest assured of concessions with regard to the use of the vernacular in singing, in accordance with their varying circumstances. And the fact is that, one after another, Bishops who have requested such privileges in recent years have been granted them.

How far the Church is now ready to go is shown by the basic assurance given to the Chinese missions that, except for the Canon, the Mass could be celebrated in Chinese.[12] Naturally, this permission lays it down as a prerequisite that there be a fitting and proper translation. In Chinese missionary circles, it is an open secret that this work was entrusted by the Holy See to the former ambassador, Dr. Wu, and the translation by Dr. Hsieh was brought to Rome in the winter of 1955-56. The expression "excepto canone" means that texts such as the Preface, the Sanctus and Benedictus, and, after the Canon, the Pater Noster are to be said or sung in Chinese. According to this decision, therefore, whatever is audible in the Mass is to be in the vernacular.

On the basis of these facts, the prospects for our proposals at this time appear to be favorable, provided that the requests of the missions are made in accordance with the needs of the various mission territories, and are presented by the proper authorities in the right form.

2. *Modification of the rites for greater simplicity*

Precise formulation

The requests should be *formulated in precise terms* and *should not ask for any disturbing changes* which would result in practically a new rite. Rather, what is needed is *a modification of some of the present rites,*

10. Translation from that given in *Herder-Korrespondenz,* 1952, 307.
11. *Acta Ap. Sed.,* 1947, 545.
12. S. Paventi, *La Chiesa Missionaria,* Rome, 1950, I, 388. Also C. Costantini, *Le missioni cattoliche,* Rome, 1949, 25.

in accordance with the needs of the time, insofar as such a modification is justified on sound missionary-pastoral grounds. The aim here should be threefold:

Greater clarity, which will bring out more obviously the exact sense and structure of the given action of worship (the Mass, Baptism, etc.), all accessory rites which conceal as much as they reveal being dispensed with. By this means, there will be attained at the same time:

Greater simplicity, making it also easier to carry out the given act of worship. Everything should be dispensed with which, in the course of centuries, has lost its original significance and cannot be given new sense and life under present circumstances.

The genuineness and sincerity in every way desirable and necessary in the liturgy will thus be assured. To render the present rites simpler and more expressive without in any way disrupting them, it would be quite sufficient to carry out fully the reforms instituted at Trent, following the golden principle then stated by Pius V that these be made "ad pristinam Sanctorum Patrum normam et ritum." This is precisely what we are trying to do today, not as scholarly archaizers, but as pastors. In this still unsettled question of the renewal of rites, we must not set aside thoughtlessly and irreverently all the developments that have taken place in the more than a thousand years separating us from the Fathers. Rather, we must consciously adopt such developments and build on them, but in such a way as not to disturb the basic ground plan of each rite, but rather to complete the structure that it implies. A typical instance of a sound development is the use of the Credo in the Mass, which, as we know, appeared rather late in the Roman liturgy. The liturgical reform of Pius V represented an excellent piece of work under the circumstances of his time, and is a good example of acting in accordance with the principle we have just mentioned. But it is easy to see how the intensive historico-liturgical studies of the last hundred years, together with the work now being done in the field of pastoral liturgy, have made possible a great advance in the task of reform inaugurated at Trent. And it is by following the above principles that we can achieve that form of Mass celebration, and of the administration of the sacraments, which is so needed in the missions, one that is simple, clear, expressive and living.[13]

Liturgical studies have now made such progress that we can sketch out a fairly concrete picture of what, for example, the celebration of the Mass might be as modified in accordance with the above mentioned

13. J. A. Jungmann, in *The Mass of the Roman Rite,* Vol. I, has indicated in so many words that an eventual revision of the Roman Ritual should follow these same principles.

principles. Even as early as the First International Congress for Liturgical Studies, which took place at Maria Laach in 1951, very notable proposals were worked out and made public[14] — proposals to which we have frequently referred in the course of this book, especially in the chapter on the celebration of the Mass. The revision of the Rite of Baptism is also a pressing missionary concern, and this was thoroughly discussed by the experts at the so-called "Little Congress" which took place just before the main Congress on the Liturgy at Lugano in 1953, under the presidency of the Relator General of the Historical Section of the Sacred Congregation of Rites, Rev. Ferdinando Antonelli, O.F.M.[15]

Any modification of the rites themselves should be accompanied by a reform of the ecclesiastical calendar. This reform should be governed by the same aims: greater clarity and conciseness to bring out more clearly the essential phases and themes of the liturgical year; a simplification of the calendar itself; the emphasizing of the temporal cycle as against the rather overloaded sanctoral. In the sanctoral cycle, a proper basic sequence needs to be worked out, so as to avoid, as so often happens now, the repetitive celebration of the same "themes," and to prevent the excessive number of smaller feasts from robbing the great feasts of their due effect. Here again, and certainly from the missionary point of view, it is better to have *multum* rather than *multa*. This question also has been already studied and discussed, and practical proposals have been worked out.[16] Indeed many of the requests made in this connection at these earlier Congresses have meanwhile been granted by Rome in the decree on the simplification of the rubrics (March 23, 1955), such as the elimination of most octaves, reduction of commemorations, greater emphasis on the ferial Masses and Offices of Lent and Advent.

Justification

The pastoral significance for the missions of the requests is quite obvious. The greater *clarity* that is asked for in our forms of worship would aid the people's understanding of doctrine, thereby greatly lessening the catechetical burden elsewhere. But the primary reason for these requests is that only on the basis of a sound understanding can the truly fruitful participation of the laity in the sacred rites be attained. Greater *simplicity* in the rites would fit in with the necessities of missionary life, while it would also aid the people to understand the sacred

14. *Herder-Korr.* 1952, 178-187, particularly 184.
15. *Lit. Jahrb.* 3 (1953), 145 ff. gives a short report of the proceedings. See also (310-322), the noteworthy proposal of Alois Stenzel, "Erwägungen zum Ritus der Erwachsenentaufe."
16. See, for example, B. Fischer, *Brevierreform*, Trier, 1950.

rites more clearly and to participate in them more intensely. The simplicity requested here would in no way lessen the possibilities of giving our celebrations the true and fitting solemnity which we strive to maintain on great feasts. *Genuineness, sincerity, naturalness* in the liturgy is obviously a most important prerequisite to the people's whole-hearted participation in it. Ceremonies which must be carried out, although their original significance has been lost and no new life infused, cannot help fostering the all too widespread notion that the official worship of the Church does not call for any *inner response and active participation*, but depends merely on the perfection with which the rubrics are carried out, since the "Church" in whose name the liturgy is celebrated, supplies all the rest. It is quite obvious what evil effects flow from such an erroneous idea, especially among the mission peoples who in many cases are strongly ritualistic and who, moreover, from time immemorial, have been under the influence of various kinds of magic.

Prospects

That the authorities of the Church have long since recognized these problems and sources of anxiety is quite evident, as is also the fact that they have set in motion, and indeed are at work on, a courageous renewal of the Roman Rite in accordance with basic liturgical principles. This work has been expressly endorsed by Rome, and its pastoral aims particularly emphasized.[17]

The impetus was given by the liturgical reforms of St. Pius X, especially by his reform of the Breviary and his statement that this was "the first step towards the improvement of the Roman Breviary and Missal."[18] In recent years, the determination of Rome was first made clear in the first permission given for the restoration of the Easter Vigil in 1951. This work by its very nature indicated and called for a re-ordering of the entire Holy Week liturgy, a reform which, of course, has since been carried out.[19] This "renewal" represents a courageous facing of, and dealing with, ritual problems, such as had not previously been attempted since the reform instituted at Trent. And, naturally, it will not be the last of such actions, for a revision of one of the elements calls for a revision of the whole.

The spirit in which this inclusive reform is to be carried out has

---

17. Note particularly the pastoral-liturgical Instruction, *Cum propositum* which accompanied the general degree of the Congregation of Rites on the renewal of the Holy Week Liturgy. See also J. Löw, C.SS.R., "The New Holy Week Liturgy; a Pastoral Opportunity," *Worship*, 30, 94-113.
18. Bull *Ineffabili*, 1911.
19. Decretum generale S.R.C., Nov. 6, 1955, *Act. Ap. Sed.* 47 (1955), 838-841.

been clearly shown in the renewal of the Holy Week liturgy: a clear-sighted return to earlier forms ("ad norman ac ritum Patrum") in the interests of clear structure and increased significance or expressiveness, and all this for the sake of more intelligent and active participation by the people. Continuous reference is made to the pastoral needs of our times; new elements are harmoniously incorporated (such as the renewal of the Baptismal Promises) to meet present needs, and dead formulae (such as the *Flectamus genua*) are given new life.

In preparation for further reforms, Rome has called for the necessary preliminary studies to be made and, for the furthering of these, for the holding of international congresses for the study of the liturgy (Maria Laach, 1951; St. Odilienberg, 1952; Lugano, 1953; Löwen, 1954; Assisi, 1956). Moreover, Rome has sanctioned the publication of the far from timid proposals issuing from these study sessions. A liturgical reordering in line with what we are requesting here is, then, no longer merely a remote possibility; it is already on the way, and gives promise of great fruit for the missionary apostolate.

3. *A more flexible conformity*

The Tridentine reform was primarily concerned with straightening out the unfortunate diversity in liturgical practice existing at that time. Up till then, each Bishop had regulated the performance of the various rites in his own diocese. After Trent, the Bishops lost this liturgical autonomy as the result of the unifying regulations issued by Rome to govern the whole Roman Rite. The great advantages of such unification are obvious, especially in these days of modern subjectivism which has to a great extent lost the spirit of reverence for tradition once so deeply ingrained in all Christians. But it is equally clear that too strict a unification runs the danger of bringing about lifeless uniformity. This problem is particularly evident in the missions, since their conditions of life are so different from those of the Western nations closer to the Roman cultural tradition, and which also do not differ from one another to the same extent as do the mission territories.

Exact formulation

Our request here is *not concerned with any liturgical self-determination,* or with the return to the bishops of the autonomy exercised before Trent. On the contrary, we are only asking here that it be made easier to obtain permission for variations in certain aspects of the liturgy involving no distortion of the basic pattern of the Roman Rite, where these are called for by the pastoral conditions of a given region, or would be particularly suited to a definite racial or cultural group.

Obviously, in each case, permission would have to be requested from Rome.

Concretely, we should like to be able to work out some closer correspondence between the liturgical gestures and the prayer gestures natural to each people: their ways of showing reverence, of greeting, etc., as also their symbolic use of color. To the Occidental, for example, a kiss is a sign of respect, but to the Oriental it is nearly the opposite, and the same with the embrace. So the Oriental would never kiss liturgical objects to which he wished to show reverence; he would rather touch them reverently to his forehead. Again, the use of saliva in the Rite of Baptism is repulsive to the Oriental mind. This does not mean that everything that seems foreign or "Western" is to be eliminated from the liturgy, but rather that appropriate elements of the gesture language of the given people be incorporated in the Rites: their customary ways of bowing, of making prostrations, of disposing themselves for prayer, of incensing, etc. And, along the same lines, some adaptation of both the shape and color of vestments might be allowed. Moreover, many peoples in the missions would find highly desirable an increase in the number of liturgical gestures, especially those assigned to the congregation. (In this connection, in the composing of texts for the people or in translating from the Latin, great sensitivity is required to the spirit of each people, of the kind shown in the truly admirable old prayers of the Chinese missionary church. There should certainly be no limping translations which immediately betray their foreign origin, nor, on the other hand, any lifeless paraphrasing.)

In all these matters of symbolic gestures, colors, etc., the wishes of the various mission territories will be quite different from one another, making it impossible to think of working out *a* Rite for all missions. What we are asking for is only the opportunity to work out various adaptations of the Roman Rite in these respects, so as to satisfy the requirements of each missionary people without destroying the basic pattern of the Rite. Every mission region would have to determine what its requirements were in this regard. And in many places, the first step would be to sharpen the vision of the missionaries themselves as well as of their charges with regard to these questions. This necessity may seem at first sight strange to the reader who is not familiar with missionary life. But many missionaries would certainly say: why should we think about a great number of minor adaptations in the rites when most of our Christians feel quite at home with the liturgy as it is? The answer is that we do not, to be sure, need this sort of adaptation or accommodation for the sake of the old Christians who, in many mission countries, live apart from the rest of the population in a kind of caste life of their own; we need it, rather, to break up this sort of "ghetto" and to get to all the people, to convert them and to make them feel really at home in the Church.

Justification

Without some adaptations in these aspects of the liturgy, a truly "popular" worship can hardly be attained. A genuinely Catholic (universal) form of worship must not only manifest the striking unity of the *Una Sancta;* it must also allow for the individuality of, the diversity among the many who are to find in the Church their true home. The analogy with the unity of belief makes this point clear: within the Church there can obviously be only one belief, one Faith which is one and the same for, let us say, the Anglo-Saxon (or American) and the Chinese. Yet the Chinese Christian is not obliged, in order to become a good Catholic, to lay aside his Chinese individuality before he puts on, as it were, his Catholic Faith. It is as a Chinese that he believes, as a Chinese that he penetrates more and more deeply into the meaning of the Faith, as a Chinese that he reacts to the Christian revelation. When in turn he teaches the Faith to others, he will and he must put his Chinese temperament and individuality to the service of the Christian revelation. Is not the same thing true of Christian worship? Clearly, it is the same Sacrifice, the same sacraments instituted by Christ that are celebrated all over the world; their being carried out within the one framework of the Roman Rite guarantees our unity; but this need not preclude a clearly discernible adaptation of the Rite to the legitimate needs of particular peoples. The Chinese Christians, in their worship, are not to feel themselves simply members of the universal Church, or of a cell in the Roman Church, but also members of the Church in China. This fundamental Christian conception was given striking expression in the early Christian liturgy, by its wonderful blending of unity and diversity. And might we not say that it was symbolized by the different gifts of the Magi when they brought the homage of the Gentile nations to the newborn Messias and King? As every individual person in the Church brings his own gifts and offers them in the one service of Christian praise, so do each of the various forms of Christian worship.

Prospects

This third line of *desiderata* can hardly be said to have received anything like the favorable attention already given to the two previously mentioned, nor does it appear to be so likely to receive a solution in the course of foreseeable developments in the pastoral-liturgical movement all over the world. Some of the objections raised to accommodation to the individual requirements of different mission regions seem very serious. For example, some say that the introduction of various living languages into the liturgy will entail an apparent weakening of the external unity of worship which has been for so long so strongly emphasized, and, this being so, it will be all the more necessary for the Church to safeguard this unity by holding to the rigorous uniformity of the Roman Rite. But, as we said above, true and vital unity is not necessarily fostered by a deadening uniformity in every detail. In fact, a recognition of the desirability of a reordering of some aspects of the liturgy in accordance with territorial needs — which reordering, of course, must come through Rome — seems to be growing in Europe itself. In this regard, it seems significant that in the Ritual for the Dioceses of Germany, (1950), for example, in various places several alternatives are left open to choice according to different circumstances. If this seems good for one and the same country with more or less uniform conditions, it would seem even more desirable for the missions.

The practical solution that emerges is that the authorities of the Church continue to ensure that the functions of the priest as celebrant be carried out uniformly everywhere, while the role of the people as participants in the liturgy be adapted to regional needs so as to make it both easy and wholehearted. If these facts are kept in mind, and no requests made that would in any way distort the Roman Rite, this third line of requests would also have a good chance of being granted. But, as in all these matters, a great deal depends on the particular way in which we present and justify our requests.

How These Requests Should be Made

It may well be that, in certain cases in the past, requests were not made in the proper form or the right manner, and were not granted for this reason. It might be said, generally speaking, that requests from the missions have not been made often enough or insistently enough; whereas in Europe they have occasionally been made without the necessary respect and, in some case, persons have gone ahead and presumed permission without waiting for an answer. Although this has happened only in isolated cases, nevertheless it has done not a little harm to the liturgical movement everywhere; *Mediator Dei* itself shows traces of such unfortunate occurrences, and not everyone realizes that these are now things of the past. In the missions, particularly, too little is known of how matters have changed and been clarified at home.

If our requests are to be granted, then, they must be made with the following principles in mind:

They must be made earnestly and insistently. Holy Mother Church judges their importance by the earnestness and consistency with which they are made. In relation to the liturgical needs of the missions and the pressing requirements for a fuller use of the liturgy as these are dictated by the world situation today, we can certainly say that, up to the present time, our requests have not been made with sufficient earnestness. The necessity for this has been particularly stressed by the proper authorities in Rome themselves. An objective study of the reports made by the missionary authorities gives the impression that the missions feel that the granting of unusual marriage dispensations is more important than anything connected with the liturgy. Indeed, as we said earlier, there have been cases where a spontaneous offer by Rome was not responded to enthusiastically or made use of, especially in regard to the preparation of vernacular rituals. We were told very emphatically in Rome that this offer was not meant as a friendly gesture, but as a clear-cut suggestion to be acted on. Yet how many missions, even now, have a ritual in their own language?[20]

Again, we must have the courage to continue to repeat our requests; each time, of course, with the same respect, but always with more earnestness and more carefully thought-out reasons. This is what Rome expects, and it is easy to see why. We missionaries are known throughout the world as professional beggars; even when we approach our own superiors, we present them with long lists of wants. And so we need hardly be shy here, just where our requests are likely to be granted. Moreover, if we do not keep coming back with a request, the authorities are not likely to believe that the shoe is really pinching. We are all certainly used to having to repeat our requests for financial aid lest it be cut off or ignored if we are silent!

The requests should be solidly founded. This is easy for the missions; all they need to do is to make clear the special exigencies of their "missionary" condition and show how, now more than ever, these require a form of worship that will have full missionary value. It is precisely when we ask for privileges that we must make our exceptional pastoral situation clear, and do so with cold facts and no rhetorical exaggerations.

Above all, our requests must go to Rome through our Bishops and superiors. The order of the Catholic Church requires this, and it is in

20. The following permission would seem to be significant of the attitude of Rome, on the one hand, and of the missions, on the other. After Rome had, in 1941, granted the privilege of translating the Ritual into the vernacular, the assembly of the bishops of the Cameroons, in 1949, requested permission to use the French ritual for everyone who understood French. Rome answered that the French ritual was to be used only for French citizens; for all others (even though they might understand French), a ritual must be prepared in their own language. *Herder-Korrespondenz*, Dec. 1952, 101 ff.

accord with the Roman way of doing things. Individual missionaries gain much more when they allow their requests to be stated for them by their superiors in Rome than they could ever gain by presenting these requests to Rome themselves.

How much Rome expects the Bishops throughout the world to take the initiative in making requests for liturgical reforms is shown by such facts as the following. As we said earlier, at the conference for theologians held at Linz in 1953, Father Löw, C.SS.R. spoke quite openly about the necessity for, and the basic principles of, a reform of the liturgy. In the discussion period that followed, the question was raised as to how quickly this reform might come about. Father Löw then repeated three times an unmistakable appeal: "The Bishops must make requests, make requests, make requests." If this is true of home countries, it is even more true of the missions, where our problems are both exceptional and exceptionally urgent. As Father Löw indicated, Rome feels that petitions particularly with regard to the liturgy should be made by the local missionary Bishops. It is they who, above all, must take an interest in the liturgical renewal and do what they can to promote it in Rome; with things as they are in the world today, it is the native episcopacy that is listened to. And when anything unusual is asked for, Rome naturally expects proof that there is a real necessity for it, and that the Bishops will point out this fact again and again, and not give up if the first request is not granted. After all, decisions in these matters are of great and far-reaching importance.

After the Bishops, it is the leading journals of missiology and missionary liturgiology that exert the greatest influence in Rome. As. Msgr. Paventi of the Congregation of Propaganda has justly pointed out, those in charge of the missions are quite conversant with the findings of modern missionary scholarship and make use of them in their advices or instructions.[21] Questions in the field of the liturgy must, therefore, be given more and more discussion in our journals of missiology. Thoroughgoing and basic investigations of the means by which the liturgical renewal could best be carried out in various missions could prove invaluable here.

Our requests must be made in a respectful and understanding spirit. If we expect of Holy Mother Church a deep and realistic appreciation of the special exigencies of our missionary work, and if, as a consequence, we make seemingly bold requests of her, it is only right and fitting that we, as loving children, show a full understanding of our Mother's

---

21. S. Paventi, "L'influsso degli studi missiologici nel governo delle Missioni," *Scientia Missionum ancilla,* Nijmegen, 1953, 1-5.

difficulties and make it as easy as possible for her to take steps that may cause her some pain. The noble speech in which the Church has for so many centuries celebrated the Eucharistic Sacrifice, all the ceremonies with which in the course of ages she has come to surround her central Mystery and, as it were, to adorn it in the ardor of her bridal love — all these have become for her as priceless pearls which she cannot easily put aside or sacrifice.

Our requests must first be concerned with matters of central and primary importance. Since this book is meant to serve not only this or that mission, but all missions, we have considered the full range of requests that might be made. But this does not imply that all these requests should be made, and made immediately, by every mission.

The most important permission to be sought for at present would seem to be the use of the mother tongue in the catechetical part of the Mass and in the singing at Mass, as well as in the liturgy of the sacraments (the Ritual). If only a good number of Bishops could be won over to the importance of making representations in Rome simply about these main points! Certainly these represent the primary goals to be striven for by those who work among peoples of high and ancient culture, and by those who work among peoples of primitive culture as well. As we have shown, for peoples of mission lands Rome has already recommended the use of the mother tongue in the administration of the sacraments. And so far as the privilege of using it in the Missa Cantata is concerned, we find that this missionary-pastoral concession was granted very early to the Iroquois mission in Canada. Obviously, then, as early as the seventeenth and eighteenth centuries, it was recognized that this kind of privilege was proper for missions among "wild" peoples, as the Iroquois undoubtedly were at that time. The catechetical part of the Mass calls for the proclamation of the Word of God to the people, and this, surely, is not a privilege to be reserved for those of higher cultures alone. In this regard, great difficulties are foreseen because of the mixture of languages in many mission fields, and this, certainly, presents a very complex problem. But should such difficulties, which can never be fully overcome, constitute an argument against the use of the mother language in worship by communities which do not suffer from this evil of confusion of tongues? After all, nobody dreams of denying the use of books to all mankind until everybody learns to read!

We should prepare now for the time when our desires may be granted. If the permissions we have been discussing were all granted immediately, we should hardly be ready in the missions to carry them out. We have to prepare for them by the liturgical formation of clergy and people, and by sound study of all the pertinent questions. So long as such preparation is not being made in each of the various mission fields, the Church is certainly not going to grant any general set of blanket concessions to "the missions", but will make her grants only in accord with the needs of particular mission territories.

We must remove the various obstacles to the granting of these permissions. Nothing could more surely prevent the speedy granting of needed permissions than such things as: a lack of "feeling with the Church"; the justification of our requests on poor dogmatic grounds; any schismatic or nationalistic tendencies displayed by unenlightened people in efforts to relieve native clergy of the burden of Latin study. Such things as these would naturally cause the authorities to look askance at our proposals, and so to continue to burden with Latin our Christian people as well.

We must show that we are sincere in our present requests by taking full advantage of those already granted. How can the authorities in Rome believe that our requests are really very urgent if we are not taking advantage of the missionary values already to be found in the liturgy as it is? If we are not doing this, we inevitably create the impression that we are more concerned with making sensational innovations than with satisfying basic pastoral needs. In this connection, it seems vitally important that we make full use of all the pastoral aids which have already been given us in the liturgical reforms already accomplished: the possibility of evening Masses, the mitigation of the Eucharistic fast, the encouragement of congregational singing, etc.

In the question of these various requests and *desiderata,* there is no doubt that we are concerned with a missionary problem of the first order. We should, therefore, as we have said, continue to bring them to the attention of our superiors and to emphasize their urgency. And not only to our earthly superiors — we should commend these problems insistently to the attention of the great missionaries and missionary patrons in heaven. Could anyone say that, until now, many prayers have been offered during the Novena of Grace that, through the intercession of St. Francis Xavier, the graces of the liturgical renewal might be bestowed on the missions in abundance, or that St. Thérèse has been besieged by urgent requests for many liturgical "roses"?

Missionary Requests Formulated at the Assisi Congress

JOHANNES HOFINGER, S.J.

That the proposals set forth in this book can be regarded as, in large measure, those of the missions generally rather than of a few individual missionaries was shown in a striking way at the International Congress for Pastoral Liturgy at Assisi, not only in the report[1] presented by His Excellency Wilhelm van Bekkum, S.V.D., Apostolic Vicar of Ruteng in Indonesia, which was received with highly significant and unusually intense approval, but also — and even more clearly perhaps — in the meeting of missionaries held immediately before the opening of the Congress itself, under the aegis of this same missionary Bishop.

This missionary meeting, although strictly private, was arranged at the request of the Committee of Organization of the Congress. Rev. Johannes Hofinger, S.J., of the Institute for Mission Apologetics in Manila, was assigned the duty of organizing a representative group from the missions to take part in the Congress itself and, at the same time, to prepare this special meeting. It proved possible to assemble quite a respectable number — more than fifty in all — of missionaries and other persons concerned in the missionary apostolate to take part in the Congress and in this preliminary meeting. Among them were some missionary Bishops and several Secretaries of missionary orders. In fact, it could be said that this particular group was outstanding among the various special groups at the Congress by reason of the number of high ranking personages in it.

During the meeting itself, the accent was decidedly on the discussions, which were concerned with bringing out as clearly as possible the task

1. The full text of this report can be found in *The Assisi Papers*, Liturgical Press, Collegeville, Minn.

and the present situation of the missions — which end was, in fact, attained. In order to assure the widest possible range and freedom of discussion, only one report was scheduled for each of the three sessions.

In the first session, Bishop van Bekkum set the tone by pointing out the *urgency* of the liturgical renewal.

The theme of the second session was the *difficulties* which the liturgical renewal faces in the missions and what can be done to overcome these difficulties within the limits of the present liturgical regulations. Rev. Josef Putz, S.J., Dean of the Faculty of Theology in Kurseong, India, gave the report. He outlined the present liturgical situation of the missions with a reassuring candor, meeting with the full agreement of the participants when he pointed to the inadequate understanding by so many missionaries of the missionary values and potentialities of worship as being the greatest single obstacle to the liturgical renewal in the missions. Both his report and the discussion afterwards brought forth very valuable suggestions, of which the most important were the following. What is needed above all is a better pastoral-liturgical, rather than a merely rubrical, training for the future preachers of the Faith, which obviously presupposes the development of qualified professors. The time for instruction of future missionaries in pastoral theology could be found during the fifth year of Theology which the Apostolic Constitution *Sedes Sapientiae*[2] recently prescribed for religious congregations, and this course would be conducted primarily from the point of view of the care of souls. It is also highly desirable that an effective institute of pastoral care in the missions, especially concerned with the liturgical renewal, be established; in fact, every major missionary territory should have such an institute. So long as this is not the case, we might consider the possibility of sending one or other of the qualified experts on pastoral-liturgical matters to the various missionary centers to awaken a proper appreciation of the liturgical renewal by means of conferences and courses, and to give the guidance needed for taking part in this renewal.

The third session was devoted entirely to a consideration of the question whether certain various important requests should be presented to the authorities of the Church, on the basis of restoring to worship in the missions its full catechetical and pastoral values. This report was presented by Rev. Johannes Hofinger, S.J., summarizing the requests to be made in much the same way as in the final chapter of this book. During the discussion that followed — in connection with a "List of Requests" that His Excellency Bishop van Bekkum had brought with him from Indonesia — certain proposals were formulated, as follows.

2. *Acta Ap. Sed.* 48 (1956) 354-365.

1. *Basic Principles*

The liturgical action should be self-explanatory, not needing many explanations. It should be the sincere action, the genuine expression, of the whole worshipping community.

It should be noted that we are fully aware of the fact that the liturgy, by its very nature, is primarily not a form of instruction, but the worship of the faithful. This in no way implies, however, that it does not contain unequalled catechetical values. But this teaching function must be carried out in complete harmony with its primary function as worship. Since, according to the present discipline of the Church, it is allowable for the unbaptized also to be present at worship, a well-designed, intelligible and communally satisfactory form of worship would also have a missionary effectiveness of the highest order.

2. *Liturgical Language*

In order that the faithful in the missions should be able to understand the liturgy more easily and be able to take their due part in it more enthusiastically, it is desirable that the mother tongue be used in the following parts:

a. The readings designed for the instruction of the people: that these be presented to the faithful directly without a previous recitation in Latin.

b. The liturgical greetings and prayers exchanged between priest and people.

c. Liturgical hymns or chants sung by the people.

3. *Holy Mass*

The Fore-Mass should again be given its catechetical character. This quality should also be brought out wherever possible in the rites of the Mass. For this purpose, the mother tongue might well be used also for the Asperges.

The prayers at the foot of the altar might be shortened, so as to begin with the Confiteor.

The pericopes could be increased. A cycle of readings for more than one year is desirable. The missionary also needs to have the privilege of choosing other pericopes in accordance with circumstances. This is particularly needed, for example, in the postponed celebration of a feast in an outlying station, when the missionary should be able to use a Mass Proper suitable to the feast.

In place of the continually changing Proper chants: Introit, Gradual, Offertory and Communion, it might be well to allow a choice of those which recur during each of the great periods of the ecclesiastical year

(Advent, Christmastide, Sundays after Pentecost, etc.) using a simple text and a suitable melody, or some particularly suitable hymn.

For the Offertory, litany-like prayers of offering in the language of the people might be worked out, resembling those of the old "Oratio Fidelium," which could be inserted after the Oremus; to these an Act of Contrition might eventually be added (*Ceremoniale*, II, 39) also in the language of the people. The symbolism marking the beginning of the liturgy of sacrifice might be brought out more clearly and strongly, perhaps by beginning with the washing of the hands; in any case by incensing even at low Masses, as is now the privilege of the Capuchins. The offertory procession of the faithful might be fostered, at least in the form of a representative procession; the priest's prayers of offering, on the other hand, might be simplified.

With regard to Communion, the rules for the Eucharistic fast might be put in terms that even the simplest mind can understand.[3] Also, the priest should be permitted, when he has gone to administer Viaticum and finds the sick person unable to communicate, to consume the Host himself, rather than to have to carry It a long way back to the church.

4. *The Ritual*

The language of the people might be more extensively used.

Baptism: the Rite of Infant Baptism, especially the first part of it, might be greatly shortened. The Rite for Adults might be rearranged and broken up into various stages, as in the early catechumenate.

Confirmation: a solemn entrance ceremony in the language of the people, with dialogue and singing, should be introduced.

The possibilities of incorporating traditional and indigenous ceremonies of betrothal, marriage, burial and seasonal customs into the Ritual should be investigated. It might be possible to have a commission established to make the necessary preliminary studies and to try out various suggestions on an experimental basis.

5. *The Pontifical*

A simplified rite might be worked out for the Pontifical Mass, which would still differ considerably from a High Mass celebrated by a single priest. Pontifical vestments could be simplified for hot climates.

6. *Holy Orders*

Minor Orders should be restored in a form suitable to present-day conditions. Above all, there should be a restoration of the Order and

---

3. This desire has not been granted in the new regulations for the Eucharistic fast of March 22, 1957.

function of Lector, to be conferred on those who now serve as catechists. At the very least, the solemn commission to teach doctrine (given to catechists and other lay helpers) should be conferred in a liturgical ceremony performed by the bishop or the priest. In addition, the restoration of a functional (permanent) diaconate, without the obligation of celibacy, might be desirable for communities without priests, particularly for the purpose of preaching and of distributing Communion.

7. The Ecclesiastical Year

In connection with the Holy Week liturgy, the missions should have greater freedom of choice of hours for services.[4] The Exultet should be sung in the language of the people. The variation of the *Hanc igitur* formula during Mass for Easter time and Pentecost should be allowed to be used also in all Masses following on the administration of Baptism.

An investigation might be conducted to find out whether the particular feasts or Mass-formularies that are connected with special seasons of the natural year (such as the Rogation Days) might not be placed at different times for countries south of the equator.

8. The Breviary

A thorough simplification is greatly desired, also the elimination of legends and of expressions that seem derogatory to peoples in the Far East ("in extremis mundi partibus," etc.)

The Office should not be a burden to the missionary, but an aid to his spiritual life (emphasis on reading the Bible, especially the New Testament).

4. This desire has now been granted in the Decree of the Congregation of Rites issued Feb. 1, 1957.

Outlines of Sermon Cycles for Missionary Use

JOHANNES HOFINGER, S.J.

THE SEASON OF ADVENT

1. *"Do penance"* (An instruction before Confession)

Twice during the year — during Advent and Lent — the Church urges us in a special way to a spiritual renewal, to penance.

    a. *Why should we do penance?* Because the coming of Christ is of value only to the penitent. It was so in the time of Christ, and it is so today.

    b. *What does true penance consist in?* In a real change of mind and heart with regard to sin, in a real turning away from sin and back to God.

    c. *How should true penance show itself?* "Bring forth fruits worthy of penance" — humble, sincere confession; a new and better life.

2. *"Be amazed, O you heavens!": the stupendous "miracle" of the Incarnation*

The amazement of the prophet Jeremias at the ingratitude of God's people: the still more amazing response of God's love to this ingratitude of men: to send and give His own Son for the sake of ungrateful mankind. Everything about this work is most amazing:

    a. *Who is this Messias who is sent to us* — True God and also true man.

    b. *How did He come* — although He is God, yet He came in such a lowly way.

    c. *Why did He descend to us,* miserable children of Adam? God Himself willed to be "punished" for us. How should we respond to this amazing love?

3. *"Blessed art thou because thou hast believed.": The faith of the B.V.M.*

The Blessed Virgin Mary gave us the Messias. And she also shows us in what spirit we must receive Him if His coming is to be fruitful for us. Here *faith* holds the first place.

a. *The faith of the Virgin.* Let us admire her faith both in receiving the angel's message, and then in adoring her Son lying in the manger. How the Virgin's faith was both reasonable and yet obscure. How important faith was to the Virgin.

b. *Our faith.* Application of the first point to ourselves.

4. *"His own received Him not"* (An Instruction in the missionary spirit.)

Our joy at the coming of the Savior is intermingled with sadness when we consider how men did in fact receive Him.

a. *"He came unto His own"* — His own both because of His creating us and because of His assuming our nature and thus becoming our Brother.

b. *"His own received Him not."* He came for all men. So many have not received Him. Pagans have not received Him. But also many Christians refuse Him. Our refusal is the practical reason why pagans refuse Him.

5. *"Freely have you received, freely give": The generosity of God and our love*

The season of Advent is not only a time of penance, but also a classic time for practicing fraternal charity. For:

a. *"Freely have you received"* — What a great and wonderful gift the Father has given us! He gave it freely, for no merits of ours, even to those who rebelled against Him, being moved by mercy. Our response.

b. *"Freely give."* We are to give freely, even to our enemies, as God has given to us. Let us give whatever we are able to give: gifts and material help, but especially our hearts. Let us give Christ Himself through prayer and truly apostolic action.

6. *"Come, Lord Jesus!" The coming of Jesus in grace and glory*

Christ has come in the flesh. But He is still "He who is to come," and His coming in grace and in glory is greatly to be desired.

a. *Come, Lord Jesus, with Thy grace* to pagans, to sinners, to all the faithful!

b. *Come, Lord Jesus, in Thy glory!* The true Christian ardently desires the glorious coming of Christ at the end of the world. The last day will be the Day of the definitive triumph of Christ; the Day of the final and complete perfecting of the Church; the Day of the completion of our redemption.

The Feast of the Immaculate Conception

1. *Our Immaculate Mother — hope of sinners:* (Instruction before Confession)

Let us celebrate this most beautiful feast of our Immaculate Mother like loving children: with pure hearts adorned with divine grace. The mystery of the Immaculate Conception is a mystery given us by God, and especially to be the consolation and aid of sinners: it was so in Paradise just after the Fall, and it is so today.

a. *The condition of our sinful first parents.* How great was their misery after the first sin. The *only hope* of our unhappy first parents was the Messias to come, whom the Blessed Virgin brought forth.

b. *The condition of a sinful Christian:* the same misery, but also the same *only hope.* With full confidence, let us come to make a sincere and contrite confession.

2. *Thou art all fair, O Mary!* (Sermon at the feast day Mass)

We come together to celebrate our gratitude. With great joy, we congratulate our immaculate Mother. In our happiness, let us consider:

a. *What wonderful gifts* our immaculate Mother received in the very first moment of her existence. She alone among the descendants of Adam came into existence without the stain of sin, she alone, from the very first moment of her life was adorned with glorious heavenly grace.

b. *Why* our blessed Mother was adorned with such great gifts. The heavenly Father wished to "prepare a worthy dwelling place for His Son." Let us notice what it is that God esteems most highly, and so gave most abundantly to the Mother of His beloved Son. The Mother actually received these gifts from her own Son. She had no Son as yet, and still she received His gifts. O wonderful Mother and still more wonderful Son! During this Mass, let us congratulate both Mother and Son, and give thanks to the heavenly Father, the final source of all these wonders.

3. *"Vitam praesta puram. Grant that we may lead a pure life":* (Instruction for the Afternoon before the Consecration to the B. V. M.)

a. *Our own excellence.* By Baptism, we share in our own way in the privilege of the immaculate Mother. Let us give wholehearted thanks for such a great gift.

b. *Our vocation.* Our baptismal innocence and grace is also to be most diligently guarded (Rom. 6, 11). Let us recall the solemn renouncement we made before Baptism: also the meaning of the gift of the white vestment and the lighted candle.

c. *Our patroness.* Our vocation is so great, so difficult for weak creatures such as we to carry out. With confidence, let us fly to our Mother for aid. The example of St. John Berchmans who signed his consecration to the immaculate Mother with his own blood.

What qualities should our consecration have to be pleasing to our Mother? Acknowledgment of our own weakness, manifestation of our confidence, readiness for vigorous efforts.

4. *"Dei Mater Alma — Loving Mother of God"* (Instruction at the Mass of the following day)

Yesterday we celebrated a great and beautiful feast; in about two weeks we shall celebrate an even greater and more beautiful one; we must prepare diligently during this time of Advent. How the recitation of the Angelus three times a day can help us in this preparation.

a. *"The angel of the Lord declared unto Mary"* — God invites her. Let us consider the wonderful mercy of God, who willed to send and to give His own Son. To carry out His work He did not need any collaboration on the part of man; yet He allowed it, He even asked for it. He sent the angel to ask for the consent of the Virgin. How did she answer?

b. *"Behold the little servant of the Lord":* mankind answers. God calls and the Virgin follows His invitation in the simplicity of her loving heart. How greatly this response differs from the spirit of pride shown by our first parents. Let us admire the same spirit of humility and love in the Son our Redeemer and His Mother, our co-Redemptrix.

c. *"And the Word was made flesh."* O wonderful exchange, an exchange of most marvellous love! What great thanks we should give, both in our words and our deeds.

THE FEAST OF CHRISTMAS
First Cycle

1. *The divine Physician is coming.* (Instruction before Confession)

a. *Our souls are sick.*

b. *Christ our Physician* — divine (omnipotent), the only One Who can cure us, most loving, self-forgetful — He is coming to you. Come also to Him.

c. *Conditions for our healing:* to acknowledge our wounds (examination of conscience), to show our wounds (confession), to ask to be cured (contrition).

2. *"I announce to you a great joy."* (Instruction for the night vigil)

a. *Who is this "Child who is born to us"?* The doctrine of the Incarnation.

b. *Why did He come?*

c. *Why will He come* again at the end of the world?

3. *Who has sent Him? Behold the gift of the Father* (very brief sermon at Midnight Mass)

a. *Behold the Father of mercies!* Adaptation of the parable of the prodigal son to the mystery of the Incarnation.

b. *Our response:* Let us follow our older Brother to the Father.

4. *How did He come?* (Instruction at the solemn morning Mass)

a. *The way in which He came:* weak, poor, suffering, humble, obedient.

b. *Why did He come in this way?* To make reparation for our avarice, comfortableness, pride, disobedience; to show us men what true wealth is, and to win it for us. Would that we would at least try to understand the lesson our Master gives us!

5. *Come, let us adore Him.* (Instruction before Benediction)

Let us go to the Word Incarnate dwelling with us in the Holy Eucharist, and let us go in the spirit of the shepherds at Bethlehem.

a. *With faith.* They saw the Child, they believed in the Savior; we see bread, we believe in Christ the Incarnate Word.

b. *With thanksgiving.* Take, O Lord, and receive us. Everything is Yours.

c. *With desire,* and especially the desire for peace, the peace of Christ.

6. *The Apostolate of the shepherds.* (Concluding missionary instruction)

We have just celebrated a most beautiful feast. Its true fruit: like the shepherds, to praise God and announce the good news of the Incarnation:

a. *With our prayers:* praise, wonder, thanksgiving.

b. *With our deeds,* especially by a right estimation of the wealth of this world, by fraternal charity, by Christian peace.

 c. *By apostolic words.*

THE FEAST OF CHRISTMAS
Second cycle

BEHOLD THE ROYAL THRONE OF THE SAVIOR!

1. *Throne of majesty.* (Instruction before Confession)

 We come together to celebrate in a fitting way the Mystery of this most holy night. What took place in this unique night, "while all things were in silence" (Wis. 18, 14)? If only we Christians would understand this mystery more fully!

 a. *Why did our Messias come?* From all eternity He has been seated on the throne of His heavenly majesty. In coming to us, He renounced His glory. Let us never forget His divine origin. Come, let us adore Him.

 b. *You also, come to Him* — by true and living faith — by the sincere confession of your neediness and misery — by a determined conversion of heart.

2. *Throne of Poverty.* (Sermon at the Midnight Mass)

 What kind of a Messias did the Jews of that time expect? Their error is quite understandable.

 a. *How "should" He have come,* considering His dignity?

 b. *How, in fact, did He come,* in His amazing love?

 c. *Why did He come in this way?* Because He came, not to seek His own glory, but the glory of His Father, to make satisfaction for us.

3. *Throne of Dishonor.* (Sermon at the Solemn Morning Mass)

 The great poverty of Bethlehem was not enough for Our Lord's love — He wanted to do more.

 a. *Where does He wish to go?* To the dishonorable throne of the Cross. By His death He wills to give us life. (John 10, 10).

 b. *Where do you wish to go?* What does love urge you to do? Love for love!

4. *Throne of Love.* (Instruction at Benediction in the afternoon)

 Especially at Christmas time, we think with holy envy of the happiness of the Blessed Virgin and St. Joseph who were so near the newborn Christ. But let us not forget our own happiness.

a. *The birth and the death of Christ are renewed on the altar.* Truly and really, but faith alone can perceive it. Yet even for the Blessed Virgin, faith was necessary.

b. *He remains in our midst in His Eucharistic presence* to distribute His gifts.

c. *With fervent hearts,* let us follow the invitation of Christ.

5. *Throne of Grace.* (Sermon at the Mass on the following day)

Yesterday afternoon, we did not set forth the full extent of the love of Christ for us in the Eucharist: He does not wish to remain on the altar, He wishes to come into your hearts.

a. *This is the final resting place* of the Word Incarnate on this earth, here He wishes to "set up His tent" (John 1, 14).

b. *Why does He come?* To reign in our hearts. But in what way? To make us like Himself, to "Christianize" us, that we may live no more for ourselves, but He in us (Gal. 2, 20).

c. For this, *our consent* is required — the free submission of a loving heart.

6. *Throne of Glory.* (Farewell instruction)

From the throne of His majesty, He came to us — to His throne of glory at the right hand of the Father He has returned, but not alone; He desires to rejoice and to reign with us forever.

a. *The throne of the triumphant Christ.* Let us rejoice greatly in the glory of our King at the right hand of His Father. But His joy has not yet reached its fulness since we, His brothers, still wander in exile.

b. *Our throne with the triumphant Christ.* This is the final purpose of the Incarnation. Then the work of Christ will be finally completed. To share this glory with Him, Christ invites us, He aids us, but He does not compel us. Would that all men would hear His voice, *including our pagan brethren!*

The Feast of Epiphany

1. *Our vocation.* (Instruction before Confession)

The Epiphany of the Lord, the other great feast of the Christmas cycle, is also a missionary feast, in which the Church celebrates particularly the calling of the first pagans to the Savior. *It is our feast!* Would that through this feast we might come to understand our high vocation more clearly, to correspond with it more perfectly! Let us consider:

a. *The blessing of the Christian calling.* The blessing of the calling of the Wise Men — this is our condition also.

b. *Our response to such a blessing.* Let us examine our conscience particularly with regard to our gratitude and our faith (prompt, living, fearless, constant, ready for sacrifice). Contrition.

2. *The Vocation of the pagans.* (Instruction at the solemn feast-day Mass)

It is not only ourselves who are called, all pagans are called also. This is the feast of the calling of the pagans:

a. *The first pagans came to Christ.* Christ thirsts for the salvation of all pagans, do you thirst for it also? The Wise Men were led by a guiding star: you must be the star of the pagans today. The Wise Men arrived only after conquering many difficulties; pagans today need your zealous help in their difficult journey to Christ.

b. *The Wise Men offered gifts.* This is what we do today in this feast-day Mass. And let us make our offering with the same devotion, not only for ourselves, but also for our pagan brothers, whose representatives we are.

3. *Come, let us adore Him.* (Instruction at Benediction in the afternoon)

The Wise Men were seeking a "King," they found a little Child, weak and poor. Yet, on the witness of the star, they believed in Him as King and Messias. So must we believe in the Most Blessed Sacrament. On the witness of faith, we believe, we adore. Thou art indeed my Lord!

a. *My Lord,* because *my Creator.*
b. *My Lord,* because *my Redeemer.*
c. *My Lord,* because *my Judge and King.*

Let us, then, consecrate ourselves to Christ the King.

4. *The Flight into Egypt.* (Instruction for the Mass of the following day)

What a great and sudden change — behold an image of, and an object-lesson in, our Christian life in this state of "journeying." Let us consider:

a. *Why the Holy Family suffered persecution?* Because it was the family of the Redeemer. Joseph and Mary suffered because of their union with Christ. So it is with the Church of Christ, so with each one of the faithful, who truly is faithful.

b. *How did they suffer?* In a completely religious spirit: holy patience, internal peace, spiritual prudence.

c. *How did God finally arrange everything for their welfare?*
After the hardships of the flight, the happy years at Nazareth.

Time After Epiphany

1. *Behold the Lamb of God!* (Instruction before Confession)

a. *The preaching of John the Baptist.* In the time of His infancy,
Christ manifested Himself only to certain chosen men. At the beginning
of Christ's public life, John the Baptist was sent to point Christ out to
the whole people of Israel. Then many Jews held a false idea of what
the Messias should be like: John shows them the longed-for Messias as
the Redeemer who takes away sin and gives grace: "Behold the Lamb
of God."

b. *The special task of the Savior:* to open to us once more the
gate of heaven, to lead us back to the Father. He has blotted out our
sins, but our task still remains to be carried out.

c. *Our task:* to acknowledge our sins sincerely (examination of
conscience, confession), to detest our sins (contrition, resolutions of
amendment).

Lamb of God, who takes away the sins of the world, spare us,
hear us, have mercy on us!

2. *Where shall we find Christ? In the Catholic Church*

The Wise Men found Christ in a house in Bethlehem. Behold
a symbol of the Catholic Church.

a. *The house at Bethlehem — a type of the Church.* If you
seek Christ, you can truly find Him only in the Catholic Church. But
you must enter in and live as a Christian in this Church.

b. *What most delights us in the Catholic Church?* The Church
offers us many and great blessings: but this is the central good: in the
Church alone can we find Christ and His grace. As the littleness of
the house in Bethlehem did not deter the Wise Men, the poverty and
imperfection that we may observe in the Church should not deter us.

c. *Christ will always remain in His Church.* Because Christ has
promised to remain with His Church forever, faithfulness to the Church
is faithfulness to Christ.

3. *Where do we find Christ? — In Scripture, in the Eucharist, in
our brethren*

In the Church, everything aids us to come to Christ, but especially
the three greatest treasures of the Church: Holy Scripture, the Eucharist,
fraternal charity.

a. *Scripture.* What is Holy Scripture? The letter written by our Father to His wandering children. What is it most concerned with? The greatest blessing given to us by our Father, that is, Christ. How is it to be read? With living faith and a great desire to find Christ and to follow Him perfectly.

b. *The Eucharist.* He is truly present, but hidden; we find Him by faith. He is present "for us," He awaits us. He becomes present in the Holy Sacrifice so that we may offer ourselves with Him to the Father and so that we may receive Him as the Father's return-gift — to unite us intimately to Himself in Holy Communion and transform us into Himself.

c. Christ is also truly present *in His brethren,* though in a different way. He is especially hidden in His brethren who labor under so many weaknesses. He is in need in His brethren. In no other way can we so truly give something to Christ as in His needy brothers. And we can even make Christ present in His brothers who are not yet converted.

4. *Christ manifests Himself to His disciples*

During His public life, Christ demanded from His first disciples complete faith, but a reasonable faith founded on solid grounds. This was the reason for His miracles. Let us consider His first miracle at Cana.

a. *What an evident and splendid miracle.* The story of the miracle and a discussion of it. Truly "it is the Lord," the Lord of all creatures.

b. *Why did He perform this miracle?* For several reasons: To sanctify matrimony; to show the power of the intercession of the Blessed Virgin and her goodheartedness; but most of all to strengthen the faith of His disciples. Having seen such a great miracle, the disciples could easily understand that Christ was working and teaching with divine power. They could believe intelligently, although they did not understand.

c. *"And His disciples believed in Him."* And rightly! Let us also believe, to whom Christ and His Church give the witness of so many and such great miracles in order that we may have faith in Him.

Suggestions for a Year's Sunday Sermons

JOSEF KELLNER, S.J.

All authorities agree that, together with the liturgy of the Mass itself, the Sunday sermon is the principal means of religious instruction for the vast majority of the adult faithful both in the home countries and in the missions.[1] Our Sunday sermons, then, must proclaim Christ's Good News in all its fullness and attractiveness to teach and encourage our people and continually to foster their loving and grateful response in worship and Christian living to the gifts that God gives us in Christ.

The following suggestions for a year's Sunday sermons will, it is hoped, give some practical aid to preachers in carrying out this principal task of the modern apostle. The fundamentals of Christian doctrine are all covered, so that the congregation attending Mass each Sunday and holyday throughout the year will receive a complete review of the essentials of the Faith.[2] These essentials are presented in seventy "themes" following the order and chief ideas of the liturgical year as brought out in the Gospel of each Sunday or holyday, without being, strictly speaking, either "liturgical sermons" or "homilies on the Gospel." Each preacher, then, can relate these themes to the special needs of his flock, bringing out the spiritual beauty of our message by emphasizing its center, Christ Himself, and the salvation He brings us, and relating it to our response in worship and Christian living.

1. As we discussed in chapter XI, the lack of a Sunday sermon in communities with no priest and no Sunday Mass except at long intervals, must be made up for in another way.
2. The necessary adaptations to mission stations visited by a priest only once a month, every other Sunday, etc., will not be difficult to make. Again, the "themes" overlap sufficiently so that if no sermon is possible on some great feasts included here, for example, that of St. Joseph, the same material can be covered in another connection.

For each Sunday and holyday, then, we give:

1.   The theme to be preached.

2.   The quotation from the Gospel which is either the text of the sermon or its point of departure.

3.   The principal aspect of the theme to be developed. Occasionally we give some additional references to Holy Scripture, and also some references, that may prove helpful in developing the theme, to *The Art of Teaching Christian Doctrine,* by J. Hofinger, S.J., (Notre Dame University Press, Notre Dame, Indiana, 1957), indicated by ATD.

ADVENT

First Sunday of Advent

1.   Our preparation for Christ's Last Coming.

2.   "Lift up your heads, because your redemption is at hand" (Luke 21, 28).

3.   By preparing for the celebration of Christ's coming in the flesh, we prepare ourselves for His last coming in glory; this is the principal task of our life in Christ, and also the principal task of the whole Church. Cf. 2 Thess. 2; —ATD 148 ff and 152 ff.

The Immaculate Conception

1.   The singular privilege of Our Lady and how we participate in it.

2.   "Hail, full of grace!" (Luke 1, 28).

3.   The Father wished to "prepare a worthy dwelling for His Son"; therefore He preserved the future mother of Christ from all stain of sin; He adorned the Second Eve with the fullness of grace from the very first instant of her existence. In a similar way, He has cleansed and adorned us in Baptism so that we might become worthy members of Christ. Cf. Esther 5, 1 ff; 15, 4-17; —ATD 13.

Second Sunday of Advent

1.   God speaks to us through Holy Scripture.

2.   "This is he of whom it is written . . ." (Matt. 11, 10).

3.   God condescends by means of our weak human language to manifest Himself to us and to open up for us the way to Him: through Holy Scripture. Far more than John the Baptist, Jesus is "he of whom it is written." He Himself appeals to the testimony of the Bible (John 5, 39), because Holy Scripture is truly written by God; God is the Author of these books which are the written message of His love for us. And here we also find out how to respond to this message. Cf. 2 Tim. 3, 16; —ATD 23-31, and 37.

Third Sunday of Advent

1. God speaks to us through Tradition.
2. "I am the voice . . ." (John 1, 23).
3. Besides speaking to us in the inspired word of Holy Scripture, God condescends to address us in the living word of the Apostolic Tradition, which witnesses to, completes, explains and unlocks Holy Scripture for us. By the living Tradition of the Church, God applies His message in a special way to our particular needs. Cf. — ATD 113.

Fourth Sunday of Advent

1. Our preparation for the Holy Feast of Christmas.
2. "Make ready the way of the Lord" (Luke 3, 4).
3. The Feast of Christ's Birth is at hand. Christ comes to make us rich and happy. We will share in this treasure and happiness only to the extent to which we have prepared ourselves by obedient faith and humble penance. Cf. Luke 3, 7 - 18.

Christmas Eve

1. Christ's redeeming love desires open hearts.
2. "Do not be afraid, Joseph" (Matt. 1, 20); "His own received Him not" (John 1, 11).
3. Christ comes to us through His revelation, through His Incarnation, through His grace. His generous love runs the risk of being refused. Let us not only open our own hearts to Him, but, as His apostles, make every effort to open other doors to Him as well: "Thy kingdom come!"

CHRISTMASTIDE

The Feast of Christmas

1. The Mystery of the Incarnation.
2. "The Word was made flesh" (John 1, 14).
3. "God made man," is the mystery of God's unfathomable love for us (Phil. 2, 6 ff): in this "most holy interchange," He gives His grace, glory, and immortality, and receives our weakness, suffering and mortality. This love calls for love, because love alone can understand and appreciate such condescension. Cf. Heb. 1; —ATD 101.

Sunday after Christmas

1. Christ, the ideal of mankind.
2. "And the Child grew and became strong. He was full of wisdom, and the grace of God was upon him" (Luke 2, 40).

3. In Christ, "the goodness and kindness of God our Savior has appeared to us" (Tit. 3, 5); Christ came not only to die for our salvation, but also to win our hearts by His wonderful attractiveness, to show us the example of a Divine life lived in visible human form. Cf. Rom. 8, 29; —ATD 102.

Feast of the Circumcision — New Year's Day

1. Christ is our destiny.
2. "And when eight days were fulfilled for his circumcision . . ." (Luke 2, 21). Christ was engrafted into the chosen people by the rite of circumcision, the image of Baptism. By Baptism, we were engrafted into the new chosen people of Christ. Hence we share in the truth and grace, the worship and destiny of Christ and His Church. Cf. Rom. 6, and 14, 7 - 9; —ATD 127 ff.

Sunday after New Year's Day

1. Christ is our Savior.
2. "His name was called Jesus" (Luke 2, 21).
3. "Jesus" means "God is salvation." Jesus, and He alone, saves us from sin and its consequences: the anger of God and eternal punishment. Jesus alleviates even our physical ills and gives them a new significance. Cf. Luke 19, 10; —ATD 98.

Feast of the Epiphany

1. Jesus, the Savior of the Gentiles.
2. "We have seen his star in the East and come to worship him" (Matt. 2, 2).
3. Christ called the Magi as representatives of the Gentiles — of us. He brought the treasure of salvation for all men. To distribute this treasure, He asks for our cooperation. By sharing our riches with others, we activate our own love for Christ and increase our own abundance. Cf. Is. 66, 18; 1 Tim. 2, 4; —ATD 116.

TIME AFTER EPIPHANY

First Sunday after Epiphany

1. The Christian Family, another Nazareth.
2. "He went down with them and came to Nazareth, and was subject to them" (Luke 2, 51).
3. The Christian family is, like the Holy Family at Nazareth, above all a religious unit, a Church in miniature: its origin and its aim is God;

its center and life is Christ; its aims are the temporal and eternal welfare of all its members. Cf. Col. 3, 12 - 17; —ATD 172 - 174.

Second Sunday after Epiphany

1. The Sacrament of Marriage.
2. "Jesus too was invited to the marriage" (John 2, 2).
3. Christ ratifies and sanctifies the natural bond between husband and wife by the Sacrament of Marriage. While the Sacrament of Holy Orders transmits the divine life to succeeding generations of men, the Sacrament of Marriage is the Sacrament of Christian parenthood. It is the wonderful symbol of the union of Christ with His bride, the Church; it consecrates human beings to cooperate with God in creating and educating new children of God, new members of the Church and of the human race. The sanctity of this Sacrament is the reason for the laws of the Church concerning marriage. Cf. Eph. 5, 21 - 33; —ATD 140 - 144.

Third Sunday after Epiphany

1. The Sixth and Ninth Commandments.
2. "I will; be thou made clean" (Matt. 8, 3).
3. Christ the Savior cleanses us and redeems us from the tyranny of our passions. Christian chastity protects the precious good of marital love (cf. 1 Cor. 7, 1 - 7) and fidelity, guards the dignity of the human body which has been consecrated by Baptism, and safeguards the control which our spiritual soul should exercise over it. Cf. 1 Cor. 6, 18 - 20; —ATD 176 - 178.

Fourth Sunday after Epiphany

1. The Church, the Ark of salvation.
2. "Then He got into a boat, and His disciples followed Him" (Matt. 8, 23).
3. In the midst of the perils and uncertainty of this world, the Catholic Church is the only Ark of salvation in which Christ can be found. Hence our gratitude and attachment to Christ who has called us into this Ark; hence also our endeavors to bring others into it. Cf. Gen. 7 and 8; —ATD 111 - 113.

Fifth Sunday after Epiphany

1. Human weakness in the Church cannot spoil God's Plan.
2. "Let both grow together until the harvest" (Matt. 13, 30).
3. Christ has entrusted the treasure of salvation to men. Because of

human weakness, "it must needs be that scandals come" (Matt. 18, 7). These scandals stain the Church and impair her work, but they cannot estrange her from her divine destiny: to lead all men of good will to God by her teaching and her guidance, by her worship and her sacraments. Cf. Phil. 1, 15 - 18.

Sixth Sunday after Epiphany

1. The Church, the Visible-Invisible Body of Christ.
2. ". . . like a grain of mustard seed . . . like leaven . . ." (Matt. 13, 31 - 33).
3. The Church is the fullness of Christ, the Word Incarnate. Christ entrusted to the Church the incomparable gifts of His redemption, His divine doctrine, His redemptive grace. But Christ also gave her a visible organization, a hierarchy, visible worship and sacraments. Like Christ, the Church, His mystical Body, has this twofold aspect: invisible and divine, visible and human. Cf. Rom. 12, 14 ff; 1 Cor. 12, 12 ff; —ATD 111 ff; 116 ff.

THE PRE-LENTEN SEASON

Septuagesima

1. Our great Christian vocation.
2. "Do you also go into the vineyard" (Matt. 20, 4).
3. God's invitation to work in His vineyard is not only addressed to the Jews, but to all peoples of all time. This vocation, as holy as that to become a priest or a nun, calls us to a magnificent service and a magnificent reward. In calling us, God is not limited as to persons, or work, or rewards. He has no need of us; He calls us only out of His infinite goodness; out of His infinite generosity, He gives us the chance also to be generous, to share in His self-giving love. And even though this call is so great, He leaves us free to accept it or not. Cf. Eph. 1, 1 - 12; —ATD 86 ff.

Sexagesima

1. Our faith: our response to God's call.
2. "The sower went out to sow his seed . . ." (Luke 8, 5).
3. The seed needs good soil to yield a rich harvest; God's Word asks that when we receive it in our hearts we give the answer which is faith. This answer is not merely a theoretical assent to some truths revealed by God, but a living and loving wholehearted readiness to follow God completely in believing and in living, even though this means great sacrifices. Cf. James 2, 14 - 26; —ATD 88, 104 ff.

Quinquagesima

1. The mystery of Christ's Passion.
2. "Behold, we are going up to Jerusalem. And they understood none of these things . . ." (Luke 18, 31 - 34).
3. We ought not to wonder at the lack of understanding of the apostles. The foolishness of Christ's Cross (1 Cor. 1, 18) is understandable only in the light of God's immense love for us and His omnipotent wisdom. His love "has not spared even His own Son, but delivered Him for us" (Rom. 8, 32) rebellious slaves; His wisdom and omnipotence has transformed such hateful things as tribulation, humiliation, pain and death into the very ransom price of our salvation and eternal glory. Cf. The Preface for Passiontide, 1 Cor. 1, 17 - 30; —ATD 105 - 107.

Ash Wednesday

1. The Christian spirit of penance.
2. "And when you fast" (Matt. 6, 16).
3. Christ, the Head, of whom we are members, gave the Father perfect satisfaction for our sins. We share in this satisfaction only insofar as we share in Christ's Passion by genuine, that is, sincere and practical Christian penance. Penance for our own sins and for those of our brothers opens the treasury of Christ's redemption. Cf. Luke 7, 36 - 50; —ATD 107 ff.

First Sunday of Lent

1. The spiritual combat and temptations.
2. "Begone, Satan!" (Matt. 4, 10).
3. Concupiscence, the result of original sin, remains in us even after Baptism. It causes our striving for virtue and holiness to be a hard struggle against Satan and his allies, including our own inclination to evil. Thus temptations give us a special opportunity to fight by the side of Christ, the great Warrior against Satan, to prove our sincere love and to win a more radiant crown. Cf. 1 Peter 4, 12 - 19; —ATD 128.

Second Sunday of Lent

1. The royal way of the Cross ends in glory.
2. "And He was transfigured before them" (Matt. 17, 2).
3. Lent is the time of penance, of spiritual combat and of renewal in Christ. To help us subdue the resistance of our natural feelings to this process, the Church, our mother, directs our thoughts to the final goal of this hard journey, and to Christ, our inspiration and example. His glory will be our glory, provided that we follow Him on the way of the Cross. Cf. Luke 24, 26; Acts 14, 21; —ATD 106.

The Feast of St. Joseph

1. The Model of Christian Fatherhood.
2. ". . . being a just man" (Matt. 1, 19).
3. Holy Scripture tells us very little about St. Joseph. But these few lines give us sufficient evidence of his greatness: his close relation to Jesus. Jesus loved, honored and obeyed him as a child does his own father. And Joseph truly was for Jesus the earthly representative of His Father in heaven. No man has ever reflected God's Fatherhood so perfectly as did St. Joseph. He is the visible pattern for every father in a Christian family. Cf. Eph. 3, 15; —ATD 172 ff.

Third Sunday of Lent

1. God's merciful forgiveness in the Sacrament of Penance.
2. "And He was casting out a devil, and the same was dumb" (Luke 11, 14).
3. God's untiring mercy has not only rescued us from the power of darkness (cf. Col. 1, 13), by Baptism, but also casts out the devil again from our souls as often as we, His ungrateful children, fall again into sin — provided that we again earnestly renounce Satan. We must gain forgiveness by deeply repenting of our relapse, we must make a firm resolution to do better, and make a sincere confession. The Sacrament of mercy is Christ's Easter gift. Cf. John 20, 19 - 23; —ATD 137 ff.

Fourth Sunday of Lent

1. The Virtue of Temperance.
2. ". . . five barley loaves and two fishes . . ." (John 6, 9).
3. Lent is the time of our renovation in Christ. To assimilate ourselves to Christ (cf. Rom. 8, 29), all our blind human tendencies must come under the control of, and be inspired by, the spirit of Christ. The goal of Christian self-discipline is Christ's life in us. In the Mass, Christ nourishes our spirit of self-sacrifice, gathering us together to offer ourselves with His sacrifice, and giving us His own flesh and blood in the "sacred banquet in which the memory of His Passion is renewed." —Cf. ATD 128.

PASSIONTIDE

First Sunday in Passiontide

1. Mortal Sin.
2. "They took up stones to cast at Him" (John 8, 59).
3. Before we were baptized we were living under the tyranny of Satan, the enemy of God and man. By Baptism we renounced Satan, died to sin and received a new divine life from God (Rom. 6). By

mortal sin we return, deliberately and voluntarily, to the tyranny of the devil and of sin; we throw away Christ's redemption; we again stone and crucify the Son of God. What ingratitude, offense, calamity and loss! Cf. Heb. 6, 6; —ATD 96 and 138.

Second Sunday in Passiontide

1. Christ enters Jerusalem in triumph.
2. "Tell the daughter of Sion; behold, thy King comes to thee, meek . . ." (Matt. 21, 5).
3. In this triumphant entry of Christ into the city of His Passion, His Messiasship is manifested and acknowledged with public solemnity. The Church invites us also to pay our homage today to Christ our Savior, and to follow Him on the way of the Cross to eternal victory. Cf. Rom. 8, 17.

Holy Thursday

1. Christ's love for us.
2. "Having loved His own . . . He loved them unto the end" (John 13, 1).
3. According to the new Order of Holy Week, the sermon is to explain briefly Christ's great love for us, shown at the Last Supper by His washing of the feet of His apostles, by His giving Himself to us in the Holy Eucharist, and by His instituting the sacrament of Holy Orders. Cf. —ATD 132 ff.

Good Friday

1. Love crucified.
2. "Behold the wood of the Cross, on which hung the Salvation of the world" (Liturgy of Good Friday).
3. Christ is crucified Love; love for us (Gal. 2, 20) and love for the Father in heaven (Phil. 2, 8). His love for us will win our love, so that we may follow Him in love and obedience to the Father. Baptized into Christ's death (Rom. 6, 3), we, too, shall crucify ourselves by penance, by patient endurance of suffering, and by unselfish service of our brothers. Thus we shall share in the incomparable fruits of Christ's victory on the Cross. Cf.—ATD 105 - 8.

The Easter Vigil

1. Renewing the grace of our Baptism: the re-enactment of Christ's Death and Resurrection.
2. "You have died, and your life is hidden with Christ in God" (Col. 3, 3).

3. Explaining this night's liturgy, we show how Baptism is participation in Christ's death and resurrection (the Paschal candle and our candles, the blessing of the baptismal water, the rite of Baptism); by the renewal of our baptismal promises, we are renewed in the grace of our Baptism on "this most holy night." Cf. Rom. 6; —ATD 125 - 129.

EASTER TIME

Easter Sunday

1. Christ's Resurrection and our resurrection.
2. "You are looking for Jesus of Nazareth who was crucified. He has risen" (Mark 16, 6).
3. "This is the day which the Lord has made," the day of the Redeemer's triumph and endless glory. Alleluia! The glorious new life which He has won for us by His Easter victory was given us in Baptism, was revivified through sincere penance and the sacrament of Penance if we ever lost it by mortal sin, is nourished by the Holy Eucharist, and will be brought to completion by our resurrection, when He will give us His own glory both in our souls and in our bodies. Cf. 1 Cor. 15; —ATD 109 ff.

First Sunday after Easter

1. The Sacrament of Holy Orders.
2. "As the Father has sent me, I also send you" (John 20; 21).
3. Christ was sent by the Father to be our Redeemer. By the Sacrament of Holy Order, He continues to carry out His redeeming work. The priest is the instrument used by Christ to teach, guide and sanctify the faithful of all times and all places on their way to the Father. The priest is also the representative of God's holy people by his prayers, sacrifices and penance. Cf. 1 Cor. 4, 1; —ATD 113.

Second Sunday after Easter

1. The meaning of the sacraments.
2. "I am the good shepherd, and I know mine . . ." (John 10, 14).
3. Christ, our good Shepherd, comes to us "that we may have life, and have it more abundantly" (John 10, 10), especially through the seven sacraments. These not only bestow actual grace, but are the outward signs producing our hidden, supernatural life: the birth, growth, renewal, nourishing, developing and transmitting of Christ's glorified life to us and to the whole Church. Cf. — ATD 122 ff.

Third Sunday after Easter

1. Heaven: eternal happiness in our Father's house.

2. "Your heart shall rejoice, and your joy no man shall take from you" (John 16, 22).

3. During the forty days after Christ's resurrection the apostles had a foretaste of the glory and joy of heaven. Heaven means the final and perfect sharing of the members, according to the individual capacity of each one, in the glory of their Head. In the triumphant Church, we shall all share in one another's happiness and in the glory Christ shares with His Father in the Spirit. This will be the final consummation of the work of grace, of the life to which we were born in Baptism. Cf. 1 Cor. 2, 9; —ATD 158 ff.

Fourth Sunday after Easter

1. The Holy Spirit, the Soul of the Church.

2 "He will glorify me, because He will receive of what is mine and declare it to you" (John 16, 14). The Holy Spirit, Who proceeds from the Father and the Son, is the Gift sent by Christ to the Church. He is her Advocate and Paraclete (Comforter). He infallibly teaches us in the Church, guides us on the way to heaven, sanctifies us in the sacraments. He gives to the members of Christ the different charismatic gifts and functions, and He makes the Church one, so that, inspired by Him, we may adore the Father in Spirit and in truth. Cf. John 16, 17 - 24; —ATD 117 ff.

Fifth Sunday after Easter

1. Christian prayer.

2. ". . . if you ask the Father anything in my name, He will give it to you" (John 16, 23).

3. Genuine Christian prayer is prayer in the Name of Christ: in union with Him, in accordance with His prayer, "through Him." Thus our prayer shares in the pre-eminence and efficacy of Christ's prayer. Cf. Matt. 15, 21 - 28; —ATD 167.

The Ascension

1. Christ returns home to the Father.

2. "The Lord . . . was taken up into heaven, and sits at the right hand of God" (Mark 16, 19). Christ came forth from the Father and came into the world. Again He left the world and returned to the Father (cf. John 16, 28). Christ's life, entirely devoted to the service of the Father, necessarily was crowned with glory at the right hand of the Father. This goal gives everything its right perspective. We are Christ's members; with Christ and in Him we shall be enthroned

in heaven (cf. Eph. 2, 6). We should look at the things of this earthly life in this glorious perspective. Our life has the same goal as Christ's! Cf. Acts 1, 1 - 14; —ATD 110.

Sunday after the Ascension

1. The Sacrament of Confirmation.
2. "And you also bear witness" (John 15, 27). Baptism is the origin, the birth of our divine life. Confirmation is the completion of Baptism; it consecrates us to become active members in the mystical Body of Christ: to bear witness to Christ through our truly Christian life, to defend and to spread Christ's kingdom. Sharing in Christ's priesthood through the sacramental character (St. Thomas), we are concerned about the salvation of others. Cf. Acts 8, 14 - 17; —ATD 119.

Pentecost

1. The sending of the Holy Spirit, the greatest fruit of the Redemption.
2. ". . . the Holy Spirit, whom the Father will send in my name . . ." (John 14, 26). On Easter Sunday, our greatest feast, we celebrated the work of our redemption accomplished by the triumphant resurrection of our Savior; on Pentecost, the second and concluding feast of the glorious season of Easter, we celebrate the chief and most wonderful fruit of the redemption: the coming of the Holy Spirit, Who is the Divine Gift, Who unites us with Christ and the Church, and with one another as well. All the vitality of the Church and of her members is His work. Cf. Acts 2; —ATD 117 ff.

TIME AFTER PENTECOST

First Sunday after Pentecost: Trinity Sunday

1. God's most profound Mystery, and that of our life in Christ.
2. ". . . baptizing them in the name of the Father, and of the Son, and of the Holy Spirit" (Matt. 28, 19). God One in nature, Three in Person: He revealed this mystery to us, not to try our faith, but rather to unveil to us, in His love, His most intimate secret, and, still more, to cause us to enter into this mystery by Baptism, in which we "become partakes of the divine nature." Cf. 2 Peter 1, 4; —ATD 119 - 122.

The Feast of Corpus Christi

1. The Holy Eucharist, the divine Food for God's children.
2. "My flesh is food indeed . . ." (John 6, 56).
3. Today's solemn procession reminds us particularly of Christ's

special presence in the Blessed Sacrament which deserves our humble adoration. But His main intention in giving us this sacrament was the remembrance, the re-enactment and the application of His redeeming sacrifice. Inseparably connected with this intention is the nourishing of the divine life in us by this most noble and effective Food. The symbolism, the rite and the manner in which this sacrament was instituted all manifest this, its significance. "Taste and see how good is the Lord!" (Psalm 33, 9). Cf.—ATD 130 ff.

Second Sunday after Pentecost

1. The Mass, the festive gathering of God and His own on earth.
2. "A certain man gave a great supper, and he invited many." (Luke 14, 16).
3. The Mass, especially Sunday Mass, is the great act of homage and thanksgiving celebrated by Christ and His brothers, the assembly of the Church, represented by the faithful present at Mass. In this festive gathering, we first listen to God speaking to us (Fore-Mass); then we answer with Christ's and our own thanksgiving gift, the Eucharistic Sacrifice (Offertory-Canon); the Father accepts it and gives our offering back to us, transformed into Christ, in the sacrificial banquet (Communion). Cf.—ATD 132 - 136.

Third Sunday after Pentecost

1. God's mercy made visible in Jesus Christ.
2. "Now the publicans and sinners were drawing near to Him . . ." (Luke 15, 1).
3. In spite of the ingratitude we would show Him, ingratitude that God foresaw from all eternity, He sent His own Son for our redemption. In Christ Who ate with publicans (Matt. 9, 11) and called sinners (Matt. 9, 13), we admire the mercy of the Father Who loved us even when as yet we were sinners (Rom. 5, 8; 1 John 4, 10). Even our sins cannot frustrate His love. Cf. Luke 15, 11 - 32; 1 Peter 1, 19; 2, 25; —ATD 106.

Feast of Sts. Peter and Paul

1. The primacy of St. Peter and his successor, the Pope.
2. "Thou art Peter, and upon this rock I will build my Church" (Matt. 16, 18).
3. Christ is the Head of His mystical Body, the Church, even after His ascension into heaven. But He gave us a visible representative to satisfy the needs of human nature: Peter and his successors, the Popes. Their spiritual power and authority, their primacy, is the basis, the

source and the guarantee of the unity of the Church. Cf. John 21, 15 - 17.

Fourth Sunday after Pentecost

1. The hierarchy of the Church.
2. "And Jesus said to Simon . . . henceforth thou shalt catch men." (Luke 5, 10).
3. Christ redeems us by the teaching, guiding, sanctifying activity of His Church. For this task, He selects and appoints special ministers and human instruments, the ecclesiastical hierarchy: the Pope, the Bishops, our priests. We honor them because they are Christ's instruments and representatives. Cf. Matt. 10, 1 - 4; 16, 18; —ATD 111 - 114.

Fifth Sunday after Pentecost

1. Christian charity: the Fifth Commandment.
2. ". . . Thou shalt not kill . . . But I say to you . . ." (Matt. 5, 21ff).
3. Christ is very strict in His teaching on the Fifth Commandment, going far beyond the forbidding of physical killing only, because this commandment is inseparably linked with the greatest commandment: to love God. From this, comes the motive for, and the measure of, our obedience to the Fifth Commandment, for the command to love God and to love our brothers is one and the same commandment. And for us, because of our union with Christ and, in Christ, with one another, the commandment of fraternal love has a still greater urgency. Cf. 1 John 2 and 3; —ATD 165; 174 ff.

Sixth Sunday after Pentecost

1. God is our Creator and Conserver.
2. ". . . if I send them away . . . they will faint on the way . . ." (Mark 8, 3).
3. God feeds and maintains us from day to day. If He were to withdraw His almighty hand, we would sink back into nothingness. Since we are His creatures, we depend completely on Him — as to our origin, our continuing to exist, our destiny. Cf. Gen. 1, 26 ff; —ATD 89 - 92.

Seventh Sunday after Pentecost

1. Living faith.
2. "Not everyone who says 'Lord' . . . but he who does the will of my Father in heaven . . ." (Matt. 15, 21).
3. Our behavior is the proof of our faith. Unless we obey God in

practice, in our lives and action, even attending Mass, prayers and devotions cannot please Him. Our deeds must be based on the principles of our faith; our faith must be activated by our deeds. Cf. James 2, 14 - 26; —ATD 105, 162, 164 ff.

Eighth Sunday after Pentecost

1. The right attitude towards property: the Seventh and Tenth Commandments.

2. "Make an accounting of thy stewardship" (Luke 16, 2).

3. God has entrusted us with material things as a means to serve Him and one another, not as a goal. Men cannot exercise unlimited ownership of things; we are all merely stewards of property; the true owner of everything is God. He has provided mankind with the necessities of life in abundance, so that everyone who works diligently should be able to provide for himself and his family. If this is not possible in fact, it is the fault of human selfishness. When we die, God will call us to give an account of our Christian use of our possessions. Cf. 1 Tim. 6, 8 - 10; —ATD 178 ff.

Ninth Sunday after Pentecost

1. Christian worship: the First and Second Commandments.

2. "And he entered into the temple and began to cast out those who were buying and selling in it" (Luke 19, 45).

3. It is essential to the dignity of human nature that we should pray, that we should acknowledge the supremacy of our Maker and Lord (cf. Isaias 1, 3), and that we willingly subject ourselves to Him. It is our great and wonderful Christian privilege to adore God "through Christ, with Christ, in Christ." Christian worship is not merely the carrying out of certain rites and words; it is the sincere submission and humble raising of our minds and hearts to God; it is worship in spirit and in truth. Cf. John 17; —ATD 169 - 172.

Feast of the Assumption

1. The Queen of heaven, the most perfect fruit of the Redemption.

2. "He has done great things for me" (Luke 1, 49).

3. Mary, the first-redeemed of all mankind, is the most sublime and the most cooperative member of Christ's mystical Body. She who is full of grace, the masterwork of the Redeemer, shows us what is the fullness of redemption. Glorified both in soul and body, our Mother and Queen is waiting for us and helping us who are striving after the same goal.

Tenth Sunday after Pentecost

1. Christian humility.
2. "Everyone who exalts himself shall be humbled, and he who humbles himself shall be exalted" (Luke 18, 14).
3. Although the Pharisee of today's Gospel speaks the truth about himself, yet he is somehow ridiculous because of his spiritual pride. All our good deeds, our merits and virtues are ultimately God's gifts, graces. We are all "unprofitable servants" (Luke 17, 10), since even our best deeds have some defects, due to our own imperfection. The more we share in Christ's merciful graces, the more are we aware of our deficiency; this makes us humble toward God, modest towards men. Spiritual pride is the most ridiculous form of self-deception. Cf. 1 Cor. 4, 7; —ATD 163.

Eleventh Sunday after Pentecost

1. Sins of the tongue: the Eighth Commandment.
2. ". . . and he began to speak correctly" (Mark 7, 35).
3. Without the wonderful power of speech, human social life would be extremely difficult. Real communication of mind and heart, trust among human beings, pleasantness and harmony in social living, the reputation of others, all depend to a great extent on the right use of this great gift of God, our tongue. The tongues of Christians, of members of Christ, temples of the Spirit, fed by the Eucharist, ought to be instruments of truth and of charity. Cf. James 3, 1 - 12; —ATD 180 ff.

Twelfth Sunday after Pentecost

1. Christian love of enemies.
2. "But a certain Samaritan . . ." (Luke 10, 33).
3. Christ is the good Samaritan who loved us even to the sacrifice of His life. God is the model of our behavior to one another (Matt. 5, 43 - 48). He loved us even when we were still His enemies (Rom. 5, 10; Col. 1, 21). Out of gratitude, we ought to "do likewise" — love our enemies and pray for our persecutors. By Christ's grace this will be possible for us. Cf. Rom. 12, 17 ff; —ATD 175 ff.

Thirteenth Sunday after Pentecost

1. Gratitude towards God and the prayer of praise.
2. "But where are the nine?" (Luke 17, 17).
3. Christ's complaint of the ingratitude of nine of the men He cured of leprosy applies still more forcefully to many Christians today who never think of showing gratitude to God for His infinite mercy. We

Christians, redeemed by the blood of Christ, should never cease to be grateful to the Father Who has "transferred us into the kingdom of His beloved Son, in whom we have our redemption" (Col. 1, 13). Our solemn community thanksgiving to the Father is our Sunday Mass, the climax of the Christian week, and this should give the quality of thanksgiving — a eucharistic tone — to our whole lives. Cf. Col. 3, 16 ff; 1 Thess. 5, 18; —ATD 167 ff, 99, 93.

Fourteenth Sunday after Pentecost

1. Trust in Divine Providence.
2. "Do not be anxious . . . for your Father knows . . ." (Matt. 6, 31 ff).
3. Jesus brings light to the darkness of all our troubles and difficulties in the Christian life by telling us: "The Father knows . . .". The Father's providence shields us from anxiety about our work — for this is the task given us by God — and comforts us in all our sufferings, which are necessary for those who try to walk the way of the Cross with Christ. Hardships will never overcome us. They are controlled by our Father; in His wisdom and love, He allows us to undergo them. He will either deliver us from them or give us the strength to bear them, and so share in Christ's redeeming work for His Church (Col. 1, 24), and therefore to a greater degree in His eternal glory. Cf. Acts 14, 22; —ATD 154, 160.

Fifteenth Sunday after Pentecost

1. Miracles, the proof of Christ's mission.
2. "God has visited His people" (Luke 7, 16).
3. God alone has power over life and death. Christ, who commands — He does not pray for this miracle — the dead to rise, thus gives convincing proof of His divine nature and mission. The greatest proof is His own resurrection from the dead. Cf. Matt. 12, 39; —ATD 105.

Sixteenth Sunday after Pentecost

1. The Christian celebration of Sundays and holydays: the Third Commandment.
2. "Is it lawful to cure on the Sabbath?" (Luke 14, 3).
3. What Christ opposes here is not the observance of the Third Commandment, but pharisaic formalism. God's command and the dignity of human nature demand not only interior submission to God, but also the exterior and social act of worshipping God. Sunday is the day of the Lord. Since the time of the apostles, Sunday Mass has been

the principal act of our religion, the solemn gathering of God's holy family. Sunday rest assures sufficient time for worship and guards us from practical materialism. Cf. Luke 4, 16; —ATD 169 - 172.

Seventeenth Sunday after Pentecost

1. The basis of all commandments.
2. "On these two commandments depend the whole Law and the Prophets" (Matt. 22, 40).
3. While the Pharisees and Scribes burden the conscience with the innumerable rules and precepts of their casuistry, Christ proclaims the twofold law of love, which ultimately is, "Love — and do what you will" (St. Augustine). This does not exempt us from the obligation of acquiring Christian knowledge, but granted this knowledge, which is not difficult to attain, Christ has given us this great law of life, clear and simple, universally applicable, giving to each obligation its proper urgency and right motivation. Cf.—ATD 165.

PRE-ADVENT SEASON

Eighteenth Sunday after Pentecost

1. The Apostolate: the Works of Mercy.
2. "And behold, they brought to Him a paralytic lying on a pallet." (Matt. 9, 2).
3. Jesus, the perfect model of Christian apostleship, is more concerned about this man's spiritual than his material welfare. The Apostolate is the generous answer of Christians to Christ's invitation to help Him in the salvation of men. It is universal, supernatural in its motive (because our brother is the son of the Father, a member of Christ) and warm-hearted ("Take courage, son"). Like Christ, we "must do the work of Him who sent us, while it is day" (cf. John 9, 4).

Nineteenth Sunday after Pentecost

1. The joyful tidings of God's Kingdom.
2. "The kingdom of heaven is like a king who made a marriage feast for his son" (Matt. 22, 2).
3. By this colorful Oriental parable, Christ summarizes his great message to us. The glory of heaven is the marriage feast; God is the king. Christ is the Bridegroom. The Church, redeemed mankind, is the bride. That is why we are at the marriage feast not only as guests. The kingdom has already come (Matt. 12, 28; Col. 1, 13), since Christ has established His Church among us. In the Eucharist we anticipate the eternal wedding feast. The last day will bring God's kingdom in its

fullness. It is our task to develop this kingdom in ourselves and in our brothers. Cf.—ATD 86 ff.

Twentieth Sunday after Pentecost

1. The Sacrament of Extreme Unction.
2. "Sir, come down before my child dies" (John 4, 49). All four Gospels show Christ as the great friend of the sick. He has not changed. In the sacrament of Extreme Unction He visits, comforts, purifies and brings to a completion His image in them before they return home to the Father. This sacrament brings to a happy conclusion what Christ began in us in Baptism and what penance has still left undone. Having received Extreme Unction, we can face our Judge with confidence. Cf. James 5, 14 ff; —ATD 144 ff; 148.

Twenty-first Sunday after Pentecost

1. God's punishing justice: Hell.
2. "And his master, being angry, handed him over to the torturers . . ." (Matt. 18, 34).
3. God's anger is not unmotivated emotion, but merely the sealing of man's own deliberate rebellion, his cutting himself off from God, by unrepented mortal sin. God does not force His salvation upon anyone; He respects our freedom of choice. The stubbornly impenitent sinner gets what he wishes. Even those who are in hell were followed all through their lives by God's mercy seeking to save them. Cf. Matt. 16, 19 - 31; —ATD 155 - 158.

Feast of Christ the King

1. Bringing the world back to Christ the King.
2. "Thou sayest it: I am a king" (John 18, 37).
3. By original sin, creatures broke away from God, not only individual men, but the whole of human society and even irrational creatures. Christ our Redeemer and King will bring all of them back, step by step. We, His followers, are to cooperate with Him in this great-hearted work. Cf. 1 Cor. 15, 26 - 28.

Feast of All Saints

1. The great harvest of Redemption.
2. "Blessed are you . . . Rejoice and exult, because your reward is great in heaven" (Matt. 5, 11 ff).
3. In the last month of the ecclesiastical year, the month before Advent, the Church meditates more than ever on the Last Things. Today she shows us an awe-inspiring view of the Church triumphant, the

glorious harvest of Christ's redemption, the brothers who have gone before us and reached the goal, which is also our goal. Their example invites us to follow Christ along the way they walked. Their intercession aids us to gain the glory they already enjoy. Cf. Apoc. 7, 9 - 12; 21; —ATD 158 ff.

All Souls' Day

1. Christian Death, the end and the beginning.
2. "And they who have done good shall come forth unto resurrection of life" (John 5, 29).
3. On this day, we remember with fraternal charity our beloved departed, with Masses and prayer, with spiritual aid (indulgences) and material alms (cf. Tobias 12, 8 ff). All belong to the same community, the Communion of Saints: we, the Church militant; they, the Church suffering; and the saints, the Church triumphant. Christian death is a death in hope (cf. 1 Thess. 4, 12). For "life is changed, not taken away" (Preface for the Dead). It is in our own hands whether the last moments of our life are the beginning of an endless life of perfect bliss. Cf. 1 Cor. 15; 1 Thess. 4, 12; —ATD 147 - 151.

Twenty-second Sunday after Pentecost

1. The Christian attitude towards public life.
2. "Render to Caesar the things that are Caesar's" (Matt. 22, 21).
3. We are pilgrims on earth; therefore earthly things have only transitory value. Lawful government is authorized by God; for this reason 1 Peter 2, 13 ff), to hold public office has, under God, a religious importance. Christian patriotism cooperates with the lawful government for peace, welfare, and material progress; it also respects the interests of every other nation in order to promote international peace and progress. Cf. Rom. 13, 1 - 7.

Twenty-third Sunday after Pentecost

1. The Sacrament of Baptism gives us divine life in the Church.
2. "He went in and took her by the hand, and the girl arose" (Matt. 9, 25).
3. By original or personal mortal sin, we are dead with regard to God (Eph. 2, 5). By the waters of Baptism and the grace of the Holy Spirit, Christ cleanses the sinner from all sins; He unites us with Himself, shares His own divine life with us, engrafts us into His mystical Body, the Church, and effectively consecrates us to the Blessed Trinity. Through Baptism, we become children of God, brothers of Christ. Filial love and gratitude oblige us to live a Christ-like life for God, dead

to sin. The fullness of glory gained by Baptism is our glory in heaven. Cf. Rom. 6; —ATD 124 - 129.

Last Sunday after Pentecost

1. Watchfulness for Christ's Last Coming.
2. " . . . know that it is near, even at the door" (Matt. 24, 33).
3. Christian life, contrary to the world's way of thinking and feeling, is essentially "open" to the age to come. This begins with "the day of the Lord," the Judge of all men and the Consummator of God's Kingdom. "Watch, therefore, for you know neither the day nor the hour" (Matt. 25, 13). Christ warns us throughout the Gospel, but especially in this chapter of St. Matthew and the one that follows. Are we ready? Cf.—ATD 151 - 154.

Index